MENDE GOVERNMENT
AND POLITICS
UNDER COLONIAL RULE

MENDE GOVERNMENT
AND POLITICS
UNDER COLONIAL RULE

*A historical study of
political change in Sierra Leone*
1890–1937

ARTHUR ABRAHAM

FREETOWN
SIERRA LEONE UNIVERSITY PRESS
1978

Distributed by

Oxford University Press, Walton Street, Oxford OX2 6DP

OXFORD LONDON GLASGOW
NEW YORK TORONTO MELBOURNE WELLINGTON
KUALA LUMPUR SINGAPORE JAKARTA HONG KONG TOKYO
DELHI BOMBAY CALCUTTA MADRAS KARACHI
IBADAN NAIROBI DAR ES SALAAM CAPE TOWN

British Library Cataloguing in Publication Data
Abraham, Arthur
    Mende government and politics under colonial rule.
    1. Sierra Leone – Politics and government
    2. Great Britain – Colonies – Sierra Leone –
    Administration
    I. Title
    325' .341'09664   JQ3121.A5   77–30064
    ISBN 0–19–711638–8

*Printed in Great Britain
at the University Press, Oxford
by Vivian Ridler
Printer to the University*

PREFACE

THIS study of government and politics in Southern Sierra Leone under Colonial Rule, is a study in the dynamics of change. Essentially, my purpose has been to give as far as possible an African interpretation to the process of change. In this, I have had to contend, in order to explode it, with what is basically a 'colonial interpretation' of African history, that continues to be perpetuated. Literature during the colonial period usually tended to justify the existing situation, and this has led to distorted interpretations of the past. What I have attempted is to explain how pre-colonial political institutions adjusted to the 'colonial situation'.

Two broad conclusions are arrived at in this study. Firstly, that in their adjustment to the colonial presence, the Africans affected the nature and pattern of the process of change, which was not a one-sided, carefully planned and directed colonial straitjacket, but a cultural synthesis resulting vitally from African reaction to that very imposition. Secondly, that *Indirect Rule* (which I have totally avoided as an analytical tool) was less indirect than we have been made to believe, so that it proves a useless or meaningless concept in the face of the objective reality (as distinct from the subjective theory) of British colonial administration. I have also avoided, as far as possible, the use of certain terms. Prominent among them is the term *native* which, in the context of the present investigation, carried colonial pejorative connotations. I have also used 'administration' in place of 'government' when referring to the colonial superstructure, which cannot be said to have been government in the strict sense of the term. Government implies consent by, and participation through representation of, the governed. Colonialism was imposed without the consent of the people, and the establishment was appointed from London, not elected by the governed!

The research was undertaken both in Britain and in Sierra Leone. I have used my MA thesis as the springboard from which to examine the process of change, since it dealt with the nature of pre-colonial political institutions. The present study is therefore a natural offshoot—indeed a continuation—of my original research.

I have been assisted by numerous persons in this undertaking, to all of whom my sincere gratitude is due. But a few deserve particular thanks. To my supervisor, Professor J. D. Fage, Professor of African History and Director of the Centre of West African Studies in the University of Birmingham, I owe a great debt. Always critical, he nevertheless created an atmosphere which gave me sustained energy to work away at my sources in an unusual manner. His meticulous editorial care has left an indelible mark on this work. I also wish to thank Mr. Christopher Fyfe, Reader in African History in the University of Edinburgh, who has been associated with every stage of my post-graduate career. Out of an informal discussion as early as 1966, he hatched this topic for me. He has readily afforded me everything I have requested of him, not least, some of the most incising criticisms of this work. I am also heavily indebted to Professor John Peterson, Head of the Department of History at Fourah Bay College, University of Sierra Leone, who originally supervised my MA programme. He has been lavish in giving me every conceivable assistance, although he had not enough time to give much attention to this study. I am also thankful to Dr. Roger Tangri of the Political Science Department at Fourah Bay College for his comments on Chapters IV and V, and to Messrs. S. J. A. Nelson and P. Squire, cartographers in the Department of Geography, Fourah Bay College, and the Ministry of Surveys and Lands, Freetown, respectively, for doing my maps for me.

For getting this work transformed from a doctoral thesis into a book, I am deeply grateful to Professor John Hargreaves of Aberdeen University, who gave me valuable suggestions for the metamorphosis. I also wish to express my sincere gratitude, in this connection, to the Afrika-Studiecentrum, Leiden, Holland, for appointing me Visiting Research Fellow for the 1974/5 academic year which gave me the time to complete this work, and also for all the facilities offered me, not least the typing of the manuscript.

Lastly, I wish to thank the Sierra Leone Government and particularly the Ministry of Education for originally granting me leave with pay, and latterly a scholarship to consummate this study. My sincere thanks also go to the staffs of the various institutions where I collected the documentary material for this study—in particular, the staffs of the Public Record Office, the Royal Commonwealth Society and the British Museum in London, Rhodes House Library in Oxford, Fourah Bay College Library and the Sierra Leone Government Archives in Freetown. I am also obliged to all who have been giving me oral information since I began research in 1969, and to many others who have helped in various other ways, but who otherwise I cannot name here.

I cannot close this preface without making an apology to fellow Sierra Leoneans in particular. It is not the traditional apology of owning up all the mistakes of fact and interpretation in the work, which I consider redundant because it is implicit in the very appearance of the work under the author's name, but my inability to have covered the whole country. This is to be explained by the very fact of how I ever came into research. With nothing but brute courage, no finance, no sponsorship, no scholarship, only the encouragement of John Peterson made me venture timidly into the first steps of research. In the circumstances, the most sensible and expeditious course was to concentrate on the area I already knew well at first hand, where I was born and bred, and to the culture of which I belong. This may be regrettable enough, but I am sure it was not of my own making, and the blame cannot be said to rest with me.

A. A.

Leiden
May, 1975

NOTE ON
PUBLIC RECORD OFFICE REFERENCES

I HAVE generally used the number of the Governor's despatch from Sierra Leone to establish the identity of the particular document without supplying the full date of the despatch. For instance, instead of 'Merewether to Harcourt, 21.2.1914, CO 267/556', I have used 'CO 267/556/112, Merewether to Secretary of State (SS), 1914'. The first number, 267, is the CO series, the second, 556, the volume number, and the last, 112, the number of the despatch from Sierra Leone, which is from Merewether to Harcourt. There is thus no uncertainty as to the identity of the document cited. In addition, I have supplied the numbers of the confidential despatches which were numbered. For example, 'CO 267/447/Conf. 45, Ag. Governor Nathan to SS, 1899'. This confidential despatch No. 45 was dated 21 June 1899. As such the number identifies the document. But there are confidential despatches which were not numbered. In this instance, the date of the despatch is supplied in full. For instance, 'CO 267/571/Conf. 17 May 1916, Wilkinson to SS'. The date sufficiently establishes the identity of the document. Sometimes, the correspondence was from some individual or institution, in which case, the appropriate name appears after the volume number, and where available, the date and year, for instance, 'CO 267/448/War Office, 28 March 1899'. The system I have adopted is especially useful after the 1930s, since the records have not been bound up into volumes yet, and are still in boxes, each containing several files. The second number supplied in the footnotes is the box number, and the third is the file number. Thus I have used, for example, 'CO 267/632/File No. 9549, Cookson to SS, 1931'.

I have followed a similar pattern with regard to the Confidential Print series. Thus I have used for instance, 'CO 879/55/570/134, Cardew to SS, 1898'. The first number is the CO series number; the second, the volume number; the third, the sub-section flagged in the volume; the last, the number of the document in that sub-section, which identifies it as confidential despatch No. 53 from Cardew to Chamberlain, received in London 30 July 1898.

I have been cautious with the use of Command Papers, usually bound up as Parliamentary Papers. Since these were to be laid before Parliament, they were usually heavily edited. Thus where the original was cancelled but not destroyed, I have used it in the CO 267 series.

CONTENTS

LIST OF MAPS

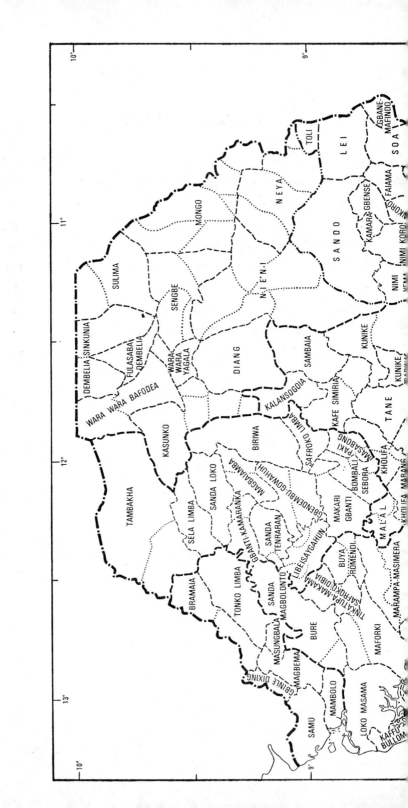

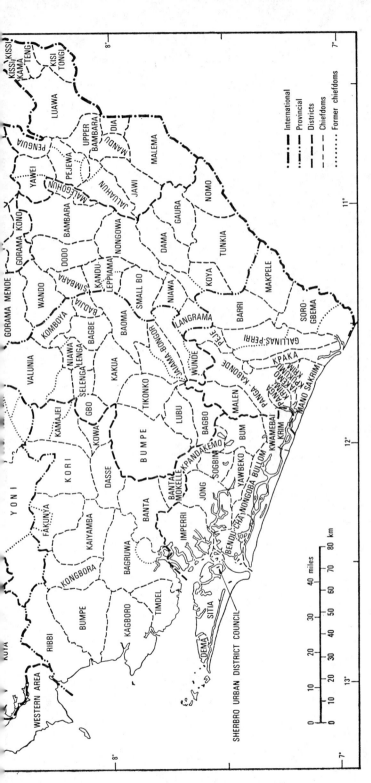

MAP I. CHIEFDOMS OF SIERRA LEONE

I

MENDEDOM

The mendenization process

THE entire southern half of Sierra Leone was, by the opening
of the colonial period and since then, generally Mende-
speaking owing to the cultural dominance of the Mende. But
earlier in the nineteenth century, the Mende were more of an
inland people, quite distinct from the coastal peoples, who were
the Sherbro in the west and the Vai in the south, although all
these peoples were mixed together. Originally, the Mende
appear to have occupied the country to the east of the Sewa
River.[1] But the first dynamic move towards the west, which is
identified with the emergence of the Kpaa-Mende, seems to
have occurred some two or three generations before the last
quarter of the nineteenth century. This was a forceful movement
based on warfare, in which the Banta, the autochthonous
inhabitants of the present Kpaa-Mende area, were either
displaced or pushed south, where they later became the
mendenized state of Bumpeh (usually referred to as Banta).[2]

After this first forceful westward drive towards the coast, a
comparatively peaceful process of mendenization set in and
became widespread by the mid-nineteenth century. However,
the subtlety of the process did not blind contemporary observers to its lasting effects. By the last decade of the nineteenth
century, Rev. William Vivian pointed out nostalgically that
the Mende have 'long overflowed their natural boundaries . . .
while the constantly advancing wave of Mende influence has
already practically inundated the land of the Sherbros'.[3] At
the same time, he classified the Vai as a Mende dialectal

[1] William Vivian, 'The Mende Country and some of the customs and characteristics of its people', *The Journal of the Manchester Geographical Society*, vol. xii,
1896, p. 4.
[2] A. Abraham, 'The Rise of Traditional Leadership among the Mende: A
Study in the Acquisition of Political Power' (University of Sierra Leone M.A.
thesis, 1971), pp. 120-3.   [3] Vivian, 'Mende Country', pp. 4-5.

group, who 'are nearest the coast and speak the purest form of
the language, and . . . invented written signs of their own'.[4]
This would suggest a greater degree of mendenization of the
Vai, and in all probability the group Vivian referred to was
not the Vai proper, but the Gallinas Mende.

By the turn of the century, it was a well-established and
recognized fact that '. . . the Mendies . . . have in fact practically absorbed all the others. . . . The Sherbros . . . have no
separate individuality but are merged in the Mendies.'[5] A
propos of this phenomenon of mendenization, the term Mende
may be used loosely to refer to the entire southern half of the
country, i.e. *Mende-speaking* peoples. Where clarity so dictates,
the necessary distinction will be made.

The process of mendenization of the coastal areas followed
certain definite patterns. One was by migration and settlement.
In a memorandum written in 1894, Darnell Davis, the Civil
Commandant of the Sherbro at Bonthe, clearly explained this
pattern. Having stated that the Mende were the dominant
group and that their dialect was becoming generally spoken,
Davis observed that the Mende were 'more energetic than the
Sherbros proper. British Sherbro is receiving frequent acces-
sions of population, not only through exiles driven hither by
war from run-away slaves, but chiefly from a swelling tide of
immigration which is flowing from the interior . . .' These
Mende immigrants were most anxious to undertake wage-
labour, even at the barest minimum of wages offered them.[6]
As their numbers increased, they elected one of themselves to
be their leader, although subject to the local chieftain in whose
territory they settled, until in time they became independent.[7]
It was in this manner that many Kpaa-Mende settlements
encroached on the Bompeh district of Sherbro territory, so
much so that by 1880, Senehun, the reputed capital of Kpaa-
Mende in the sense that the king resided there, was technically
Sherbro country under Chief Richard Caulker.[8]

---

[4] Vivian, 'Mende Country', p. 16.
[5] CO 267/448/War Office, Notes by Major A. R. Stuart, 28 March 1899.
[6] CO 879/8/32/19, enc. 2, memo by Darnell Davis.
[7] CO 267/510/A. Walker, enc. 2, Sept. 1908, petition from people of Bompeh
town; CO 267/510/Major E. D'H. Fairtlough, 3 Oct. 1908; C. Fyfe, *A Short
History of Sierra Leone* (London 1962), p. 96.
[8] CO 879/17/214/18, enc. 5, report by William Budge, 1880.

Oral tradition also has it that the part of Kpaa-Mende known today as Kongbora chiefdom was a bride-payment of Sherbro territory made to the Kpaa-Mende King Gbenjeh by Richard Caulker in return for giving the latter one of his daughters in marriage.[9]

Sometimes there was a whole diaspora such as led to the infiltration of the settlement of Mattru at the mouth of the Jong River. The Mattru people who now inhabit it were originally refugees from Palima in the upper Bum district where they are said to have violated a law of a secret society. Consequently, they escaped and sought refuge with the *So Kana* of Subu, a Sherbro town under the jurisdiction of Chief James Tucker. Strengthened by increasing numbers, they attempted to oust the *So Kana*, but the latter succeeded in pushing them westward into the Cha district. The *So Fa* of Cha mediated in the dispute, paid the *So Kana* 'five slaves', and arranged for the renegades to return to Mattru. They accordingly returned, and have since formed the principal portion of the inhabitants.[10]

The second important pattern in the process of mendenization of the coast was the 'buying of war' from Mende mercenaries, that is, 'they were often called in to fight in the neighbouring wars, rewarded if they were victorious, with a share of the captives and plundered goods'.[11] The Sherbro and Vai countries were constantly embroiled in local squabbles resulting in wars, and Mende warriors were called in to help on both sides.[12] The Mende mercenaries stayed on to possess the territories they were hired to conquer. As Vivian sardonically put it, 'now the Sherbros are rudely awakened to the Nemesis'.[13] The Mende mercenaries, by their superior strength, gradually acquired the ascendancy over their erstwhile employers.[14]

A contemporary graphically epitomized this process of

[9] Ngolotamba Lamboi, 'History of Madam Yoko: Kpaa-Mende Chiefdom' (unpublished MS., 1915); also personal interviews, December 1969.

[10] CO 879/25/332, 'Particulars relating to the Tribes and Districts of Sierra Leone and its Vicinity', by T. G. Lawson and J. C. E. Parkes, 1886, p. 41, hereafter cited as Lawson and Parkes.

[11] Fyfe, *Short History*, p. 95; Governor's Despatches to the Secretary of State, 117/1875, Sierra Leone Government Archives, hereafter cited as 'Despatches, SLGA'; Governor's Aborigines Letter-books, 44/1887, SLGA, hereafter 'GALB'.

[12] CO 879/15/175/11, Rowe to Secretary of State, 1879.

[13] Vivian, 'Mende Country', p. 5.

[14] Lawson and Parkes, p. 40.

cultural absorption: their '. . . language is dying out. In a few
years more, the Mendies will have achieved a quiet and blood-
less conquest of the whole district between Mano Salijah [the
Vai boundary in the east] and the Bompeh river [the Sherbro
boundary in the north].'[15] This in effect has come to mean that
the entire southern half of Sierra Leone is Mende-speaking and
can be regarded as *de facto* Mende.[16]

The Pattern of Warfare

In the nineteenth century, war was a commonly observable
phenomenon, and warfare has been described as a cultural
pattern.[17] Because of this, the Mende were described by Dr.
Clarke, who never visited them, as a 'wild savage people,
continually at war amongst themselves and against their
neighbours . . .'[18] This is, however, a one-sided, if not distorted,
picture, for warfare was common everywhere in the entire
hinterland. This must not, however be taken to imply a state
of general anarchy, for as a Liberian noticed while travelling
in the hinterland in 1868, it was 'the practice of exaggerating
every petty affair into the proportions of a universal war . . .'
which gave the impression of chronic instability.[19]

A number of hypotheses have been advanced as to the origins
or causes of this stress on warfare. Little and McCulloch (the
latter influenced by the former) contend that from the north,
'invaders forced their way into the country and waged war
against anyone opposing their right to settle there . . . This
helped to establish warfare as a principal form of activity and
institution.'[20] It is likely that this idea may have originated

[15] Vivian, 'Mende Country', p. 5.
[16] On this cultural absorption generally, see also N. W. Thomas, *Anthropological Report on Sierra Leone*, I (London: Harrison, 1916), p. 7; D. T. P. Dalby, 'Language Distribution in Sierra Leone', *Sierra Leone Language Review*, 1, 1962, pp. 62–5; F. W. H. Migeod, *A View of Sierra Leone* (London 1926), pp. 203–4.
[17] K. Little, *The Mende of Sierra Leone* (London 1951), p. 24.
[18] R. Clarke, *Sierra Leone* (London 1843), p. 164; also J. A. B. Horton, *West African Countries and Peoples, 1868* (Edinburgh U.P. 1969), pp. 86–7.
[19] Benjamin Anderson, *Narrative of a Journey to Musardu, the capital of the Western Mandingoes* (New York 1870), p. 11.
[20] Little, *The Mende*, p. 28; M. McCulloch, *Peoples of Sierra Leone* (London 1950), p. 7; also D. J. Siddle, 'War Towns in Sierra Leone: A Study in Social Change', *Africa*, xxxviii, 1968, p. 49.

with Goddard, whose official report describes 'invaders . . . from the north'.[21]

This interpretation has recently been questioned by the suggestion that Mende warfare may have derived from their apparent historical connection with the Mani.[22] A third hypothesis is that advanced by Siddle, that the Mende cultivation of warfare was a response to the socio-economic changes that accompanied the peopling of the country four centuries before the establishment of European rule.[23]

It is possible to put forward yet a fourth hypothesis, that both the Mende addiction to weaponry and their characteristic courage derived from their need to kill off wild animals when they originally settled their country.

However, although in the nineteenth century most of their polities were warlike in character, the Mende states came into existence peacefully through the amalgamation of settlements, and not through conquest by an immigrant group with superior military techniques. It was in the nineteenth century that war was significantly used to establish Mende states. The Kpaa-Mende represent the most important manifestation in this direction.[24] Thus the generalization that African kingdoms came into existence by conquest, and that the impetus was given by an immigrant group, does not apply here. As Vansina plausibly points out:

From the nucleus, a state extended itself by actual military conquest or threat of conquest. How the nuclei themselves first became organised as kingdoms is more obscure. We cannot assume that this was through military action, if only because the potential military force of the early kingdom was composed of its own citizens, but by conviction that a kingdom was the best and indeed the only way to regulate the political life of the community.[25]

More specifically, these wars were fought for particular reasons. Nearly all contemporary literature describes these wars as *tribal wars*. Yet a closer examination of the literature

[21] T. N. Goddard, *The Handbook of Sierra Leone* (London 1925), p. 53.

[22] A. Abraham, 'Some Suggestions on the Origins of Mende Chiefdoms', *Sierra Leone Studies*, N.S. 25, July 1969, p. 36.

[23] Siddle, 'War Towns', p. 48.

[24] Abraham, 'Traditional Leadership', Chaps. II, VI, and *passim*.

[25] J. Vansina, 'A Comparison of African Kingdoms', *Africa*, xxxii, 4, 1962, p. 329.

reveals the misleading nature of the description. 'The contestants were not "tribes", but individual chiefs and their [followers].'[26] These wars tended mostly to take on the character of alliance systems. Thus it could be that many of them assumed a magnitude and dimension which were not uncharacteristically out of all proportion to the causative issues at stake— hence the exaggerations. 'The Mendies', noted Governor Rowe in a despatch, 'are a fighting tribe, and the different clans furnish contingents of so-called war-men, in all directions, and though these men are good friends at home, they fight well against each other when away.'[27] This was certainly a matter of principle, not anarchy.

A very illustrative circumstance was explained by Administrator-in-Chief Berkeley to Secretary of State Kimberley. Tom Kebbi Smith, a man of humble origin who by dint of personal effort succeeded in carving out political authority for himself through his wealth in Imperreh in the Sherbro, granted land to one of his dependants in 1875. Lahai Golay, a Chief of Mongray in the same country, asserted claims over the same piece of territory, and sought to evict the tenant, who appealed to his overlord for protection, after a riot.

The mischief was not confined to the persons immediately implicated in the quarrel. As not infrequently happens in the country, it became engrafted on another war which since . . . 1869, had with varying degrees of activity, been existing in adjacent districts (viz: Big Boom, Lubu and Bompeh [Bumpeh] countries). Lahai Gooray, backed by the Mongrays, applied to Buri, a chief of Bompeh, for assistance. Smith, on the other hand, applied to Momodu Groah, a chief who had been at feud with Boom in the old war; and the chiefs thus appealed to, along with their respective adherents, renewed hostilities against each other.[28]

---

[26] C. Fyfe, *Sierra Leone Inheritance* (London 1964), p. 226.

[27] CO 879/24/318/23, Rowe to SS, 1886. In 1888, Garrett, on a mission to the Gallinas, reported to the Governor that Ndawa was fighting against Makaya, both of them warriors under Makavoray's jurisdiction, but they had been hired by different parties—CO 879/27/350/53.

[28] Parliamentary Papers (hereafter PP), vol. lii, 1875 (printed for HMSO, 1876), Papers Relating to Her Majesty's Possessions in West Africa, Berkeley to Kimberley, p. 6. Also, N. Darnell Davis, *Chiefs and Their Wars in West Africa* (printed for private circulation, 1876), pp. 5–6; A. Abraham, 'The Pattern of Warfare and Settlement Among the Mende in the Second Half of the Nineteenth Century', *Kroniek van Afrika*, 2, 1975.

Since these wars were not tribal wars, it is possible to seek explanation for them in other quarters. Observers during the period have stressed the importance of capturing slaves—that the wars were fought principally to capture slaves.[29] So-called 'domestic slavery' certainly existed, and in fact it was a principal institution of the social fabric. As will presently be apparent, the institution was not abolished by law until 1928.

In the nineteenth century, much of the insecurity to which the Europeans drew attention in West Africa, and 'which they like to think was its dominant characteristic was a direct result of the [trans-Atlantic] slave trade or a result of the European penetration of Africa'.[30] It was the Europeans who introduced the demand for slaves on the coast, and their continued presence on the African coast from the fifteenth century onwards is to be seen as part of the direct cause of the capture of slaves.

Yet to assume that the major cause of wars in pre-colonial Africa was the capture of slaves is both exaggerated and jejune. It is not unlikely, while the trans-Atlantic demand lasted, that sometimes wars may have been inspired by consideration of the profits to be obtained from selling prospective captives. With reference to the Mende in particular, Malcolm notes that 'the professed causes of wars were various'.[31] Certainly the prospect of such profits might be expected to have increased the vehemence of the wars begun for quite other reasons. As arms constituted one of the principal commodities of exchange, a whole series of arms races was generated. To assert that Africans had nothing to fight about except the capture of slaves is absurd, for as will be apparent presently, there were genuine political and economic reasons for these wars. A missionary traveller in nineteenth-century Yorubaland pointed out that these 'wars generally start because of political reasons'. The slave trade came in later and encouraged their continuance.[32]

As Professor Fage explains, 'what were called "slave raids"

[29] See for instance, CO 267/359/126, Rowe to SS, 1885; CO 267/383/Secret 23, enc. memo by Parkes. Cardew throughout his governorship emphasized this point. The Yoruba wars too, and indeed most African wars at this time, were described simply as extended slave-raiding campaigns.

[30] M. Crowder, *West Africa Under Colonial Rule* (London 1968), p. 15.

[31] M. J. Malcolm, 'Mende Warfare', *Sierra Leone Studies*, xxi, Jan. 1939, p. 49.

[32] J. D. Omer-Cooper, 'The Question of Unity in African History', *Journal of the Historical Society of Nigeria*, III, 1, December 1964, pp. 108–9.

by Europeans, not only by imperialists such as Goldie and
Lugard, but also by such a serious historian as Olderogge in
his study of slavery in the Songhai empire . . . were really
campaigns of conquest designed to build up the state and the
economy. They concentrated on the acquisition of people
simply because land and other resources were useless without
an adequate supply of labour.'[33]

However, by the late nineteenth century, one notices an
apparent self-perpetuating tendency in these wars, whatever
the reasons for which they were begun. '. . . The willingness
with which war was entered upon seems to show that the people
liked it for its own sake . . .', observes one writer.[34] Having
become a profitable occupation, warfare led, perhaps directly,
to the emergence of a professional class of warriors. This, it is
reasonable to suppose, abetted the incidence of wars, as the
warriors had to be occupied somehow. The profitability of
warfare seems to have stemmed from the widespread insecurity
generated by the political and economic rivalries of the late
nineteenth century, and thus in part accounts for the rise of
professionalism in warfare.[35] The circle, once complete,
became a vicious one. Rivalries led to wars; wars created
insecurity; insecurity became conducive to professionalism, as
enough income would be obtained from war-booty; the presence of a professional class of warriors exacerbated rivalries as
war would readily be 'bought'.

In 1880, T. A. Wall, the Civil Commandant of the Sherbro,
paid a surprise visit to a local ruler, Kpawoh Jibila, who frankly
confessed that 'trained up to war, he had no other occupation
and was obliged to resort to it for a living . . .'[36]

The Bumpeh (Banta) people too, created a state whose
raison d'être was warfare. '. . . War was their trade. They knew
nothing else, and did not know "book" like English people.'
They practised this art with almost criminal tenacity.[37] Thus

[33] J. D. Fage, *States and Subjects in Sub-Saharan African History* (Johannesburg
1974), pp. 13–14.
[34] Malcolm, 'Mende Warfare', p. 49.
[35] E. A. Ijagbemi, 'The Freetown Colony and the Development of "Legitimate"
Commerce in the Adjoining Territories', *Journal of the Historical Society of Nigeria*,
V, 2, June 1970, p. 153.
[36] PP, vol. xlvii, 1883, Correspondence respecting the disturbances in the
neighbourhood of British Sherbro.
[37] CO 879/17/214/18, enc. 5, report by Budge, 1880.

warfare became a system in itself, a cultural phenomenon, reinforcing its self-perpetuating nature, and making it difficult for the leaders to control the war-men.

Berkeley, the Administrator-in-Chief, observed to Secretary of State Kimberley that 'the prevalence of native wars in the districts adjacent to Sherbro is in general to be attributed to the existence of a numerous class of persons following no useful industries, but making their trade in pillage, slave-catching, and slave-dealing; and ready at all times to lend themselves to whatever enterprise affords opportunity of following their propensities'.[38]

King Mbriwa of Bumpeh complained that he was saddled with the responsibility of a great party of warriors under sixty-nine chief warriors, who had helped him against his usual rival, the Tikongoh people under Makavoray, and who refused to go to their homes and still lingered about his country. The old king was clearly tired of them, and wanted to be rid of them, if possible, with the assistance of the Freetown administration.[39]

Even when they belonged to a warrior of great reputation, the war-men availed themselves of any opportunity for 'private practice'.[40] In 1874, for instance, Mbalahina, a warrior belonging to the Kpaa-Mende King Gbanya, led an unauthorised raid on Mano Bagru in retaliation of an attack made by that town's chief against certain Kpaa-Mende towns. Gbanya promised to retrieve the losses and to release the captives, which promise T. G. Lawson, the Government interpreter, felt was very altruistic, because Gbanya always honoured his promise to the Freetown administration. Yet it took him time and difficulty to redress the loss, because the warriors 'scattered as soon as they made plunder of any place' and it would 'take some time to see them or obtain' any of the looted property from them.[41]

In 1888, while Captain Crawford was leading a frontal attack against the warrior Makaya for persistently raiding land adjoining 'British territory', and in one instance actually attacking the customs post at Sulima, Makavoray, 'supposed

[38] PP, vol. lii, 1875, p. 6.
[39] CO 879/17/214/18, enc. 5, report by Budge, 1880.
[40] See *The Times*, 26 December 1882.
[41] CO 267/326/43, minute by T. G. Lawson, 1874.

to be his father', was also attacking Makaya from the rear. In an interview with Governor Hay, Makavoray 'expressed his thanks for the action taken as Mackiah had for long been disturbing the peace of the country . . .'. Apparently, everyone was disgusted with Makaya—even his 'father'. This shows again the self-perpetuating nature of the wars.[42]

However, it would be a distortion to use the self-perpetuating nature of these wars as the only plausible explanation of their occurrence. Grievances, legitimate or fabricated, in the eyes of the contestants, had to occasion a particular war. The self-perpetuating nature accounts for the picture of incessant disturbances that emerges during this period.

If it is possible to exclude the pretexts advanced by the contenders as the reasons for the wars, and to supply a rational explanation, it is reasonable to seek further interpretation in economic and political causes. Indeed the wars reflect the complicated social, political, and economic changes that were taking place at the time.

It has been suggested that the wars of the late nineteenth century were economic wars.[43] As 'legitimate trade' expanded, especially in palm produce, many chiefs took to trading. This necessitated rivalries as one chief tried to get control of a trading centre or of trade routes, and the rivalries in turn led to wars. Thus, paradoxically, 'legitimate trade', far from bringing peace and security, contributed a major cause of the wars.

Those who already held so-called 'domestic slaves' added fresh numbers to them from war-captives to work on their farms and collect other 'legitimate' produce for them. This kind of labour force, misleadingly called 'slavery', became a paramount social institution when the chiefs realised that they could make greater profits by keeping the 'slaves' to work their farms for them than by selling them. 'This realisation soon led to competition, and the various local rulers began to look for ways of increasing their slave holding. So the desire to produce more slaves to help produce the "legitimate" commodities became one of the major incentives for war . . .' Thus the so-

---

[42] CO 267/375/9, encs. 3 and 10, Hay to SS.

[43] Fyfe, *Inheritance*, p. 226; Fyfe, *Short History*, pp. 109–15, 122–6; Ijagbemi, 'Development of "Legitimate" Commerce', pp. 243–56; A. M. Howard, 'Economic History', in J. I. Clarke (ed.), *Sierra Leone in Maps* (London 1966), p. 74.

called abolition of the slave trade by the European powers is
more apparent than real. Ironically, far from abolishing it, the
European powers merely diverted it within Africa itself, as the
need for more and more labour to collect, prepare, and transport the new 'legitimate' export crops necessitated wars to
gain captives for labour. Political and economic rivalries led
to overt hostilities.[44]

It might be further added that the wars reflected an economic
situation in which there was a shortage of man-power in relation to growing opportunities for enrichment by production
and larger-scale organization. This particularly applied to
growing opportunities for trade, especially in palm produce,
and thus the wars would aim at increasing each group's labour
force at the expense of its rivals.

It is also possible to interpret these wars as a military
projection of domestic power politics and trans-territorial
diplomacy. Dynastic power struggles were translated into force
when opposing factions invoked mercenary alliances to espouse
their individual causes. Two allies would turn enemies and
fight if one were guilty of a breach of diplomatic protocol.
An ally 'left in the lurch' would resort to war for redress as an
important instrument of international arbitration. Two political rivals in a state of negative physical confrontation would
readily espouse the causes of opposing factions in an attempt to
establish their relative strength. In this sense, therefore, the
wars of the period can be seen as an instrument of politics.
However, to assert that a consistent pattern in this system was
that contiguous towns tended to be rivals, as John Davidson
claims, is a broad generalization that drastically oversimplifies
the complex situation. The single example of Bumpeh and
Tikongoh (both of which belonged to different states, and were
only fortuitously contiguous) is certainly a very facile and
inadequate basis for such a claim.[45]

The war mentioned earlier which broke out between Tom
Kebbi Smith and Lahai Golay had political undertones in the

[44] Ijagbemi, 'Development of "Legitimate" Commerce', pp. 252–3; A. G.
Hopkins, 'The Lagos Strike of 1897: An Exploration into Nigerian Labour
History', *Past and Present*, 35, Dec. 1966, p. 138.

[45] J. Davidson, 'The Southern Mende Chiefdoms and the Expansion of
Sierra Leone 1849–1898' (Seminar paper, Birmingham University CWAS, Nov.
1972).

context in which it was fought. Lahai Golay's ally was Lahai Sheriff.

The quarrel between Lahai Serifoo and Tom Cabby Smith is founded, without doubt, upon the possession of a horse-tail which is the sign of sovereignty in the Mongray country.[46] The horse-tail in question had been in the possession of Lahai Serifoo's father, the King of the country, up to his death, and on his death, it appears that Tom Cabby Smith who is an ambitious and avaricious, as well as an industrious man, intrigued for the possession of the horse-tail, and so successfully that some chiefs with due ceremony offered it to him, with the sovereignty of their country. . . . The Mongray people did not join in this coronation of Smith but disowned allegiance to him, and claimed the surrender of the horse-tail. He, on the other hand, says that they must become subject to him. And so they go on fighting.[47]

Bumpeh and Tikongoh, two powerful states in the upper Bum basin, were traditional rivals. In fact, they were said to have been 'at feud for so long as can be remembered . . .'[48] although this is probably a slight exaggeration, for another account dates the beginning of their hostilities to 1872.[49] Both Bumpeh and Tikongoh had powerful mercenaries, who were usually engaged by the Bum and Lugbu chiefs lower down the river to assist in their wars stemming from domestic politics. In 1876 Bumpeh and Tikongoh commenced hostilities against Lugbu and Bum respectively, 'because having formerly been engaged . . . to assist them in their wars against each other, they had not been consulted when the last treaty was made with the Government'.[50] A formidable war-party from Bumpeh against Lugbu only retreated at the request of Wall, Acting Commandant of the Sherbro.[51] The political nature of these conflicts is further underlined by the fact that these states 'do not, however, come down on independent expeditions, but are only attached to one of the local chiefs'.[52]

[46] 'The elephant's tail is . . . symbol of considerable importance, as it represents high chieftainship and sovereignty in its holder . . .', CO 879/15/175/28, Rowe to SS, 1879.

[47] Davis, *Chiefs and Their Wars*, p. 6.

[48] CO 267/330/28 Dec. 1876; CO 267/329/59, Rowe to SS.

[49] CO 267/344/60, report by Laborde, 1881.

[50] CO 267/330/160, Rowe to SS, 1876.

[51] CO 267/330/170, Rowe to SS, 1876.

[52] CO 267/329/59, Rowe to SS, 1876.

The Gallinas country too, was convulsed in disturbances throughout the 1880s, which continued in spite of the administration's vain attempts to arrest their progress. To the officials, the wars represented nothing other than engagements to capture slaves. Yet the situation is in many respects comparable to the nineteenth-century Yoruba wars, which were basically struggles for succession to the imperial authority of Old Oyo.[53]

Governor Rowe realised in 1888 that 'the condition of affairs is . . . arising from the strife for the succession to the authority of the late Prince Manna as Massaquoi . . . '.[54] The chiefs involved in the struggle solicited the alliances of mercenaries consisting not only of Mende, but of Temne also.[55]

The Gallinas state seems to have reached its height under King Siaka and his successor King Manna during the early and mid-nineteenth century. It is said that 'the elders of the tribe were known as Massaquoi . . . meaning . . . "learned man" of the tribe'. However, the name Massaquoi by the mid-nineteenth century had a new meaning in the evolution of the political state system—that of the title of the imperial crown.[56]

The Gallinas state as it was in the nineteenth century was created by war,[57] and was based upon serfs, who brought an increase in man-power in addition to wealth.[58] King Manna's power following that of King Siaka was owed in an appreciable degree to his numerous bands of mercenaries, whom he paid with money obtained from the sale of slaves to Pedro Blanco, a notorious slaver in the Gallinas. By dint of personal effort, Manna consolidated his superior position over all the other rulers in the Gallinas. By the time he died in 1872, the *Massaquoi Crown* was a most coveted imperial position. Manna personally left behind considerable wealth and property.[59]

King Manna was succeeded by his brother Jaya, who in

[53] See J. F. A. Ajayi and R. Smith, *Yoruba Warfare in the Nineteenth Century* (Cambridge 1964).
[54] CO 879/27/350/2, Hay to SS, 1888.
[55] CO 267/358/67, Rowe to SS, 1885.
[56] S. M. Despicht, 'A Short History of the Gallinas Chiefdoms', *Sierra Leone Studies*, xxi, Jan. 1939, p. 5.
[57] Ibid., *passim*.
[58] 'Guide to Pujehun District,' *Sierra Leone Studies*, xvii, Feb. 1932, p. 54.
[59] CO/267/367/68, memo by Rowe on Hay's despatch, 1887.

political ability and astuteness was no match for the late king. He was blind, senile, frail in frame, feeble and politically effete, helplessly confined to his house and town for several years, and he drank 'almost anything', so that he was in a state of almost perpetual inebriation.[60] He thus created an ideal situation for political intrigue. Moreover, with the decline in the slave trade, the economic base of the state was seriously undermined. The subordinate rulers became virtually independent of any imperial control, and Jaya was *de facto* king in name only.

Political intrigue precipitated wars, and by 1885, there emerged two clear contestants for the honour—Boakei Gomna (mendenized form of Governor), the most influential of the upper Gallinas chiefs, and Fawundu of the lower Gallinas. Boakei Gomna was as ambitious as he was industrious, and having robbed the blind man of the state crown, he was further accused of having caused him to be murdered. It made no difference to the power situation whether Jaya was alive or dead, except that the throne, which had been *de facto* vacant, now became *de jure* vacant.[61]

The two factions hired mercenaries from the interior whose actions traversed the entire country. The actual occasions for hiring these warriors were trivial ones. The factions also entered into complex alliances, which, together with the power situation, were too fluid and confused to admit of easy analysis here. The chiefs admitted that if a *Massaquoi* were crowned, an end would be brought to the disturbances. But Governor Rowe, on leave and apparently anticipating Cardew's protectorate proposals, objected to any power being made paramount other than the British administration based in Freetown. No rational solution being found for a peace settlement, the administration decided on an expedition. A very effective campaign was conducted against the latest invading mercenary warrior, Makaya, in 1889, destroying his capital Largoh, and most of his towns.

The nature of these wars did not take on the character of bloody casualties, except when Europeans were involved, deploying their superior fire-power against the Africans, as

---

[60] CO 267/335/182, Edwards–Loggie report, 1878.
[61] CO 267/358/67, CO 267/359/126, Rowe to SS, 1885.

will be shown in Chapter II. Otherwise, the general picture
has been well described thus:

The wars of these people are, however, not attended with any
sanguinary results, they consist mainly in surprising a few individuals where they can be suddenly come upon. Sometimes, the roads
are waylaid wherever their respective traders are supposed to pass.
These, together with other petty annoyances, constitute their
principal mode of warfare. The large walled towns are seldom
taken. Pitched battles are seldom fought; and even when these
people may be said to take the open field, most is done by some war
Chief by way of displaying his individual prowess.[62]

Settlements

'War in fact, being such an essential part of the life of the
people . . . seems to have dictated to a great extent the method
of their living. The layout of the normal Mende town of that
period illustrates this.' Malcolm further continues that inside
the towns 'the round houses . . . were crammed together in the
closest possible space, eaves touching eaves on all sides, so that
in pouring rain, a man could pass right through the town
without getting wet'.[63] This pattern was not only characteristic
of Mende towns, it was fairly general in the hinterland. In the
Liberian interior the 'houses are huddled together in a close
and most uncomfortable proximity; in some parts of the town
scarcely two persons can walk abreast'.[64] Also in the hinterland
to the north of the Freetown Colony, Winterbottom observed
that with this kind of settlement layout the whole village was
burnt down if one of the houses was set alight.[65]

Every war-town was stockaded by a number of war-fences,
of which there were two types.[66] The most common was called
gɔɛɛ, which was made with sticks and logs of wood. These fences

[62] Anderson, *Journey to Musardu*, p. 116, see also Abraham, 'Warfare and Settle-
ment'; W. R. E. Clarke, 'The Foundation of Luawa Chiefdom', *Sierra Leone
Studies*, June 1957; N. C. Hollins, 'A Short History of Luawa Chiefdom', *Sierra
Leone Studies*, June 1929; Protectorate Literature Bureau, *Kailondo Kɛɛ Ndawa*
(Bo 1953).

[63] Malcolm, 'Mende Warfare', p. 47.

[64] Anderson, *Journey to Musardu*, p. 15, also pp. 66–7.

[65] T. Winterbottom, *Account of the Native Africans in the Neighbourhood of Sierra
Leone*, I (London 1803), p. 81.

[66] I am grateful to late chief Musa Tangar of Daru for elucidating this point,
personal interview, August, 1970.

were arranged in tiers. A contemporary description of Mongray on the Jong River graphically illustrates the character of these stockaded towns more generally.

I found Mongray to be a town capable of holding 5,000–7,000 people. The houses, circular huts of mud, closely packed, roofs thatched, streets winding narrow irregular passages, 4 to 9 feet wide, surrounded by a triple stockade, fully 20 feet high of posts 6 to 10 inches in diameter, many of them green, growing (having taken root while planted), well interlaced and tied with supple jack, the tops trimmed and brushed as an English hedge right and left and overhanging, through this fence, a small door on the river side was the only entrance about 4 feet by 2. The opening in the outer fence was not opposite to the opening of the inner. The construction and door of the second fence and of the inner one were identical with that of the first. A space of about 15 feet separated each fence and encircled the town, nothing was grown here; it was a black swampy ooze, unoccupied except by the sheds of the guards who keep and were then keeping, constant watch. On the land side of the town, a formidable ladder and pen protect the door in the outer stockade. In some instances the door is defended by several boulders (a foot in diameter) suspended above it, and in one instance the passage from the door in the outer stockade to that in the inner was connected by a covered way, not unlike the interlaced wires of a rat-trap.[67]

A second type of war-fence was called *daa*. This was a solid wall about a yard thick made of sticks and mud. The outside was thoroughly plastered with animal dung, and finished with a polish of palm oil so that rain water would drain off it, and leave the wall perfectly undamaged. In 1879 William Budge, Manager of the second Eastern District of the Colony, was commissioned by Governor Rowe to undertake a friendly mission into Mende country. At Kwellu he saw the *daa* type of fortification:

The town is protected by an outer and an inner wall, each three feet thick and about 12 feet high, built of a tenacious mixture composed of fine clay, sand and gravel. . . . The copings of both walls were roofed with thatch throughout to protect the material

[67] PP, vol. iii, 1876, Papers Relating to Her Majesty's Possessions in West Africa, p. 34; cf. similar description for the Liberian hinterland in Anderson, *Journey to Musardu*, pp. 15, 53, 63.

of which they are composed from being soaked into and gradually washed away by the rains . . .[68]

In certain instances both types of fortification would be used in one defence strategy. The strength of such defensive fortification cannot be exaggerated. Governor Rowe, during one of his expeditions into Mende country, came across 'stockades . . . further fortified by mud walls at Tyama-Wuro [Taiama Wulo], there being two encircling walls, the inner 15 feet high and *12 feet thick at its base, impervious to rocket and small cannon shot* . . . and fenced with well-tied stakes on the top'.[69]

In between the walls or stockades ditches were dug out, some of which Rowe described as '6 feet wide and fully 8 feet deep'.[70] Stakes and pike-staffs would then be erected in them.

There was, however, an interesting material difference between stockades in upper and lower Mende. The reasons would seem to lie perhaps in ecological and demographic factors. While making the first trip ever by a white man into the upper Mende countries in 1890, Alldridge noticed this difference:

The towns being usually built upon a low hill surrounded by dense bushy thickets it became only necessary to cut a narrow lane through this impenetrable vegetation on both sides of the town for the entrance and the exit, these lanes being of considerable length were divided into sections and a high palisade erected at each section having a wicket gate which was the usual customary solid slab of hard wood cut from the spur of some large tree—this style of defence offered great resistance to native warfare. The wicket gates are so exceedingly narrow and low that it is frequently with difficulty that I could get my body through the opening and in any case before the bearers [carriers] could pass through with their loads, the slabs had to be broken from the massive wooden lintels and many side posts removed . . . as many as ten sections on both sides of the town had to be passed.[71]

That ecological and demographic factors partly accounted for the difference can be illustrated by another parallel.

---

[68] CO 878/17/214/18, enc. 15, report by Budge, 1880.
[69] PP, vol. lii, 1876, p. 60 (emphasis supplied).   [70] Ibid.
[71] CO 267/388/329, enc. 1, report by T. J. Alldridge, 1891; for the Liberian hinterland too, see Anderson, *Journey to Musardu*, p. 50, who describes a town 'surrounded on all sides by impenetrable jungle, which is considered a sufficient barrier from all attacks'.

Winterbottom, writing about the Africans in the neighbourhood of the Colony of Sierra Leone very early in the nineteenth
century, observed that in Susu and Mandingo countries, which
were further inland to the north-east, the towns were surrounded by walls or palisades for defence. But in Bullom and Temne
countries closer towards the coast and in the tropical rain
forest belt at the time, the towns were defended 'merely by the
intricacy of the path leading to them'. The fortifications of the
Susu and Mandingo towns were of two types: bamboo stockades, and brick walls with thatched roofs. This corresponds
exactly to the Mende types.[72] Apparently, as the century progressed, the coastal forest belt was deforested by human activity, so that by the latter part of the century, it was necessary
to erect artificial defences. But in the upper Mende countries,
the forest was still thick enough to afford a natural defence.
This, of course, would also disappear in time through human
activity.[73]

The war-town was the smallest unit within the political
structure. Since it was a product of war, there seems to be a
direct functional relationship between war and the nature of
the settlements in terms of the political structure. And the
nature of the settlements is to be examined meaningfully, only
within the context of the political state systems. But before
moving on to such an analysis, it is necessary to examine the
question of 'slavery' as an important institution in Mende
society. 'Slaves', contends one authority, 'provided in fact the
basis of the social system.'[74]

The Institution of 'Slavery'

The popular European idea about 'slavery' in Africa is
parochial, misconceived, and erroneous. 'The domestic slavery

[72] T. Winterbottom, *Account of the Native Africans*, p. 87. Another interesting
parallel is to be found among the Yoruba. Since the country spreads from forest
belt in the south to savana in the north, there were also two types of fortifications
like those just described. The descriptions are very similar. See *Yoruba Warfare*,
Chap. III.

[73] Anderson explains for the Liberian hinterland that repeated farming destroyed the forest which 'is the chief reason why all the barricades . . . are formed of
earth and clay instead of the large stakes that are used by the natives in the
vicinity of Monrovia' (*Journey to Musardu*, pp. 61–2).

[74] Little, *The Mende*, p. 37.

of western Africa', wrote J. C. E. Parkes, Secretary for Native
Affairs, in a memorandum, 'is so peculiar that it is best to
leave it alone . . .' At the Colonial Office, the margin was
annotated, 'Quite Right!'[75]

Contemporary observers, more familiar with chattel or
plantation slavery in the New World, necessarily tended to
view forms of African 'slavery' as being usually oppressive. As
Oroge explains,

> . . . slavery, viewed as a social status, did not always connote the
> lowest class of Yoruba society. While in the New World the slave
> was in some respects a slave to every freeman in the community, . . .
> a slave in Yorubaland was only a slave to his master and could even
> be master of a number of freemen.[76]

This category of 'unfree' people included such a range in the
social structure as wide as 'the lordly executive' who had
immense authority and could be taken for a prince, to the
'lowly chattel slave or menial'.[77] This is quite true of several
other parts of Africa, where the institution tended to function
similarly.

The origin of this institution has so far posed a problem
among historians. Walter Rodney is emphatic that slavery in
West Africa was a direct response to the Atlantic slave trade,
and goes on to say that 'to speak of African slavery as being
ancient and to suggest that this provided the initial stimulus
and early recruiting ground for slaves exported to Europe and
the Americas is to stand history on its head'.[78] But J. D. Fage,
on the other hand, has been arguing recently that 'slavery, and
the making, buying and selling of slaves were means by which
certain privileged individuals in West African society, or
persons who wished to gain or to extend positions of privilege
in that society, sought to mobilize the wealth inherent in the

---

[75] CO 267/400/14, enc. 3, memo by Parkes, 1893.
[76] E. A. Oroge, 'The Institution of Slavery in Yorubaland with Particular
Reference to the Nineteenth Century' (Birmingham University PhD, 1971),
pp. 2–3.
[77] Ibid., pp. 2, 31, 81.
[78] W. Rodney, 'African Slavery and Other Forms of Social Oppression on the
Upper Guinea Coast in the Context of the Atlantic Slave Trade', *Journal of African
History*, vii, 3 (1966), p. 440.

land and the people on it, and that *this process had already gone on some distance before the Europeans arrived*.[79]

In sub-Saharan African society, the 'starting point' from which to discuss the question of 'slavery' must be the premiss that the extreme shortage of people and therefore labour, relative to the abundance of land available, is the key to understanding the development of institutions of servitude. 'I would argue', writes Professor Fage, 'that the African systems which the nineteenth- and twentieth-century Europeans labelled "slavery" may not have been very different in kind, and were certainly analogous in purpose, to the systems of human dependence that emerged in early Mediaeval Europe.'[80] Enslavement was a crucial step in the economic and political mobilization necessary for the development of a state. New demands were placed on African societies by the growth and development of foreign trade; labour was critically short, yet there was abundant land with incalculable potential that could produce goods for trade; there was need to operate systems of administration over large areas to enable more profits to be realized from trade and tribute without the danger of interference from outsiders. Once this process was set in motion there was need to increase the labour force of a state, and it became necessary for the ordinary man to seek voluntary dependence in order to escape the dangerous exposure that not infrequently resulted in involuntary servitude.

Studying the Ashanti in the 1920s, R. S. Rattray exposed not only several categories of so-called slaves, but also the fact that even those categories closest to the European notion of a 'slave' had rights, not unlike those of the 'ordinary privileges of any Ashanti freeman'. Moreover, he concluded, 'a condition of voluntary servitude was, in a very literal sense, the heritage of every Ashanti', and to remain unattached to a master was an open invitation to involuntary servitude.[81]

Because people were always a key resource in this mobilization process, the main index to wealth and security was the possession of people. Indeed, a man became a basic unit of the

---

[79] J. D. Fage, 'Slavery and the Slave Trade in the Context of West African History', *Journal of African History*, x, 3 (1969), p. 398 (emphasis added).

[80] J. D. Fage, *States and Subjects*, pp. 10–11.

[81] R. S. Rattray, *Ashanti Law and Constitution* (Oxford 1929), Chapter 5.

economy, an accepted currency. This argument undermines the traditional view that slavery and the slave trade caused incalculable socio-economic devastations in West Africa.[82] Indeed, 'slavery' and other forms of dependence, far from destroying the economies of West Africa, were in fact a function of its modes of economic production as will be shown presently for the nineteenth century.

What has, however, bedevilled a clear understanding of this phenomenon is the question of terminology. Although there were several categories of dependence, these have usually been described—all of them—by the term 'slaves', and this carries connotations derived from the New World. Thus Walter Rodney sees every category of 'slavery' 'as well as agricultural serfdom and personal service . . . as "forms of social oppression" '. But he adds that 'in many cases the oppression was extremely attenuated', and then admits that 'the word "slave" was used . . . so loosely as to apply to all the common people . . .'.[83] Thus it is a problem defining terms. As Hopkins explains:

Many of the 'slaves' recorded by foreign visitors may well have been . . . loyal, if subordinate, citizens of the state, while others, though formerly of slave status were in practice integrated into the household and were virtually indistinguishable from freemen. At the same time, it is important to recognise that slave labour was present in West Africa long before the rise of the Atlantic trade, and that some slaves were bought, sold and otherwise used like the chattel slaves of the Americas. A substantial minority of the population in certain areas occupied a position of legal subordination and practical dependence which was less advantageous than that enjoyed by freemen. Not all slavery was a misnomer.[84]

But in most instances, it was a misnomer as it was applied indiscriminately by nineteenth-century observers

to all sections of the dependent labour force, thereby creating the impression that there was one rigidly defined and wholly underprivileged group whose sole concern was to perform all the menial tasks of the community. This view oversimplifies what now appears to have been a more complex situation. In reality, slaves constituted

---

[82] Fage, 'Slavery', *States and Subjects, passim.*
[83] Rodney, 'African Slavery', p. 432.
[84] A. G. Hopkins, *An Economic History of West Africa* (London 1973), p. 23.

only part of the labour force which also included serfs and free-men.[85]

Thus the use of the term 'slave' appears to be clearly inade-quate or inappropriate. What was called a 'slave' could have been a subject, servant, client, serf, pawn, dependant, or retainer. To describe them as 'domestic' is equally inappro-priate, for seldom were these dependants kept wholly within a household. As a labour force, they were kept more on the land than at home, and their settlements usually comprised 'open villages'.

The category of dependence, and therefore the status and treatment, depended on the methods by which the dependants were acquired. This has been well analysed for Ashanti and Yoruba,[86] where there were complicated hierarchies. In Sierra Leone, however, the situation seems less complex, and depen-dence was by choice, inheritance, or purchase.[87] This last cate-gory was usually made up of captives of war who could be sold, and is the only one that really approximates to 'slaves'. But it must be remembered that not only 'slaves', but freemen too were sold for debt and other serious offences.[88] The captives of war did the heavier farm work, and at first had few rights. They could be disposed of or used according to the behest of the mas-ter. If, however, they gave good service, in time they would be attached to a 'house', and given land to cultivate for their own profit. Their children were automatically 'slaves of the house'—i.e. they belonged to the family of the master and were an integral part of it. They were entitled to retain the profits from their own labours.[89] This possibility of upward mobility within dependent categories meant that the status of depen-dence could in time get lost in the extended family system.

The dependants who were attached to a household generally enjoyed more rights and shared a number of privileges with freemen. In the contemporary accounts of Sierra Leone, these are usually referred to as 'domestics', which is our main concern here as the least servile category of dependence. In this regard,

[85] A. G. Hopkins, 'The Lagos Strike', p. 139.
[86] Rattray, *Ashanti Law and Constitution*; Oroge, 'Slavery in Yoruba'.
[87] C. B. Wallis, *West African Empire*, p. 212.
[88] K. Crosby, 'Polygamy in Mende Country', *Africa*, x, 3, 1937, p. 252.
[89] CO 267/604/Conf., 20 June 1924, Slater to SS.

it has been said of Sierra Leone that '. . . a slave . . . in fact means a domestic servant in a feudal relation to the "owner" '.[90] The servant eventually gets absorbed into the extended family of the master, and with this upward social mobility, one sees a direct relationship between a dependant situation and the extended family. But the extended family itself is indeed a basically dependant situation with strong personal kinship ties. Thus household servitude could be seen as an aspect or an extension of the extended family system when by the upward mobility non-kinship personal ties became transformed and accepted as kinship ties.[91]

That this could be, and that it was usually possible for it to be so, is to be explained partly by the absence of classificatory kinship terminology among the Mende. First or second cousins and close friends with no degree of consanguinity were all loosely referred to, and refer to themselves, as brothers or sisters. Moreover, not only is a father's brother a father, but every male within the father's age-group is regarded and addressed as father; the same principle applies to the mother and her age-group too. Thus the kinship terminology itself works in favour of obscuring the nature of the exact relationship between persons which gets blurred with time and generation.

Voluntary dependence or servitude by choice also helped this development, by the system of 'pawning'. This reduced a man first to a position of dependence within a household, until he eventually got absorbed into the extended family. For instance, a freeman heavily in debt, and facing the threat of the punishment of being sold, would approach a wealthier man or chief with a plea to pay off his debts 'while I sit on your lap'. Or he could give a son or some other dependant of his 'to be for you', the wealthy man or chief. This in effect meant that the person so pawned was automatically reduced to a position of dependence, and if he was never redeemed, he or his children

---

[90] R. Lewis, *Sierra Leone* (London 1953), p. 73 n.

[91] This theory is not altogether new. Rattray in his *Ashanti Law and Constitution* first put it forward, perhaps, when he stated that many 'slaves' were simply extensions of the family. *Ibid.*, Chapter 5. See also Allan and Humphrey Fisher, *Slavery and Muslim Society in Africa* (London 1970). In 1897, certain rulers petitioned the acting Governor Caulfield that their 'few domestics' were servants not 'slaves', and part of their families, and therefore should not be made to leave them— CO 879/49/533/79, enc.

eventually became part of the master's extended family. By this time, the children were practically indistinguishable from the real children of the master, since they grow up regarding one another as brothers.

By the last quarter of the nineteenth century the institution of domestics was an established and integral part of the family and society. By the 1880s economic changes in particular were working in the interest of perpetuating the institution as a way of recruiting much needed labour. By this time it was said that the institution existed with the 'willing consent of the slaves themselves'.[92] The service rendered to the master was more in the nature of a voluntary one.[93]

Pinkett, in a despatch to Derby in May 1883, tried to correct the current mistaken ideas:

Domestic slavery in these parts is not what writers paint; the slave lives as well as his master and sure I am that hundreds of slaves come to Freetown [where slavery and slave-dealing were prohibited by law] and willingly go back to their masters. The native canoes that from the neighbouring territories bring produce are often unquestionably manned by slaves who come and go without any wish to change their condition.[94]

Even Governor Cardew with his anti-slavery humanitarianism and military impatience exhorted that the administration should proceed with caution to deal with the question of 'slavery', as it would be 'undesirable' suddenly to uproot an institution 'which from time immemorial appears to have been embedded in the manners and customs of the natives'.[95] As late as 1923, Captain Stanley, a Provincial Commissioner, opined in a minute that 'both master and slave see nothing wrong in domestic servitude'.[96]

It seems as if the institution operated similarly in most parts of Africa. David Livingstone, writing about East Africa, explained that

Among the coast tribes [in touch with slavers] a fugitive is always sold, but here [in the interior] a man retains the same rank he held in his own tribe. The children of the captives even have the

---

[92] CO 267/330/27, minute by A. W. L. Hemming, 1876.
[93] CO 267/417/Conf. 36, Cardew to SS, 1896.
[94] PP, vol. xlvii, 1883, p. 15; see also Wallis, *West African Empire*, p. 212.
[95] CO 267/409/Conf. 45, Cardew to SS, 1894.
[96] CO 267/604/Conf., 20 June 1924, enc. 5.

same privilege as the children of their own captors. . . . The Revd. T. M. Thomas, a missionary now living with [king] Moslekatse, finds the same system prevailing among his Zulus or Matabele. Mr. Thomas says that 'the African slave brought by a foray to his tribe, enjoys from the beginning, the privileges and name of a child, and looks upon his master and mistress in every respect as his new parents. He is not only nearly his master's equal, but he may, with impunity, leave his master and go where he likes within the boundary of the kingdom: although a bondman or servant, *his position . . . does not convey a true idea of a state of slavery*; for by care and diligence, he may soon become a master himself, and even more rich and powerful than he who led him captive.'[97]

In Sierra Leone 'slaves' of the second generation were always considered to be 'slaves of the house'. They had farms allotted to them, and not infrequently married into the family of their 'master', and rose to positions of trust, and became headmen of towns and even chiefs. More usually, as in Yoruba, dependants became masters themselves having a number of dependants.[98]

By the 1880s to the 1890s it was even observed that the status of these dependants was far better than that of a day-labourer in Freetown. The working relationship with the master was institutionalised so that the dependant gave five days of labour a week to his master, and used the remaining two days on his own private farm. This farm was also observed to be always in a better condition than the master's.[99]

The dependants of the same house could not be sold except for some serious offence, but punishments as such were not meted out to persons because of their status, but because they were first and foremost criminals. In the majority of cases, dependants associated freely with the children of the house as equals and were treated with respect if they were older. The dependants themselves preferred this kind of paternalism, which had nothing whatsoever of the nature of the cracking whips

---

[97] Quoted in M. Gluckman, *Custom and Conflict in Africa* (Oxford 1955), pp. 29–30.

[98] CO 267/604/Conf., 20 June 1924, minute by Stanley; Harry Luke, *Cities and Men, III* (London 1956), pp. 10–11; Hopkins, 'Lagos Strike', pp. 139–40; R. Lewis, *Sierra Leone*, p. 73.

[99] CO 267/400/14, enc. 3, memo by Parkes, 1893; cf. Oroge, 'Slavery in Yoruba', p. 200, where he says that the 'slaves' were so well-off that they had no desire to change their condition.

which called slaves to work on the plantations in America.[100]
Captain Wallis personally observed:

I have known cases where a 'slave' has run away from his master,
gone to Sierra Leone [the Colony] and finding the outside world
too hard for him, has of his own free will returned to his former
employer and home. These men who have left their masters in the
interior and have come down to the coast towns have to work a
great deal harder for a livelihood than they did in the bush.[101]

These dependants were so attached to the 'house' that it was
not uncommon for them to take employment in Freetown or
Bonthe and, having obtained some hard cash, to return with
the proceeds to their masters, and resume their occupations
under them. While conducting much of the trade for their
masters with the Colony, they generally did not avail themselves of the opportunity to be 'free' by claiming their freedom.
Indeed, Cardew himself agreed that 'their servitude is not of
an irksome nature'.[102] From the close of the nineteenth century
onwards, it was a matter of great difficulty to establish a
distinction between a 'slave' and a freeman.[103]

The innocuous nature of the system can further be illustrated
by the restraints imposed by custom upon the master in the
matter of punishing the dependant for committing offences.
No master had a right to imprison a dependant without first
obtaining permission from, or the authority of, the chief. The
chief took cognizance of two factors upon receiving the application: whether in reality the dependant was the master's, and
whether the offence was serious enough to warrant his being
put into the stocks.

In most instances, the chief assumed the innocence of the
dependant, and the master had to prove his guilt. This did
not arise in cases of grave offences, such as malicious damage to
the master's property. The chief took custody of the dependant,
to see if by firm but considerate action his character could be
changed. The results were invariably salubrious, and he was
returned to his master. In a circular to District Commissions

---

[100] CO 267/400/14; Little, *The Mende*, p. 38; Luke, *Cities and Men*, p. 11; Winterbottom, *Account of Native Africans*, p. 127.

[101] C. B. Wallis, *West African Empire*, p. 212.

[102] CO 267/417/Conf. 36, Cardew to SS, 1895.

[103] CO 267/484/140, enc. Probyn to District Commissioners, 1906; also Little,
The Mende, p. 38; Report of Tour by Major Pearce, 1909 (SLGA), p. 20.

in 1906, Governor Probyn urged the observance of customary laws with regard to the rights of dependants. In pre-colonial times, a master who put a dependant into the stocks without the prior authority of the chief was liable to a fine, and Probyn urged the revival of this custom.[104]

When Sir Harry Luke, as acting Governor, affixed his signature to the law which emancipated 'slaves' in 1928, he 'emancipated a quarter of a million people from one of the least oppressive forms of servitude in the history of human labour'.[105]

This account in no way presumes a euphemistic interpretation. It is plausible to argue that accounts during the colonial period would have tended to be biased in favour of an institution which, if condemned by the officials, would have meant condemning themselves for not having destroyed it. Yet the accounts of the pre-colonial and colonial periods present much the same picture. Indeed, while this account holds true as a general rule, there were certainly exceptions of abuse, and consequently there were defections of dependants from their masters to the Colony in order to gain their freedom. But these were isolated cases, and in any case, there was no mass exodus.[106] This would suggest that generally there was no mass ill-treatment of dependants. Were this the case, masters would have been faced with a sudden flight of their dependants, to their social and economic detriment. As early as 1803, Winterbottom summed up the general position of the institution thus:

Their [the interior peoples] domestics are in general treated by them with great humanity, and it is not uncommon to see the heir apparent [son] of a headman sitting down to eat with the meanest of his father's people, and in no wise distinguished from them by his dress. . . . No one can be sold as a slave, except such as have been first bought, without having some crime imputed, and being condemned by a trial or palaver. The property of masters in the children of their slaves is very much circumscribed, and the power of selling them without a palaver is taken away by the custom of Africa.[107]

---

[104] CO 267/484/140, enc. Probyn to DCs, 1906, Cf. Oroge, 'Slavery in Yoruba', p. 135: 'The master had the power of sale over his domestic slave, but . . . this power could not be exercised "without considerable difficulty".'

[105] Luke, *Cities and Men*, p. 11.

[106] See e.g. CO 267/345/206, Havelock to SS, 1881.

[107] Winterbottom, *Account of Native Africans*, p. 127.

Despite the harmless nature of this kind of servitude, dependants constituted an important indication of wealth:

The chief aim and the greatest desire of man and woman too amongst the Mende tribes is to possess slaves; it is at once the gauge to Native respectability and position, and the owner of such property rises in local importance in proportion to the number of slaves which he or she may have acquired.[108]

Evidently, women too belonged to this category, for they were dependants of their husbands and the larger a man's bevy of wives, the more important and wealthy he was considered to be.

These dependants were usually engaged in economic production. Agriculture depended on their labours. They were also responsible for collecting and cracking palm kernels and extracting palm oil. Kenneth Little explains that 'probably the growing importance of agriculture in place of warfare itself helped to improve the slave's position by providing him with an economic role'.[109] But this proposition is based on the false assumption that a straightforward dichotomy existed between war and agricultural production, as many contemporaries emphasised. Yet in 1876, when warfare was reported to be rampant, Governor Rowe fined the Mende who conducted the Keningbo raid 10,000 bushels of rice, because 'the country is one immense rice farm'.[110]

Indeed, even while war was still going on, the captives were set to work on farms to produce more wealth for their masters and the chiefs. Little, explaining this further, certainly puts the cart before the horse, when he advances that 'it is also possible that the availability of slave labour established rice growing over any other kind of economic activity as the pre-dominant form of agricultural industry'.[111] 'Slave labour' or no 'slave labour', rice was always grown as the staple food. More labour would only have meant more production and possibly surpluses that could be used in economic transactions and in accumulating wealth.

[108] CO 267/388/239, enc. 1, Report by Alldridge, 1891. This was the same in Yoruba country where 'for both economic and social reasons, every Yoruba normally aspired to acquire slaves'. Oroge, 'Slavery in Yoruba', p. 180.

[109] Little, *The Mende*, p. 39.   [110] PP, vol. lii, 1876 (C. 1402), p. 50.
[111] Little, *The Mende*, pp. 37–8.

War was not incompatible with the economic production function of the very captives of war. Rather than a dichotomy, one sees a stable co-existence between the two phenomena. 'Slave labour', therefore, was surely productive. But contemporaries argued as to whether it was productive or not. The question rather should have been how productive or how economic.

Dr. J. C. Maxwell, acting Governor in 1921, and an administrator with considerable experience, argued the economic point in favour of the abolition of the institution of dependence. 'It is unnecessary to elaborate the point here that slave labour is wasteful labour. This has been proved repeatedly in all parts of the world . . .'[112] It appears, however, that Dr. Maxwell was only rationalizing his opposition to the system without advancing specific illustrations of the wastefulness of dependent labour as proved in the Sierra Leone context.

Captain Stanley was perhaps more realistic in his opinion that he did

not find that agriculture is more vigorously conducted by the tribes among which servitude hardly exists; on the contrary they are as a rule poorer, cultivate less land, and have smaller reserves of foodstuffs than is usually the case with tribes among whom servitude is practised. . . . It is not impossible that with *servitude in its present state and form*, the average slave is made to work just a little harder than he would do if he enjoyed his freedom but in order to get him to do this, the average master works also a little harder than he would otherwise do.

This opinion was 'unquestionable'.[113]

Dependent unpaid labour was not wasteful or inefficient. West Africa had faced a historical shortage of labour which it was unable to solve by the development and use of machinery. The alternative would have been to hire labour and pay wages. This, however, would have been expensive, and the recourse to dependent labour was a 'deliberate choice'. Dependent unpaid labour was cheaper to acquire and maintain than the cost of hiring wage labour. In terms of cost-benefit analysis, now accepted as applicable to pre-industrial societies, the employers

[112] CO 267/604/Conf., 20 June 1924, Slater to SS, p. 5.
[113] Ibid., p. 14 (emphasis added). Also Little, *The Mende*, p. 38.

found dependent labour more advantageous.[114] Indeed many colonial regimes early in this century were faced with the same problem, and they not infrequently resorted to forced labour. The legal abolition of the institution of 'slavery' by the colonial regimes was more apparent than real, for in the final analysis what dissolved it was not legislative action, but changing socio-economic circumstances during the colonial period which rendered dependence irrelevant.

The Political System

Dependence was an important feature of society, and dependants, who were mostly engaged in carrying out various economic functions, usually inhabited 'open villages' supporting a war-town.[115] Security was an important priority, although it appears that the lives of the ordinary people outside the war-towns do not seem to have been fundamentally disrupted. A typical settlement consisted of *'walled towns and open villages or towns surrounding it'*.[116] These tended to be the centres of population concentration, and the settlements were set more widely apart.[117] In upper Mende, Alldridge discovered it 'to be a custom, at the great centres, to build three large circular towns within a few yards of each other, each containing some hundreds of huts, and each encircled by several war-fences. There is generally a large open space in front of these towns, which is called the Korbangai, and is used for public gatherings.'[118]

The war-town was the smallest unit of local administration, and was under the jurisdiction of a chief who had had some military experience. Malcolm explains further that 'there were two or three war chiefs . . . [who] were retired warriors, and did not themselves fight, or even go near the scene of battle unless a victory was reported, but they acted as the brains of the undertaking'.[119]

[114] Hopkins, *Economic History*, pp. 21–7.
[115] Cf. Anderson, *Journey to Musardu*, pp. 39–41.
[116] CO 267/344/60, report by Laborde, 1881.
[117] N. C. Hollins, 'A Short History of Luawa Chiefdom', p. 12.
[118] T. J. Alldridge, 'Wanderings in the Hinterland of Sierra Leone', *The Geographical Journal*, iv, 1894, p. 128.
[119] Malcolm, 'Mende Warfare', p. 49.

In a recent analysis of stateless societies, Robin Horton sees the 'large compact village' (which was characteristic of Mende settlements), as the 'type 3' variety of a 'three-fold social typology' of 'stateless social organisation'. Type 1 is the over-publicised 'segmentary lineage system', and type 2, the 'dispersed, territorially defined community', which results from a 'single-minded adjustment to subsistence farming'. But the type 3 kind of settlement 'results from a partial neglect of the organizational demands of farming in the face of those of efficient defence', and were thus usually fortified or stockaded.[120] Thus the structure of Mende settlements reflected military priorities. Even if the enemy succeeded in entering the town, they would sometimes find it very difficult to fight, or would get lost or dispersed once inside. It was this structure which appeared to Governor Rowe to suggest the existence of 'independent republican townships'.[121] But this interpretation can easily be misleading, as it could be to consider the Mende political system in the nineteenth century as a stateless one. And so is the view advanced by Barrows that, with the imposition of British rule, the 'war-town gave way to the chiefdom as the basic unit of social and political interaction' when the Colonial administration decided to 'grace . . . collections of war-towns' with its recognition as chiefdoms.[122] This is admittedly an over-simplification of a complex political structure. It suggests the absence of any centralized authority of importance, and this is all the more surprising when a recent writer can so categorically assert that no centralised system of government existed in Sierra Leone before colonial rule, and that it was 'colonization [which] . . . brought in a system of centralised government . . .'.[123] This can only be described as a wild assertion based on assumptions without any investigation.

Perhaps, within the context of Horton's plausible analysis, it is possible to agree that the society could and did move from

[120] Robin Horton, 'Stateless Societies in the History of West Africa', in J. F. A. Ajayi and M. Crowder (eds.), *History of West Africa*, vol. I (New York 1972), pp. 78–119.

[121] CO 267/330/28, Dec., 1876, Rowe to SS. Also Malcolm, 'Mende Warfare', p. 47.

[122] W. Barrows, 'The Position of the Contemporary Mende Chief' (University of Western Ontario symposium on Sierra Leone, Mar. 1971), p. 4.

[123] G. Collier, *Sierra Leone: Experiment in Democracy in an African Nation* (New York & London 1970), pp. 69, 72.

a stateless one into a centralized system without any drastic discontinuities, for types 2 and 3 contain 'germs from which state organization and ideology could sprout'. This might have been the case with the Mende, but Mende war-towns were not prototypes of Italian or Greek city-states, because they remained within the basic administrative structure of whichever 'country' they belonged to. Centralization was achieved without colonial rule, and certainly by the nineteenth century the Mende were in no sense a stateless people. In the Mende context trade and war were, perhaps, the most important factors in the transition to larger state systems.

Above this basic structure one discerns what was perhaps loosely referred to as 'the country'—walled towns and open villages and their 'fakais'. These latter were much smaller farming villages of no strategic importance, and which hardly attracted war-parties. They seem to have been widely scattered over the country. A ruler with clear territorial jurisdiction exercised authority over walled and open towns and 'fakais'.[124] Perhaps the equivalent of a 'fakai' in the upper regions, although much larger, was an ordinary town which was 'really a clearing among the big vegetation, which forms its natural walls . . .'.[125]

As William Budge explained in 1879 during a visit to Jama ('a collection of walled towns, nine in all, with two large open villages'), 'the principal chief was absent. We were kindly received by Vanjawa, the chief left in charge. Population here between 7,000 and 8,000 souls.'[126] Similarly Taiama, consisting of sixteen towns under a *Kolay*[127] 'who possessed all authority',[128] was said to be the 'metropolis of Tyama [Kpaa-] Mendi country . . . [and] supposed to have a population of over 10,000 souls'.[129] Wende, Ndawa's capital, consisted of thirteen towns; Kailahun, as typical of the upper regions, three fenced towns; Largoh, Makaya's capital, nine; Tikongoh, three; Pujehun, two; and so on. It is reasonable that this second tier,

---

[124] CO 267/344/60, Report by Laborde, 1881.

[125] Alldridge, 'Wanderings', p. 127.

[126] CO 879/17/214/18, enc. 5; see also CO 267/386/570, enc., 1890, for a description of Jama under Quee which consisted of twelve towns by then.

[127] CO 879/25/331, Karbekeh to Hay, 25 March 1887; CO 267/344/60, Report by Laborde, 1881.

[128] PP, vol. lii, 1876, Rowe to SS.　　　　　　[129] Despatches, 82/87, SLGA.

which may roughly approximate to what is today a chiefdom, was not constituted of only one 'settlement' of walled towns and open villages. A number of 'settlements' could actually constitute this second structure. In the absence of good communications, the expansion of a chiefdom over any considerable expanse of territory created a veritable imperative for the delegation of authority. Thus this structure emphasizing rank and differentiation of function was not a colonial invention, as some have assumed,[130] but an indigenous development.[131]

Above this second tier was the last echelon in the political structure; its units will be referred to as states, whose rulers were the real kings, although the title was used very indiscriminately by contemporaries. Although they are here called kings, the designation of the states as such follows the Vansinian theory.[132] On the basis of the available evidence, and the discernible differences already referred to, there were about nine states by the 1880s, which can be divided morphologically into two, for convenience categorized as territorial and personal-amorphous states. This tentative terminology is based on the nature of the territoriality. But, on the basis of the power and authority of the kings, the amorphous state was something of a personal state. Among the former can be listed Sherbro, Gallinas, Lugbu, Bumpeh, and Kpaa-Mende, while among the latter will be included the states of Nyagua, Mendegla, Makavoray, and Kai Londo. Krim is not included as a separate state because it was originally part of Sherbro. The name in Sherbro means 'immigrants'. By the late nineteenth century, their language 'which is Bolome is at present slightly different due chiefly to contamination with the dialect used by the Mendes . . . who had had intercourse with them'. The position of the territory was politically ambiguous, as there was strong Gallinas influence too. It is highly likely that *Zoro Kong* was the title of the ruler, like other Sherbro rulers. The situation, however, was quite a fluid one.[133] In the map appended to Winterbottom's book, the Sherbro are shown to border the Vai, while the Krim are not shown as a separate group.

[130] e.g. Barrows, 'Mende Chief', p. 5.
[131] Abraham, 'Traditional Leadership', pp. 44–5.
[132] Vansina, 'African Kingdoms', p. 342 n.
[133] C. R. Morrison in *Sierra Leone Weekly News*, 14 Oct., 1933; also Revd. Dr. Max Gorvie, personal interview, May 1972.

Thus, although the Mende have a common language and a common culture, they never evolved a common political state. The distinction of the political divisions among them has hitherto been completely blurred by reference to all the Mende system as a 'fluid state system', which description is actually true only of the personal-amorphous states.[134] These states had no very sharp lines of demarcation, and depended on the character of the king. Vivian was actually referring to the personal-amorphous states when he explained that 'the real cue to the present division comes from territory claimed by a given King and his subordinate headmen. As, for instance, Tikonko Mendi applies to any one who comes from any town or village over which Macavoreh, the Chief of Tikonko, exercises jurisdiction.'[135] The subjects identified themselves with the king, rather than with the state, and the state was only held intact and stability maintained according to the ability of the king. To the people, the king personified the state, and the two offices were indistinguishable to them. The state was readily identified only by reference to the king.

On the other hand, the territorial states did not depend for their stability on the character of the king as did the personal-amorphous states. The state existed and survived in spite of the king, who was more or less a *primus inter pares*, and did not assume that very dominant position with infinite power and authority reputed to belong to the king in the personal-amorphous state. In Bumpeh, for instance, there was an accepted plurality of rulers. Chiefs who were technically subordinate to the king in this state could be equally powerful if they had the force of character. It does appear to be generally the case that the Chief elected to head the capital of the state invariably becomes the king.[136]

These kings were generally titled rulers, such as *Beh Sherbro* of the Sherbro, *Massaquoi* of the Gallinas, *Kolay* (?) of the Kpaa-

---

[134] Cf. Paula Brown, 'Patterns of Authority in West Africa', *Africa*, 21, 4, Oct. 1951, p. 275; K. Wylie, 'Innovation and Change in Mende Chieftaincy', *Journal of African History*, 2, 1969, p. 295; Barrows, 'Mende Chief', p. 3; K. Little, 'The Mende Chiefdoms of Sierra Leone', in D. Forde and P. M. Kaberry (eds.), *West African Kingdoms in the Nineteenth Century* (London 1967), pp. 239–59; K. Little, 'The Political Function of the Poro, II', *Africa*, xxxvi, 1, 1966, p. 64. Even Davidson ('Mende Chiefdoms') does not perceive this distinction.

[135] Vivian, 'Mende Country', p. 16, also p. 24.

[136] Cf. the Gallinas, CO 879/25/331, 1887, Hay's interview with the Chiefs.

Mende, although there may have been a good number of exceptions. It is doubtful what the titles of the kings of Bumpeh were. In the Sherbro this titularization of the rulers was highly developed, and went even further down to the lowest echelons of the administrative hierarchy. All the territorial chiefs under the suzerainty of the *Beh Sherbro* had titles, viz.: *Ta Bompay* of Nongoba, *Sei Bureh* of Torma-Bum, *So Kong* of Imperreh, *Sei Kama* of Jong, *So Fa* of Cha, *Ya Kumba* of Tasso (Kagboro) which titular rulership merged and identified with the Caulkers since the eighteenth century. In some instances, even heads of towns were titled, such as *Do Fama* of Mattru, or the *So Kana* of Subu.[137] In the personal-amorphous states (which geographically belonged to the interior) the kings were literally 'maha mahu mahangaa', i.e. chiefs above chiefs. They were generally referred to as *Mendemahu*, connoting a ruler over an appreciable Mende territory. In all the states, the kings were addressed as 'Maada', i.e. grandfather.[138]

The territorial states admittedly had a markedly more complex kingship system than the personal-amorphous states. In both types of states, the office of king was not hereditary.[139] Election determined the incumbent to the office,[140] but the territorial states had a more elaborate system of investiture.[141] The election was carried out after due consultation with the chiefs and territorial heads, the 'big men' or 'elders'. As early as 1796, Dalton, a slave trader in the Gallinas, describing the country to Macaulay, stated that 'Each town or district sends delegates to a congress which elects a king, who has to do their will. It is seven years since the last king died. . . . The choice of king has to be unanimous which presumably explains why no king has been chosen.'[142] In 1903, the 'big men' of Gaura were still lamenting the death of Gbatekaka when King-Harman

[137] Lawson and Parkes, p. 41; 'The Caulker Manuscript, Part I', *Sierra Leone Studies*, iv, Oct. 1920, p. 17; CO 267 series, 1870–1890; T. J. Alldridge, *A Transformed Colony* (London 1910), pp. 268–73.

[138] Interviews at Vulunia 1969; Jawe, 1969; Gaura, 1972; Sembehun Junction, 1972.

[139] Winterbottom, *Account of Native Africans*, p. 124; Abraham, 'Traditional Leadership', *passim*.

[140] CO 267/501/61, enc. 3, Report on Native Law and Custom, 1908; CO 267/467/36, King-Harman to SS, 1903; Alldridge, *Transformed Colony*, pp. 268–73.

[141] Alldridge, loc. cit.

[142] Information kindly supplied by Christopher Fyfe.

visited them and asked them to 'proceed to the election of a new chief in accordance with their own law'. Meetings were then held by the sub-chiefs and leading men to come to a unanimous decision.[143] Age was a very significant factor in determining selection to high political office. 'Young men are not wanted as chiefs. Any age under forty is rightly considered too young. Men of experience are needed.'[144]

The same applies to women.[145] In customary law, women are treated as minors. As late as 1907, the Sherbro District Report for 1906 described the election of a woman in Bullom as 'most injudicious . . . and not in accordance with their native traditions'.[146] It was not uncommon, however, to have women as town or village heads.

The acquisition of political authority was not circumscribed and limited to only a particular class of persons. In both types of state systems, the process of acquiring power was open to anyone who qualified for it in spite of family or ethnic affiliations. 'Almost any influential person might make a bid for a Mendi chiefship . . .'[147] The acquisition of high political office was a flexible process except with regard to women.[148]

In the territorial states, the elaborate investiture by the elders led perhaps directly to the maintenance of important state regalia. The staff of office which William Budge saw with Movee, the Kpaa-Mende King, in 1879, was 'a stout walking stick with heavy brass mounting . . . borne by a messenger', and was the symbol of authority.[149] The Edwards–Loggie mission of 1878 described the Gallinas state regalia thus: 'The state property consisted of a white metal crown . . . a crimson robe richly laced with gold, a very fine ivory war-horn, heavily ornamented with silver, and the staff of state'.[150] The staff of state itself was described by Dalton to Macaulay as 'a gold-headed cane' which took the place of the deceased king at 'palavers'.

This is not to suggest that in the personal-amorphous states

[143] CO 267/467/36, King-Harman to SS, 1903.

[144] Migeod, *View of Sierra Leone*, p. 112; Hollins, 'Mende Law', p. 28.

[145] See Chapter V below.

[146] CO 267/495/299, Sherbro District Report, 1906.

[147] J. S. Fenton, *An Outline of Sierra Leone Native Law* (Freetown 1933), p. 4; see also Davis, *Chiefs and their Wars, passim*.

[148] Abraham, 'Traditional Leadership', *passim*; see also Chapter V below.

[149] CO 879/17/214/18, enc. 5, report by Budge, 1880.

[150] CO 267/335/182, Edwards–Loggie report, 1878.

there were no state regalia or symbols of authority—only that
they were not as elaborate. In fact an elephant's tail was very
widely and quite commonly used as a symbol of authority. By
the close of the century, too, the coastal areas had come to
accept the top hat as a symbol of authority![151]

In terms of the actual exercise of day-to-day administrative
authority, the kings wielded power almost equal to that of their
chiefs. Laborde noted that although 'Movee is practically the
king of the [Kpaa-Mende] country . . . in reality he has no
more power outside his own town than any other chief'.[152] The
kings did not interfere with the administration of their chiefs
over their direct and immediate subjects. As late as 1903 the
chiefs of Jong 'deprecated any interference on the part of the
Government between themselves and those subject to them'.[153]
The king was responsible for the external relations of the state
and also for war, and he heard appeals from his chiefs or
against his chiefs. Thus the idea of 'independent Republican
Townships' is more apparent than real. The king was also
responsible for conducting the election of his chiefs.[154]

Restless and turbulent chiefs could create immense problems
for the kings. Makavoray, for instance, had trouble with Ndawa
and Makaya. Both were in fact his wards, and he was their
'father'. When both were hired to fight wars in the coastal
areas, Makavoray found it difficult to control them, although
they were sub-rulers under him. Ndawa stated to Rowe that
'Makavoray is my father, but I am not in his hand . . .'.[155] In
fact Ndawa built his own settlement at Wende of which he was
the chief. So did Makaya at Largoh.

Thus the kings themselves were basically chiefs of their own
war-towns or 'settlements' to which their active jurisdiction
was limited. It does appear, however, that the kings of the
personal-amorphous states could exercise greater powers than
those of the territorial states.

[151] Alldridge, *Transformed Colony*, p. 271 and illustration. The use of European
dress—hats, coats, etc.—as signs of regal authority in the coastal areas was also
true of the Temne. See A. M. Falconbridge, *Narrative of Two Voyages to the River
Sierra Leone* (London 1802), pp. 12–51.
[152] CO 267/344/60, report by Laborde, 1881.
[153] CO 267/467/36, King-Harman to SS, 1903.
[154] Ibid.; CO 267/495/299, Sherbro District Report, 1906; Alldridge, *Transformed Colony*, p. 270; CO 267/367/68, memo by Rowe, 1887.
[155] CO 879/24/318/23, encs. 2, 8, 9, 10, Ndawa to Rowe, 1887.

Nevertheless, the 'rule of law' obtained. Kings, chiefs, and subjects alike obeyed the same laws of custom. No ruler could exempt himself from the rules of customary law simply because he was appointed principal head-chief over his subjects.[156] Subjects had a right to appeal against their chiefs. If, however, there was a dispute between a king and his subject, the subject had a right to appeal to a neighbouring king, which was not considered an indignity.[157]

The statement that the power and authority of the kings possessed 'all the ingredients of monarchical absolutism',[158] is a gross exaggeration and a downright inaccuracy.

. . . their position and powers are not narrowly defined, and vary somewhat according to the personality of the chief or of the other 'big men'. . . . It may confidently be stated that a Mende chief is not a despot, but a constitutional ruler—custom rather than strict law framing the constitution. Custom forbids him certain acts and insists that in an important matter he should only act after consultation with his 'big men'.[159]

Writing about the Liberian hinterland, Benjamin Anderson noted that 'tyrannical and bloodthirsty' the African rulers sometimes appeared to be, but much allowance must be made for this, because 'this character is artificial'. The outward appearances were only meant to prop their authority by inspiring 'terror and respect'.[160] Commenting on the government, Winterbottom wrote:

The government in Africa is in general monarchical, at least in name; for it must be acknowledged that in most cases the power of the aristocracy [elders] considerably overbalances that of the king . . .[161]

African political systems were in general democratic, whether the society was 'monarchical, i.e. chiefly, or whether it was republican, i.e. chiefless'. Two important concepts of democratic government were common to them—the representative

[156] A. Bokhari, 'Notes on the Mende People, II', *Sierra Leone Studies*, Mar. 1919, p. 54.
[157] Ibid., p. 53.
[158] Collier, *Sierra Leone*, p. 79.
[159] Hollins, 'Mende Law', p. 26.
[160] Anderson, *Journey to Musardu*, p. 86.
[161] Winterbottom, *Account of Native Africans*, p. 124.

principle and government by discussion.[162] Lord Hailey emphasised this point:

African sentiment attaches special importance to the due observance to the procedure by which all members of the community
concerned are able to have some voice in determining issues which
are of major interest to it. It is rare to find in British colonial Africa
any instance in which the indigenous form of rule previously in
force could be described as autocratic and there are not many cases
in which it could be described as authoritarian.

But he goes wrong when he says that there was no machinery to enforce obedience to orders.[163]

By the 1880s there was a discernible decline in the coastal territorial states. The territorial chiefs under the *Beh Sherbro* were virtually autonomous, perhaps only accepting him as their titular head, but probably equalling him in the actual exercise of authority. Thus instead of one unitary Sherbro state, the territorial divisions and their chiefs assumed virtually autonomous importance. This was particularly the case with Krim. The *Beh Sherbro* was more of a figurehead. This contrasts with the previous century when he was said to 'have the most power in these parts'.[164]

Equally, the Gallinas state was in decline owing to the persistent succession wars. Chief Abdul Lahai of Juring told Administrator Hay in 1887 that there was no real successor to King Manna Siaka, and that if one were elected, the troubles would cease. Hay thought that this was an urgent necessity. All the other chiefs agreed with Lahai.[165] Nevertheless, a successor was not elected.

At the same time, there appears to have been a certain amount of state-building going on in the personal-amorphous states. Nyagua, Kai Londo, Makavoray, and Mendelga were powerful kings who attempted to maintain the stability of their states, and to expand territorially by conquest. No contemporary kings in the territorial states assumed any comparable positions. While the kings of the personal-amorphous states

[162] T. O. Elias, *Government and Politics in Africa* (Asia Publishing House 1961), pp. 19–20.
[163] Lord Hailey, *Native Administration in the British African Territories*, IV (London 1953), p. 2.
[164] N. Owen, *Journal of a Slave Dealer* (London 1930), p. 47.
[165] CO 879/25/331, Hay's interview with Gallinas Chiefs, 1887.

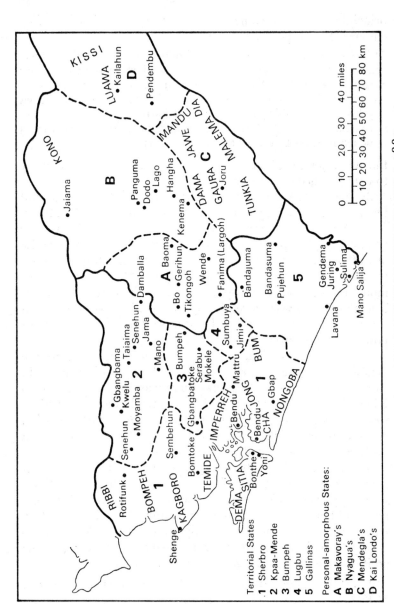

KISSI

LUAWA
• Kailahun
D
• Pendembu

KONO

MANDU
JAWE
DIA
DAMA GAURA MALEMA
C
• Joru

B
• Jaiama

Panguma •
• Dodo
• Lago
• Hangha

Kenema
• Baoma
A
• Gerihun
Bo •
• Tikongoh
Wende •

Dambaila

Fanima (Largoh)
TUNKIA

• Bandajuma
Bandasuma •
• Pujehun
5

Gbangbama •
Kwelu • Taiaima
Senehun •
Jama
2
• Moyamba
Mano •

Senehun •
Sembehun •
Bumpeh •
3
Gbangbatoke •
Serabu •
Mokele •
Sumbuya •
Jimi •
4

Gendema
Juring •
• Suima

• Lavana

Mano Salija

RIBBI
Rotifunk •
1
BOMPEH

Bomtoke •
TEMIDE / IMPERREH
• Bendu
Bendu •
• Mattru
JONG
BUM
CHA
NONGOBA
• Gbap
1

KAGBORO
Shenge •

DEMA SITIA
• Bonthe
Yoni •

Territorial States
1 Sherbro
2 Kpaa-Mende
3 Bumpeh
4 Lugbu
5 Gallinas

Personal-amorphous States:
A Makavoray's
B Nyagua's
C Mendegla's
D Kai Londo's

0 10 20 30 40 miles
0 10 20 30 40 50 60 70 80 km

MAP 2. TENTATIVE RECONSTRUCTION OF MENDE STATES, *c.* 1880

were dominant imperial figures, the kings of the territorial states were just one category of powerful chiefs. The decline of central authority in the territorial states led to a corresponding increase in the power and authority of the district chiefs.

This decline in the territorial states is partly to be explained by the presence of a European power on the coast. The coastal states needed to be strong and well organized, properly to conduct trade with the interior. Up to the nineteenth century the trade was mostly in 'slaves'. With active British interference the trade declined, and this perhaps in part accounts for decline of the coastal states. Moreover, it may be hazarded that the gradual infiltration and subsequent absorption by the Mende was also partly responsible.

But over and above this, the British actually discouraged the revival of any strong states on the coast. When Administrator Hay suggested to the Colonial Office that the title and office of the *Massaquoi* be revived, so as to avert the troubles that had afflicted the Gallinas for years, the substantive Governor, Rowe, then on leave in Britain, bitterly opposed it and carried the day. He suggested that only his recommended course of action would be to the advantage of the British.[166]

It would no more be to the advantage of the British Government to put someone to occupy the position formerly held by Prince Manna [the *Massaquoi*] than it would be to restore the King of Sherbro who existed at the time of Turner's Treaty [1825]. . . . In my opinion it is undesirable in every way that there should be a Native as the Massaquoi—the Governor of Sierra Leone or his representative should be the only person allowed to fill that position. I feel sure that any restoration of the Massaquoi in the person of a man who attempts to exercise power will produce trouble.[167]

Indeed, Rowe was anticipating the colonial occupation. Any attempt to revive any strong powers would be dangerous to the mission. The fragmentation of the coastal states was in the interests of the British. This fragmentation produced the same dynamic social forces as the state-building processes in the interior states. In short, the society was in a state of flux. Into this fluidity *Pax Britannica* was projecting its ubiquitous head by 1890.

[166] CO 267/367/94, minute by Rowe, 1887.
[167] CO 267/367/68, memo by Rowe, 1887.

II

CONTACT AND INVASION

Nature and extent of British influence in the late nineteenth century

ONE of the most astonishing facts about the European advent is that despite five centuries of their presence on the coast, their direct influence had hardly penetrated the heart of Mende country—no more than about thirty miles from the coast. What little influence there was, was limited to the coastal periphery. Within the context of European cultural influence in the interior, it is reasonable to categorize Creole influence as British too. Although the slave trader was the 'frontiersman' through whom European influence penetrated the interior, the Creoles too, for whom a settlement had been established on the Sierra Leone peninsula as part of the anti-slavery campaign of the late eighteenth century, generally took up trade in the nineteenth century, venturing up the navigable waterways, which, however, did not extend much beyond twenty-five miles inland.[1] Yet they acted as cultural agents. Having been brought in from divers places at various times and away from heterogenous forms of oppression and slavery, the Creoles were an amalgam of different societal norms, who having been divorced from their own societies, had to evolve a culture of their own. By the time of their centenary in 1887, the Creoles possessed a distinctive culture, heavily imbued with British values, although aspects of traditional African life are still discernible in their way of living. But the 'upper class' Creoles in particular not unusually evince the enigmatic character of being both the European and the African at one and the same time.[2]

[1] C. H. Fyfe, 'European and Creole Influence in the Hinterland of Sierra Leone before 1896', *Sierra Leone Studies*, N.S. 6, June 1956, pp. 113–23; Fyfe, personal communication to the present writer, 10 May 1972.

[2] On the evident duality of the Creole character, see Lemuel Johnson, *The Devil, the Gargoyle and the Buffoon*: *The Negro as Metaphor in Western Literature* (New York 1971), Ch. II; Graham Greene, *Journey Without Maps* (Penguin, 1971), Part

Brought up under British humanitarian paternalism, the Creoles were the first Africans to adopt systematic western education and professions. Dressed as Europeans, they were able by their mere presence in any part of the hinterland to exercise some amount of western influence.

But the communication system did not entice them into any adventure appreciably beyond the heads of navigation on the rivers. There was no 'gateway' into the interior of Sierra Leone to compare with the Gambia or the Niger. Like the slave traders before them, the Creoles had no incentive to venture deeply into the interior. The slave trader found convenient shelter for his hideous trade in the irregularity of the coastline with its mesmerizing inlets, while the Creoles could buy what they wanted readily on the coast.

Yet even taking British influence to include Creole influence, its geographical spread was no more than about forty to fifty miles from the coast by 1880. Within this limit, however, there were physical signs of European cultural influence. When Budge went on his mission into Mende country in 1879, visible signs of 'the influence of some civilising agency from Sierra Leone' did not fail to attract his meticulous attention. At Moyamba, Chief Hagba introduced Budge to his house with a 'sitting room plainly furnished, with a few cane-bottomed chairs, a fir centre table with cover, a small side table, a couch of plain deal with cotton print cover, pillow and swab . . .'

At Senehun, Budge received a 'pleasant surprise' for which he was quite 'unprepared', although it was 'by no means an unwelcome one'. Creole traders were already well established in this town, and they lived in their own 'quarter' as distinct from the 'native quarter'. King Movee, successor to Gbanya of Kpaa-Mende who died at a ripe old age in 1878, ushered the visitor into the room specially prepared for him.

I found here a roomy four-posted bedstead, hung with clean white curtains; a patchwork coverlet spread over a thick wool mattress, beautifully clean sheets, bolster and pillows. Toilet table, looking glass, toilet ware, and in short, everything requisite for comfort and convenience.

I, Ch. III. The Creoles generally have a nostalgic fever for 'home', i.e. Britain, and persist in aping European culture and Victorian values with irrational religious tenacity even where factors of ecology, climate, and nationalism—and, one may add, simple commonsense—would have dictated otherwise.

At Taima, Budge discovered that the most powerful chief, Gombu Pien, lived in a two-storied wooden house which was built for him by a carpenter called Collier, presumably a Creole.[3]

From the 1850s onwards, Creole traders had been establishing themselves at points in the interior plain so that by 1880, settled Creole establishments were present at Mabang, Moyamba, Senehun, Mo Toppan near Sumbuya, Mano Bagru, Mokele, and Shenge. These traders sent out agents with goods further up into the interior to important centres like Bumpeh and Tikongoh. 'Yet even allowing for the movement of such agents, Creole influence seems by 1870 to have scarcely covered the whole flat plain of the Mende country, hardly begun to penetrate its uplands.'[4]

Before 1880, no European had ever gone into Mende country beyond Senehun East, about a day's march from Taiama. Even in 1896 when the Protectorate was declared, 'the settled area of influence had not extended beyond the country known to the eighteenth century slave-traders'.[5]

Early attempts at expansion

The lack of any sustained attempt to extend direct European influence in the interior reveals the limited purposes of the British administration in Freetown. The Colonial Office steadily disapproved of annexation.

The tiny enclave of the Crown Settlement of Sierra Leone based on Freetown depended in a very great measure for its survival on the good-will of the interior kings whose kingdoms bordered it on all sides, and on one of whose territories the settlement had been planted after the land had been acquired from him. Within the Colony itself, there was no groundwork for economic viability, and, therefore, for political survival, for the British Government insisted that the settlement should pay for its own administration. Besides, the vicissitudes of interior politics affected the fortunes of the Colony; wars were said to

[3] CO 879/17/214/18, enc. 5, Report by Budge, 1880. Cf. the Liberian hinterland: 'the king has a frame house at Totoquella, with a piazza surrounding it, all of native construction. He also uses chairs, tables, beds, bedsteads, looking-glasses, scented soap, colognes, etc.' (Anderson, *Journey to Musardu*, p. 45).

[4] Fyfe, 'European and Creole Influence', p. 122.

[5] Ibid., p. 123; CO 267/344/60, Report by Laborde, 1881.

lead to the cessation of trade flowing into the Colony, and therefore of colonial revenue and profits.

Thus early in the nineteenth century, there arose a conflict
in policy between, on the one hand, the British Government's
insistence on barely preserving, and if possible contracting, the
existing responsibilities in West Africa, and on the other, the
men-on-the-spot, the frontiersmen, chafing restlessly to extend
colonial jurisdiction over the adjoining hinterland.

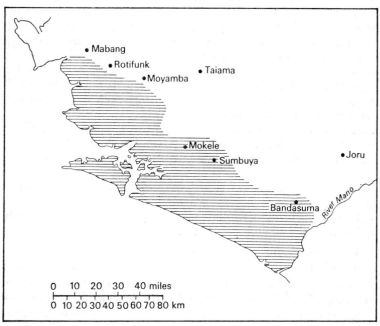

MAP 3. APPROXIMATE EXTENT OF EUROPEAN INFLUENCE, c. 1880

When Charles MacCarthy, an army officer, took charge of
the Colony in 1816, he had a threefold policy. One was to
increase the revenue of the Colony by extending its frontiers
and imposing customs duties. He revived British claims to the
Gambia, and got the Isles de Los ceded to the Colony. In 1820,
he persuaded the Caulkers to lease the Banana Islands for an
annual payment of 250 bars.[6] These seemed moderate expansionist moves.

But in Major-General Charles Turner, Governor from 1825

[6] Fyfe, *A History of Sierra Leone* (London 1962), pp. 131–3.

to 1826, the Colony found a hot-headed frontiersman and expansionist, with an almost entirely military approach to things. Taking advantage of the anti-slave trade spirit of the British Government, Turner used the suppression of the slave trade as a smokescreen to justify his imperialistic tendencies. In a logically reasoned despatch, Turner, after stating that the whole of the coast from Senegal to Liberia was involved in slave-dealing except the territory under his jusisdiction, added:

Should I succeed generally, as I have already done in certain districts in satisfying these [independent African] chiefs that other pursuits are more for their advantage and better for their country, than civil war and their slave dealing, and that they should prefer us to any other Nation to trade with and for their better security against the influence of the slave ships, claim our protection, I cannot see any just cause of complaint which such an arrangement on our part can give to any European state.

. . . such an arrangement . . . must promote in an unlooked for degree every object contemplated in our intercourse with Africa. In short, it would in a few years make a large portion of Western Africa altogether English. . . .

The annexation of these [Caulker] territories is the simplest measure possible. I make them govern themselves, and should any chief prove refractory, he is put down immediately by furnishing his rival with a few muskets and ammunition . . .[7]

In the year before, Turner had seen his chance. The Sherbro country was seething with ancient hostilities and the Caulker civil wars. Chief George Caulker asked Turner to mediate. On reaching Plantain island where the Sherbro chiefs were assembled, Turner made it distinctly known that he would do nothing unless the chiefs pledged themselves to give up the slave trade and cede their territories to the Crown. They were to receive British protection and become British subjects in return.[8]

The 'convention' Turner concluded with the Caulkers was thorough and complete in its unequivocal transfer of sovereignty. Drafted by officials, the preamble stated as a matter of fact the idea that, in the civil wars, the 'ultimate object [of the Mende] . . . is to exterminate the present possessors of the soil by the sword, or by selling them into slavery . . .'.[9] The preamble

[7] CO 267/71/17, Turner to SS, 1826.
[8] Fyfe, A History, pp. 156-7.   [9] PP, vol. xlvii, 1883.

further stated that the signatories[10] 'of their own free will and accord' asked for protection, despite the fact that Turner made the cession almost as an ultimatum, a condition, for his intervention in the disputes. In the end, the signatories

for themselves . . . their heirs and successors, for ever ceded, transferred and [gave] over . . . the full entire, free and unlimited right, title, possession, and sovereignty of all the territories and dominions to them respectively belonging, being situate between the southern bank of the Camaranka River on the north . . . and the line which separates the territory of King Sherbro from those of . . . the Gallinas on the south together with all and every right and title to the navigation, anchorage, waterage, fishing and other revenue and maritime claims in and over the said territories and the rivers, harbours, bays, creeks, inlets and waters of the same.[11]

While the transfer of power was so absolute, the territorial definitions were so vague that the convention was bound sooner or later to give rise to serious political, legal, and diplomatic complications. But as it turned out the treaty was never put to the test at the time. Earl Bathurst, Secretary of State for the Colonies, on first being informed of the negotiations, wrote back that the annexation would not be sanctioned because the British Government would not 'consent to any arrangement which might be construed into a desire of territorial aggrandisement. You will communicate therefore', the despatch instructed, 'to these chiefs with whom your negotiations . . . have been conducted . . . that their connection with Great Britain must be confined to one of Amity and friendly intercourse. . . .'[12]

Evidently, this decision sounded the death-knell of Turner's treaty despite the latter's powerful economic argument. But the death was more apparent than real. Half a century later, the treaty was to be salvaged and revived, and was to involve much practical and forensic wrangle. In the meantime, with

[10] 'Banka, King of Sherbro, on the part of his tributary Kings, Chiefs, and Headmen, Kong Kuba, Prince of Sherbro, Sumana, King of Bendoo, Ta Bumpay, King of Bullom, Solocco, King of Bargroo, Suwarrow, King of Char, Kenefarre, Chief of Sherbro Island, Will Adoo, Chief of Jenkins, Ya Comba, Queen of Ya Comba, by her lawful representative and next of kin, Thomas Caulker, Chief of Bompey and George Caulker of Tasso and the Plantain Isles, on behalf of themselves, their tributary chiefs, headmen and people.'

[11] PP, vol. xlvii, 1883.

[12] CO 268/20, 67, Bathurst to Turner, Dec. 1825.

explicit instructions to Campbell, Turner's successor, to annul the annexations, Turner's treaty was safely, if temporarily, set aside.

In 1831, therefore, Governor Findlay inaugurated the inoffensive policy of extending indirect influence by signing treaties of friendship with local kings and chiefs in the vicinity of the Colony. These rulers undertook, in return for annual stipends or presents, not to make war or molest traders. But the efficacy of these treaties left much to be desired. The signatories might retreat to distant parts of their territories where they would remain uninfluenced by the administration. Moreover, in most instances, the administration lacked the ability to enforce the treaty regulations, for instructions from London prevented the officials getting embroiled in any local matters that might result in war.[13]

This British policy of non-annexation was changed in 1861 when under another restless Governor, it was circumvented with impunity, whether by chance or by design. Hill, as an army Colonel, was determined to win a military decoration. He meddled frivolously in the affairs of the territories bordering the Colony from the Northern Rivers to the Gallinas. He interfered in the Port Loko election of 1857; led an abortive expedition to Maligia in Kambia which ended in a military fiasco; ostensibly to protect traders, he fraudulently annexed part of Koya while assuring the chiefs it was being leased; finally, in 1861, he was presented with a singular opportunity for annexing part of Sherbro.[14]

During the 1850s, the pressure of French encroachments in the Sherbro became very apparent. As their influence increased, the French were determined, if need be, to use force. In 1857, an unfortunate incident brought the French squadron to the Sherbro and the town of Bendu, Chief Thomas Stephen Caulker's capital, was bombarded, ostensibly because a French trader had been insulted. Finding himself sandwiched between British and French interests, either of which savoured of a loss of sovereignty just in the offing, the chief decided upon the lesser of the two evils: he offered his country to Hill.[15] '. . . Knowing

---

[13] Fyfe, 'European and Creole Influence', p. 117.
[14] Fyfe, *A History*, pp. 276–8, 308–12.
[15] Ibid., pp. 285–6; Fyfe, *Inheritance*, p. 188.

that I could never consent to the French having Bendoo . . .', Caulker wrote to Hill, 'I now offer this place to your Excellency . . . which I have the whole and sole right to . . . *Grasp* at this offer and send down at once, or the French will be in possession of the most prominent part of the Sherbro which is Bendoo.'[16] The Governor immediately gave orders for hoisting the Union Jack there before he himself went to Bendu.

Hill sent emissaries to the Bagru and Sherbro Island chiefs, in order to conjure a request for protection from them, thus making it appear that the chiefs had voluntarily ceded their territories to the British Crown. Having thus deftly stage-managed the situation, he went to Bendu himself in November 1861. At Hill's instigation, Chief Caulker and the Jong Chiefs ceded not only Bendu, but some 200 square miles round it. Then the Bagru and Sherbro Island Chiefs fixed their marks on a treaty of cession which had been drawn up in advance. When he told the Colonial Office what he had done, Hill stated specifically that the initiative had come from the chiefs, who had begged him to take over their country. The justification for taking over the territories which Hill argued powerfully—to keep the French away from valuable dockyard timber, and to suppress the slave trade (although this had not been practised in the Sherbro for ten years)—won over the Colonial Office into somewhat reluctantly ratifying the treaties.[17]

For the first time, the Colonial Office accepted the threat of a foreign power as a partial reason for side-stepping its former policy. The suppression of the slave trade was an equally vigorous argument—whether it was true or not was beside the point—in the cession of Sherbro. Two decades later, the suppression of the slave trade was an anachronistic argument for a more aggressive policy towards the interior. The French menace had become more apparent, and if anything, and if somewhat reluctantly, was alone thought to be sufficient ground for abandoning the old policy.[18] But the real reasons for annexations in the 1880s were economic. The world depression of the

[16] CO 267/270/23, Caulker to Hill, 1861, quoted in Fyfe, *Inheritance*, pp. 188–9.
[17] Fyfe, *A History*, pp. 308–10.
[18] Fyfe, *Inheritance*, pp. 201–2; D. H. Perraton, 'The Man on the Spot: British Officials in late nineteenth century Africa', in *Theory of Imperialism and European Partition of Africa* (Centre of African Studies, Edinburgh University Seminar Proceedings, 1967), p. 152.

1870s was sufficient by itself to make officials and the men-on-the-spot openly advocate political aggrandisement in order to maintain economic stability—a policy officialdom had shied away from in earlier decades, but a policy which they would now find far-fetched reasons to justify.

The problem was quite delicate, and intricately interwoven with the interior politics of the indigenous Africans. To the officials generally, the interior was just a melting pot of turmoil and interminable 'inter-tribal' warfare—the issues at stake too complex, unfamiliar and of little direct interest to the Colony unless trade was affected or British subjects were molested.[19] The officials therefore took a very oversimplified view of the situation and came out with ready-made solutions that proved very inadequate. Although, with some exceptions, the general rule, as has been noted, was non-intervention, the establishment of permanent residents in areas beyond British jurisdiction was bound to bring with it official commitment, as traders pushed up the heads of navigation on the rivers. But the climate of British opinion at Whitehall was strongly opposed to any extension of responsibilities.[20]

The financial crisis of the Colony and the move to the interior

The financial position of the Colony in the 1870s was precarious, since it depended mostly on the fortunes of trade. The revenue depended on the volume of exported produce and also on the prices that the produce would fetch in Europe. If one fluctuated, the revenue of the Colony was adversely affected. Moreover, the amount of customs revenue was directly related to both trends. Lower prices or a lesser volume of trade would result in less imports and therefore in less customs revenue.

When therefore the Great Depression began in 1873, the Colony was thrown into financial embarrassment. Imports dropped catastrophically from £411,935 in 1872 to £326,011 in 1875, while exports were correspondingly £936,750 and £350,202. This downward trend continued throughout the 1870s.

[19] Creoles were British subjects.
[20] J. D. Hargreaves, 'The Evolution of the Native Affairs Department', *Sierra Leone Studies*, N.S. 3, Dec. 1954, p. 168.

Explaining this general economic phenomenon, Hopkins writes:

During the last quarter of the nineteenth century legitimate trade passed through a period of crisis, as the prosperity of West African trade was undermined by acute market problems in Europe, where changing conditions of demand and supply had a profound and adverse effect on exports from the West Coast. . . . Increase in the supply of oils and fats was not matched by a corresponding increase in demand. In England the financial crisis of 1873 signalled the advent of the so-called Great Depression, a period when wholesale prices of raw materials in general, and of palm produce in particular, tended to fall. . . . By about 1880 . . . the continuing fall in prices was a reflection solely of the collapse of the European market for palm produce.[21]

Palm produce constituted the bulk of the Colony's exports, and with the depression crisis, the Colony entered into serious fiscal problems.

In the heated debate for saving the Colony from financial collapse in the later 1870s, the beginnings of a policy that was to involve the administration in the affairs of the interior, a policy from which it later became impossible to escape, are clearly discernible. The immediate objectives were intended to be those of practical economic value. Yet the administration began to entagle itself in a political morass.

In 1874, the results of Governor Hennessy's economic reforms did not equal his expectations. Looking, perhaps, for cheap popularity, he abolished direct taxation, including house and land tax, as soon as he assumed office in 1872. He was still using a tariff structure that had been introduced by Governor Kennedy nineteen years earlier, and by 1874 this was complicated and injurious to commercial operations. The customs revenue anticipated for 1874 was £54,865, as compared with £72,905 for 1873, while the actual revenue for 1874 was £43,983 as compared with £62,845 for 1873. Hennessy moreover abolished most of the existing duties while increasing those on three or four commodities only, such as spirits, tobacco, and ammunition.[22]

[21] A. G. Hopkins, 'Economic Imperialism in West Africa: Lagos 1880–92', *Economic History Review*, 21, 1968, pp. 585–6.
[22] CO 267/326/35, Rowe to SS, 1874.

Traders who got embroiled with the inhabitants in local political affairs urged active intervention by the administration to annex the adjacent territories from the Isle de Los to the Shebar River. William Grant, for instance, made such a suggestion to the Colonial Office, adding that the collection of duties in the annexed areas would alleviate the Colony's difficulties and increase its revenue.[23] This was necessary because duties levied on goods entering the Sierra Leone Colony could hardly produce much revenue so long as goods entering immediately adjacent areas paid no duties at all.

There was, however, a two-fold opposition to this line of policy. Governor Berkeley saw the logic in the argument of the traders, and thought that 'to espouse unconditionally the cause of the merchants . . . in their quarrels with the natives, would be a line of policy likely to meet with general approbation'. But he was wary of recommending such action 'in as much as I believe, in many instances the subjects of this Government are at fault'.[24] The Colonial Office was not yet ready to accept any political responsibilities. Dr. Blyden after his visit to Falaba in 1872 expressed apprehension that the French might claim the Great Scarcies, especially as negotiations to exchange the Mellacourie for the Gambia from France had proved abortive on account of the Franco-Prussian war of 1870. The Colonial Office was quite explicit on the point that the government would not object to the extension of French influence 'provided there is no exclusion of British trade . . .'.[25]

There were further complications to the problem. Despite Hill's annexations of 1861, British jurisdiction in the Sherbro was very hazy. Lord Kimberley recognized that 'B[ritish] Sherbro . . . is somewhat of a "terra incognita" . . .' and was bewildered by 'the very undefined way in which the limits [of British jurisdiction] are laid down'.[26] Moreover there were internal disturbances that affected the areas which were technically under British jurisdiction, at the same time as the economic condition of the Colony and British Sherbro continued to deteriorate. There was the Keningbo war in the

[23] CO 267/327/6 Oct. 1874, Havelock to SS.
[24] CO 879/8/82/16, Berkeley to SS, 1874.
[25] CO 267/327/6 Oct. 1874, Havelock to SS.
[26] CO 267/327/43, Kimberley to Holland, 1874; CO 267/329/2, minute by Meade, 1876.

Caulker country, and renewed disturbances in the Jong country because of the disputed territory between Tom Kebbi Smith and Lahai Sheriff.

Governor Kortright was converted to the opinion of the traders, and he attributed the loss of revenue to 'the native wars'. But more practically, he argued that the loss of revenue to the administration was due to the fact that a slice of territory, Jong territory, in dispute between Smith and Sheriff, broke into the territory under British jurisdiction, and that through it goods passed into British Sherbro without paying duty. He therefore advocated its acquisition and that of Shenge territory. Two advantages would accrue. Firstly, customs duties would be collected, and secondly, 'by prohibiting the importation of arms and ammunition [the administration might] cripple the resources of war of the contending chiefs'. R. Meade at the Colonial Office agreed to the suggestions for the acquisition of the Sherbro seaboard 'to allow us to place customs officers and collect duties'. But, he concluded, 'we do not want to increase our responsibilities in other matters or to *govern* more than at present'.[27]

The policy followed since the cessions of 1861, of signing friendly treaties with chiefs of surrounding districts binding themselves to maintain the peace and to refer their disputes to the Governor for arbitration, was now seen to be useless. The treaties were worth less than the paper on which they were written. Lord Carnarvon minuted: 'I doubt much the expediency of these "treaties" with native chiefs. They are more likely to entangle than benefit us . . .'[28] A more positive policy was clearly seen to be necessary. The crux of the whole matter lay in the financial insolvency of the Colony.

Governor Rowe and intervention in interior politics

The initiative of following a more practical policy with regard to the interior, was seized by Governor Samuel Rowe, an army surgeon who had worked in Lagos and the Gold Coast, and who was appointed to act in Sierra Leone in 1875, when Kortright

[27] CO 267/328/111, Kortright to SS, 1875; CO 267/328/153, minute by Meade, 1875.
[28] CO 267/328/111, minute by Carnarvon, 1875; CO 267/329/59, Rowe to SS, 1876.

went on leave. His activities may be said to have laid the foundations of official British penetration. In 1876, as the economic situation worsened, William Grant whipped up sufficient support for a petition signed by 300 people (and Grant claimed there were more) pleading that the 'acquisition of, at least, the seaboard of those adjacent native territories . . . would have secured the Sierra Leone trade and revenue from the fluctuation and peril to which both seem at present to be exposed'. The petition further drew attention to the fact that the inhabitants had evaded tax ever since the increase in duties on tobacco and spirits. The signatories were abundantly unambiguous in their opinion that only the acquisition of the sea-board territories would secure prosperous development of Sierra Leone trade.[29]

The Colonial Office, apparently eager to avoid a diplomatic fracas with the French, was not ready to consider any acquisition of territory to the north of Sierra Leone. To the south, however, they favourably considered

the Lt-Governor being authorised to enter negotiations with a view of obtaining from the native chiefs of the territory lying to the south of Sierra Leone between Calmont Creek and the Cockboro river the power of appointing Customs Officers and levying customs dues. . . . Dr. Rowe has recently been instructed to endeavour to make an arrangement of this nature with regard to the Shangay territory between Cockboro River and the Yaltucker River.[30]

Upon his assumption of duty, Rowe became very active in demonstrating British power. The recent Keningbo and Kebbi Smith wars were seen to be part of the causes of the Colony's economic paralysis. To cure the latter, the adjacent territories must, in colonial terminology, be 'pacified'. In a characteristically high-handed fashion, Rowe dealt firmly with the culprits of the Keningbo war, and he personally led two expeditions to the Bagru and Mongray river basins. He renewed treaties with chiefs surrounding British territories to keep the peace and to open trade routes. After his startlingly quick successes, Rowe was in an advantageous position vis-à-vis the inhabitants. It is thus understandable that the terms of his agreement with them represent him as something of a bully—it was in fact a dictated agreement. The document was not a treaty, because, as Rowe

MAP 4. THE SHERBRO, *c.* 1880

himself explained, the terms were not binding on the British Government. But by the terms, the signatory chiefs were made, *inter alia*, to agree that

in case of any infraction . . . of the promises now made by us the signatories of this agreement, the Chief or Headman so breaking his plighted word shall be considered to be the enemy of the Queen's government, and . . . he shall be considered to have forfeited the right to the government of his country; and . . . Her Majesty shall be considered in consequence . . . to have acquired the right to

remove him from his government . . . or punishing him in such
other way as may seem good to her and taking possession of his
country . . . or appointing another person to govern it . . .[31]

Rowe believed that a threat to hand over their territories to
British rule was the most powerful deterrent to compel the
chiefs to desist from fighting. Although they were only meant to
be a 'threat', the terms of the agreement herald a new era in
the relations between the inhabitants and the British officials.
The administration was imposing its own peace, and the resulting political entanglements were to lead eventually to the
declaration of the Protectorate.

One immediate consequence of the agreement with Rowe
was the commencement of hostilities by Bumpeh and Tikongoh
against their erstwhile allies, Lugbu and Bum, because they
were not consulted when the agreement was signed by them.
The war-party Bumpeh sent against Lugbu retreated only at
the request of Wall, the acting Commandant of the Sherbro.[32]
The traditional dynamics could not be arrested by any super-
ficial action on the part of the administration.

Rowe's policy, evinced in his late action, was one of instilling
fear of British might into the people, which the Governor
explicitly acknowledged: 'My action in the Mongray river
supplemented by that in the Bagroo has made an impression
on these people, which the execution of Caulker, Kinigbo and
Vana has I hope completed.' The chiefs were threatened with
loss of their territories if they did not desist from fighting.[33]

Having completed his political task, Rowe had to convert his
success into economic benefit from the Colony. He argued that
'by all the country rules of justice, the Caulker family were
responsible for [the Keningbo] war, and liable to be charged
with any expenses consequent upon it'. Rowe's argument is
reminiscent of that of the British Government that the American
colonies must pay for the benefits they gained after the Seven
Years' war. The Mende mercenaries who conducted the Keningbo raid were fined 10,000 bushels of rice. 'The Bompeh and
Cockboro countries had also been large gainers by the action
of the Sierra Leone government . . .' and must be made to pay

[31] CO 267/329/59, enc., Agreement with the neighbouring Tribes in the
Sherbro, 8 May 1876.
[32] CO 267/330/160, Rowe to SS, 1876; CO 267/330/170, Rowe to SS, 1876.
[33] CO 267/329/59, Rowe to SS, 1876; CO 267/330/170, Rowe to SS, 1876.

a share of the expenses. Thus, in spite of the punishment of the culprits, Rowe obtained the right to collect customs dues along the seaboard. He wanted fiscal, not political, jurisdiction. Thus, as he explained, although 'the population generally would have been only too glad that the country should be transferred to British rule', the agreement of 1876 did not propose any such action. But the right was acquired of levying duties over the seaboard, and arbitrating in certain quarrels without any possession of land.[34] The Colonial Office was in perfect agreement as long as the holding of a strip of land for customs purposes 'would involve no corresponding responsibilities inland'.[35]

Despite the inaccuracy of the local contemporary analysis that the interior wars were responsible for the economic crisis, and the universality of the world depression at the time, Rowe at last found the opportunity, with ample rationalization based on local events, to consummate a policy which the traders had talked the Colonial Office into believing in. Neither the Governor nor the traders professed any primary political motives. Their interests were economic, and they took care to avoid political entanglements. Yet as is commonplace in human affairs, the division was artificial, and would not long survive the division. The supposed panacea of extended jurisdiction was indeed a political act inspired by economic motives. Yet it did not bring relief to the Colony's more deeply rooted economic ills, which continued in spite of efforts to cure them. Matters were further aggravated in 1878 by a recurrence of wars in the interior which created a general state of anxiety and hysteria on the part of the traders.

The Bum and Sherbro countries were disturbed by a serious raid led by Canagboh, described by Rowe as 'a notorious ruffian, and supported by the Bompey [Banta] tribe'. While refusing a request from certain chiefs until they proved adamant to lead an expedition against Bumpeh, Rowe was in fact seeking permission to lead an expedition to the head of the Bum River. Two traders also complained of losses by the raid. But Rowe insisted that the raid was not even near British territory, and was not conducted by any chief in treaty

[34] PP, vol. lii, 1876, pp. 49–51.
[35] CO 267/330/27, minute by Hemming, 1876.

relations with the British. It was the familiar story of British traders moving beyond British territory, and expecting to be protected. The administration did not want to stretch its responsibilities.

However, when he made a visit to the disturbed areas, Rowe advised the chiefs to arrest Canagboh and hand him over to the administration. But he wished to take an active part in the capture of Canagboh, by leading an expedition to enforce the demand, and to confine Canagboh 'as a political prisoner and bandit' in the Freetown gaol. 'The effect will be very great and the peace . . . would be confirmed for years.' As the example of Canagboh proved, Rowe was underestimating the dynamics of the politically fluid situation.

For conducting similar wars, Canagboh was handed over to the Commandant at Bonthe, Darnell Davis, by the Bum Chiefs in 1875. He was sent on to Governor Kortright who decided that as he was not a British subject and had not committed crimes on British soil, he should not be imprisoned, but should reside with the Government Interpreter under a sort of house arrest. Davis was convinced that Canagboh had reformed his ways, but then one day he stealthily disappeared. 'Mr. Davis was always an optimist with respect to the negro', reads an annotation in the margin of the despatch reporting the incident. It is unlikely that the removal of Canagboh was alone sufficient to arrest the situation.

However, the Colonial Office was hesitant. 'It would be a departure from our settled policy whereby we do not undertake, except in very exceptional cases, to interfere actively beyond our borders . . .' But, it was cautioned, sanction must be given for an expedition, if British territory were violated.[36]

Political missions and African reaction

Having been baulked of a much desired personal adventure, Rowe resorted to the alternative of sending political missions to the interior kings and chiefs, and this expedient became an aspect of official policy towards the interior in the following years. But Rowe justified himself by concrete examples of the general condition of the neighbouring countries, which was not

[36] CO 267/334/33, Rowe to SS, 1878.

conducive to the Colony's economic recovery. There was a general state of anxiety and apprehension. Gbanya of Kpaa-Mende died; Kebbi Smith died too, and plunder and trouble were feared in the Bum country; there were reports of dissensions among the Caulkers and a possible recourse to arms; traders in the Bum feared another raid by Canagboh; there were rumours of wars in the Kittam and the Gallinas. Messrs. L. Edwards, Assistant Colonial Secretary, and J. C. Loggie, acting Commandant of Sherbro, were thus commissioned to survey the area in general.

The mission was reported to be successful. At Yengema, Bumpeh, Chief Seppeh, one of those involved in the latest Canagboh dispute, was warned 'in earnest language that if peace did not come to their country, the time would shortly be when the land would pass out of their hands'. Rowe had apparently schooled them.[37] As a result, messengers from Bumpeh, Tikongoh, Kpaa-Mende, and the Gallinas visited the Governor to reaffirm the pledges of peace that their leaders had made to the commissioners. In a farewell message to them, Rowe said that 'the Great Queen of England . . . does not want your country or anything from you. . . . She has many countries in her dominion, far larger and wealthy than yours. If she wanted your country, it would be very easy to take it in 3 or 4 months' time.'[38] Rowe was systematically applying his policy of 'threat'.

However, despite sending messengers, Bumpeh remained an obstacle to the penetration of colonialist ideas, and was determined to maintain its traditional culture and role. Bumpeh resented the interference of the administration in its traditional feuds particularly with Tikongoh. According to a report by policemen on their way to Tikongoh, they were led to the place where warriors usually assembled before hostilities. There, they found 400–500 warriors, among them Canagboh! The warriors stated that

They see no reason of the Governor's interfering with them and the Tekonkohs; that they have large debts to pay, and without war, they cannot obtain money to pay their debts . . . Why is the Governor so anxious for us to leave off war? We are not making war

[37] CO 267/335/182, enc. Edwards–Loggie Report, 1878.
[38] CO 879/15/175/1, enc. 4, Rowe to SS, 1879.

against whitemen, nor do we take war to the Queen's country. If any of the Queen's subjects is killed, it is those who through their hard head force themselves into our country. If the Governor wishes us to leave off war altogether . . . let him remove all the men of warships and boats from the waters.

The Bumpeh were apparently unconcerned about punitive expeditions which burnt down their towns.[39]

It is reasonable to suppose that, while pledging themselves to fulfil any promises as requested by the British officials and agents, the interior states did not yet envisage the British administration as a threat to their sovereignty. They thus continued to conduct their affairs as time-honoured customs dictated, quite oblivious of any obligations they might have incurred with the administration. In short, they did not as yet treat the administration with any appreciable degree of seriousness. The readiness with which they pledged themselves to accept the demands of the administration lulled the latter into a false sense of security, while allowing the states to continue their affairs with little disturbance. The policemen to whom the Bumpeh warriors spoke so candidly were not white men. Had they been, the warriors would easily have pledged themselves to obey the Governor, a promise not meant to be honoured.

Solving the financial crisis—acquisition of 'fiscal jurisdiction'

Meanwhile a Departmental Committee was appointed by the Secretary of State for Foreign Affairs, the Secretary of State for the Colonies, and the Chancellor of the Exchequer in 1877, to enquire into the economic depression of the Colony, and to suggest remedies.[40] But the Edwards–Loggie report in 1878 was the first objective local analysis of the situation. It drew attention to the fact that the traders themselves were not agreed as to the causes of the depression, since they expressed their own biases. 'It might be said in explanation that the wave of trade depression is over the whole world, and that West Africa is suffering in common with the rest; but there are

[39] CO 879/15/175/28, enc. 6, Report of Policemen on their journey to Tekonkoh, 1879.
[40] CO 267/333/20 July 1877, report of Departmental Committee.

certain local circumstances which in a measure partly explain the causes of this depression.'

The traders were not united, and there was consequently cut-throat competition. Every year, new entrepreneurs started commercial ventures with little or no capital, and entered into competition with established firms. Mostly Creoles, these traders pushed up the rivers, and were content with quick returns and small profits.

Secondly, chiefs, formerly content to receive presents from traders, now turned 'middlemen' themselves. Some therefore prevented traders venturing beyond certain points on the rivers, and importing certain commodities, notably salt, into certain areas.

Lastly, the report concluded, the unsettled state of the Bum prevented local producers from coming down to the coast for fear of being plundered.[41]

The report of the Departmental Committee was much narrower in its perspective, which examined the crisis simply within the context of the diminishing revenue of the Colony. Since nearly all revenue was derived from customs, it argued, the imposition of more customs duties in 1871 had led to smuggling. It was estimated that about £10,000 annually was being lost to revenue in smuggling.[42] Traders moved to rivers where they paid no duties, and this led to a decline in trade and consequently in revenue.

The report suggested that any reduction of duties would not help revive trade because traders paid no duties in the rivers. It recommended that the Colonial Office confirm the treaties of cession signed by Rowe in the Scarcies, and annex the coastline south of the peninsula from the Chief of Bompeh (Sherbro), Ribbee, and Cockboro (Kagboro), in substitution of the treaties made in 1875.

The conditions of the Colony and its urgent necessities are such that, in the absence of an annual grant from Parliament, there would appear to us to be no alternative but to revert to the scheme . . . of protecting the customs revenue of the Colony by securing as much of the adjacent coastline as may be necessary for the purpose.[43]

[41] CO 267/335/182, Edwards–Loggie Report, 1878.
[42] CO 267/337/3, minute at the CO, 1879.
[43] CO 267/333/20 July 1877, Report of Departmental Committee.

Accordingly Rowe was requested by the Colonial Office in 1878 to negotiate new treaties with Bompeh and Ribee chiefs, since Turner's treaties of 1825 had not been ratified. Customs revenue would then be collected to alleviate the fiscal distress of the Colony. But the Treasury made it 'distinctly understood that they are not prepared to hold out the prospect of any . . . subsidy in aid of the policy of acquiring fresh territory, however limited in extent, in order to maintain the present Customs Duties'.[44]

It was, however, discovered that more smuggling was being done in the Bum-Kittam region by traders such as the notorious John Harris. From 1855, onwards, Harris steadily established himself in the Sherbro despite several setbacks. A very daring adventurer, his ships had at one time been seized by the Liberian officials for breaking their customs regulations. Only through Hill's intervention were they released. Smuggling, in fact, was generally commonplace among traders since they would make more money thereby.

After the difficulty of obtaining the consent of the Foreign Office to the extension of jurisdiction over the Scarcies and Ribee districts, the Colonial Office was reluctant to approach it with further requests to acquire the Bum-Kittam mouths. To try and save the situation, it was thought most advisable to enlist the cooperation of Chief Tucker of Nongoba Bullom, who controlled these rivers. 'Fortunately,' according to the Edwards–Loggie report, 'he thinks a great deal more of the British Government than he does of the British trader, and would prefer to retain his stipend than to receive double its value from private individuals.'[45]

In the desperate bid to save the Colony from fiscal collapse, Rowe discovered, somewhat fortuitously, that Turner had signed treaties in 1825 and 1826 which gave jurisdiction of the Bum-Kittam district to the British Government. But these had not been ratified. Turner, however, had not informed the Chiefs that the treaties had been disavowed. Could Rowe legally enforce the treaties now to save the Colony and bring Harris to fiscal justice?

[44] CO 267/336/7 Sept. 1878, CO to Rowe.
[45] CO 267/335/182,. Edwards–Loggie Report; CO 267/337/3, minute at the CO, 1879.

After a protracted forensic wrangle and numerous minutes, the law officers gave their opinion that the Treaty of 1825 'ought to be regarded as valid and now in force'. The Colonial Office was careful to tell the Foreign Office that with the latter's consent, while the Governor would be instructed to assert claims in the future to the whole of 'Turner's peninsula', the immediate objective of invoking the treaty was to exercise only such jurisdiction as would check smuggling. Sir Michael Hicks-Beach cautioned in a letter to Rowe: 'Her Majesty's Government are extremely reluctant to sanction any extension of jurisdiction in West Africa beyond what may be absolutely necessary.'[46]

Rowe agreed that it was unnecessary to negotiate new treaties with chiefs of the seaboard in order to exercise fiscal jurisdiction. On the basis of Turner's Treaty of 1825 as recently interpreted by the Law Officers, he simply proceeded to station constables on the coast thus claimed between the Sierra Leone peninsula and British Sherbro.[47]

Thus, Turner's Treaty, long considered dead, was revived when it promised to be useful in fulfilling the objects of pragmatic policy. The promulgation of the Treaty was intended to be of practical value. The more ill-defined the policy, and the more fleeting the relations with the inhabitants, the greater the utility. As such, in similar circumstances, quite different interpretations of the same policy would be used to justify British action and perpetrate British interests.

In 1881, Wall, the Civil Commandant at Bonthe, arrested people from Bramah for assaulting constables, since, under Turner's Treaty, Bramah was legally within British jurisdiction. Wall was acting logically to uphold Turner's Treaty, but practically it was impolitic. The Acting Administrator-in-Chief, F. F. Pinkett, carefully got the prisoners discharged on a nolle prosequi.

The inland extent of the territory ceded by Turner's Treaty was sufficiently vague to lead to unpleasant complications if it were logically upheld. A. W. L. Hemming at the Colonial Office minuted that 'We intend to make use of the treaty for our fiscal purposes, but if it gives us authority over an unlimited

---

[46] CO 267/399/14 Mar. and 16 July, 1879.
[47] CO 267/340/Conf. 10 Mar. 1880, Rowe to SS.

extent of territory, we are not going to exercise that authority'. And Meade concurred: 'All we shall do is to exercise control over the mile or half mile of the seaboard.' Lord Kimberley was succinct in his opinion: 'I agree.'[48]

Apparent peace: result of Rowe's policy?

For about a year or two, there was a conspicuous absence of wars in the interior. This was universally acknowledged to be the result of Rowe's policy. In 1879, Revd. J. B. Bowen, described by Rowe as 'a negro clergyman himself a Mendi who was educated at the Church Mission Schools in Freetown', made a visit to Taiama and reported his impression in a letter to J. C. Loggie, the acting Commandant of the Sherbro.

The impression which forcibly strikes a stranger as he travels among the natives is as if the whole of the surrounding tribes are under British rule. The Colonial Government has inspired a wholesome fear into them, and as a consequence, the country was free from disturbances . . . At Teyama Wah, I was told that the Queen's children, meaning British subjects, were feared throughout the country . . . The wild natives have all learned thus to respect British subjects. This is the effect of the late Bagroo expedition by [Rowe].[49]

Having been brought up under colonial missionary tutelage in Freetown, Revd. Bowen's diagnosis was no different from that of Colonial officials, although he was himself a Mende.

Ostensibly to bid Rowe farewell before he went on leave in 1880, Mende Chiefs from Taiama, Senehun and other parts accompanied by a 'numerous following of Wives, Dancing Girls, and attendants' arrived in Freetown after Rowe had left. The Administrator-in-Chief, Streeten, readily attributed this gesture to the success of Rowe's policy. Hemming expressed his opinion about the people that 'their present attitude [of peace] is the result of the policy so actively carried out by Sir S. Rowe of sending missions to various districts to induce the natives to give up fighting and live peaceably.'[50]

This success was more apparent than real, for soon after-

[48] CO 267/344/Conf. 7, 7 May 1881.
[49] CO 267/337/130, enc. Bowen to Loggie, 28 May 1879.
[50] CO 267/340/104, Streeten to SS, 1880.

wards, another complicated and elaborate war broke out. It seems as if the main reasons for the lull must be sought, not in the policy of the administration, but in the dynamics of the traditional system. On the whole, it is quite apparent that the interior chiefs were more interested in the presents they received from the administration than in binding themselves to any treaty obligations, which they always treated according to their convenience. It is also reasonable to suppose that signatures were affixed to treaties without any real understanding of either the treaties themselves, or their implications. But since the signing was usually accompanied by presents, the chiefs most readily affixed their marks. Thus British action must not have been the true cause of the lull.

Revd. Bowen drew attention to the fact that most of the chiefs in the 'Mabanta country' 'have the impression that the Colonial Government has not noticed them . . . I think presents taken up to these people by a Government official would secure their confidence in the good intention of the Colonial Government for the welfare of their country.'[51]

It does seem that the fear of British power as reported by contemporaries, was also more apparent than real. Indisputably of course, the presence of a British official or steam boat, would bring a halt to the progress of a war. But it would only be temporary. Accounts seem to over-estimate the fear of British power, and indeed, the persistent recurrence of wars that demonstrations of British presence or power were supposed to halt, illustrates this point. The Edwards–Loggie mission reported that the steam launch on the Bum

has had a very beneficial effect. It has impressed upon the tribes . . . the important fact that the arm of the Government can reach them even in their head-waters in a few hours . . .[52]

The Departmental Committee set up to examine the causes of the depression in the Colony also reported in similar vein:

It is . . . owing to the existence of British establishments at Sierra Leone, and the fear of the British power thus engendered in the minds of the natives that the merchants are now enabled to carry

[51] CO 267/337/130, enc. Bowen to Loggie, 28 May 1879.
[52] CO 267/335/182, Edwards–Loggie Report, 1878.

out their transactions, in the rivers beyond the settlement with safety . . .[53]

Even Administrator-in-Chief Streeten was led into the same belief that '. . . with a view of preventing any threatened disturbances . . . the presence of a white man will probably succeed . . .'.[54]

The Africans were well aware that no official presence or action at this time was permanent. Thus while the demonstration of British power could bring a temporary lull to the progress of a stormy war, it could not permanently arrest the dynamics of traditional power-politics. As soon as the demonstration faded away, the war continued. And so while the officials liked to think that their actions had had 'a good moral effect' to assure peace for years, they found themselves constantly intervening to maintain the very peace they had assured themselves was permanent. Peace missions, presents, and gunboats only momentarily interrupted, but did not generally or permanently arrest, the dynamics of traditional society.

The Gbellie war and the mission of Laborde, 1881

As soon as Rowe went on leave, Streeten found himself making arrangements for another peace mission to halt the progress of the Gbellie war. Hemming minuted on the appointment of Laborde to lead the mission: 'It is very desirable to maintain the influence which has been acquired for the Sierra Leone Government with these interior tribes by the efforts of Sir S. Rowe and his agents.' Concerning the objects of the mission, Streeten informed Laborde:

You must constantly keep three things in view—the furtherance of peace and good relations with the Chiefs of the countries through which you pass—promotion and increase of trade—and to impress upon the people the desirability of opening roads and keeping them clear for traffic by which the second object will be greatly facilitated.[55]

Thus according to the contemporaries, interior politics affected the economic fortunes of the Colony. Therefore the administration resorted to political gestures in the interior in order to

---

[53] CO 267/333/20 July 1877, Report of the Departmental Committee.
[54] CO 267/342/266, Streeten to SS, 1880.   [55] Ibid.

maintain economic sanity in the Colony. In actual fact, the crisis of the Colony was a universal problem. As such, what seemed to elude official analysis was the fact that an expedition attended with presents to collaborating rulers would not obliterate decades, let alone centuries, of historical development. The sanguine reports which attended all such involvements were soon belied by subsequent events.

Gbellie, whose proper name was Kabague, the chief of Mosso, had instigated the war 'that at present threatens to be a most serious affair . . .'. Apparently, after rendering assistance to the Yoni Temne in one of their wars, Gbellie fell out with their leader, Gbenga, and subsequently declared war on him. The war became thoroughly complicated, as many chiefs and warriors, both Mende and Temne, got involved. The Taiama Chiefs unsuccessfully attempted to make peace. Mende Chiefs joined the Yoni party of Gbenga, and consequently the war became a 'mixed one', both in ethnic composition and in the issues at stake.

Many of those who joined the war did so to pay off their grudges against their more prosperous rivals. There was fiercer competition and jealousy among chiefs near the coast than among those up country. Laborde was informed that the old chief Momodu Sesay of Kwellu was supporting Gbellie. At Kwellu, however, Momodu Sesay assured Laborde that he was not connected with the war, and added that he believed that the report had been disseminated by the chief of Gbangbama, Ali 'alias Yonah'. Yonah in fact hated Momodu Sesay because of the latter's wealth in money and dependants.[56] Indeed, this was not a 'tribal war', nor was it a war fought solely to capture 'slaves'.

The administration was careful not to get entangled in the politics of the interior. But slowly and imperceptibly, it was coming to find itself in a position from which it was unable to disentangle itself. As colonial influence spread, traders ventured further inland. Mostly Creoles who were British subjects, they expected to be protected. At Senehun, Laborde warned them that Rowe's object in his policy towards the hinterland was not to encourage them to venture into the interior, but rather to get the people to come down to the 'waterside' with

[56] CO 267/344/60, letter by Laborde to Governor, 1881.

their produce and 'get into contact with more civilised Society'. The administration's interests were fiscal ones, and it was conscious of the undesirability of getting politically involved in the interior.

Nevertheless Lord Kimberley was elated at Laborde having weathered the storm.

There can be no doubt that the organization at not infrequent intervals of missions of this description is likely to be attended with beneficial results, both as regards the establishment of friendly relations with the native tribes and the development of the commercial resources of the interior.[57]

From 'fiscal jurisdiction' to political annexation

In the next few years, confirmations of existing treaties were made and the policy of occupying the coast for financial reasons was pushed to its logical conclusion—the virtual annexation of the entire coastline to Sulima.

This was accomplished by 1883. Moreover, Mende rulers of Bumpeh, Lugbu and Tikongoh entered into a treaty in 1881, binding themselves to remain at peace with one another, and to refer their disputes to the Governor for arbitration.[58]

The administration had begun to move into the hinterland. This movement may be thought of as a political act necessitated by economic considerations. There is thus a direct relationship between the economic crisis of the Colony and the political move into the interior which culminated in the proclamation of the Protectorate. As Cox-George explains:

It was in connection with the perfection of the customs administration that the Colonial Government was thrice induced [1826, 1847, and 1853]—each period being one of intensified search for revenue— to extend its territory to gain fiscal control of the adjacent coastal and riverine areas. . . . This movement was revived in the seventies following the difficult financial experiences of those years and culminated in the extension of the boundaries of the territory and of its fiscal jurisdiction . . .[59]

The policy of confirming existing treaties was the work of

[57] CO 267/344/60, letter by Laborde to Governor, 1881.
[58] CO 267/345/168, Treaty with Native Chiefs, 6 Feb. 1881.
[59] N. A. Cox-George, *Finance and Development in West Africa: The Sierra-Leone Experience* (London 1961), pp. 92–93; cf. Hopkins, 'Economic Imperialism', pp. 605–6.

Havelock. The rationale behind it all was to maintain the influence of the administration and to arrest any wars that might erupt. He entered into a treaty with Thomas Neale Caulker, regent chief of Tasso and Plantain Islands, and Richard Canray Bah Caulker, chief of Bompeh and Ribbee to uphold Turner's treaty. Both chiefs were to continue receiving their annual stipends of £100 and £50 respectively. Other chiefs not under British jurisdiction also entered into treaties—Momodu Karimu of Bramah, Movee of Senehun (successor to Gbanya), Sorie Kessebeh of Rotifunk, and Canray Mahoi, sub-chief of Ribbee. It was 'deemed expedient to engage the services of [these] chiefs . . . for the better government of their respective districts . . . [They would] be paid annually . . . ten pounds each.'[60]

These chiefs were 'only subsidised to maintain order' in their respective territories, although not under British jurisdiction.[61]

In the following year, 1882, Havelock got Chief William Tucker to sign a declaration reaffirming British jurisdiction and political sovereignty over his territory as in the terms of Turner's treaty of 1825. His stipend was increased from £40 to £60 a year. Havelock further decided

to grant a yearly stipend or salary of ten pounds each to two brothers of Chief Tucker's, who act under him as sub-chief. The family of the Tuckers is very numerous, and the Chief is unable to exercise complete control over them. By taking the two most influential and intelligent of the brothers into the pay of the Government, I hope to attach them to the interests of the Government and to strengthen the hands of the Chief by securing to him their support in the performance of any service which the Government may call upon him to render.[62]

The fact that the stipend of £60 to be paid to Chief Tucker was to be paid 'to the person for the time being holding during Her Majesty's pleasure the office of the Chief of Bullom and Shebar . . .'[63] shows that the administration was interfering in the traditional political process.

---

[60] CO 267/356/267, Havelock to SS, 1884 (Sherbro Treaty of 19 Dec. 1881).
[61] CO 267/355/269, Havelock to SS, 1884.
[62] CO 267/349/213, Havelock to SS, 1882.
[63] Quoted in E. Hertslet, *Map of Africa by Treaty*, I (London 1895), pp. 52–3.

At the same time, King Jaya of the Gallinas and his sub-chiefs ceded territory at the mouth of the Moa river extending half a mile inland from the high-water mark. By 1883, the annexation of the entire coastline was complete. In June, 'Queen' Messie and the chiefs of Krim country ceded all their territories which 'borders and adjoins the Atlantic Ocean'. When Pinkett accomplished the annexation, Lord Derby was bewildered: 'It is awkward to have these little annexations going on.' But he was convinced by the Colonial Office that it was no new annexation, 'merely a step towards the completion of what has already been decided', namely, the establishment of fiscal control over the coastline.[64]

Incipient fragmentation—effect of annexation and stipends

One interesting point that emerges from these annexations is the striking ignorance of the officials about the traditional territorial units, which led them into the first attempts to give sovereign identity to sections of a state, however unconsciously. Admittedly, the Sherbro state was in a period of decline at the time, and the various sections had emerged strong enough to be fairly reckoned as states. Caulker country included Ribbee, as was stated in the confirmation treaty of 1881. Yet the same treaty classed the sub-chief Canray Mahoi as not under British jurisdiction, while Richard Canray Bah Caulker was! The same anomaly applies to the chief of Rotifunk, whose territory was part of Caulker country but was also classed as not under British jurisdiction.

In the Gallinas too, the authority of King Jaya was no more than a farce, while his sub-chiefs exercised real power. How-ever, the treaty of annexation recognized separate territorial units as belonging to particular chiefs, for example Fawundu, who in fact was a contender for the kingship. Certainly these sub-chiefs exercised local authority, but within the structure of the Gallinas polity. The treaty, however, set about definitively recognizing geographical units as under the sovereign rule of individual sub-chiefs. Thus the maps neatly define 'Queen' Messie's territory, Fawundu's country, and Jaya Siaka's country as distinct states. Of course at this time, the inland

[64] Quoted in E. Hertslet, *Map of Africa by Treaty I* (London 1895), pp. 50–4; CO 267/352/100, Havelock to SS, 1883.

extent of the states was not the concern of the Colonial administration. It was preferable to keep it both vague and undefined. Thus it was common to have portions of a state under British jurisdiction and the rest not under it. In the long run, the effect on the exercise of political authority was to restrict the king to the area under British jurisdiction, while his sub-chiefs became autonomous and in time were elevated to a position similar to that of their king both in British eyes and in fact.

Stipends also tended to have a weakening effect on the exercise of authority by the kings and chiefs. Once in the pay of the administration, the rulers tended to be morally obliged to it. Moreover, stipends tended to introduce the rulers more rapidly to the demands of a cash economy, so much so that certain coastal chiefs even sent to ask for their stipends in advance. Gradually and unwittingly, the chiefs and rulers were mortgaging their sovereignty.

Before 1880, these stipends were paid haphazardly and were only institutionalized after an audit query to Rowe. Chief William Tucker, for instance, was receiving a stipend of £40 a year, although it was not stipulated in the treaty of 1853. The Colonial Office suggested that the list made out for 31 December 1879 should be taken as the starting point for the future (like a rent roll), and the local authorities were to furnish the Audit Office annually with a return of any additions or deductions made. It was then found to be both necessary and desirable to appoint a Secretary for Native Affairs.[65] By 1883, £1234 was being paid annually in stipends—principally in return for engagements on the part of chiefs to protect traders. At this time, probably only one real Mende was a 'stipended chief'—Movee.[66]

The bloody Sherbro expeditions of 1882–3

The brief respite which followed Laborde's mission was shattered by two affrays in the Sherbro in 1882, both of which may be partly explained by the tactlessness and impetuosity of Laborde himself. As this situation came under control, and

---

[65] CO 267/340/74, CO 267/241/221, SS to Gov. 1880.
[66] CO 267/351/36, minute by Hemming, 1883.

frantic efforts were being made to find a lasting solution, more wars erupted in the Gallinas, which were so serious that the administration was bound to move in actively. The jittery men-on-the-spot and the irrational frontiersmen (from the African point of view at least) created a panicky situation which resulted in much needless involvement.

The problems intended to be solved far outran their limited resources and capacities at the time and therefore had to await the full deployment of the machinery of colonial rule in all its institutional forms.

After the Kebbi Smith wars, some chiefs resolved to revive the defunct Jong chiefship, with its title *Sei Kama*, to restore order. They invited Laborde, the acting Commandant at Bonthe, to take part in the coronation, which was scheduled for April 27. Laborde failed to turn up, but the ceremony was duly performed. Then on May 10, Laborde belatedly turned up, and addressed the chiefs 'as to the deception played on me in asking me to be present at the coronation when the King was already crowned'. Laborde felt insulted. To add insult to injury, one Momodu drew Laborde's attention to the fact that his interpreter was incompetent and was mistranslating the Commandant's message. Laborde took this as a 'presumption' and ordered the 'insolent' intruder to be arrested. Then a row followed, in which the official boat containing presents for the king was ransacked, while Laborde escaped.[67]

Meanwhile, after Laborde had reported the incident, the Governor took advantage of a man-of-war being in harbour, and with thirty police led an expedition to Jong. An indigenous account states that the Governor decoyed and arrested three chiefs. Then a Dr. Jarrett of the Governor's party provoked an incident, by firing a shot at dancers who did not come and prostrate themselves before His Excellency. The official account says that the people shot a constable in the knee, and without command, the whole line opened fire. The Governor denied burning down the town of Mattru and killing several people. He set fire 'to those huts . . . which I was told belonged to persons concerned in the outbreak'. Yet in his report on the

[67] R. P. M. Davis, *History of the Sierra Leone Batallion of the Royal West African Frontier Force* (Freetown 1932), p. 6, says that the meeting became 'extremely abusive and offensive'.

proceedings in the Jong, Lt. Baker, who commanded H.M.S. 'Foam', said that they 'set fire to the town'.[68]

C. H. Hopwood, a Liberal M.P. who asked a question about this incident in the British House of Commons, wrote to the Colonial Office drawing attention to the inconsistencies of the official version, and inferring that there was a serious contradiction or suppression of fact in the official version. The explanation given as to the origin of the whole affair was very naïve— that the people 'cast a slur' on his dignity and slighted Laborde. Hopwood asked his question 'in order that enquiry may obviate such dreadful acts as shelling defenceless men and burning villages in the future'.[69]

In his 1903 *History of Sierra Leone*, Crooks concluded that there is 'little doubt that the collision with the natives was owing to the lack of discipline in the constabulary . . .'.[70]

Havelock, who could not really justify the action, explained the incident in very irrational Eurocentric terms:

. . . my opinion is, that the outbreak was the result of sudden impulse taking effect among a number of people already predisposed to excitement. Anyone who has had experience in dealing with savages or semi-savages, knows that such people are very prone to act upon sudden impulse and that it is very difficult to discover any precise ground for acts they may commit when there is present some cause for excitement.[71]

This answer suited very well a public believing in its own innate racial superiority with a mission to 'civilize' barbaric humanity. This attitude reduced whatever feelings of remorse there were for such barbarous treatment of the local inhabitants.

However, *The Times* came out with a more plausible explanation:

. . . Differences with the natives nearly always arise from the want of knowledge on the part of the British officials. Their usual term of office is so short that they have no time to learn the peculiarities of the neighbouring tribes and of British relations with them. . . . Most of the governors . . . entering upon their short official career

[68] PP, vol. xlvii, 1883, p. 30; CO 267/350/House of Commons, 31 Oct. 1882; CO 267/350/Admiralty, 27 July 1882; *The Times*, 4 November 1882.

[69] PP, vol. xlvii, 1883, p. 8.

[70] J. J. Crooks, *History of the Colony of Sierra Leone* (London 1903, new impression 1972), p. 256.

[71] PP, vol. xlvii, 1883, p. 14.

. . . initiate a policy of their own, frequently the direct opposite of that of their predecessor. The natural result of this want of uniformity in our attitude towards the natives is mistrust, restlessness, and too often risings, which have to be put down with bloodshed and burnings as in the present case.

This analysis was claimed to be the work of a British trader in the Sherbro with over twenty-five years' residence.[72]

Havelock declined to make a comment, but 'for myself . . . it has been my aim . . . to follow . . . the policy of my predecessor . . .' Rowe, whom *The Times* report gave as the only exception to its rule about governors.[73]

However much the officials might have been at fault, the Colonial Office was firm in their support, since they all thought of the Africans basically as savages. Hemming confessed in a minute that '. . . It is very difficult to judge whether Mr. Laborde acted rightly or wrongly' and he noted that the constabulary fired without orders. 'But I imagine that, as a rule, these chiefs require to be treated somewhat like Irishmen, i.e. that attempts at conciliation unsupported by a show of power are simply laughed at, and that a somewhat high-handed policy is the only attitude that is really respected.' Hemming had no qualms when he suggested congratulating Havelock on his 'warlike demonstration'.[74] In fact Havelock ordered Lt. Baker to stay at York island after the expedition for a few days, as the Governor 'was of the opinion that the presence of a man-of-war would have a good moral effect'.[75] Hemming was of like opinion. 'The operation . . . will . . . have a beneficial effect by showing that the Colonial Government can, if it chooses, strike an effectual blow into these interior districts.'[76]

After this expedition, the chiefs sent a letter expressing their regret at the occurrences, and urging the administration to take them under its protection.[77] Yet the indigenous account of the occurrences reveals that the Governor asked Chief Tucker of Bullom to tell the Jong chiefs and people that if they did not

---

[72] *The Times*, 26 Dec. 1882.
[73] PP, vol. xlvii, 1883, p. 17.
[74] CO 267/348/108, minute by Hemming, 1882.
[75] CO 267/350/Admiralty, 25 July 1882.
[76] CO 267/348/108, minute by Hemming, 1882.
[77] CO 267/348/144, Havelock to SS, 1882.

surrender and 'admit their faults in writing, His Excellency will come again and destroy them. The people therefore did accordingly.'[78] The requests by the inhabitants for British protection thus seem to be well stage-managed. As a matter of necessity, a 'colonial psychology' gradually to prepare the minds of the potential colonists to accept foreign domination was slowly taking root.

Theoretically, the Jong country was under British jurisdiction as a result of Turner's treaty. But the British Government was not prepared to accept responsibility for the logical limits of this. It was

not desirable to carry out the theory of British protection to the extent of setting up a Government establishment. . . . It might perhaps be sufficient to explain to the chiefs that they are to all intents and purposes already in the position they desire, and that as long as they behave properly, they will enjoy the benefits to be derived from protection of the Government.[79]

The Mattru expedition was part of a wider complex of problems with which the administration had to grapple. While aspects of the war between Seppeh of Yengema (Bumpeh) and Gbellie of Bongeh appeared in the previous proceedings, the expedition and show of force could not arrest the progress of the war, the dynamics of which were buried in the social system. Temporarily, it ended with the expedition against Kpawoh Jibila[80] of Talia, an outrage involving unjustifiable brutality and inhumanity.

The occasion for this bloody expedition was a raid on a village within British jurisdiction, and the robbery of the official pay boat proceeding to Barmany with the sum of £19. 8s. 1d. Kpawoh Jibila was made a scapegoat after the machinations of the traders had succeeded in enlisting official support for them.[81]

However, as the Colonial Office realized, the situation was more complex. It could not meaningfully be reduced to a single oversimplified incident. The issues at stake were deeply rooted in the traditional system, and the wars were just symptoms.

[78] PP, vol. xlvii, 1883, p. 5 (original edited).
[79] CO 267/348/144, Havelock to SS, 1882.
[80] Variously spelt in the documents Gbow, Gpwoe, Gbpowe, Gbpow.
[81] PP, vol. xlvii, 1883.

The role of the traders created a situation of 'frontier irrationality': just the situation Hopwood had cautioned the Colonial Office to avoid. Hopwood gave his opinion on the issue of enlisting the weight of the administration behind one of the contestants in this purely African struggle which had nothing to do with the disaffection of the people to the administration, because 'their disputes and quarrels are amongst themselves':

This may be right or wrong, but I feel it my duty to mention it, for I presume Your Lordship would desire that the Government *should keep aloof as much as possible from the quarrels among the natives, the complications and rights of which it is difficult to understand.*[82]

In the present case, the 'complications and rights' were not understood, and the administration exerted itself in the wrong direction.

Less than a fortnight after taking over the Colony from Governor Havelock as Administrator-in-Chief, Chief Justice Pinkett led the expedition against Kpawoh Jibila in April 1883. By disposition, 'warlike ambitions lurked under the robes of this judge . . .'[83] The acting Commandant at Bonthe informed Pinkett about reports from traders that an attack on Sherbro was imminent. For the past two decades, traders had commonly scared administrations with such rumours.

In June 1882, after signing a friendly treaty with the administration, Chief Seppeh of Yengema had quarrelled with Chief Gbellie of Bongeh, another signatory. Havelock had requested Seppeh to desist from any further attacks, but Seppeh had said he was acting in the interest of the administration and asked for permission to continue the struggle for three years. However, a 'native account' reports that it was Gbellie who asked to wage war on Seppeh for three years, and in this the administration supported him. This account goes on to say that £300 worth of goods was to be distributed under the Governor's orders to neutral chiefs to support Gbellie, and many oaths were administered to them. Havelock had tacitly admitted this when he had asked Laborde 'to settle the dispute by peaceful negotiation or failing so to obtain joint action from loyal chiefs to punish Seppeh and assist Gberry'. There had been no hope

---

[82] PP, vol. xlvii, 1883, p. 9 (emphasis added).
[83] Fyfe, *A History*, p. 441.

of an immediate settlement, so Chiefs Tucker and Jibila had been asked to mediate.[84]

Peace had still seemed a far way off. Tucker and Jibila secretly sympathized with Seppeh, and when the negotiations had broken down Jibilia had openly sided with Seppeh. Meanwhile, Gbellie had been making false representations to the Commandant to the effect that Seppeh had had hostile intentions against the administration. Most of the traders and Laborde had sympathized with Gbellie. Jibila had incurred their displeasure when he openly sided with Seppeh. Jibila had drawn the attention of the Commandant to the chicanery of Gbellie and had been arrested for disobedience, while Gbellie had taken and destroyed several of his towns.[85]

Thus the disturbance had spilled over into what was 'British territory'. As such, without any malice in the first instance, Jibila had become involved in acts which 'constituted an offence against the Government . . . and threatened the peace of our settlement' during the course of his operations against Gbellie and his allies.[86] Havelock, while in Britain, had felt that the reports were exaggerated, and that the alleged activities of Jibila might have been concocted by the traders through a trap they set, since they had 'long desired, and . . . have strongly urged on the Government, the use of severe measures of repression . . .'. Havelock had elaborated this point:

Traders in the Sherbro and in all other places similarly situated, are prone to invoke the exercise of force by the Government, on every occasion, in which they become exposed to risk, or in which they suffer loss, through the action of the natives. In the majority of cases, the risk or loss incurred may be traced to the imprudence or misconduct of the traders themselves. . . . They do not hesitate to circulate unfounded reports and to make untrue statements.[87]

Hopwood had transmitted an explanation of the disturbances from S. B. A. Macfoy, one of the most important of the Sherbro traders. In the covering letter, Hopwood had explained that 'the reasoning in it is directed to show that the local Government has been deceived by Gberri, who has availed himself

[84] PP, vol. xlvii, 1883, pp. 6–7.
[85] CO 267/353/112, memo by Havelock on Pinkett's despatch, 1883; CO 267/354/9 Aug. 1883, Havelock to SS.
[86] CO 268/353/112, memo by Havelock, 1883.
[87] CO 267/352/93, minute by Havelock, 16 May 1883.

of the confidence of the Government in order to advance himself and prostrate his rivals'. In the final analysis, the Colonial Office was convinced that enough corroborative evidence pointed to the fact that indeed 'Mr. Pinkett was misled by the statement of interested persons'.[88]

On 19 May 1883, Pinkett sent a despatch to the Colonial Office saying that he was moving to Bonthe on account of the raid on Mosaipeh in British territory, and the offensive attitude of chief Kpawoh Jibila, to reduce the latter's 'fortress' of Talia. Havelock was perturbed at the nervousness of Pinkett in accepting reports from the Sherbro. 'In describing Gpow's village of Talliah, a nest of mud huts with a fence of stakes round it, as 'this much dreaded Frontier', Mr. Pinkett conveys an exaggerated opinion.'[89] Pinkett, however, was decided upon action at all cost and for whatever reason.

The expedition was thorough in its work of destruction. After destroying some of Jibila's towns, his capital Talia was assaulted. *The Standard* of 18 June described the holocaust:

. . . No less than one thousand five hundred warriors were assembled [at Talia]. . . . The rocket batteries and field guns, under the command of Captain Jackson, R.A. did great execution. The friendly natives who accompanied the expedition fought with much zeal against their ancient and powerful foe. . . . The town was entirely destroyed and Gbpowe himself only escaped with great difficulty . . .[90]

It was reported that Jibila's power was completely broken, and that all the towns under his control were seized from him by his foes.[91] After the report was received at the Colonial Office, Havelock expressed the opinion that the description of Jibila as 'a notorious robber chief' (which was the same description used by *The Standard*) and other epithets were not justified. 'Certainly, the chief was a warrior of distinction, but not much worse off than his neighbours in the recent history of Sherbro.' Surely, he was not hostile to the administration.[92]

A reward of £50 was offered for the apprehension of Jibila.

[88] CO 267/254/9 Aug. 1883, minute at CO.
[89] CO 267/352/95, minute by Havelock on Pinkett's despatch of 19 May 1883.
[90] *The Standard*, 18 June 1883.
[91] CO 267/352/96, 99, Pinkett to SS, 1883.
[92] CO 267/352/96, minute by Havelock, 1883.

Apparently, he fled to Sahun, and because its inhabitants could not surrender him, Pinkett petulantly led another expeditionary force ostensibly to dislodge him. At Kortumahun, where there was a bloody encounter, *The Standard* of 26 June reported that 'it is believed that most, if not all, of the inhabitants must have perished in the conflagration'. The newspaper continued:

. . . The enemy are routed, flying for their lives, but the work of death still goes on. . . . No quarter is given or expected; the wounded are murdered as they fall and the horrible custom of mutilation follows. . . . Our allies took many prisoners, the males being ruthlessly killed in cold blood. . . . Inside the town, the sight was ghastly in the extreme. In a small space, one officer counted 82 dead . . . evidently the work of a single shell . . . [Talia] was razed to the ground.

The march to Sahun was fruitless. The expedition found all the towns deserted and burnt. The force went up to Bahol 'in support of our friends', further up the Bum than any British force before, 'but there was not fighting to do'.[93]

Sir Henry Holland, M.P., gave notice to ask the Under Secretary of State whether the report in *The Standard* was correct, and whether he would cause an enquiry to be made as to the truth of the allegations. This caused considerable unease at the Colonial Office. Hemming minuted that the report was probably exaggerated, but that there was probably also an under-current of truth, as the 'native allies' took such a prominent part. When questioned about the savage barbarities of the 'allies', Pinkett dishonestly replied: '. . . The vanquished naturally fled out of the other side of the place. What was done there I cannot say.'[94] But Major Talbot, Officer Commanding the troops, who commanded the expedition, affirmed that Talia was razed 'to the ground'.[95]

Generally, Havelock did not approve of the armed expedition, which went 'a good many miles beyond the farthest limit of British jurisdiction'. Lord Derby cautioned Pinkett to desist 'from all hostile operations, unless as a measure against aggression, without previous instructions from home'. Havelock was

93 CO 267/352/99, Pinkett to SS, 1883.
94 CO 267/354/House of Commons, 26 June 1883.
95 PP, vol. xlvii, 1883.

D

apprehensive that unsatisfactory consequences might ensue. It was the policy of Her Majesty's Government not to undertake operations on behalf of traders trading beyond British territory. Now that Pinkett had set the precedent, traders would expect and demand a repetition of the expedition in their interest. This would then lead to an undesirable extension of British jurisdiction.[96]

But Pinkett was quite categorical about his solution to the Sherbro problem: 'There will be no permanent cessation of these tribal wars, unless it is thoroughly understood that not only in British territory, but also in the neighbourhood no war will be permitted.'[97] Moreover, he suggested deposing Chief W. E. Tucker for sympathizing with Jibila, which he termed 'treachery'.[98]

Evidently, the Colonial Office would not agree to the suggestion. 'Not only would it be very difficult to replace [Tucker and his family], but such a measure would probably give rise to a state of anarchy in the country and would thus make it necessary for the Colonial Government to assume direct administration of its affairs.'[99] This it could not do.

Nor was the Colonial Office convinced that 'expeditions such as those of Mr. Pinkett do much permanent good. . . . British territory must be defended if attacked, but beyond that, I do not think we ought to go or that we can gain any advantages by going', wrote Hemming. Havelock's mediating policy was commended.[100]

Events did not vindicate Pinkett either, for once he was back in Freetown, news was received that Seppeh and Gbellie were still fighting, and that Jibila was recuperating military. However, Havelock returned and took charge of the Colony.

Trade depression, interior wars, and 'Protectorate' suggestions

The severe commercial depression of 1884 and 1885 drew the attention of interested parties to the question of peace on the

[96] CO 267/352/99, minutes on Pinkett's despatch, 1883.
[97] CO 267/353/129, Pinkett to SS, 1883.
[98] CO 367/352/80, Pinkett to SS, 1883.
[99] Ibid., minute at CO.
[100] CO 267/353/167, minute by Hemming, 1883.

borders of the Colony, since wars were held to be a major
cause of the depression. But the part played by 'tribal politics'
was often exaggerated. As Hargreaves explains:

The principal items of the Colony's export trade to Europe were
wild crops, requiring little cultivation, but varying amounts of
labour at harvest time: rubber, palm kernels, palm oil, and kola
nuts. The total value of these exports declined sharply in 1884 and
1885, but very largely because of falling prices; the quantities of
palm products and kola nuts exported in 1885 were actually greater
than in 1883. . . . The most general cause of hardship was the international depression of trade in 1883–6, and the consequently intensified competition. . . . Sierra Leone would have suffered a serious
trade depression even if perfect peace had reigned in the interior;
but merchants are often reluctant to seek remote and complex
explanations of their circumstances when simple ones are at hand,
and apparently within the power of governments to remedy.[101]

Thus Manchester merchants and others interested in trade
with Sierra Leone, sent a petition to the Colonial Office urging
that only Rowe could deal effectively with the Sherbro problem. Rowe himself suggested three methods. Firstly, to keep
a fixed frontier, beyond which action should be avoided, but
which should be so far inland as to embrace the producing
areas and keep trade routes open. Secondly, to appoint officers
in districts important to the peace and trade of Sierra Leone, who
would exert strong influence on the people. Thirdly, that the
Governor and experienced officers should make frequent visits
to encourage the friendship of chiefs and to pay them stipends
and give presents. Rowe recommended this third alternative
as the most expedient. In fact he was just going back to his old
policy. He accepted an invitation to return to Sierra Leone as
Governor to settle the problem.[102]

Yet the problem persisted, especially as the struggle for
the Gallinas Crown took a dramatic turn in a sudden realignment of forces by the contending parties. Officials at the
Colonial Office began to give serious thought to the declaration
of a protectorate over the disturbed areas.[103] In fact, Rowe and

[101] J. Hargreaves, *A Life of Sir Samuel Lewis* (London 1958), pp. 41–2.
[102] CO 267/357/4 Nov. 1884, 1 Dec. 1884; CO 267/361/21 May 1885, Rowe
to SS.
[103] CO 267/360/189, minute by Hemming, 1885.

the traders had advocated this policy before. With the economic imperative still looming large, Anderson minuted that 'real financial stability can only be looked for from a maintenance of peace in the producing area. Disturbances in that area we now take no notice of till we begin to feel their effect financially. . . '. He also suggested declaring a protectorate, so that the ready presence of officers of the administration would serve to nip any trouble in the bud, as was being done on the Gold Coast. 'The only alternative,' he concluded, 'is to withdraw. . . . That is admitted to be impossible, and the sooner we make up our minds to the inevitable, the better.' Hemming, however, did not favour expansion. He probably only wanted a protectorate to consolidate existing economic interests.[104]

Although this policy was not thereupon implemented, there existed a situation by 1886 whereby it was impossible for the British to withdraw. Rowe's suggestion for declaring a protectorate was not followed, not because of opposition to the policy *per se*, but because all that was desired was 'peace on our immediate borders without the trouble and responsibility involved in annexations and protectorates'. Yet this proved impossible to achieve. Punitive expeditions and the 'dire consequences of ignoring all agreements signed with the Queen' proved ineffectual to halt the dynamics of traditional society.[105] This meant that sooner or later, a protectorate had to be declared. As opinion was already crystallizing in favour of a protectorate, and as it was admitted to be impossible to withdraw, perhaps it could be said that the declaration of a protectorate was then only a matter of time.

With the realignment of forces in 1885 which threw the Gallinas into war, Boakei Gomna was supported by Jabati and Henry Tucker, while Fawundu was supported by Momoh Jah and Momoh Kaikai. The war was conducted by Mende and Temne mercenaries hired by each party. Rowe proceeded to the Gallinas and got the principal participants in the current war to parley. Both Boakei Gomna and Fawundu stated their case, and Rowe decided that there should be a general treaty of peace. In May, the agreement was signed at Bandasuma in the Barrie country. The signatories undertook to maintain

[104] CO 267/365/323, minute by J. Anderson, 1886.
[105] Ibid.

peace, open up trade routes, and submit their disputes to the Governor.[106]

In Colony circles, the Governor's activities in Barrie country were applauded, because they were thought to promise new vistas of economic expansion. The *Sierra Leone Church Times* was of the opinion that 'the future prosperity of this settlement depends on the opening up of the countries beyond to its commerce, and the development of the resources of those countries . . .'. Barrie country was a gateway to the 'commercial *El Dorado*' of the interior countries.[107] Yet by December 1885, the paper was already lamenting that the severe commercial depression had not eased, and reported graphically: 'The future of the Colony is not very encouraging. The prospect is cheerless. Trade is *nil*.' It took up the recipe brought out earlier in the *Contemporary Review* that

The administration pursue on the whole, a traditional policy which they have inherited from vitiated sources. . . . Administrators espouse local passions and views. . . . The sole object of Great Britain should be to reconcile the disputes of the various tribes, to extend her trade and influence into the interior, and to endeavour to establish some native powers strong enough to deal with the people and keep order. . . . In order to accomplish this, it will be necessary to make some considerable alteration in British policy and in its administrative system.[108]

As the economic crisis deepened, the inhabitants of the Colony sent a memorial praying for the enlargement of the Colony by a policy of peaceful annexation. The memorialists requested an imperial loan to accomplish the plan. Rowe supported the adoption of this policy. Naturally, this was repugnant to official policy. But Rowe emphasized that the proposal must be seriously considered if the Colony was to continue to be self-supporting.

Rowe's personal proposals

Rowe proposed first and foremost the definition of the vague boundaries of the territories acquired by Turner's treaties, and

---

[106] CO 267/358/67, Rowe to SS, 1886; CO 267/359/124, 125, 126, Rowe to SS, 1885; *Sierra Leone Weekly News*, 23 May 1885.
[107] *Sierra Leone Church Times*, 17 June 1885.
[108] Ibid., 16 Dec. 1885.

the maintenance of a 'clean track' through them, so that trade, 'on which Freetown depends entirely for its revenue', would follow. The actual exercise of jurisdiction would be limited. Beyond the peninsula and the mile of seaboard, action would be confined only to punishing crimes of murder and robbery with violence, preventing the passage of slave caravans, and punishing the selling of persons into slavery. Rowe further suggested that the easiest and least costly way of obtaining peace in the producing areas on which the volume of trade and therefore colonial revenue depended, was 'to make use of the existing Government of the Country, to advise the native Chiefs in their rule, and to support or remove them as their behaviour justifies'. Rowe further suggested the appointment of political officers.

Rowe had a formidable reputation at the Colonial Office for his knowledge of the neighbouring countries, and his suggestions won sympathy in some quarters. 'The object of his present proposals is . . . to establish a fixed and definite policy which shall ensure the maintenance of the authority and influence of the Colonial Government and secure trade and revenue . . .', said Hemming, who went on to add that there was a widely extended 'protectorate' on the Gold Coast reaching a long way back from the coast, 'and yet we scarcely ever have any troubles in it . . .'. He concluded:

. . . . I hardly think we can afford to reject lightly a policy which [Rowe] declares to be an 'absolute necessity'. He is fully aware of the repugnance which must naturally exist to any serious extensions of our responsibilities, and would not . . . advocate these measures so strongly if he did not feel very sure that . . . the prospective advantages infinitely outweighed any possible inconveniences.

The Colonial Office was not definite, however, in its approval or rejection of Rowe's proposals. It asked for 'insertion in the agreements which have been or may be made by the Government of Sierra Leone with all the chiefs in the districts of a clause binding them to impose no restrictions on trade, and to refer all their disputes with their neighbours to the Governor of Sierra Leone whose decision shall be final'. No responsibility for the defence of the people was to be undertaken in cases of attack by other people, and interference with 'the internal economy and institutions of the people' was to be avoided.

These were rather small concessions to Rowe's proposals, and the British Government seems only to have been concerned with the Colony's economic interest. Although still vacillating, the Secretary of State for the Colonies was 'unwilling to recommend any increase of territorial responsibilities'. This aptly sums up the main constant in the policy of the Colonial Office at this time.[109]

Persistence of Gallinas wars and the Makaya expedition

While Rowe was hamstrung by the indecision of the Colonial Office, peace was also not to be known. In April 1887, Ndawa and Makaya, allies of Boakei Gomna, took war to the Gallinas and the Kittam, and their warriors captured several towns.[110] The Administrator, J. S. Hay, was informed in a conversation with Chief Abdul Lahai of Juring, that there were war and troubles because there was no real successor to the authority of the *Massaquoi*. Hay thought it very urgent to have a *Massaquoi* appointed to stop the disturbances.[111]

Rowe was opposed to the idea. He believed that it would no more be to the advantage of the British Government to get a *Massaquoi* appointed than it would be to revive the King of Sherbro who existed *de facto* at the time of Turner's Treaty.

Rowe further argued that should a *Massaquoi* be restored it would be improbable that chiefs like Fawundu, Boakei Gomna, and Abdul Lahai would obey his authority. Therefore the administration would be bound to support him, and in so doing more trouble was likely to ensue than in dealing with the individual chiefs.[112]

It is reasonable to infer that Rowe's real reasons for opposing the restoration of the *Massaquoi* were not expressed, since no concrete evidence was brought out to substantiate his claim that more trouble would ensue. Besides, Hay, who was in the field, was convinced, as were most other chiefs, that an end would be brought to the troubles if a real successor were found to the

---

[109] CO 267/362/23, Rowe to SS, and minutes, 1886; CO 879/24/323/43, enc. memo by Rowe, 1886.

[110] CO 267/387/Tel., 16 Apr. 1887, Hay to SS.

[111] CO 879/25/331, Hay to SS, 1887 (conversation with Gallinas Chiefs).

[112] CO 267/367/68, memo by Rowe on Hay's despatch, 1887; CO 267/367/94, minute by Rowe, 1887.

Massaquoi. The troubles were dynastic—a manifestation of power politics. Rowe himself later admitted this.[113] A plausible inference is that since he was an advocate of some kind of protectorate, the restoration of any strong indigenous authority would serve to obstruct the colonial designs he entertained. As such, he not only opposed the *Massaquoi*, but the *Beh Sherbro* too!

Meanwhile, Hay was instructed by telegraph to strengthen the police for the defence of the threatened places within British jurisdiction. Hay accordingly strengthened the police at Lavana, Cassie, Sulima, Salijah, and established a post from which to patrol between places within British jurisdiction. The Colonial Office was in favour of severely punishing the 'miscreants' and 'marauders', but was apprehensive of the War Office's unwillingness to sanction the employment of troops.[114]

Freetown, however, was hopeful that the War Office would sanction a military expedition to the Gallinas, similar to the one led by de Winton in 1887 against the Yoni Temne. When this expectation seemed to be protracted indefinitely, traders began to put on pressure for an expedition. The Palma Trading Company petitioned:

The long looked for long talked of expedition under Sir Francis de Winton has not yet put in an appearance, and the interior natives and the disaffected of the Treaty chiefs are thus emboldened to harass and plunder the country more and more to the entire stoppage of all legitimate trade.[115]

Similarly, traders in the Sherbro resented the inert policy of Her Majesty's Government in dealing with 'refractory tribes' and drew attention to its invidious nature—'whereas it fails to impress the natives with the benignity of a powerful Christian Government, it acts as an incentive contrary to its intention and emboldens them to commit further outrages'. The petition continued:

That by reason of the turbulent, aggressive and insulting attitude assumed by these chiefs, there seems to arise a stern necessity for a prompt and vigorous action on the part of Her Majesty's Govern-

[113] CO 879/27/350/2, Rowe to SS, 1888; Governor's despatches to the Secretary of State, 62, 1888, hereafter 'Despatches', SLGA.
[114] CO 267/367/Tel., 16 and 20 Apr. 1887.
[115] CO 267/373/Palma Trading Company, 1 Mar. 1888.

ment that would have the effect of putting an end to these tribal wars and the consequences that follow it.

. . . Savage minds respect power alone . . . physical force, or the demonstrations of physical power, would be, should be, and ought to be the 'experimentum crucis'.

. . . Deportation from their home and country seems, in our opinion, the only punishment dreaded by native chiefs . . .[116]

G. H. Garrett, Officer in charge of the Sulima police, expressed a similar opinion. He found the opinion prevalent that the British only had naval power, and would not fight inland where there would be no ships to support them. Like the merchants, he suggested that

. . . pacification of the country . . . will be [achieved by] the removal of Mackiah, and the breaking up of Boccary Governor's party at Bahama . . . the construction of a good wide road connecting the navigable heads of all the rivers from the Manoh river in the south northwards . . . a station at each river head and weekly patrols from one to another . . .[117]

While no direction was being given for positive action in the Gallinas, the men-on-the-spot seized upon a number of local remedies. Rowe, true to his old policy, believed that contact would yield fruitful results. He stressed that communication with powerful chiefs beyond the Colony's frontier and with turbulent districts would be a very wise policy. When King Makavoray and others visited him in 1878 and 1880, the result was that

the years following showed a considerable increase in the quantity of produce exported from the Sherbro district, a result which is considered by myself and the Sherbro merchants to be the direct effect of these visits and which is shown in the direct return of the duty received at Sherbro on exports from that place . . .[118]

Rowe therefore advocated an institutionalization of the payment of frequent visits to such powerful kings in order to ensure economic benefit to the Colony.

Meanwhile, Ndawa, one of the recent raiders, was killed.[119] Garrett was convinced that it was possible to restrain Makaya

---

[116] CO 879/27/350/37, enc. petition from Sherbro merchants to SS, 1888.
[117] CO 879/27/350/67, enc. Garrett to Rowe, 1888.
[118] CO 879/27/350/53, Rowe to SS, 1888.
[119] CO 879/27/350/53, enc. 1, Inniss, O/C Sulima to Rowe, 1888.

from his wars, but 'until Boccary Governor is either killed or permanently removed, there can be no peace in that district'.[120]

The chiefs of the lower Gallinas were inveterate opponents of Boakei Gomna. The Colonial Office was convinced that there was ample evidence against Boakei as the leading spirit behind the restlessness of the Gallinas. Although realizing that it would be a 'somewhat high-handed measure' to seize and exile Boakei Gomna and George Gbapo, the Colonial Office was quite unambiguous about there being 'no other or better way of pacifying the country', since it was impossible to persuade the War Office to undertake a punitive expedition. The Secretary of State for the Colonies therefore sanctioned the arrest and banishment under special ordinance of Boakei Gomna and George Gbapo to the Gambia.[121]

Hay, for his own part, suggested the destruction of fortifications around the towns as one method of ensuring peace. Rowe, however, cautioned that these fenced towns were a double-edged weapon, providing 'as much a protection for the weak who take refuge in them, as they are the strongholds of the strong who plunder and rob . . .'. Thus, unless the administration was prepared to give protection to the weak by administering the whole of the district through which Hay proposed to destroy the fences, the undesirable result would be to leave the weak at the mercy of the strong.

A special service officer, Captain Coupland Crawford, was sent to the 'Sulima District' as acting manager in 1888. With his forty-seven police, he was instructed only to repel an attack, but not to take any offensive. Eager for military command and resolved to fight, Crawford experimented with minor punitive expeditions on behalf of British 'allies', quite contrary to his instructions. Hay was not particularly opposed to this. Both were resolved to punish Makaya not only for instigating the raid on the customs post at Sulima, but because they were convinced there was no other way to maintain the peace. At the end of 1888, there were rumours of threats to overrun the Bum and Kittam districts by Makaya. This would have been 'disastrous to British interests'. After 'mature consideration', Hay determined 'to punish this freebooter who has for long not

---

[120] CO 879/29/361/7 and enc. Garrett to Rowe, 1888.
[121] CO 267/271/Conf. 22, minute by Hemming, 1888.

only harried the country in the vicinity of the jurisdiction, but last year made a raid within it'. Thus Crawford, with the support of about 800 disorganised 'friendlies', attacked Fanima on 2 January 1889, and the following day stormed Largoh, releasing about 600 captives who were held there. Makaya then fled inland.[122]

After the high-handed action of Crawford in sacking his capital, Largoh, Makaya fled to Nyagua, seeking protection. Although Nyagua hesitated for a time, 'because some up country chiefs were adverse to it', he later agreed to surrender the warrior.[123] Nyagua's route to the coast was blockaded by an encampment of warriors at Wende, apparently remnants of Ndawa and Makaya, and the king was quite willing to hand over Makaya if the obstruction were removed. Nyagua reaffirmed that he had no grievances against the administration, and that all that he required was to live in peace with the administration and get the trade route open to allow his subjects free and unimpeded commercial intercourse with the coast.[124]

Wende, the capital of the late Ndawa, was a cluster of thirteen towns. Garrett stormed the settlement and released 3,000 captives who were held there. Hay was sanguine that 'a prosperous country is placed in direct communication with the coast, the results of which should have an important effect on the trade of the Colony'. The Governor believed that with the co-operation of the chiefs, a permanent solution had at last been found to end the disturbances.[125] Garrett reported to the Governor from Bandajuma that 'peace was definitely and fully concluded between the whole of the Chiefs of this district, and I do not anticipate having any further trouble'. Most significant was the reconciliation of Nyagua to Makavoray. A little dispute concerning the blockade at Wende, technically in Makavoray's jurisdiction, existed between them. Both of them embraced and shook hands after the peace arrangement.[126]

[122] CO 267/376/136, enc. 1; CO 267/376/145, 158, 1889.
[123] A. Abraham, 'Nyagua, the British and the Hut Tax War', *International Journal of African Historical Studies*, V, 1 (1972), p. 95.
[124] CO 267/376/136, Nyagua's representative Bokari to Commandant of Bonthe, 1889; CO 267/376/145, Hay to SS; CO 267/376/158, enc. Garrett to Governor, 1889.   [125] CO 267/376/158, Hay to SS, 1889.
[126] CO 267/377/268, enc. Garrett to Governor, 1889.

A more forceful policy: Police, roads, and more treaties

By 1889, the horizon of a more forceful and less amorphous policy is apparent. Symbolically, the onslaught against Largoh and Wende was ample demonstration. Ndawa was dead, Makaya banished to the Gold Coast; Rowe too had died on his way home. Sir J. S. Hay was now in full control, and he was quite conscious of the need for a new forceful and dynamic policy towards the hinterland. On examination, it is clear that Hay did not initiate a new policy. He effected what had long been advocated, and his activities moved the interior people only one stage away from a British Protectorate. The new approach was a triple emphasis on roads, policing, and a greatly increased number of treaties.

The para-military aspect of the new approach was not Hay's invention. After the Yoni expedition of 1887, de Winton came out with proposals for the establishment of a policing system to watch the frontier. On his own initiative, he left a frontier post at Robari, which was more or less experimental. The War Office became jittery, and began to press for the withdrawal of the post. But the Colonial Office was convinced that further raids would be prevented, as well as their consequentials— renewed military expeditions. Hay certainly favoured the retention of the post as 'the moral effect of the small detachment of troops . . . is very great'. He suggested that for some time to come, the post must be retained, and any withdrawal was 'most inexpedient' with the 'discovery of a considerable traffic in slaves in the neighbourhood . . .'.[127] The garrison was thus retained.

De Winton, however, submitted detailed proposals in a memorandum. 'I am convinced', he began, 'that the occupation of certain advanced posts beyond the borderline is the only means of securing peace and tranquillity along the frontier.' Friendly relations with the neighbouring people would be established, and trade would be encouraged. Strategically, in the case of an attack from the interior, 'the colony would occupy a far stronger position than in the present unsettled state of many of the neighbouring tribes on the border'. De

[127] CO 267/373/War Office, 12 Apr. and 5 Sept. 1888; CO 267/376/164, Hay to SS, 1889.

Winton saw no more opportune time than the Yoni expedition. The defeat inflicted on the Yoni showed the people all along the coast 'the power of England'; they would thus fall in with any arrangement proposed 'lest the same fate befall them'.

There was to be no political occupation in the scheme. In fact, 'the general conditions of the country remain undisturbed . . .'. There was to be a division between police and constabulary. The former would carry out police duties at Freetown under a magistrate; the latter were to be placed under an Inspector-General with four Inspectors and four Sub-Inspectors. De Winton estimated that 250 men would be sufficient to cover the frontier. Rowe had been afraid of getting politically involved in the interior and had been bothered about how a military officer stationed inland could escape exercising political influence. Nothing was done immediately with the proposal.[128]

The road-making policy too had been advocated by Garrett while he was stationed at Sulima, and also by Rowe. With Hay, however, these proposals were brought together in a firm policy, which he forcefully suggested to the Colonial Office.

My recommendations comprise the opening of a road from KAMBIA on the GT. SCARCIES to the Manoh River, our South-Eastern boundary, passing through the different important towns between the two points. The increase and reorganisation of the police whereby a body of 100 men under an officer should be available for duty as *Civil Police* in Freetown, and an armed constabulary consisting of 150 men with a complement of officers, who would be stationed at important points on the proposed frontier road whose duty it would be to keep a constant patrol . . . thus preventing any sudden inroad of the slave hunting expeditions of the so-called 'war-boys', and the officers of the force specially selected for tact and intelligence, added to military training, would exercise great influence amongst the Chiefs, and help them to decide any points of difference between them.

The third and last suggestion is the appointment of two of the three Travelling Commissioners,[129] which plan has already met Your Lordship's approval. . . . one in charge from the MANOH river to as far as the KITTAM, the other to supervise the Bompey and Shaingay district. The intervening country between the

---

[128] CO 879/27/350/1, enc., memo by de Winton, 1888; CO 879/27/350/7, Rowe to SS, 1888.   [129] See CO 267/367/9, Hay to SS, 1887.

KITTAM and the BARGRU might well be divided between the Police Inspectors proposed to be stationed at Mafwe and Bendoo.[130]

J. C. E. Parkes, Secretary for Native Affairs, added a memorandum outlining the duties of the Frontier Police. They were to maintain free transit along the frontier road and keep peace between it and the settlements. Crimes of murder and robbery with violence should not be condoned, and slave caravans were to be impeded.[131]

Although the proposals would initially be expensive, the establishment of peace and order was expected to lead to an increase in cultivation, with a consequent improvement of trade and revenue. With this promise of economic benefit, the Colonial Office approved of the proposals.[132]

With the approval of his policy proposals, Hay became firmer in his attitude to Chiefs. In the Gallinas, he told the chiefs that

Headquarters	Inspector	Sub-Inspector	Sgt.-Major	Pay and quarter-master Sgt.	Drill Instructor	Pay clerk	Rank and file
Songo Town		1	1	1	1	1	40
Robari District	1						30
Rokell							5
Mamaligi							10
Senehun							5
Kwellu							15
Taiama							10
Sherbro District							
Bonthe	1	1					40
Mafweh	1						30
Bandasuma (upper Kittam)							10
Bumpeh Mende							5
Bandasuma (Sulima river)	1						30
Gorahun							10
Largo							10
	4	2	1	1	1	1	250

De Winton's proposal for frontier police distribution.

130 CO 267/371/340, Hay to SS, 1888.
131 Ibid., enc., memo by Parkes, 1888.
132 CO 267/371/340, minutes at CO, 1888; also Alldridge, *The Sherbor*, pp. 266 ff.

things had changed and that the administration was 'determined to restore peace and order in the Districts', and would no longer condone breaches of agreements. He threatened that if they did not implicitly obey the orders they received thenceforth, he would either fine or imprison them. Hay reiterated this new emphasis and determination of the administration, and at Jimmi actually 'lectured' the chiefs, adding that they would be severely dealt with for disobeying his orders in the future.[133]

Apparently, there was applause from several quarters for the destruction of Makaya. Chiefs as well as their messengers visited Hay, who wrote that they 'are now subservient to my wishes, and execute the orders received with energy and promptitude'. Hay believed that confidence had been restored to the minds of the people throughout the country. He placed a premium on keeping open communications with the interior, and on getting the chiefs to open up the roads, foster trade, and protect traders.[134]

Chiefs at once agreed to commence work on the roads immediately, which Hay assured them was not with any object of taking control of their country from them. He requested Momoh Kaikai to rebuild Bandajuma, which had been captured by Makaya, and to erect a block house to quarter police, and to keep certain crossroads in permanent good order throughout the year. Momoh Jah showed much enthusiasm in undertaking this project, and a little over a month later, on 26 February 1889, the building was completed, without expense to the administration. The people were frantically improving the new road to Jimmi and clearing farms in the neighbourhood, as well as rebuilding the town.[135] The cost of the new road from Kambia to the Manoh river was estimated at £2,000, but the enthusiasm of the chiefs and their people was enough to accomplish the task in much less time and at no cost to the administration.[136] Hay's frontier road, in fact, 'delimited . . . the traditional sphere of influence, never before officially recognised'.[137]

[133] CO 267/372/476, Hay to SS, 1888; CO 267/375/23, 34, 40, Hay to SS, 1889.
[134] CO 267/375/23, 34, 41 enc. 2; CO 267/376/128, Hay to SS, 1889.
[135] CO 267/375/2, 3, 7; CO 267/376/135, 150, Hay to SS, 1889.
[136] CO 267/375/34, Hay to SS, 1889; Governor's Aborigines Letterbooks, Jan. 1889, passim, hereafter GALB, SLGA.
[137] Fyfe, 'European and Creole Influence', p. 122.

In these arrangements generally, the grant of stipends added an economic focus to its political function. Hay intimated to the chiefs that in future payment would be 'dependent on the way in which they keep this new road'.[138]

Concerning the police, Hay dismissed all rumour that they were intended to take the country from the chiefs. He assured the latter that the police were only to 'act as soldiers to protect them from the inroads of their enemies from the interior, and that there would be no interference with their manners and customs . . .'. When Makavoray requested that a few police be stationed at Tikongoh, albeit temporarily, Hay was particularly delighted: '. . . his very request for constables goes to prove that he recognises the fact that his interests will be best served by carrying out the instructions he receives.'[139]

Up to this time, and perhaps for the next few years until formal rule was declared, the chiefs did not realize that they were gradually losing their sovereignty, although they were not unaware of the changing pattern. The policy throughout this period was intended to surround the Colony with amenable neighbours and to protect them from turbulence, but without directly assuming political control.[140] Although, as subsequent events were to prove, this policy was a 'Trojan horse', the chiefs acquiesced because they saw clear advantages, even if they were only short-term advantages. The traditional rivalries and jealousies among the chiefs ensured a warm welcome for Hay's new peace policy. Each chief would lay the blame for the wars that erupted on his rivals, and in enthusiastically keeping Hay's proposals, the chiefs probably thought that the administration was a kindly benevolent agency watching over African interests. They conceived of the administration as an ally, not a tyrant ready to abrogate their sovereignty. Evidently, no king or chief would sign away his sovereignty for a pension of £10 a year.[141] Thus it was very common when a conflict arose to enter a quick appeal to the Governor to attempt to marshal the support of the administration. Little then did the Africans realize that the 'British were not interested in

[138] CO 267/375/67, Hay to SS, 1889.

[139] CO 267/375/10, 18, Hay to SS, 1889.

[140] PP, vol. lx, 1899; Sir David Chalmers, *Report on the Subject of the Insurrection in the Protectorate of Sierra Leone, 1898*, vol. I, p. 12, hereafter 'Chalmers Report'.

[141] See CO 267/395/312, enc. 1, report by Alldridge, 1891.

conflict resolution *per se*, but more in creating alliances by penetrating the local conflict arena as a third party. . . . The party that joined them won the immediate battle, but both [eventually] lost their independence.'[142] Nor could they foresee that their casual relations would be transformed into the 'master–servant relationship of Colonial rule'.[143] Thus chiefs who exploited the new situation in the mistaken belief that it was in their interest were rudely awakened to the danger when the full effect of the deployment of the Frontier Police, as the paramilitary arm of the administration's new policy, came to be gradually felt between 1890 and 1895.

In the meantime, the administration continued to woo the chiefs into a false sense of security by forging alliances through treaties.

However, these treaties were not just a political by-product of the Colony's economic needs. The French were established to the north of the Colony, and throughout the 1880s were gradually extending their sphere of influence. A convention to delimit British and French spheres was made in 1882 but was not ratified. Then the Berlin Conference of 1884–5 laid down the principle of 'effective occupation' as the basis for claiming territory. Moreover, in 1889, there was a 'border' incident which necessitated the reopening of negotiations with Paris. An aggreement was signed settling several West African boundary disputes, and preserving the 1882 delimitation.[144]

Moreover, the publication of the Carnarvon Commission's report on British naval defences (1879–82) suddenly revealed that the naval defences of the British Empire depended on the maintenance of fortified coaling stations where armed steamships could be supplied. Freetown was the only adequate coaling station on the West African coast, and therefore a vital concern of imperial strategy, which must be protected from the French.[145] The report, however, took time to sink in, and not until the French threat of expansion in the north did the British Government attempt to hold its own.

In 1888, Hay made the Colonial Office aware of the French

[142] T. B. Kabwegyere, 'The Politics of State Formation: The Nature and Effects of Colonialism in Uganda' (Essex PhD thesis, 1972), p. 79.
[143] John Hatch, *History of Britain in Africa* (London 1969), p. 165.
[144] Fyfe, *A History*, p. 486.
[145] Ibid., pp. 438–9.

threat. Already there were treaties of friendship and alliance
existing with many 'tribes' in the vicinity of the Colony. But

as recent events have, however, taught us that other nations are not
inclined to adopt a similar policy, and may even in the face of our
treaties of friendship obtain the cession of countries which we cannot
afford to lose . . . I venture to suggest that I may be permitted to
enter into arrangements with the chiefs in the districts around,
that they will neither cede nor sell their lands to any Foreign
Power [France implied] without the consent of Her Majesty's
Government.[146]

The Colonial Office realized the danger Hay was pointing out,
and as Hemming minuted:

Practically, such treaties could not be pressed against any power
which might induce the chiefs to break their engagements and cede
their territories, but at the same time they would no doubt afford
some sort of check to any such action taking place.[147]

After reference to the Foreign Office, the Colonial Office agreed
to Hay's proposal, and approved of the draft treaty he attached,
which was to be printed in advance for the chiefs to sign.[148]
Thus the immediate object of Hay's treaty policy was to afford
a diplomatic instrument in the British bargaining with the
French over boundaries.

The treaty boom began in 1890. The year before, two Travelling Commissioners had been appointed on the recommendation of Hay. Garrett was to make treaties in the north, while
Alldridge was to make treaties in the south.[149] The standard
treaty which the chiefs were made to sign contained four points.
Firstly, that there should be peace between the subjects of the
chief and Her Majesty's subjects. Secondly, British subjects
should have free access to all parts of the chief's territories, and
any dispute arising therefrom should be submitted to the Governor whose decision should be final. Thirdly, the chief should
not enter any war or acts of aggression 'by which the trade of
the country with the British Colony of Sierra Leone shall be
interrupted'. Lastly, the chief was not to cede any part of his
territory to any other foreign government 'except through and

[146] CO 267/372/Conf. 26, 1888, Hay to SS.
[147] Ibid., minute by Hemming, 1888.
[148] CO 267/376/144, CO approval; CO 267/379/FO, 1889.
[149] CO 267/380/Alldridge, 1889; CO 267/380/Garrett, 1889.

with the consent of the Government of Her Majesty'. So long as the terms were kept, the signatory was entitled to an annual present, the amount of which was added to the treaty in long hand.[150] This stipend was usually of £5 or £10 a year, depending on how important the officials thought the signatory was.

The first standard 'Friendship Treaty' to be signed by a Mende ruler was that signed by Makavoray on 25 March 1889, after he had requested constables. But Hay 'did not feel justified in interfering with his liberty of action with respect to his foes in the interior'. This was of course contrary to the third clause of the treaty. He was recommended to get an annual stipend of £10 in February 1890.[151] Exactly two months later, Nyagua signed the second treaty. After a meeting at Bandajuma in an attempt to resolve the differences among the various chiefs and to establish peace, Garrett reported that 'peace was definitely and fully' established among all the rulers so that he anticipated no further trouble.

The most important rulers there were Makavoray and Nyagua, who shook hands after the peace arrangement, as already noted. It was then that Nyagua signed the treaty similar to Makavoray's.[152]

The rest of the treaties in Upper Mende were negotiated by Alldridge. With the French threat looming large, Hay was frantic to get the task of binding treaty-less chiefs completed as soon as possible 'in consequence of the limited time at our disposal before the rainy season, and the extreme desirability of having the greater number of Treaties completed before then'.[153]

Hay's instructions to Alldridge give a full exposition of the situation and the reasons for the mission:

Having regard to the opening up of communications with the interior chiefs and entering into Treaties with them . . . visit the Barrie, Toonchia, Gaura, Damala, Jawveh, Kono, Kissi, and Onymar Boussie [Loma] Districts and enter into Treaties . . . with the paramount Chiefs.

. . . The object of your journey is *mainly to prevent any Foreign*

[150] CO 267/372/Conf. 26, enc. (draft form of treaty).
[151] CO 267/376/165, Hay to SS, 1889; CO 267/381/47, Hay to SS, 1890.
[152] CO 267/377/268, enc. Garrett to Governor, 1889; Goddard, *Handbook*, Appendix I.
[153] CO 267/381/Conf. 7, Feb. 1890, Hay to SS.

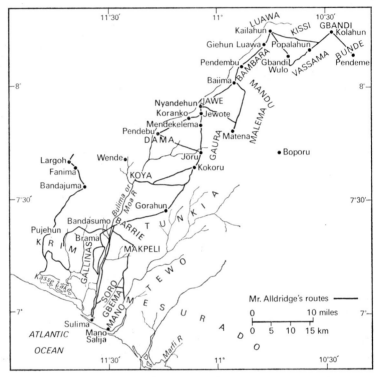

MAP 5. ALLDRIDGE'S ROUTE INTO THE HINTERLAND

Power from further surrounding and hemming in the Colony and that the sphere of British influence should be extended as far as possible consistently with the due observance of the Anglo-French Agreement . . .

You will therefore in all your negotiations avoid anything that may be regarded as an infringement of the right of either the Government of the Republic of France or that of Liberia.

You will all along endeavour to impress upon the chiefs the strong desire which Her Majesty's Government have of opening up their country and developing their resources, and you will impress upon them the strong necessity of their making good broad roads from their towns to central stations, and communicating frequently with the Government.

. . . You will gather all the information you possibly can as to the productions of the country, the requirements of the people in the shape of European articles of merchandise, and generally such information as would assist in the development of its resources.[154]

These instructions reveal mixed strategic and economic motivations and objectives. But Alldridge himself stated in quite over-simplified terms that the object of his mission was to invite the chiefs 'to accept the privilege of entering into friendly treaties with the British Government'.[155]

The first 'white man' in Upper Mende

Alldridge began his hinterland journey from Sulima, and moved roughly in a north-easterly direction. On his first trek, he concluded treaties with twelve rulers, 'nine of them being . . . the Rulers of twelve distinct countries . . .'. There seems to be a certain inconsistency in the signing of these treaties. The remaining three treaties were made with 'sub-chiefs whose individual allegiance to the English Government, I considered it was desirable to secure, apart from that of their paramount chiefs . . .'.[156] If twelve treaties were signed, and three with sub-chiefs, then it is difficult to swallow the explanation that the nine 'paramount chiefs' ruled over 'twelve distinct countries'. Alldridge's report seems to convey a picture of political

---

[154] CO 267/381/Conf. 7, enc. 1, instructions to Alldridge.

[155] Alldridge, *The Sherbro*, p. 165.

[156] CO 267/383/248, enc. Alldridge to Governor, 1890; CO 267/382/159, 182, Alldridge to Governor, 1890.

fragmentation, which the administration was in later years to encourage as a systematic policy.

An ardent 'frontiersman', Alldridge used high-handed tactics to make or to operate the treaties. Having already contravened his instructions to sign only with 'paramount chiefs', he did not hesitate to threaten the chief of Dama to sign. By the time Alldridge got up as far as Kailahun, the news had spread that the chiefs closer to the coast had already signed treaties. Perhaps this partly explains the relative ease of Alldridge's task.[157]

Alldridge suggested arresting the chief of Tunkia, and the chief of Nomo (the latter not a treaty chief at all) as political prisoners, because of their intention to go to war with the Gola. Parkes felt it impolitic, for even within treaty stipulations, 'we can advise but we cannot compel them to do so'. The Colonial Office was in agreement with Parkes.[158]

Meanwhile, the chiefs realized that a new day was dawning, but were probably not yet aware that they were to lose their independence.[159] When King Mendegla wrote to chief Abdul Lahai of Juring in Arabic that 'the power of the English is unnumbered . . . the whole of the power of the Governor is known to us by Captain Crawford' (who sacked Fanima and Largoh) he was probably expressing a hope that there was now a powerful arbitrator to whom recourse could easily be had in case of dispute.[160] Many rulers as such readily accepted the arbitration of the colonial officials. Alldridge, on his second tour in 1891, settled a long-standing dispute between Kai Londo and Momoh Babawo of Pendembu. He arbitrated and gave neither party the right, so as not to compromise anyone in the eyes of the other. Both accepted.[161]

Thus many rulers accepted Hay's new policy in all good faith. To aid and foster the success of this policy, Mendegla resorted to a traditional instrument of ensuring permanent peace. He initiated a special 'Peace Poro'. 'Nothing of very great importance ever takes place until a "porroh" has been

[157] CO 267/383/248, enc. Alldridge to Gov., 1890.
[158] CO 267/395/312, encs. 1 & 2, Alldridge to Governor and Parkes to Governor, 1890.
[159] CO 267/383/248, enc. Alldridge to Gov., 1890.
[160] CO 267/377/173, enc. 2, Mendegla to Abdul Lahai, 1889.
[161] CO 267/388/133, enc. Alldridge to Gov., 1891.

sent down . . .', wrote Alldridge. When he arrived at Banda-suma, where he had asked the chiefs to assemble in order to explain his mission to them, he discovered that 'all of the chiefs whom I met there had already accepted the "porroh", which so far as I could learn, had reference to a permanent peace being maintained in the country . . .'. The Poro had already spread over a radius of nearly one hundred miles from Men-degla's capital, 'which will . . . show how an important chieftain like [him] is able to make known his laws whether for good or for bad, over a very considerable area of country'.[162] Thus the colonial 'pacification' of the country was not merely achieved from without. However, Mendegla was unwittingly aiding the process of colonial occupation, though he did not live to see it. While acting in good faith, the rulers were being deceived by the administration, for as subsequent events proved, it did the exact opposite of what it had professed all along.

Thus with these beginnings, the 'colonial situation' assumed an essentially spurious character. The disparity between pro-fessed policy and actual practice has generally been demon-strated by Brunschwig.[163] The gulf between facts and theories, particularly after the formal declarations, constitutes 'blatant hypocrisy'.[164]

Treaties in Middle Mende

Meanwhile, Hay himself was busy getting treaties signed in the middle Mende belt. In 1890, he journeyed through areas coming under British influence from the Gallinas, through Jimmi, Mofwe, Tikongoh, Bumpeh and across Kpaa-Mende. In December, a large assemblage of chiefs and people gathered at Tikongoh, where Quee of Jama, Hotagua of Bo, and Goam-bay of Mattru, together with Kargobai of Damballa, signed treaties similar to Makavoray's. Hay kept falsely assuring them that

Whilst the Government earnestly desired to assist and advise them on all matters calculated to improve the condition of their people

[162] CO 267/383/248, enc. report by Alldridge, 1890.
[163] H. Brunschwig, *French Colonialism, 1871–1914: Myths and Realities* (London 1966).
[164] G. Balandier, 'The Colonial Situation: A Theoretical Approach', in I. Wallerstein, *Social Change: The Colonial Situation* (New York 1966), pp. 38–9.

and the country, *there was not the slightest desire or intention of either taking control of the latter out of their hands*, or of interfering in any way with domestic institutions.[165]

Hay was then accompanied by such important rulers as Makavoray, Momoh Jah, and Hotagua to meet the Bumpeh rulers.

Hay was well aware of the fact that the Bumpeh afforded a bulwark to colonial penetration.

They have for years past been almost unapproachable and it has therefore been my aim in my intercourse with them to assure them of the goodwill of the Government and its desire to draw closer the bonds of friendship between us. . . . I suggested that they should enter into a similar treaty, as that signed by Chief Makavoray.

This was the first occasion in that decade that the Bumpeh rulers had come to meet the 'Officer Administering the Government'. Hay reported that there were four rulers over Bumpeh, all of whom signed the treaty, Mbogbawova, Seppeh, Demeawah, and Gubloh, 'the former being recognised as the paramount . . .'.[166]

In January 1891, Foray Vong, Dandeh, and Degbeh signed on behalf of Taiama. The only other treaty signed was with Fakondo of Baoma. No treaties were signed with the rest of the Mende.

Immediate implication of the treaties

The following were those listed in 1895 as having signed treaties:[167]

> Madam Yoko of Senehun
> Foray Vong of Taiama
> Quee of Jama
> Mbogbawova of Bumpeh
> Kargobai of Damballa
> Makavoray of Tikongoh
> Nyagua of Lower Bambara
> Kpawoh Lalama of Gorahun Tunkia

[165] CO 267/386/570, Hay to SS, 1890 (emphasis added). CO 267/385, 386, *passim;* CO 267/386/549, Hay's address to Chiefs at Mofwe.

[166] CO 267/386/554, 580, Hay to SS, 1890.

[167] CO 267/418/156, enc., Treaty Chiefs, 1895; see also CO 267/386/580, Hay to SS, 1890, and Goddard, *Handbook*, Appendix I.

Mendegla of Gaura
Vandi Saawai of Jawe
Hotagua of Bo
Fakondo of Baoma
Kabba Sei of Mandu
Momoh Babawo of Upper Bambara
Kai Londo of Luawa
Joseh of Koya
Braima Jah of Jimmi
Canray Nancy of Mofwe
Duwo Nyeami of Malema
Wono of Gerihun.

Conspicuously absent from this list are the three 'sub-chiefs'—Kpawoh of Kokoru, Samawa of Gorahun, and Gbatekaka of Kpuwabu—with whom Alldridge signed treaties on his first trek. In the particular case of Gbatekaka, the absence of his name is in spite of the fact that apart from having signed a treaty, he had been unanimously elected to succeed Mendegla on his death in September 1890. Also absent from the list is Hakawa of Dama, who was probably dead at the time.

The pattern of this treaty-making was very haphazard, for there was no consistency in the status of the signatories. For instance, Gaura, Nomor, Dama, Koya, Jawe etc. were all part of Mendegla's polity, yet their chiefs were made to sign treaties, and their rulers were regarded as equally 'paramount' as Mendegla. On the other hand, important divisional rulers in the Kpaa-Mende state, such as Vonjo of Mongere, were not made to sign any treaties. The recognition of divisional chiefs as 'paramounts' may be said to have been part of what later became a general policy of fragmentation. In this muddle, the distinction between king and chief, the latter being the subordinate of the king, was lost. For even if the king is to be regarded as 'paramount chief' within the colonial context, the colonial power now arrogating suzerainty to itself, there was still an important shift in the balance of traditional power. By signing treaties with their subordinates, the British detached the allegiance of the chiefs from their kings. This undermined the kings. This same effect is seen on the Gold Coast at the same time.[168] Not only were the kings undermined, this process also

[168] See W. Tordoff, *Ashanti Under the Prempehs, 1888–1935* (London 1965), p. 388.

fragmented the states, and the geographical extent and quali-
tative exercise of regal jurisdiction was contracted to fit the
uniform pattern that was now being imposed. The traditional
system was being moulded to fit the 'colonial situation'. This
muddled picture of contradictions was the result of the direct
activities of the colonial officials.

After this frenzied treaty-making, Hay envisaged the up-
country treaty-chiefs from the Jong to the Manoh rivers 'as a
federation to ensure the future peace and advancement of the
country, they being guided in their action by the advice of the
Government'. The administration was underplaying its role
as the dominant power, and the whole arrangement was
presented to the chiefs as a kind of partnership. Alldridge
looked forward 'with pleasure to [Kai Londo's] becoming an
important and powerful ally to the Government' after signing
the treaty. Thus Hay proposed holding annual meetings of all
the chiefs 'to show that the Government is sincere in its desire
to assist them in all that is calculated to improve their country'.[169] All these pronouncements were a hollow farce. In the light
of what subsequently happened, the chiefs and people were just
being deceived. Having been baited into swallowing the hook
of the 'colonial psychology', the people were later awoken to
the falsity of the ostensible British altruism as it had been
preached to them but which in fact was a cover for ensuring
the economic survival of the Colony. The activities of the military arm of the new policy, the Frontier Police, made the chiefs
aware that certainly in the alliance of equal partners, the British
were more equal than the Africans. The men-on-the-spot seem
to have been conditioned in their aims and beliefs 'more by
their social background and by the local circumstances in
which they found themselves than by the policies which they
were instructed to follow from Whitehall'.[170]

The Frontier Police and the invasion of African sovereignty

Enlistment for the Frontier Police began on 1 May 1890, and
recruitment was mainly done from the interior in districts

[169] CO 267/386/580, Hay to SS, 1890; CO 267/395/312, enc. 1, Alldridge to
Gov., 1892; CO 267/386/588, enc. Hay to SS, 1890. See also Little, *The Mende*,
p. 56.
[170] D. H. Perraton, 'The Man on the Spot', p. 161.

bordering on the Colony.[171] Within six months, 32 stations had been established, which literally dotted the entire length of the frontier road created by Rowe to demarcate the Colony's sphere of influence. Some stations were, however, found in a few towns nearer the coast.[172] The Frontier Police were to repel attacks from without, and prevent dissensions from within, and thus preserve the integrity of the borders. They were not to 'mix themselves up in any inter-tribal disputes, or interfere in any way with the domestic institutions of the natives . . .'. They were also to encourage the chiefs to get their people to open up the roads to the interior markets and to bring down produce. They were instructed always to be polite to the people and to 'do all in their power to gain their respect and confidence'.

In the *Standing Orders and Regulations*, Major Moore concluded that 'all breaches of discipline in the way of taking undue advantage of the natives will be generally punished'.[173] In short, as Hay outlined, their duties 'are intended to be merely those of a frontier force'. While adding that 'they may stop the transit of large slave caravans', Hay insisted to the officer-in-charge that he should see that 'they do not overstep the bounds I have laid for them'.[174]

Alldridge drew attention to the general desire of chiefs with whom he had signed treaties to have police quartered in their towns. This was natural, for having accepted the British *pax* in good faith, the presence of the police would serve to remind potential peace-breakers or past rivals that a more powerful ally was at hand. Hay favoured the idea of extending the area of police activity, but the proposal was kept pending because of 'the lack of means at our disposal'. At the moment, therefore, 'action must be confined to a periodical police visit to our *new allies* . . .'.[175]

Within a year, Hay pressed to have the Frontier Police

[171] CO 267/385/466, Hay to SS, 1890; CO 267/382/198, Hay to SS, 1890.

[172] CO 267/385/466, enc. Report by Moore, Ag. Inspector-General of Police, 1890.

[173] Al. Moore, *Standing Orders and Regulations of the Sierra Leone Frontier Police Force* (London 1890), pp. 54–6.

[174] GALB, 100/89, SLGA.

[175] CO 267/382/182, Hay to SS, 1890; CO 267/383/248, Hay to SS, 1890 (emphasis added).

increased, because 'I have recently reluctantly arrived at the conclusion that the force is not only under-officered, but under-manned'. Men had to be withdrawn from their stations when any special patrol was called for.[176] In May 1891, Hay recommended that the force be enlarged by at least one European Officer and fifty non-commissioned officers and men, 'having in view the large extent of country lately placed by the Timini and Mendi chiefs under our immediate control'. This was approved by the Colonial Office.

The increase was necessary because 'the presence of constables around the country exercises a wholesome influence over the chiefs', and information would be gathered 'enabling the action of the chiefs to be carefully watched'.[177] Already, officials were regarding the territories of the treaty-chiefs as British.

Although quite aware that the treaties were friendly treaties in which the signatories were made to believe that they were allies, Alldridge wrote of 'new territories placed under the protection of Her Majesty's Government',[178] and Hay, of territories 'under our immediate control'. As it turned out, having acquired territorial influence, the officials began to act as if Britain were already sovereign, particularly with the deployment of the Frontier Police. This may be seen as the direct result of the policy followed, even if it was not the orginal purpose of that policy.

As early as January 1891, Hay made it clear that 'the chiefs should not be left to act altogether without the advice of the Government'.[179] While making the rulers believe that there was no interference with their traditional system, the officials behaved in a manner, after the treaty-boom of 1890–1, which suggested that the days of African sovereignty were close to an end. The dichotomy between professed policy and naked practice, mattered little in the approach of the British to establish colonial dominion over the hinterland.

The Frontier Police as one important arm of the new approach, usually did no credit to the administration because of incessant abuse of their powers.[180] Complaints began as soon

[176] CO 267/385/466, Hay to SS, 1890.
[177] CO 267/395/312, enc. 1, Alldridge to Gov., 1892.
[178] CO 267/392/Alldridge, 6 Oct. 1891.
[179] CO 267/388/15, Hay to SS, 1891.
[180] J. H. Mannah-Kpaka, 'Memoirs of the 1898 Rising', *Sierra Leone Studies*,

as they made their debut. The chiefs of Mofwe complained to Hay in 1890 'that constables from Jimmi have been in the habit of catching people in their territory on the Bum river'.[181] In the same year, Kai Londo reported that Police Constable Henry Collier, while acting as escort to Alldridge, 'ravished one of his wives'. A plethora of reports against 'extorting money from people against their will under various pretexts,' taking people against their will as they did to some of Yoko's people, 'flogging people indiscriminantly', giving badges to people 'to act as constables', kept bombarding the Governor's office.[182] The activities of the Frontier Police thus contradicted the very *raison d'être* of their establishment.

Particularly in the matter of their instruction to stop large slave caravans in transit, the operations of the Frontier Police were a source of much vexation. Yet the fact that the administration did not seem really to understand the true nature of the so-called 'slave' system existing at the time, made it readily accept the exaggerated reports from the Police. In March 1893, Governor Fleming suggested that the most likely way 'to put down slavery than anything else' was to acquire as much of the country as possible.[183] In June, while Fleming was away, J. J. Crooks, the Administrator, issued *Instructions to Police Regarding Overland Slave Traffic*, which seems to suggest that the Frontier Police acted in the matter much as they pleased, irrespective of their instructions.

The *Instructions* reiterated that the Police have 'only a right to take steps to stop the transit of slaves' in specified towns and districts. The transit of slaves was defined to mean 'slaves either chained or in shackles', or (this was added later) 'otherwise in restraint', who were being taken or driven along the roads in the districts enumerated. The instructions added:

The Police are on no account to enter the house or yard of anyone to search for slaves as they have no right to interfere excepting where slaves are being actually transported . . .

N.S. 1, Dec. 1953, pp. 37-8; J. D. Hargreaves, 'The Establishment of the Sierra Leone Protectorate and the Insurrection of 1898', *Cambridge Historical Journal*, xii, 1, 1956.

[181] CO 267/386/549, Hay to SS, 1890.

[182] GALB, 107/89, 519/90, SLGA, Native Affairs Department Letterbooks, 291/93, SLGA, hereafter NADL.

[183] CO 267/401/113, Fleming to SS, 1893.

Otherwise, the *Instructions* concluded, 'they have no right to interfere in any slave questions in the places where they are stationed'. The enactment of these instructions shows that much brutality and unwarranted interference were being used. Crooks hoped that with the instructions, 'greater care is now being executed in the matter'.[184]

Scattered in small detachments without any central direction and 'no European Officer', the Frontier Police were bound to be unruly. After the Sofa expedition, the Police were unable to maintain order. Cardew, who had taken over as Governor in 1894, proposed to strengthen the Police in the disturbed districts, and to distribute them 'on the principle of having a central main body of adequate strength under an Inspector, and small outlying posts at different points with constant patrolling from the main body . . .'. Cardew was fully aware that the existing distribution of Police in small bodies in isolated posts without adequate supervision—such supervision that existed was mainly by sub-Inspectors and non-commissioned officers—would make them 'apt to exceed their authority, and grave acts of irregularity are likely to occur', as was already most prevalent.[185] When he made his first tour into the interior in 1894, Cardew emphasized as his 'principal object' the aim of securing 'the full fruits of the recent [Sofa] expedition by the proper organisation and distribution of the Police . . .'.[186]

The Governor proposed increasing the number of privates from 300 to 500. The Force would then be divided into five Companies lettered A to E, each consisting of an Inspector, a sub-Inspector, four Sergeants, four Corporals, and 100 privates. One Company would be in Freetown, and 'one each in the districts of SANDA-LOKO, FALABA [in the north], MONGHERRY and SULIMA [in the south]'. By this re-organization, Cardew aimed at making the military power of the administration felt throughout the interior, for it would be possible, so he argued, to marshal 250 men on any remote point on the frontier within three weeks in case of any disturbance.

The system of scattering police in small detachments was most objectionable and fraught with many evils, the men get out

184 CO 267/402/195, and enc. 1, Crooks to SS, 1893.
185 CO 267/408/88, Cardew to SS, 1894.
186 CO 267/408/Conf. 27, Cardew to SS, 1894.

of hand, they deteriorate as a military body, they become mixed up in the intrigues of the natives . . . often behave extortionably [*sic*] and are always open to the temptations of bribes.[187]

'A' Company was stationed in Mongere district with headquarters at Mongere, while 'B' Company was stationed in Sulima district with headquarters in Bandajuma.[188] Appreciating the acts of oppression of the people by the Frontier police, Cardew took 'drastic steps' to stop the malpractices, dismissing thirty men for misconduct in 1895.[189]

Cardew was perhaps unduly touchy about the 'slave question', as were nearly all the officials, who took insufficient cognizance of the difference between slaves who were being sold, and dependants. It became necessary to amend the instructions to the Police regarding the slave traffic because 'the instructions have been a direct incentive to the Slave Traffic . . .'. Since the police were only to operate in the districts and towns named therein, traders embarked on the traffic in the exempted areas. Thus Cardew amended the instructions to include 'the whole of the territories under our sphere of influence'.[190]

Himself an army Colonel, Cardew was an impatient man with an essentially military approach. No wonder he emphasized the military aspect of the administration's policy towards the hinterland. Having thus fully deployed the armed force, the chiefs who had signed friendly treaties were now undeceived, when they were made to realize that the administration would treat them no longer as allies, but as subordinate authorities who had to obey the orders of the administration whether they liked it or not. In short, they were suddenly made aware, during Cardew's time, that they had unwittingly sold away their sovereignty.

When Cardew gave orders for the suppression of the slave traffic, King Nyagua stated that he would like to consult his chiefs and headmen before giving a reply, in compliance with traditional constitutional law. Cardew forcefully replied that

[187] CO 267/409/180, Cardew to SS, 1894.
[188] CO 267/412/265, Gazette Notice, Frontier Police Districts.
[189] CO 267/415/111, report on Frontier Police, 1895.
[190] CO 267/408/117, Cardew to SS, 1894; CO 267/409/155, Cardew to SS, 1894.

'in any case he must understand *the orders were final and would be carried out*'.[191] The whole idea of alliance, which the chiefs had been made to believe was the nature of the relationship with the administration, was brutally and unilaterally thrown overboard.

Similarly, in March 1895, Cardew 'censured Kai Lundu for not obeying my instructions to come to Vahun' during the Governor's second tour. Cardew was annoyed to learn that Kai Londo was contemplating ostracizing the police stationed at Kailahun by depriving them of supplies, so that they would be forced to evacuate his territory, if the administration did not assist him in fighting his enemies. Evidently Kai Londo had realized the chicanery of the British, and further contemplated handing back the stipends he had received so far, and thus reclaiming his territory. The King was at last suddenly made aware that the police, ostensibly there to assist him, were in fact an instrument of domination by the administration. But his position had become precarious, like that of other rulers, all of whom were now victims of the projection of European force into Africa. Cardew threatened Kai Londo that 'his position would become intolerable . . . especially if the Government were to bring the pressure of the Frontier Police to bear against him. This line of reasoning appeared to have a good effect.' The good effect was only in the sense that the king was in an impasse, i.e. it was impossible at this stage to resist the military force of the British. Cardew, however, cushioned the precarious predicament of the king by giving him false assurance that there was no idea of permanent expropriation of his traditional sovereignty.[192] But there was sufficient military force to back the administration in this brutal approach.

The hinterland was by now a virtual British territory. Cardew was only waiting to have the Anglo-French boundary settled before he formalized the existing situation. When this was done, Cardew suggested the 'desirability of declaring a Protectorate over the whole territory within the boundary'. While he had to work out the details of the administration to be adopted, he emphasized that whatever the form, 'I do not think it should be maintained at the expense of the colony, and

---

[191] CO 267/408/131, Cardew to SS, 1894.
[192] CO 267/417/61, Cardew to SS, 1895.

therefore later on, the question as to the best means of raising
a revenue within the Protectorate must be decided on'.[193]

In August 1895, an Order-in-Council was passed in accordance with the Foreign Jurisdiction Act of 1890, making it

lawful for the Legislative Council for the time being of the Colony
of Sierra Leone by ordinance or ordinances to exercise and provide
for giving effect to all such jurisdiction as Her Majesty may . . .
have acquired in the . . . territories adjacent to the Colony of
Sierra Leone.[194]

This formalized and legalized, in the eyes of English law, the
colonial occupation.

Conclusion: the economic imperative and the colonial occupation

The beginnings of the policy which ended in the colonial
occupation of the hinterland are to be seen in the desperate
efforts of the administration to save the Colony from economic
paralysis. Thus there appears to be a direct functional relationship between the economic depression of the Colony and the
first political overtures in the interior. The reasoning behind
the move, namely that the economic crises was caused by the
wars in the interior, was not necessarily correct or valid. Yet the
men-on-the-spot were so convinced about the verity of the false
local economic analysis which was propagated by the traders,
that the administration, while unwilling to disobey policy by
interfering in the interior, gradually found itself, in the effort
to maintain peace on its frontier, bogged down in the morass
of the interior politics, from which, by the late 1880s, it became
impossible for it to disentangle itself.

By this time, the officials were aware that the colonial occupation, however inadvertent in origin, was not far from being a
reality. When the French threat appeared in the northern
sphere of influence, it became an urgent necessity to get the
rulers consciously allied to the British—hence the treaty boom
of 1890–1. But while the eventual objective might have been
manifest to the officials, they carefully cajoled the chiefs into a
policy that ended in taking away their rights. By treaty-making,
exploitation of existing conflicts, use of violence, bribery in the

[193] CO 267/417/Conf. 36, Cardew to SS, 1895.
[194] CO 879/49/533/8, enc.

form of stipends, 'the inductive system', i.e. the machinery to induce compliance and acceptance of colonial domination at the local level,[195] the 'colonial psychology', the process of colonial occupation was accomplished. The rulers, by accepting the Grecian gifts of the British in all good faith, unwittingly aided the process of the colonial occupation, particularly as they were being constantly assured that there were no imperialistic intentions. They were victims of British diplomatic machinations.

When Cardew took office, he relied on the Frontier Police, which had already caused apprehension among the rulers, to make the latter aware that the idea of alliance between them and the British was a myth of the past. He astonished them by the proposals of the Protectorate administration, which threatened to undermine the fabric of their society. The consequent 'Mende War' of 1898 has to be examined within this context.

[195] Kabwegyere, 'State Formation', Chap. III.

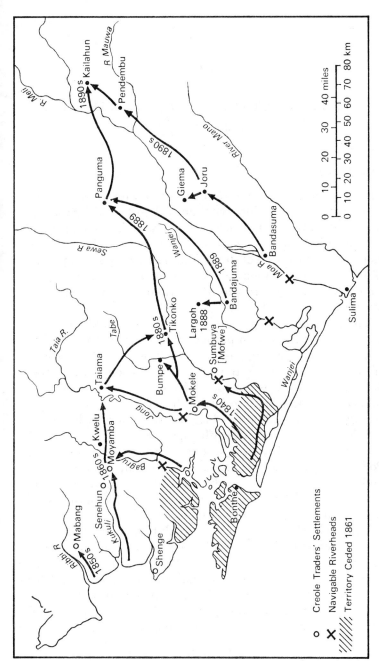

MAP 6. SPREAD OF EUROPEAN INFLUENCE AFTER 1880

Creole Traders' Settlements
Navigable Riverheads
Territory Ceded 1861

III

FRAUDULENT PROTECTORATE
AND WAR

Local pressures

THE steps in the declaration of the Protectorate were a dex-
terous manoeuvre of chicanery and bad faith on the part of the
British administration, which escalated at a meteoric pace after
the treaties of 1890–1 had been signed, and left the rulers and
their people in utter consternation. The new policy approach
of the early 1890s emphasized the re-organizing and strengthening of the military arm with the invidious explanation that it
was meant to protect the people.

The vocal pressures for establishing a Protectorate were local
in origin. The traders, in particular, were the vanguard of this
pressure group.[1] In 1893, there were disputes among the chiefs
of the Scarcies region to the north of the Colony. A Mr. Davis
drew attention to this state of affairs and petitioned that political agents be appointed to further the economic interest of the
Colony by settling diputes which obstructed trade. Parkes, the
Creole Secretary for Native Affairs, was enthusiastic and 'really
desires to establish . . . a species of Protectorate, by placing
Political Agents in such portions of adjacent territories as are
under, what is called the British sphere of influence'. The
report of the 1865 Parliamentary Select Committee which
recommended a general contraction from West Africa, was by
this time clearly an anachronism both to Whitehall and to the
men-on-the-spot. Governor Fleming agreed fully with Parkes
that to maintain the British hold in West Africa, officials were
necessary to watch over the indigenous people and 'check
their barbarous customs'. Fleming preferred reducing the
Frontier Police to pay for the Political Agents, but the Colonial
Office was adverse to any reduction because of the recent

[1] Chap. II, *supra.*

experience in Lagos where the Hausa constabulary undertook an expedition that saved the colonial administration there from what would have been 'a very serious expenditure' had regular troops been employed.[2] Parkes's Protectorate proposals were perhaps the first comprehensive document of its kind representing the general ethos of the Colony at the time. A loud anomaly was that 'we exercise all the authority incidental to a Protectorate without venturing to declare that it is one'. Parkes thus wanted to make *de jure*, a situation that existed *de facto*. The 'robber-baron policy' of taking the coastal strip for fiscal purposes was, he pointed out, doomed to failure. In view of 'the energy of our neighbours, the French, the struggle of the native tribes . . . [and] the necessity of maintaining at least a little of that commercial activity which existed in the past . . .', something concrete and positive had to be done. He suggested appointing five Political Agents who would not displace existing African governments, but should only 'advise and direct' the local rulers.

But should the declaration of the Protectorate not be approved, Parkes recommended the appointment of the five Political Agents, who would confine their actions to:

(1) visiting and directing the Chiefs as to the cleaning of roads and towns and the improvement of agriculture, (2) seeing that their Treaty stipulations are strictly adhered to, (3) assisting them to settle such native palavers as they cannot settle themselves, (4) using their moral influence to prevent the burning or torture of persons for witchcraft.

In addition, the Governor should call a 'sort of durbar' of the Chiefs every dry season to discuss matters germane to colonial interests that were always said to be for the better government of the country. Parkes concluded that this scheme was a responsibility the administration had shirked long enough, but that events were so fast approaching a crisis point that 'the consideration of some definite policy for the future cannot be much longer delayed'.[3]

Fleming wanted positive action, and was quite clear that Parkes's alternative suggestion would not be much good.

[2] CO 267/400/47, Fleming to SS, and minutes by Hemming; Despatches, 12/93, SLGA.
[3] CO 267/400/47, encs. 5 and 6, Parkes to Col. Sec., 1893.

According to the terms of the treaties, moral influence or a cessation of stipends were the only instruments of control to get the rulers to stop the slave-traffic and other abhorrent customs repugnant to 'our notions of advancement and progress'. Only the existence of active jurisdiction would make any 'real impression' on the people.[4] Alldridge was emphatic that 'the country is now ripe for annexation, which would bring about much needed reforms, greatly to be desired, more particularly in connection with the traffic in human beings'.[5]

While the Colonial Office was undecided about the matter, the men-on-the-spot did not fail to act. In August 1893, the Executive Council voted unanimously to have a Protectorate proclaimed 'over all the territories included in the sphere of British influence'. The French had already diverted the Niger trade, and a similar occurrence was feared in the Sierra Leone hinterland. To preserve the economic nerve-centre of the Colony, peace and security were necessary to encourage agriculture and trade. Only a Protectorate would ensure this. But the Colonial Office was hesitant. The Foreign Office was still conducting negotiations with respect to the Anglo-French boundary, and it was feared that if a Protectorate were proclaimed, the objectives might be misunderstood. The Foreign Office assured the Colonial Office that the French would not misunderstand British motives so long as 'no Territory should at present be included the title to which is still disputed'. The Colonial Office was content, therefore, once the French regarded the area in question as a British sphere, to permit the Sierra Leone administration 'without any further announcement or proclamation, to continue to exercise, as hitherto, the functions of Protection as far as convenience and circumstances may permit'.[6]

Governor Cardew

In 1894, Col. Frederic Cardew took charge of the administration of the Colony. With more vigour and enthusiasm than any

---

[4] CO 267/401/125, Fleming to SS, 1893.
[5] CO 267/401/113, enc. 2, Alldridge to Gov., 1893.
[6] CO 267/403/Conf. 49, Crooks to SS, 1893; CO 267/405/FO, 14 Oct., 14 Nov., 2 Dec. 1893.

of his predecessors, Cardew stood for action and change.
With promptitude, he took decisions on many long-standing
projects. He was a regular soldier—like most of his predecessors—but he was more forceful and dynamic, and approached
most matters in a remarkably military manner. For five years,
he had been Resident Commissioner in Zululand, a Protectorate, and on arrival in Freetown, he lost no time in bringing
further pressure on the Colonial Office for a Protectorate in
Sierra Leone. His early methods, however, evinced caution, but
as events moved fast enough, he was prone to abandon his
previous restraints.

Addressing the Colonial Office, Cardew advocated an administrative machine similar to that of Zululand, *mutatis mutandis*.
'The leading principle', he wrote, '. . . should be the administration of the country as far as possible by native law and custom
through the chiefs.' Customs and offences 'altogether repugnant
to our ideas of humanity and civilisation' should be abolished,
or tried by a court of chiefs presided over by a District Commissioner. But offences relating to the slave-trade and 'slavery' should be tried by the District Commissioner alone. The
Protectorate administration should be distinct from that of the
Colony, the only link being the Governor, who in Cardew's
conception, as in Rowe's, should be the new 'paramount chief
of the interior'.[7]

Arguing for the Protectorate, Cardew had 'no hesitation in
asserting that the source and origin of all native wars is the
slave traffic'. To ensure peace and the cultivation of land, the
Protectorate was imperative.

The more powerful and warlike Chiefs derive their whole revenue
from the sale of slaves. They prey on the less warlike, because more
industrious, tribes around them until all the neighbouring region
which is within their sphere of action becomes a desert. In the chief
town of each chief, there are traders generally from the Susu country
and Futa Djallong whose principal stock in trade are guns and
powders which they get from Freetown and Port Loko. These they
advance to the chiefs for the promise of slaves in lieu, often a chief
becomes heavily in debt to these traders, and to discharge his debts
he sells some of his or what is more generally the case, he organises a
raid on some neighbouring tribe . . .

[7] CO 267/409/Conf. 45, Cardew to SS, 1894.

If the Frontier Police were augmented to extirpate the slave-trade, 'the extra outlay would be more than compensated by the increased trade that would result'. Thus, the lynch-pin of Cardew's proposals was economic—stop wars caused by slave trading and increase trade and revenue.[8]

The Colonial Office was impressed by Cardew's forceful arguments, but while the outcome of the Anglo-French boundary negotiations was still being awaited, it assured the Governor that his proposals would form 'the basis for ultimate action'. In the meantime, however, 'the proper course will be to pass an Order in Council under the Foreign Jurisdiction Act as has been done in the other West African colonies, giving the legislature of Sierra Leone, the power of making laws for the adjoining Protectorate'. Measures for consolidating British authority would then be gradually introduced in order 'to be acceptable to the inhabitants'. The Colonial Office warned Cardew that in view of the large extent of territory to be so controlled with the limited means of the administration, *the general assent of the people is indispensable to the success of any laws* that may be introduced'.[9] This apparently did not imply consent for the proclamation of the Protectorate.

The Colonial Office cautioned against haste, but Cardew lost no time in re-organizing the Frontier Police. On his second tour of the hinterland in 1895, he reported favourably that the vigilance of the police had 'practically stamped out' the slave-trade, although 'there may still be private and illicit dealing in domestic slaves'. The Susu and Fula traders would not risk capture and confiscation from the regular patrols.[10]

In the meantime, Cardew briefed the chiefs about the 're-forms' he was going to introduce. He expected to develop the interior by economic rather than by political means. The first step should be to increase the demands for European merchandise among the people, so that, to satisfy their wants, they should be forced to cultivate more. Already the demand for trade rum and gin was increasing, which Cardew deprecated 'from an ethical point of view . . . but the principle is sound and must result beneficially as long as it is applied to more useful and

---

[8] CO 267/409/Conf. 45, Cardew to SS, 1894.
[9] Ibid. (emphasis added).
[10] CO 267/416/53, Cardew to SS, 1895.

less demoralising articles of commerce'. Traders were expected to play a crucial role in this culture.[11]

Alldridge, who had now taken charge of Sherbro district, explained to the chiefs and people that a 'healthier' system was to be introduced for their 'greater happiness and freedom'. In short, three institutions were to be guillotined—the slave-trade, 'the staking of persons', and that economic nuisance of a 'PORO' which 'from selfish motives' placed an embargo on palm trees, thus diminishing commerce and causing loss of revenue.[12]

To goad the rather cautious Colonial Office to accept that circumstances had matured earlier than was expected for declaring a Protectorate, Cardew stated that the chiefs and people 'appeared to acquiesce in the scheme as it was unfolded to them and many expressed approval of it'.[13] Three months later, while on leave in Britain, Cardew took the opportunity, after discussing the matter with the Colonial Office officials, to elaborate his proposals in more detail. The power and authority of the African rulers were to be severely curtailed as many matters were to be removed from their jurisdiction. Although aware that land could not be alienated under the traditional system, Cardew proposed that the Governor should have power to assign locations for 'Native Chiefs' and 'tribes', to authorize occupation of waste or uninhabited land by colonists from the Colony or elsewhere for settlement, and to deal in mineral rights and the acquisition of land for all administrative purposes. Cardew hoped that 'domestic slavery' will 'gradually disappear' because the development of the Protectorate will alter the conditions of life. No legislation was therefore proposed, but in the meantime, the law was not to take cognizance of 'slavery'.[14]

The new administration was estimated to cost £5,000 for a start. Already, the cost of the Frontier Police—£19,000 a year—was a serious burden on the Colony's precarious revenue. Money therefore had to be found. 'The most prolific source of revenue' was calculated to be a house tax, to be gradually introduced, those nearer the coast paying first. In 1894, Cardew had reported that he envisaged no opposition to

[11] CO 267/417/Conf. 32, Cardew to SS, 1895.
[12] CO 267/416/32, enc., Alldridge to Gov., 1895.
[13] CO 267/425/Conf. 23, Cardew to SS, 1895.
[14] CO 879/43/497/34, Cardew to SS, 1895.

the tax.[15] In 1896 the Governor was saying quite another thing. Since the 'whole administration hangs' on the house tax, 'firm dealing' was necessary to exact it, 'for the West African negro has a traditional dislike to direct taxation such as a house tax'. Therefore 'it is necessary to have sufficient force to uphold the authority of the Government . . .'. Cardew did not expect much trouble in collecting the tax, but 'the sure way to prevent such trouble is to have the necessary show of force'. The Colonial Office was baffled by the apparent inconsistency,[16] but had nevertheless given approval for declaring the country on the British side of the Anglo-French boundary agreement on 21 January 1895, as formally under the protection of Her Majesty.[17] In August 1895 an order-in-Council had been passed in accordance with the Foreign Jurisdiction Act of 1890, making it legal for the legislative council of the Colony to make laws for the adjacent territories in which Her Majesty was said to have acquired jurisdiction.[18] Twelve months after, while Cardew was on leave, a Proclamation was issued in the Colony by the Officer Commanding the Troops, Lt.-Col. A. L. Bayley, declaring that it was 'best for the interests of the people . . . that the territories adjacent to the colony of Sierra Leone . . . are now under the protection of Her Majesty'.[19] This Proclamation was issued not in the Protectorate it established, but in the Colony.

The details of working out the new administrative mechanism were left to Cardew when he returned to the Colony. A fortnight later an ordinance was passed to establish 'a definite system of jurisdiction and administration in place of the chaotic one that has hitherto prevailed'. The Governor was convinced that this was a 'sincere endeavour to legislate for the best interests of the natives'. This measure was speeded up 'on the grounds of urgency, as it is necessary to take immediate steps to have its provisions made known to all the native chiefs, as a preliminary to appointing District Commissioners and the necessary Judicial and Administrative staff . . .'.[20]

[15] CO 267/409/Conf. 45, Cardew to SS, 1894.
[16] CO 267/427/Conf. 53, Cardew to SS, 1896.
[17] CO 879/49/533/9, SS to Cardew, 1895.
[18] CO 879/49/533/8, enc. Order-in-Council for the jurisdiction of the Hinterland.
[19] *Sierra Leone Royal Gazette*, 1896.
[20] CO 879/49/533/30, Cardew to SS, 1896.

Why the Protectorate?

To contemporary officials the Protectorate was quite justified. Cardew's stance has already been shown. Contemporaries are unanimous in asserting that the Protectorate was proclaimed because of the incessant disturbances in the interior and in order to stop slave-raiding.[21] This sounds humanitarian enough, but the economic imperative was perhaps a most important factor. Captain Wallis stated bluntly that 'for the last three-quarters of a century we have been continuously contending with the native races in order that *we might benefit from the commercial and other wealth* in which this part of the continent abounds'.[22]

Alldridge said that the disturbances and slave-raiding 'prevented the expansion of trade, and consequently of revenue. . . . This was a most serious state of things, that called loudly for British intervention.'[23] This was a justification only within the context of imperialist ethics. Thus Hay adopted 'a firm and greatly extended policy for the interior'.[24] According to a recent writer, however, with the hinterland providing most of the Colony's exports, 'the Protectorate was established to safeguard this economic base and to facilitate exploitation of its resources'.[25] Considering the French threat which was both economic and political (military), it is possible to agree with John Hatch's verdict that 'the need rather was to defend established markets and territories already economically or politically controlled against the dangers which suddenly arose from rivals to Britain's commercial and military supremacy'.[26] It is therefore not improbable that the Protectorate itself was an economic proposition.

Modern writers have also tried to justify British intervention by explaining that the African societies could not withstand the pressure exerted by the Europeans on the coast. Thus by

[21] Alldridge, *The Sherbro*, p. 5; idem, *A Transformed Colony* (London 1910), pp. 294–5; Wallis, *West African Empire*, p. 24; K. J. Beatty, *Human Leopards* (London 1915), p. 108.
[22] Wallis, *West African Empire*, p. 6.
[23] Alldridge, *The Sherbro*, p. 5.
[24] Ibid.
[25] A. M. Howard, 'Economic History', in J. I. Clarke (ed.), *Sierra Leone in Maps* (London 1966), p. 74.
[26] Hatch, *Britain in Africa*, p. 175.

the close of the nineteenth century, the societies were on the verge of collapse, and British intervention was necessary 'to re-establish an equilibrium which they themselves had disturbed in the first place'.[27] While it is admitted that the Africans could not withstand the military onslaught of the Europeans, major structural changes within African societies had to await the full deployment of the machinery of colonialism in the 20th century.[28] The Sierra Leone evidence suggests that the British presence encouraged the political fragmentation of the indigenous states, and quite consciously prevented any political re-organization so as to facilitate the colonial occupation, which was in the economic interest of the Colony. The societies were not on the verge of collapse; nor did Britain intervene to save them. The coastal states, although in a state of relative decline, were on the verge of internal re-organization which the British halted, while the interior states witnessed a period of political state-formation up to the time of the colonial occupation.

Standard treaties as the basis of the Protectorate

Hay's treaty boom is said to have secured the future of the hinterland.[29] These treaties, as already noted, did not imply or connote any abrogation of sovereignty. The 'whole process of treaty-making was hardly more than a farce. According to Lugard, "treaties were produced by the cartload in all the approved forms of legal verbiage impossible of translation by ill-educated interpreters". Another European agent, Major Thurston, has asserted that he [found treaty-making] "an amiable force".[30] The aggressive intentions of the British to colonize the hinterland were cloaked in all sorts of devices, and the chiefs and their people were constantly deceived into believing that no such intentions existed up the official sleeves. This was so because outright acquisition might have precipi-

[27] A. G. Hopkins, 'Economic Imperialism', p. 604.
[28] Ralph Austen, 'The Abolition of the Overseas Slave Trade: A Distorted Theme in West African History', *Journal of the Historical Society of Nigeria*, v. 2, 1970, pp. 263 and 269.
[29] C. B. Wallis, 'In the Court of the Native Chiefs in Mendi land', *Journal of the African Society*, xvi, 1905, pp. 398-9.
[30] J. C. Anene, *Southern Nigeria in Transition, 1885-1906* (Cambridge 1966), pp. 62-3.

tated caustic wars, which the Colonial Office might not have been ready to finance.

In point of fact, the use of these treaties as the basis for declaring the Protectorate was a downright fraud. Sir David Chalmers, the Royal Commissioner who investigated the causes of the 1898 war, recognized this when he stated:

In . . . treaties . . . the character of the chiefs as the owners and sovereigns of territory and as independent contracting powers is unequivocally and universally recognized. The chiefs are generally well aware of this. In a few of the later treaties there is found a provision for the English Crown assuming sovereignty and full control of territory in the event of the chiefs not fulfilling their treaty engagements.[31]

Sir Samuel Lewis drew Cardew's attention to the fraudulent basis of British rule when the Protectorate Ordinance was being passed. Not that he opposed the protectorate—indeed, he was an ardent advocate of it—but as a lawyer, he was concerned about legal finesse. He pointed out that no evidence had been adduced to prove the jurisdiction which Her Majesty was said to have 'acquired'. Since it was not by conquest, it would be wise to show that it rested on the consent of the chiefs, which need not necessarily be written in a document. But Cardew ruled the lawyer out of order.[32]

But it was a clearly recognized fact that the basis of the British Protectorate was a fraud. Both colonial and international lawyers have tried to justify the position and to make it assume legality. In 1896, the Attorney-General Mr. Crampton-Smyly, apparently conscious of the fraudulent basis, tried to give an air of dishonest legitimacy to it by declaring that 'the effect of proclaiming a Protectorate over territories of this kind is the same as if these territories were expressly ceded to Her Majesty or had been acquired by conquest . . .'.[33] According to the Foreign Jurisdiction Act, 1890,

whereas by treaty, capitulation, grant, usage, sufferance and other lawful means, Her Majesty the Queen has jurisdiction within divers foreign countries . . . it is and shall be lawful for Her Majesty the Queen to hold, exercise, and enjoy any jurisdiction which Her Majesty now has or may at any time hereafter have within a foreign

---

[31] *Chalmers Report*, Vol. I, p. 9.   [32] Hargreaves, *Samuel Lewis*, p. 88.
[33] CO 879/49/533/30, enc. 2.

country in the same and as ample manner as if Her Majesty had acquired that jurisdiction by the cession or conquest of territory.

This piece of legislation recognized but did not confer the power to acquire jurisdiction,[34] although it legalized the exercise of such jurisdiction if it existed *de facto*. Although Roberts-Wray says that in English law there is no question about the right of the Crown to acquire jurisdiction in the exercise of prerogative powers without the intervention of the legislature,[35] there is reason to believe that there was such a question, hence the Foreign Jurisdiction Acts.

Indeed, treaties are vulnerable as a basis for acquiring jurisdiction unless this is expressly and explicitly stated therein. 'It is conceivable that the informality or terms of the document would give rise to doubt as to whether "treaty" or "grant" fitted the situation. In that event there is virtue in "other lawful means".'[36] This would imply that a formal document need not be necessary as long as the inhabitants or their representatives or rulers manifest abundantly a desire or wish to surrender their sovereignty. Even accepting this interpretation, the Protectorate in Sierra Leone cannot be said to have been 'lawfully' acquired. The treaties did not surrender sovereignty, nor was the consent of the chiefs and peoples distinctly manifested.

However, once the situation exists *de facto*, and continues to do so, then legal rationalizations can multiply. Writing about India, W. E. Hall rationalized thus:

> . . . in matters not provided for by treaty a 'residuary jurisdiction' on the part of the Imperial Government is considered to exist, and the treaties themselves are subject to the reservation that they may be disregarded when the supreme interests of the Empire are involved, or even when the interests of the subjects of the native [rulers] are gravely affected. The treaties really amount to little more than statements of limitations, which the imperial Government, except in very exceptional circumstances, places on its own action. *No doubt this was not the original intention of the treaties*, but the conditions of English sovereignty in India have greatly changed since these were concluded . . .[37]

[34] Sir Kenneth Roberts-Wray, *Commonwealth and Colonial Law* (London 1966), p. 104.

[35] Ibid., p. 103.   [36] Ibid., p. 112.

[37] W. E. Hall, *Treatise of International Law*, 7th Edition (Oxford 1917), p. 27 (emphasis added).

Thus whatever forensic polemic that may have arisen and whatever the rationalizations, it is reasonable to infer that the fundamental assumption, accepted as a moral postulate, that Africans would necessarily benefit from European colonialism, was behind the Foreign Jurisdiction Act, which remedied difficult anomalies between British practice and British law. To us at least, the Protectorate in Sierra Leone remains a fraud, and the Foreign Jurisdiction Act the most hopelessly naked of imperialistic documents, legalizing—in the eyes of English law—fraud, coercion, force, violence, and all sundry devices to subject the African peoples. The legal vindication presented today is perhaps more a subject of English and Colonial law than of African history.

The Protectorate Ordinance

The precipitancy with which Cardew passed the Protectorate Ordinance of 1896 without first submitting the draft for the comment of the Colonial Office generated imperfections to which the Colonial Office raised serious objections. The result was a series of amendments, which made it necessary to get the original Ordinance and its amendments re-enacted in a second Ordinance usually referred to as the Protectorate Ordinance, 1897.

The basic problem in the scheme of administering the Protectorate was, as Hargreaves has said, 'how to ensure respect for the fundamental values of the imperial power within the structure of Native Society'.[38] Cardew was not particularly fond of Africans, whom he regarded as ignorant and uncivilized, nor was he impressed by their institutions, which appeared crude to him. But if only for administrative and economic convenience, it was necessary to permit the chiefs to rule in accordance with their own laws and customs, but only in so far as 'they are consistent with humanity and civilisation'. In his address to the legislative council on the passing of the 1896 Ordinance, the Governor showed concern about maintaining social cohesion. Indeed, he aimed at separating the administration of the Colony from that of the

[38] Hargreaves, *Samuel Lewis*, p. 73.

Protectorate because, if the laws of the Colony were introduced into the Protectorate,

there would be an abrupt subversion of their laws and customs which would result from bringing to bear on the natives the jurisdiction of the courts of the colony, and all our various methods of administration, which are adapted for more civilized communities, and the consequent injustice which would be done to the Native Chiefs, who would thus be deprived of their authority, and the income which they now obtain from the fees and forfeitures connected with their jurisdiction.[39]

Yet it is doubtful whether the alternative arrangement for the administration of the interior as embodied in the Protectorate Ordinance was much of an improvement. The new administrative innovation did not dispel the misgivings of the chiefs and people, as Cardew rightly feared.

The provisions of the original ordinance enacted in 1896 dealt a severe blow to the power and authority of the rulers. Their power-base was undercut because their sovereignty was lost to the British Government. To symbolize this the title of *King*, which had hitherto been often used in the treaties, was carefully excluded from the provisions of the ordinance. In its place was substituted 'paramount chief', defined as 'a chief who is not subordinate in his ordinary jurisdiction to any other chief'. Authority now effectively derived from the colonial administration, which foisted a uniform pattern of rulership on the people—kings and their sub-chiefs being equally recognized as Paramount Chiefs.

Three types of Court were established. The first was the 'Court of the Native Chiefs', but was severely limited in its jurisdiction. The composition was not interfered with, and the emoluments from the exercise of their truncated juridical powers still went to the chiefs. In general, criminal jurisdiction (with minor exceptions) was removed from the province of this type of court, which was to hear civil cases arising solely between 'Natives', a 'native' being defined as 'any member of the aboriginal races or tribes of Africa ordinarily resident within the Protectorate'. Cases involving a title to land or 'arising out of tribal and factional fights' were also removed from the jurisdiction of the court.

[39] *Sierra Leone Weekly News*, 12 Sept. 1896.

The second category of Court was that of the 'District Commissioner and Native Chiefs', which 'shall consist of the District Commissioner and such two or more chiefs as shall be selected by the District Commissioner'. This Court had jurisdiction over the criminal offences expropriated from the 'Court of the Native Chiefs', and could inflict capital punishment. But the decision of this Court was 'vested exclusively in the District Commissioner', so that the chiefs were merely assessors.

The third type, the Court of the District Commissioner, had jurisdiction in all civil cases arising between non-natives, or a native and a non-native; cases involving a title to land, 'although arising exclusively between natives'; criminal offences committed by non-natives; and crimes of witchcraft, slaving, 'tribal fights', 'notwithstanding that the person charged is a native'. Women were generally to be exempted from the sentence of whipping. The District Commissioner further had the power and authority to settle any matter within his District 'having their origin in Poro Laws, Native rites or customs . . . or any other matters which if not promptly settled might lead to breaches of the peace or occasion disaffection on the part of the natives . . .'. This was deemed necessary, according to the Attorney-General, because the ' "poroh" custom, which while beneficial in many ways, is open to great abuses, besides being . . . decidedly dangerous to a constituted authority'. The Court was to be guided by English legal procedure, but was not bound by it.[40]

Dealing in slaves was specifically prohibited and made unlawful, and any accessories would be guilty 'of an offence'.[41] According to the explanation of the Attorney-General, the law did not interfere with 'domestic slavery', and the object of the law was to discourage, 'while not forbidding, the system of domestic slavery'.[42]

The sale or transfer of land by a 'native' to a person not a 'native' was declared unlawful. The Governor was, however, empowered to assign locations to the Chiefs 'for the use and occupation of their tribes', to acquire lands for public service,

[40] Protectorate Ordinance 1896, Parts II and VI; CO 879/49/533/30, enc. 2, Attorney-General to Governor, 1896.
[41] Protectorate Ordinance 1896, Part III.
[42] CO 879/49/533/30, enc. 2, Attorney-General to Governor, 1896.

and to authorize the occupation of waste or uninhabited lands 'by such person or persons as he shall think fit'.[43] Cardew explained to the legislative council on the passing of the ordinance, that the lands section was 'especially intended to protect the interests of the natives . . .'.[44]

To finance this scheme of administration, the Protectorate itself had to raise the requisite revenue. As from 1 January 1898, every chief was made liable to pay to the District Commissioner 'in respect of every house . . . [within his] jurisdiction', except those occupied by non-natives or those in the service of the administration, an annual house tax at the rate of ten shillings for each house with four or more rooms, and five shillings for each house with three or less rooms. The tax was to be paid in coin, unless there was no alternative but to accept kind. Defaulters, including Chiefs, would have taxes levied on their goods and chattels. In addition, licences to trade were to be taken out as from the 1 January 1897.[45]

In executing the provisions of this Ordinance in the hinterland, 'the Governor and all officers and persons acting under his authority, or acting *bona fide* for the purpose of promoting peace, order and good government . . . are hereby indemnified, freed and discharged in all matters, acts, and things whatsoever done or performed under the said authority . . .'.[46]

In spite of the very erosive nature of the Ordinance on the traditional powers of the chiefs, Cardew believed that they 'will [still] be in a position of considerable authority and importance, and when occasion requires, besides exercising jurisdiction, their advice can be sought by the District Commissioner on the native affairs generally of their district'.[47] This appears to be a gross over-simplification of the erosive effect of the new scheme when it is considered that much of the traditional area of judicial operation of the chiefs had been forcibly taken away from them. Indeed, questions involving witchcraft and 'slavery' perhaps formed the general bulk of the criminal proceedings of a chief's court. Within the limitations now imposed, which confined the jurisdiction of chiefs to civil and only minor criminal

---

[43] Protectorate Ordinance 1896, Part IV.
[44] *Sierra Leone Weekly News*, 12 Sept. 1896.
[45] Protectorate Ordinance 1896, Part V.   [46] Ibid., Part VI.
[47] *Sierra Leone Weekly News*, 12 Sept. 1896.

cases, the former powers of a chief were probably reduced by more than half, in terms of the seriousness of the cases dealt with. It was also made an offence by section lxxxii of the Ordinance for any chief to exercise jurisdiction in any matters other than the residue now relegated to him by the ordinance. To crown it all the District Commissioner could banish any person, subject to the approval of the Governor, if he found it expedient for the 'Security, Peace, and Order of his District' while the Governor, subject to the approval of the Secretary of State, was empowered 'as occasion may require *to depose any Chief who is unfit for the position and to appoint a fit and proper person to be Chief in his place*'.[48] As such the traditional legitimacy of the authority of the Chief was instantly undercut. Thus while Cardew did not apparently realize it, the effect of this Ordinance was not much different from what he originally feared would have resulted had the laws of the Colony been introduced, for as Sir David Chalmers observed, 'in many of the provisions of this ordinance . . . the Local Legislature went far beyond any historic basis existing at the time of the enactment'.[49]

To implement the new administrative proposals Cardew issued an order-in-council on 20 October 1896 dividing the Protectorate into five districts, namely Karene, Koinadugu, Ronietta, Bandajuma, and Panguma. Already it was thought advisable to include in the Protectorate areas which though technically in the Colony, were 'not accustomed to civilised ways and modes of thought . . . and have practically remained in the same condition as the inhabitants of the Protectorate'. It was thought, besides, that there would be a great tendency on the part of the inhabitants to emigrate into such areas so as to avoid the house tax which would be levied in the Protectorate.[50] Thus the territory south of the Peninsula to Imperreh, but not including it, was removed from the Colony and added to the Protectorate. Cardew also at once appointed Frontier Police officers to acting District Commissionerships, Assistant-Inspectors Barker and Carr in the Ronietta and Bandajuma districts respectively, and Inspector Sharpe in Karene district.

[48] Protectorate Ordinance 1896, Part VI.
[49] Chalmers Report, I, p. 17.
[50] CO 879/49/533/22, Cardew to SS, 1896.

Two civilians, Messrs Hudson and Griffith, were to be appointed to the other two districts.[51]

Cardew proposed to have Frontier Police Officers seconded to the appointments as District Commissioners because 'from their knowledge of the country, their experience of the natives, their previous military training . . . and the knowledge they acquire in the Army of military law and the principles of evidence [they] are very well suited for such appointments . . .'. These Officers were to continue using their uniforms 'from a governmental point of view, as Natives have a great respect for officials who wear a uniform . . .'. In December the Colonial Office approved of their appointments as District Commissioners, Inspector W. S. Sharpe, Inspector E. D'H. Fairtlough, Assistant-Inspector C. E. Carr.[52] All three were the type of men Cardew wanted, for as he was a soldier himself these appointments suggest that his was a military administration behind a civilian screen. A District Commissioner's Staff consisted of a Clerk, a Gaoler, an Interpreter, and from four to ten Court Messengers who 'will be employed in serving writs, summonses, etc., and also in the collection of taxes; the men of the Frontier Police will also assist in carrying out these duties'. For a start Ronietta had the largest number of Court Messengers (ten) 'to make up for the paucity of the Frontier Police'.[53]

Objections to the 1896 Ordinance

Apart from the fact that there were 'numerous defects in the language'[54] due to the haste with which the Ordinance had been drawn up, the Colonial Office objected to two provisions in particular—lands and taxation. Two months after the Ordinance was passed, the first amendment was made to clarify to the chiefs and people that the tax was to be paid at the beginning of 1898 and not at the end of that year, as the officials who explained the Ordinance to them had informed them.[55] The second amendment was made in December. The section

[51] CO 879/49/533/30, enc. 2, Attorney-General to Gov., 1896; 36, encs. 1 & 2, Order-in-Council and Attorney-General to Gov., 1896; 37, Cardew to SS, 1896.
[52] CO 879/49/533/37, 48, Cardew to SS; 49, Chamberlain to Cardew, 1896.
[53] CO 879/49/533/32, Cardew to Chamberlain, 1896.
[54] CO 879/49/533/52, Chamberlain to Cardew, 1896.
[55] CO 879/49/533/46, encs. 1 and 2, Attorney-General to Gov., 1896.

dealing with lands vested all mineral rights in the Crown. Chamberlain objected that 'as Her Majesty does not claim any property in the soil . . . this section cannot be allowed to stand'. Concerning rumours that thousands of square miles of land were being granted in concessions, Chamberlain would not 'allow, without enquiry, large tracts of land to pass into the hands of speculators'. This was to prevent the legalizing of concessions of dubious validity—the documents were signed by persons who were incompetent, or if competent, had been made to sign out of ignorance of their effects, or for an unfair consideration, or by downright fraud. This part of the Ordinance was revoked.[56]

The taxation policy—the pivot on which the new administration rested—was the subject of much controversy. Drawing comparisons with other parts of Africa where direct taxes were being paid, Cardew argued that the tax to be levied was extremely light and that it was within the means of the people to pay it.[57] For the remaining part of 1896 the expenditure was estimated at £1500; for 1897, £9244. Revenue anticipated for 1897 was a paltry £350, but Cardew computed that there would be a derivable revenue of £20,000 from house tax in 1898. To set the new administrative machine working, however, Cardew suggested drawing on the reserve fund of the Colony which was £42,629, since other colonial territories such as Bechuanaland, Zululand, and the Niger Coast Protectorate were heavily subsidized to get their new administrations running.[58]

At the Colonial Office, it was felt that 'Col. Cardew is going too fast . . .'.[59] Owing to administrative and cultural difficulties, it was felt to be impossible to give effect to the scheme simultaneously in all five districts, unless the handful of officials 'were considerably strengthened at heavy cost'. Moreover, conditions in the other parts of Africa where direct taxes were being levied were not the same as in the Sierra Leone Protectorate, which was more comparable to the Gold Coast, where,

[56] CO 879/49/533/44A, Chamberlain to Cardew, 1896; CO 879/49/533/54, encs. 1 and 2, Attorney-General to Governor, 1896.

[57] *Sierra Leone Weekly News*, 12 September 1896.

[58] CO 267/426/Conf. 43, 1896; CO 879/49/533/50, Cardew to Chamberlain, 1897; CO 267/427/Conf. 53, Cardew to SS, 1896.

[59] CO 267/426/Conf. 43, minute by Mercer, 1896.

it was argued, a poll-tax once imposed had proved to be a dismal economic fiasco.[60] There was also objection to the payment in coin because 'the use of coin appears to be practically unknown in the Protectorate'. According to a minute at the Colonial Office:

There is a considerable danger that the system would break down and that the revenue would fall much below expectations. There is also a serious moral danger in attempting to collect a tax which might not be understood and which the natives would be tempted to evade or resist. I think that Col. Cardew's arrangements are much too ambitious and premature, and that he has adopted a wrong line in not devising some means of interesting the native chiefs and headmen in the administration so far as taxes were concerned.[61]

But Cardew did not think much of the people and their institutions. To him he was at the time dealing 'with a people that are practically savages—some are cannibals—quite illiterate and very degraded by ignorance and gross superstition . . . accustomed to the most despotic sway on the part of their chiefs . . .'.[62] However, the Colonial Office allowed him to use only £5000 from the reserve fund and advised him to implement his proposals in three districts only—Karene, Ronietta, and Bandajuma. The caution of the Colonial Office was explicit though succinct:

If your scheme were to fail, the failure would be disastrously expensive . . . the natives should be familiarised gradually with the new duty of paying taxes, and that the first operations should not be so extensive as to make it impossible to guard against oppression or evasion.[63]

Cardew felt that there would not be much difficulty in collecting the tax. He estimated that the cash in circulation was about £18,000 and that this would increase when public works employing labourers, such as the railway, were started. He agreed, however, that chiefs should receive a rebate on taxes collected, and that for at least two years Koinadugu and Panguma districts should not be made to pay the tax.[64]

[60] CO 879/49/533/40, Chamberlain to Cardew, 1896.
[61] CO 267/426/Conf. 43, minute by Mercer (?), 1896.
[62] CO 879/49/533/55, Cardew to Chamberlain, 1897.
[63] CO 879/49/533/40, Chamberlain to Cardew, 1896.
[64] CO 879/49/533/50, Cardew to Chamberlain, 1897.

Although there were no official reports about dissidents, rumours reached Cardew three months after the promulgation of the Protectorate Ordinance that 'some Chiefs are going to protest against the house tax'. Cardew was ready to use 'coercion to enforce its payment'. While aware of the limitations to the full implementation of his scheme, Cardew had 'every hope of its success'. Confining it to three districts for a start reduced the estimated expenditure to £6000. The Colonial Office agreed to Cardew's readjustments, and even allowed an extra £1000 from the reserve fund, but added a strong reminder that no assistance from Imperial funds should be counted upon.[65] In April 1897 Cardew submitted a draft ordinance to the Colonial Office, embodying all the amendments. It was approved, and was passed as the Protectorate Ordinance 1897, superseding that of 1896. The chiefs were granted a rebate of 5% on amounts collected.[66]

The house tax and African apprehensions

Opposition to the house tax was neither covert nor limited to those on whom it was imposed. The Freetown press with its traditional horror of direct taxation used the emotionally pregnant term, hut-tax. The Sierra Leone Chamber of Commerce petitioned that the people were too poor to pay the tax, and that rather than pay, they would desert their habitations and abandon agricultural pursuits to the detriment of commerce. Merchants in the Sherbro protested that because of the dissatisfaction among chiefs and traders 'particularly in consequence of the imposition of the "hut-tax", which is generally felt to be oppressive', there was much interference with trade. The Europeans on the spot ventured to forecast that the tax would yield little revenue. The Manchester Chamber of Commerce too felt that the tax should not be imposed. But the Colonial Office could not accept this view.[67]

[65] Ibid.; CO 879/49/533/60, Chamberlain to Cardew, 1897.
[66] CO 879/49/533/71, Cardew to Chamberlain 1897, and enc., Chief Justice to Governor, 1897; CO 879/49/533/72, 75, 82, Cardew to Chamberlain, 1897, and enc. 3, Attorney-General to Administrator, 1897.
[67] CO 879/49/533/77, Manchester Chamber of Commerce to SS, 1897; CO 879/49/533/80, SS to Manchester Chamber of Commerce; CO 879/49/533/82, enc. 3, Attorney-General to Administrator, 1897.

There seems to be a certain ambivalence in Cardew's whole approach to the taxation policy. While persistently proclaiming that the system would work without trouble, he insisted on a show of force at the same time. Before the tax was actually to be collected he sought the approval of the Colonial Office to augment the Frontier Police by fifty more privates, thus increasing the establishment of each Company from ninety to one hundred privates. Without this,

the Government will not be in the commanding position which is so necessary in order to fully collect the revenue. . . . I do not anticipate there will be any active opposition . . . but unless there is a good show of force . . . the natives may passively resist the authorities collecting the tax, and do all in their power to evade it. I think we should be prepared for such an eventuality, and the best way to do this is to have a sufficient force of police on the spot.

The approval was readily granted.[68] Cardew thus expected some kind of resistance which he was determined to suppress. The Protectorate Ordinance of 1897 'as far as I can ascertain, is working smoothly', wrote Cardew, but, he added, 'the crucial test will come when the house tax is levied, but with an adequate police force. . . . I have no apprehension as to the result.'[69]

To the chiefs and people who were to be taxed, the Protectorate Ordinance came as a profound shock. The previous equality in dealings with African rulers was swept away when the Ordinance abrogated African sovereignty. The officials had previously all along assured the rulers that there were no intentions to 'take their country' from them. The Ordinance suddenly revealed that the erstwhile friendly and benevolent agency was a ruthless sequestrating and buccaneering tyrant. The whole organization which shattered the now almost traditional equilibrium in Eurafrican relations in fact threatened to destroy the very fabric of society. The reaction of the chiefs and people is graphically epitomized by Fyfe:

The elaborate provisions . . . set out in . . . reassuring . . . style . . . interpreted by government messengers who tended to garble a complicated statement they scarcely understood themselves . . . alarmed rather than reassured them. Many never heard it read . . .

[68] CO 879/49/533/73 and 74, Cardew to Chamberlain, 1897, and Chamberlain to Caulfield, 1897.
[69] CO 267/431/Conf. 18, Cardew to Chamberlain, 1897.

... Instead of feeling their rights safeguarded, the chiefs felt them suddenly undermined ... A clause prohibiting sentences of flogging women was understood to forbid a man to beat his wife ... The lands clauses ... were taken as a threat to deprive them of their land, trading licences of their right to trade, the Hut Tax of their homes ...

Nor did they know what authority government had to rule and tax them ... Most treaty chiefs had done nothing more than promise friendship ...

They felt degraded at having to share their jurisdiction with a District Commissioner who had power to punish them, in court where their own subjects could have them brought to trial. The slaves on whose labour they depended were no longer under their control ...

... the chiefs felt deprived of redress, for they had lost their traditional channel of complaint.[70]

On his previous tours in the hinterland Cardew seems to have restricted his statements more to the question of slavery and only hinted at the proposed taxation in 1896. He did 'not himself seem to have attached importance to the consents of the chiefs'. Promulgation of the Ordinance was more effective than the abrogation of the amended clauses like that on lands.[71]

Petitions

Throughout 1897 an avalanche of petitions bombarded the administration, mostly from northern chiefs. All petitions and representations requested that the house tax be revoked on grounds of poverty. This was good tactics, for it was the only rational appeal the administration would have listened to. But it fell on deaf ears.

During Queen Victoria's Diamond Jubilee celebrations a number of northern rulers sent a petition expressing their apprehensions. The Ordinance implied 'a total dispossession of their country' as they believed they had no more power over their lands and property. They were completely flabbergasted because they were 'not aware that they have done anything to merit such great calamity from their friends and benefactors'. They claimed to have practically stopped the slave trade so

[70] Fyfe, *A History*, pp. 552–4.
[71] Chalmers Report, I, pp. 15 and 23.

that the 'few domestics' left to them were part of their families and should not be encouraged to leave them. In this setting the houses in the towns were owned by 'not more than half-a-dozen chiefs and headmen', on whose shoulders the burden of taxation would fall unsquarely. Besides, the houses were not worth the tax imposed on them. The petitioners were confounded at the loss of their jurisdiction, and it was a 'pending scourge', 'terrible punishment', and 'serious disgrace' to be flogged and handcuffed 'sometimes for the most trivial cases, in the presence of their wives, servants, and children'. These petitioners writing at the end of 1897 were not aware that the lands clauses had been repealed in December 1896.[72]

Other petitions followed similar lines. But more importantly it was requested that the tax be reduced or rescinded. Some chiefs got a cable sent to Chamberlain[73] while others sent him a petition through the Administrator. The reply was brusque: the tax was for the benefit of the people and their country. A group of rulers brought a deputation to see Cardew personally when he was on leave. They waited till he returned in November 1897, and they presented their petition. Their revenues would now go to the police and the District Commissioners, since they were only left with a tiny fraction of their criminal jurisdiction. The country, too, was said to be 'under the virtual rule of the police'. Cardew's reply was not reassuring. He dismissed the points violently, sometimes in technical language quite impossible to translate. On the allegation that chiefs would be liable to flogging, he replied: 'Punishments are directed not against classes of persons, but classes of offenders.' Cardew considered his concessions, such as paying five shillings all round on houses and the exemption of villages of under twenty huts, very liberal. He emphasized that he 'expected them to give loyal obedience to the orders of the Government'.[74]

Only few petitions from the south, however, conveyed the feelings of the people. As early as 20 October 1896 Bumpeh chiefs sent a petition that they were too poor to pay the tax. In

---

[72] CO 879/49/533/79, enc., petition of Nemgbana, Dick Wola, Alimamy Seneh Bundu, Bey Suba, Alkarley Kozar Bubu, Kombor, Alkarley of Port Loko, Bey Coblo, Alimamy Sater Lahie, Alimamy Annamordoo, Bey Farmarr, to Caulfield.

[73] CO 879/49/533/84 and 86, Chiefs to Chamberlain and Chamberlain to Caulfield, 1897.

[74] CO 879/55/570/2, and enc. 1; Chalmers Report, II, pp. 584–7.

December they sent another petition in which they pleaded: 'We are not in any way opposing the Ordinance, but we are really poor and not in a position of paying . . .' It was a three-sentence petition.[75] The same month another petition was sent by the Gallinas and Kittam chiefs, sixty-four in all, to Sir Samuel Lewis with the request that he should place it before the Governor in a constitutional way, saying they were too poor to pay the tax. With the promulgation of the Ordinance,

we see ourselves in bondage, we are not free, we know that our country did not take by conquest, only we gave the queen to protect it we find now that she took it from us. . . . If we know that such will be the case, we might not agree to sign treaty His Excellency Governor Havelock, we ask him all these things, he deny . . . .[76]

Only Madam Yoko, installed by the administration as ruler of Kpaa-Mende and 'distinguished for her unqualified loyalty and support of the English Government', provisionally accepted the Ordinance. Hers was the only communication in which no 'deprecatory expressions' were used against the Ordinance.[77]

The Protectorate was achieved by fraud and the people knew it. While the Temne chiefs entered into a vocal opposition the Mende chiefs said little; revolt was fermenting cryptically. All the petitions imply that the fabric of society was being violently destroyed. The innovations presumed tenets of English law and Western ethical values quite out of place in the historic experience of the people. The most revolutionary innovation was the radical interference between rulers and ruled. In this must be sought one of the most crucial roots of the subsequent revolt.

Resentment

Apart from three chiefs who owed their positions to the Freetown administration—Madam Yoko of Kpaa-Mende,

[75] Chalmers Report, II, pp. 569–70. Cf. W. L. Barrows, 'Local-Level Politics in Kenema District' (Yale University PhD, 1971), p. 51: 'No deluge of protest found its way to Freetown; there was in fact very little indication that the interior people realised that anything had changed. At least, one petition of protest did, however, reach the eyes of the administration.'

[76] Chalmers Report, II, p. 573, and i, p. 20.

[77] Ibid., I, p. 19, and II, pp. 571–2.

Nancy Tucker of Bagru, and Thomas Neale Caulker of Kagboro—the general atmosphere in Mende country was one of resentment.[78] There were ample indications of trouble and in July 1897 the Colonial Office warned Cardew:

when the time comes to consider native taxation afresh, it may be found necessary to reduce the hut tax or possibly to repeal it altogether, and you should avoid committing yourself to the retention of the tax.[79]

Chief W. B. Tucker of Nongoba Bullom went to Freetown in 1897 to take out letters of administration of estate. He was advised by 'principal officers of the government and members of the municipality' not to take out such a letter of administration, which could only be done by a British subject and not a 'Native chief or King—having a country or territory'. If he did, the 'rights of himself, his heirs, his families, people and country will be taken away and [he] will be considered a British subject . . .'. The chief explained all this in a private letter, dated 29 April 1897, to J. A. Williams, a Creole trader in Gambia in his chiefdom. He further intimated to his friend that he intended writing on behalf of the 'Native Chiefs stating our rights to our land under Protectorate to Her Majesty's Government . . . and the inconsistency of licence being imposed upon us . . . and house taxes'.[80] Being one of the very few educated Protectorate chiefs, Tucker did not understand the Protectorate to imply abrogation of the sovereignty of the rulers over their subjects and lands. The interference in the internal affairs of the rulers was a revolutionary new concept, impossible to comprehend.

The Sherbro chiefs used the Poro, the traditional instrument of social control, to impose economic sanctions against the Colony. It was reported that the *Beh Sherbro*, Gbanna Lewis, had established a post at Kapala 'for the purpose of preventing traders from passing to and from, while natives are stopped from transacting business in general with the middlemen'. When this matter was discussed in the Executive Council it was decided to use force to solve the problem. The District Commissioner of the Sherbro informed the chiefs at a meeting in May that if they did not remove the obstruction to trade,

[78] Chalmers Report, I; p. 24.

[79] CO 267/433/161, Chamberlain to Cardew, 1897.

[80] CO 267/441/Conf., 12 December 1898, enc., Tucker to Williams.

they would be severely dealt with. The *So Kong* of Imperreh said that he would first have to confer with the *Beh Sherbro* because he took his instructions from him. Although invited to do so, the *Beh Sherbro* himself did not attend the meeting. But immediately after, Acting Governor Caulfield was informed that the *Beh* sent out further instructions that no trade was to be transacted. Caulfield recommended his detention.[81]

Two Ordinances were passed to protect trade and detain Gbanna Lewis. In December 1897, Cardew saw the *Beh Sherbro* and the *So Kong* and

carefully explained to them their position with regard to the Protectorate . . . as they belonged to the Colony they were exempted from the house tax, but that also for the same reason they had no jurisdiction as chiefs, except in the case of any portion of their territories lying within the Protectorate . . .[82]

Chief Tucker's territory also technically formed part of the Colony. Yet to be told that they had no jurisdiction as chiefs over their own countries was a most objectionable circumstance that was bound to provoke active resistance.

There were several deputations to Cardew concerning the Protectorate Ordinance, but he was very peremptory in dismissing them. Momoh Kaikai, Momoh Jah, Momoh Fofi, Francis Fawundu, all from the Gallinas, Sandi of Tikongoh and other Bum chiefs, not satisfied with the oral reply of a deputation sent in February 1897, decided in January 1898 to see Governor Cardew. He at first declined to give them an audience and insisted that they should see their District Commissioner, Carr. A short while later the Governor changed his mind, and invited them to see him at Government House, 'with a view to explaining to them, their obligation to pay a lawful tax and the reasonableness of it'.[83] The Chiefs, apparently because they had not gone to see Carr, were suspicious of the invitation and turned it down, preferring instead to write.[84]

However, Momoh Kaikai and Sandi did afterwards see Cardew, who later wrote that '. . . after reasoning with them

[81] CO 267/433/Conf. 35, Caulfield to SS, 1897.
[82] Chalmers Report, II, evidence of Cardew, p. 549.
[83] CO 267/437/Conf. 4, Cardew to SS, 1898; Chalmers Report, II, pp. 335–7.
[84] Ibid. Evidence of Fawundu, pp. 336–7.

and pointing out to them the serious consequences that would devolve on them if they remained recalcitrant, . . . they have promised to do their best to collect the house-tax from their people . . .'.[85]

Cardew v. Fawundu

As for Francis Fawundu, he had a confrontation with Cardew, and the incident abundantly illuminates the exact nature of the existing situation, and the real causes of resentment of the new plan of administration. Fawundu, educated at one of the Mende Mission Schools in the Sherbro, informed J. C. E. Parkes in a letter that he would rather be official in his dealing with Cardew.

. . . I shall be glad to receive in *writing* anything which your Governor desires to say to me on business of our foreign relations. My reasons for such a request is this, in your reply . . . to my letter of the 6th instant, I observe the following which I now quote to you, namely, 'I am directed by His Excellency the Governor to inform you that he has fully explained the ordinance to you all when you came with Bai Sherbro (Bannah Lewis) of Yonni.'
Whilst not admitting here that was 'in regard to certain clauses of the Protectorate Ordinance' my letter of that date purported to have shown, I have to respectfully mention to you, that His Excellency Your Governor remembered it appears to me to have told you only what he said or did on that occasion . . . but not what we the persons spoken to by him said, particularly I, as to our agreements respecting thereto or otherwise. It would not be anything hard on my part to call on your Governor, if he desires it, or should I need it and he consent to receive me; but on business (political or other wise) relations, I prefer treating with him in writing.
. . . the circumstance in which I have now found out that my country, subjects, and myself, is placed by your Queen and Governor—Your Queen whom my predecessors and myself in office have been treating with through Her Representatives respectively sent out here from time to time as a 'Good Friend'—of course this treatment being mutual—is very very painful and distressing to my mind. My almost every moment expression is 'can a friend treat his friend so?' . . .

And Fawundu signed 'King of Manoh'.[86]

[85] CO 267/437/Conf. 5., Cardew to SS, 1898.
[86] CO 267/437/Conf. 5, enc. 1, Fawundu to Parkes, 1898.

As Cardew correctly interpreted the letter, Fawundu 'takes the stand of a Chief independent of this Government except in the matter of "foreign relations" and will not admit that he is subject to the Queen'.[87] The whole idea here is that the relationship as construed between the British and indigenous kings, was one of partnership or association, although admittedly the British were the senior partners. In 'foreign relations' the kings had no objection to the British taking over that function, for which there were traditional precepts, but it was most inadmissible that the British should so suddenly and fraudulently assume responsibility for the 'internal affairs' of the indigenous states. There was no precedent for this in traditional law and its enforcement was inconsistent with any previous Anglo-African relations. This indeed was the real position, which Cardew was most loth to admit, or to be made to face.

On the receipt of Fawundu's letter Cardew asked Parkes to inform him that his letter was 'disrespectful and insubordinate', and that the position of independence he was asserting was inadmissible. Particularly disquieting to Cardew was Fawundu signing as King of Manoh, and thus 'arrogating' to himself 'the position of an independent power'. At less than a day's notice, Fawundu was directed to apologize for the 'disrespectful and disloyal tone' of his letter. In the letter conveying Cardew's opinion, Parkes, the Secretary for Native Affairs, aided the Governor in perverting the legal and legitimate situation by emphasizing that the position Fawundu had taken 'is ridiculous, [since you] further state that you will remain a subject of the Queen and under the authority of His Excellency the Governor'. He regretted that Fawundu was 'ill-advised' and ordered him to withdraw his letter and thereafter 'quit Freetown to return to your country within twenty-four hours'. He added a warning note that should the king ignore the orders, 'His Excellency will consider you unfit for the position of a chief and recommend your deposition'.[88]

On the same day, Fawundu replied:

That in signing myself King of Manoh . . . my people who crowned me called me their King in succession to my father though your

[87] CO 267/437/Conf. 5, Cardew to SS, 1898.
[88] Ibid., enc., Parkes to Fawundu.

Government used to call me Chief. To me, all has been, and means the same thing.

Before today, I never knew and yourself Mr. Parkes know it truly, that I was never told I am a British subject. I have known myself always to be a 'friend' as my fathers were, of the Queen of England. . . . Now when I go back to my people who sent me here to your Government, I shall tell them. Because it is their daily charge of my predecessors and myself that we had sold their country, hence the present change, when in reality it had not been so.

After reminding Parkes of the numerous titles of 'Kings' and 'Queens' in the various treaties, he concluded: '. . . judge me fairly from the inference to be drawn . . .'.[89]

Cardew considered the 'attitude' expressed in the letter as 'impertinent' and therefore declined to accept it as an apology. Moreover, as he had 'repudiated being a British subject', which was indeed a disingenuous interpretation of his letter, Cardew 'considers you unfit for the position of chief in your country and he deposes you from such position from this date [20th January 1898] subject to the approval of . . . the Secretary of State. . . . After this you will not exercise any jurisdiction in your country, and if you do, it will be regarded that you have committed an offence against the law and you will have to take the consequences.' The Colonial Office approved entirely because, as Cardew pointed out, it was necessary to make a 'severe example' of Fawundu 'as a deterrent to others', when 'under the present circumstances . . . the attitude of the whole of the chiefs in the Protectorate is one of opposition to the payment of the house tax'.[90] Fawundu was thus probably the first serious victim of the new order. The source of legitimacy for traditional authority was now abrogated by the Colonial administration, and transferred to English law. The key to any meaningful understanding of the subsequent war is amply demonstrated in this confrontation between Cardew and Fawundu.

Collection of the Tax

By the time the tax was due to be collected, Cardew was already aware of the existing spirit among the chiefs. He was fully

[89] CO 267/437/Conf. 5, enc., Fawundu to Parkes.   [90] Ibid., enc.

aware that it was necessary for the administration 'which has now entered on a struggle with these people, to compel them to pay a tax which has been lawfully imposed and without the revenue from which it will be impossible to carry on the Government of the country. . . . I believe if we show force, we shall have no difficulty in the future.'[91] Cardew thus wanted to use force to overcome the resistance of the people to what appeared to them to be an illegitimate expropriation of their rights. While the chiefs were indisposed to collect the tax, the officials proceeded to collect on instructions 'with an oppressive severity'. Chalmers was convinced that all the officials 'came to the conclusion that the exercise of *force*, peremptory, rapid, and inflexible, was the element to be relied on in making the scheme of taxation a success'.[92]

The Acting District Commissioner of Ronietta district, Dr. T. Hood, reported to Cardew in late January that Madam Yoko had subscribed £60, but he believed it was personally contributed by her on behalf of her favourite sub-chiefs, 'to make the officials think an effort is being made by her people'. In actual fact, the people were not willing to pay, and Hood was not blind to the general apathy: 'The majority of her sub-chiefs are not loyal to her, and pay little attention to her orders until my assistance has been rendered.' Hood, like the Colonial Office before him, felt that the tax would be easily collected if the chiefs were enlisted to the taxation cause and thus gave the necessary instructions to their subordinates. Cardew had made no serious effort to achieve this. And his answer to Hood's report was characteristic: he at once sent the Adjutant of the Frontier Police, Captain Moore, to relieve Hood of his administrative duties.[93] Moore called a meeting of chiefs at Kwellu, the headquarters of Ronietta, and Fula Mansa, the Paramount Chief of Yoni Temne, informed him that the chiefs had taken an oath to resist the tax. His immediate answer was to arrest some ten or twelve chiefs.[94]

Cardew informed the Colonial Office that since the beginning of the year, there had been many instances of the people

[91] Ibid., Cardew to SS, 1898.
[92] Chalmers Report, I, p. 24.
[93] CO 267/437/Conf. 6, Cardew to SS, 1898, and enc., Hood to Secretary, Native Affairs.
[94] Chalmers Report, I, pp. 25–7.

gathering together, armed with 'trade guns, swords, and cut-lasses to resist the authority of the District Commissioners and the Frontier Police'. There had been no physical confrontation as yet, but 'as they are liable to bring about a breach of the peace', he had ordered the people to be disarmed and their arms confiscated. To limit their use of arms, an ordinance was passed increasing duties on guns and powder.[95]

In the Bandajuma district District Commissioner Carr called a meeting of the chiefs at Mofwe and asked them to pay the tax. The chiefs pleaded extreme poverty and want of young men to till their fields and gather produce, but Carr insisted that they must make a symbolic gesture of their general approbation of the tax policy. After 'hanging heads' for a few days the chiefs maintained their same position. 'Mr. Carr learnt from informers . . . that they had all agreed *not* to pay or attempt to pay for their respective countries.' Carr's reply, too, was force. He arrested the four principal chiefs present, took them to Bandajuma, and dispersed about 4000–5000 supporters of the chiefs.[96] This sounds ridiculous. However, the people bitterly resented the arrest of their chiefs and according to Chalmers, 'there was onimous talk about what might happen'. One of the chiefs admonished the people not to make a disturbance. The arrests were illegal even within the terms of the Protectorate Ordinance.[97]

Cardew was not apprehensive of armed conflict as Carr would use the police to disarm the people. But he requested a company of the 1st Battalion West India Regiment to proceed at once to Bandajuma before the rainy season began, as the 'moral effect would be great'. Two weeks later Cardew said the situation was not so serious, and the troops would only be sent in case of emergency.[98]

There was general maltreatment and extortion, and the effect of the Frontier Police disarming the 'natives' can better be imagined than described, considering the past record of the force. 'There were very many examples of cruel and flagrant abuse of authority, utterly unsanctioned by the law.' Momoh

Jah was arrested in March by a sergeant and twenty Frontier Police, and much property and cattle was looted, 'an example likely to provoke retaliation'.[99] While it cannot be denied that in at least one case in the Ronietta District, where a Frontier Policeman was maltreated, and one in Bandajuma, where the Medical Officer was mobbed, the people defended themselves,[100] the atrocities committed by the officials of the administration were out of all proportion to the circumstances. The Governor, too, convinced that the 'natives' were not prepared to pay, sanctioned their maltreatment. Chief Momoh Kaikai, who promised to be loyal to Cardew and did not take any open part in the war, complained passionately to Cardew of violation at the hands of the police. Cardew dismissed the appeal on the grounds that he believed the chief wanted to evade the tax.[101] At Bumpeh, the police fired and wounded a chief.[102] The precise extent of the barbarities committed against the chiefs and their people may never be known, but it may be assumed that it was of such dimensions as to convert apathy to active resistance.

Outbreak of War

Meantime, in the north, Bai Bureh was successfully harassing the administration by his guerrilla war tactics adopted in defence against British aggression. The news of his success spread round the country although it was exaggerated in the Press. J. C. E. Blakeney, acting District Commissioner of Panguma, thought that 'agitators' were spreading these 'false rumours' which were inciting the people in his district to resist. He apprehended trouble even though his district was exempted from the tax. Reports reached Blakeney that Nyagua and other chiefs were holding secret meetings at Kenema and 'that Nyagua was urging them to give him every assistance in driving the white man out of the country', and was collecting war

[99] Chalmers Report, I, pp. 44–5.
[100] Cf. A. Abraham, 'Bai Bureh, the British and the Hut Tax War', *International Journal of African Historical Studies*, vii, 1, 1974.
[101] Despatches, 45/96, 52/96, 53/96; Native Affairs, 28/98, SLGA.
[102] Chalmers Report, I, p. 46.

materials. Blakeney thought it imperative to arrest Nyagua, and Cardew sent reinforcements.[103]

In April 1898 Cardew felt he could deal effectively with the Bai Bureh war in the north, and requested a Commission to try persons concerned in the 'insurrection now existing in the Protectorate'. The commission was to have Supreme Court powers but no jury, since most people in the Colony sympathized with the 'insurgents'.[104] Then on 27 or 28 April there was a simultaneous outbreak in major centres in the south, accompanied by mass killings of British subjects and the plundering of trading stations.[105] Within a week the whole country was practically up in armed resistance. Captain C. B. Wallis who was then in the Bandajuma district, gathered that the chiefs of Bumpeh and the neighbourhood instigated the disturbances. On 27 April Wallis estimated that about 1,500 insurgents from Bumpeh attacked his party at Kambia, 'who appeared to have been repulsed' after about four hours fighting. He reported simultaneous disturbances in Imperreh and Mofwe.[106]

The following week Kwellu was reported captured by insurgents who were advancing on Songo Town in the Colony.[107] In fact Songo Town was not molested. Contemplated attacks on Bonthe were rumoured but it escaped attack from the warriors because of the arrival of warships there on 1 May.[108] Sub-Inspector Johnson at Kwellu reported the attack on that post to the Frontier Police Adjutant, Captain Moore, on 5 May:

. . . *The whole of the natives rebelled* against the Government, they have raid [*sic*] the whole of the country from Upper Mendi to Rotifunk. The war came from Nyagwa, Big Bompeh, Ticongoh, Bongeh. . . . A large war gathered at Mokassi . . . will join with chief Foray Vong war from Kwalu.[109]

Then on 8 May he reported again: 'Enemy put fire on Kwalu. Only Kwalu, Gbangbama and Moyamba for the English',[109] because they were under the sway of Madam Yoko, who was unflinching in her loyalty to the administration.

[103] CO 267/438/Conf. 29, enc., Blakeney to Colonial Secretary, 1898.
[104] CO 267/437/Conf. 27, Cardew to SS, 1898.
[105] Chalmers Report, I, p. 46; CO 267/438/Conf. 32, Cardew to SS, 1898.
[106] Ibid.   [107] CO 267/438/Tel. 4 May 1898, Cardew to SS.
[108] CO 267/438/Conf. 35, Cardew to SS, 1898.
[109] CO 267/438/Conf. 37, enc. 2, Johnson to Moore, 1898 (emphasis added).

The Mende war had a peculiarly brutal, indiscriminate, and xenophobic character, which contrasts dramatically with the Bai Bureh war in the north. The latter was a kind of conventional war fought only against the troops of the administration and organized on lines of guerrilla tactics. With very few exceptions, there was no general onslaught against innocent persons. But the character of the Mende rising reveals a lamentable story of cruel murder and brutal massacre of innocent persons. Unsuspecting officials, missionaries, traders and their families (Creole, European, and American alike) were seized and killed and their property looted or destroyed. It was estimated that about 1000 suffered in this way, although the exact number can never be known.

The major centres of missionary activity, Shenge, Rotifunk, Mano Bagru, and Taiama have the singular irony of being the scenes of systematic butchering of the missionaries and the destruction of mission buildings and property. The Chief of Shenge, Thomas Neale Caulker, 'who was really a usurper, having obtained his position by false representations', and was 'recognised as such by the Government',[110] was one of the first victims of the attack. The two missionaries at Taima, having been utterly confused by the Chief Foray Vong, were allowed to be decapitated on 8 or 9 May, although the Chief had promised them protection. The traders and officials of the administration, their wives and children, were indiscriminately massacred, their property looted and destroyed. Hughes, the Creole Assistant District Commissioner of Sherbro, was killed in Imperreh. Panic-stricken British subjects and foreigners poured into Bonthe, which was now protected by warships.

A few were lucky enough to escape. Madam Yoko and Nancy Tucker, the imposed chief of Bagru, were smuggled under Frontier Police cover into the barracks at Kwellu. Another serious attack was mounted on the place on 13 May, in which the attackers were beaten off, leaving behind over 100 dead, including two of their leaders, Lahai Mboma and the Chief of Kangahun.

In the Gallinas many trading factories were abandoned in frenzy, and company agents and Creoles assembled at Mano

[110] Governor's Confidential Despatches, 94/1911, enc., Fairtlough to Colonial Secretary, SLGA.

Salijah, which was easily defensible, until they were rescued by H.M.S. *Fox*. An attack on Panguma was anticipated by the arrest of the king, and in Bandajuma, Momoh Kaikai only gave support after the Government forces had successfully withstood the attack on the town. All these mesmerizingly horrible incidents occurred within a fortnight. The pattern everywhere was one of 'parties of warboys raiding round and plundering and murdering any Creoles or Frontier Policemen they could get hold of . . .,' as District Commissioner Fairtlough put it. Only Kwellu, Bandajuma, and Panguma, district capitals, were strong enough to hold their own. Thereafter, the resistance petered out and the administration counter-attacked. Within two months it was virtually all over, but the Temne war under Bai Bureh in the north lasted until November, when the war-general surrendered.[111]

Nyagua and the *Beh Sherbro*, Gbanna Lewis, were arrested early in May. Nyagua had co-operated with the administration all along, and as recently as twelve months previously, had assisted Captain Fairtlough with about 400 warriors under his head warrior, Dɔni, in an expedition against the Kissi. Lt. Birch, who acted as District Commissioner after Fairtlough, reported that he 'was unable to give any information with regard to the part he took in the recent disturbances. I can only state that . . . I found him willing to carry out my orders.'[112]

The Frontier Police attacked Nyagua's towns, burnt them, and killed many people. Then on 4 June, following these unprovoked atrocities, actual fighting occurred. It is reported that twenty-seven chiefs participated, but by 8 August they had begun to surrender. There was little evidence for legal proceedings against Nyagua himself. So he was detained on the advice of the Attorney-General. [113] Fairtlough, however,

---

[111] For a detailed account of the course of the war, see ibid.; Fyfe, *A History* pp. 572–7; Wallis, *West African Empire*, pp. 87–200; Alldridge, *The Sherbro*, pp. 304–33; R. A. Corby, 'The Mende Uprising of 1898 as it related to the United Brethren in Christ Missions' (Western Illinois University MA, 1971), pp. 20–34; J. S. Harrison, 'The Twenty-Seventh of April: The Sierra Leone Wars of 1898' (City College of the City University of New York MA, 1972), pp. 93–102; J. H. Mannah-Kpaka, 'Memoirs', pp. 28–39.

[112] CO 267/446/Conf. 32, enc., memo on political prisoners in Freetown gaol, 1898.

[113] See A. Abraham, 'Nyagua, the British and the Hut Tax War', *International Journal of African Historical Studies*, v, 1, 1972, pp. 94–8.

claimed falsely that the 'insurrection started in the Pangoma district', with Nyagua heading the 'prime movers'.[114]

Gbanna Lewis had a year before his second arrest used the Poro to impose economic sanctions on the Colony, for which he was arrested. When the deluge of resistance burst out in the south, Alldridge, the District Commissioner of the Sherbro, reported that Gbanna Lewis was the brain behind everything. On 14 May, Alldridge reported to the Governor that he

sent for him and he came over yesterday, and I suggested that as he disclaimed everything, that he should proceed to town [Freetown] . . . and make his explanations to Your Excellency in person. . . . The object [of the resistance] appears to be the massacre of all Sierra Leoneans [Creoles] and Europeans, and thoroughly it is being done. The country is destroyed as regards Trade—several traders being killed and places burnt.[115]

Gbanna Lewis was arrested by order of the Governor on 7 May, he being 'treated as a suspect, but against whom, there seemed to be no evidence'.[116]

Pressures for withdrawal of the tax

Ever since the reported attack on Kwellu and the purported advance on Songo Town, the 'present difficulty' of the Colony was proportionally increased, which 'constitute[d] a reason for taking the matter of the tax in hand at once'. Mr. Davitt, M.P., asked Chamberlain 'whether . . . the Government can see its way to instruct the Governor to take immediate steps to inform the natives that the tax will be discontinued', in view of the previous experience when Hennessy had abolished direct taxation in the Colony in 1872. Chamberlain denied any knowledge of the annual celebration of the occasion as 'Pope Hennessy's Day', although Cardew had told him of it. The Secretary of State stated that he would not consider abolishing the tax while the people were still in arms. But he admitted that the tax caused the disorder. When Davitt tried to corner the Secretary of State, who was obviously protecting his Ministry and Cardew, by supplementary questions, he was constantly

---

[114] CO 267/440/Conf. 68, enc., Fairtlough to Colonial Secretary, 1898.
[115] CO 267/438/Conf. 34, enc. 2, Alldridge to Governor, 1898.
[116] Chalmers Report, I, p. 49.

obstructed and cried down. He succeeded, however, in getting over to Chamberlain: 'May I ask whether the Right Hon. gentleman does not consider that it would be a sane and Christian way of stopping the rebellion to take off the tax?' The Speaker cried 'Order, Order'.[117] Two days later, however, Cardew was telegraphed to reconsider the tax. At a meeting of the Executive Council to consider this telegram, the members, no doubt under Cardew's powerful influence, unanimously agreed that it would be inexpedient either to suspend the tax temporarily or to grant any concessions in respect of it, since this would savour of the administration capitulating to the resistance movement. Any concessions would only be granted if the resistance movement were 'thoroughly subjugated'. The telegraph he sent back to Chamberlain added the infelicitous note: 'Have reason to fear that all aliens, white or black, in Mendi districts from Mano river to Ribbi river have been killed.' Mercer at the Colonial Office found it rather difficult to reconcile this news with the refusal to withdraw the tax, and he minuted:

If we decline to make any concession and enforce the tax, this must be for other than financial reasons: for apart from the cost of the operations the natives, if disaffected, could easily retaliate by not sending down produce. They have adopted this policy before.[118]

The merchants, too, tried to get the Colonial Office to prevail on Cardew to withdraw the tax or make appreciable concessions. But with his powerful rhetoric, the Governor would not budge from his former position, and argued against the merchants. He put forward the view that the administration of the Colony was a matter of indifference to the traders, as long as commerce was good. He overtly accused them and the 'Public Press' of directly inciting the inhabitants of the Protectorate not to pay the tax. At the time when the administration seemed hard-pressed by the war, Cardew stood firm in his conviction that any concessions whatever would be misconstrued by the people. When the administration stood at an advantageous position, he would consider concessions.[119]

[117] CO 267/439/Tel. 4 May 1898, minute by Mercer; CO 267/443 House of Commons, 3 May 1898.
[118] CO 267/438/Tel. 8 May 1898, minute by Mercer.
[119] CO 267/438/Tel. 9 May 1898, Cardew to SS.

In justifying himself and the hut tax, Cardew accused the Creoles of instigating the war, since they were averse to direct taxation. He came out with the startling suggestion that instead of being abolished, the house tax should be extended to the Colony.[120]

The end of the war

By June, Cardew was hopeful that the administration was gaining the upper hand, and came out with proposals to deal with the resistors. The Governor suggested different treatments for the Temne and the Mende since their wars were characteristically different. While he recommended that a general amnesty should be granted to the Temne once Bai Bureh was taken, he determined to deal with the Mende with great firmness as he would accept 'no condonation of the murders . . .'. A special Commission Court would try all cases of murder. On 15 June, an Order-in-Council gave the District Commissioners of the three districts of Panguma, Ronietta, and Bandajuma, powers in all criminal cases.[121]

After the formation of a flying column under Col. Woodgate which left Freetown on 9 May and captured several towns, naval operations on the coast, and several arrests, the rains set in. The Mende were vastly inferior in weapons, and Cardew knew that they would not hold out a sustained effort. Another column under Col. Cunningham left on 31 May.[122] In July, Alldridge led a punitive expedition to the Sherbro mainland and after razing several towns, suggested the destruction of the crops just maturing for harvest, as a further reprisal.[123]

Cardew, feeling confident that the administration was clearly gaining the upper hand, ventured the following proposals for the re-establishment of the authority of the administration after the rains:

I propose that about five columns of such strength as O/C Troops may consider suitable should start next November from such points as Port Loko, Songo Town and Bonthe, and completely

[120] CO 267/438/Conf., 28 May 1898, Cardew to SS.
[121] CO 267/439/Conf., 9 June, 1898; CO 267/439/126, Cardew to SS, 1898.
[122] CO 267/439/Conf. 56, 23 July 1898; Cardew to SS; Chalmers Report, I, p. 51.
[123] Enclosures in Despatches, 65/98, SLGA.

traverse the Protectorate by various routes which should be so determined and the march of the columns so combined as to enable two or more to act in concert, if necessary, in those portions of the Protectorate where on political and military grounds it is necessary that a superior force should be shown. . . . Simultaneously . . . boat expeditions should be sent up the rivers and creeks . . .
I attach very great importance to the necessity of moving . . . columns in the manner I have proposed . . . for . . . especially all along the eastern boundary, the natives have had no evidence of the power and resources of Her Majesty's Government other than the presence of isolated posts here and there consisting of three or four men of the Frontier Police . . . and many parts are still very disaffected, especially in the Panguma and north-eastern portion of the Bandajuma districts.[124]

By the following month the administration had succeeded in reasserting its authority, although the war in the north was not yet at an end. It was reported that many chiefs were suing for peace. Cardew availed himself of the circumstances to vindicate his position. When the resistance was thoroughly overcome, 'the natives will have learnt their lesson and there will . . . be no more trouble about the collection of the house tax'. He added that the chiefs were already yielding in all directions and while 'many of the chief actors . . . are [still] being apprehended', there was 'practically no opposition' except in Panguma and the remoter parts of the Bandajuma district.[125] It was reported that 'a remnant of Mendi insurgents have re-occupied and stockaded Tungea', against whom Cardew gave orders to the Officer Commanding the Troops to send a force.[126]

In September Deputy Judge A. G. Bonner, accompanied by the Acting Attorney-General, proceeded to Kwellu to hold court there, after the District Commissioner had reported that with a very few exceptions, 'all the insurgent chiefs have surrendered' in the Ronietta district.[127] Early in October, two patrols of Frontier Police captured 650 'Insurgents', but seventeen were detained, including Foray Vong of Taiama.[128] In all, sixteen captives were condemned to death; the

[124] CO 267/439/Conf. 56, 23 July 1898, Cardew to SS.
[125] CO 267/440/155, Cardew to SS (4 Aug. 1898).
[126] CO 267/440/Conf. 73, Cardew to SS (17 Sept. 1898).   [127] Ibid.
[128] CO 267/440/220, Cardew to SS (6 Oct. 1898).

Executive Council confirmed fifteen of these sentences. Nine were executed.[129]

While the sentences were being passed on the captives at Kwellu, '. . . a number of headmen of towns had arrived in Bonthe to tender their submission on behalf of the Imperri country. . . .' At Bonthe Bonner condemned twenty-one persons to death. Cardew, after learning that the people were sincerely desirous of coming to terms, decided to proclaim a free pardon to all those who had participated in the war. But seventeen were executed for murder at Bonthe.[130] In Bandajuma 107 were tried for murder, of whom sixty-five were convicted and forty-two acquitted. Of the sixty-five, thirty-five had their sentences commuted, while the rest were executed.[131] All in all Cardew reported on 2 December that 180 captives had been tried, 112 convicted, sixty-seven acquitted or discharged, and one had escaped. The death sentences were confirmed in sixty-six cases—and the rest reprieved. All these trials were for murder, which Cardew would not condone, although he did pardon 'rebels'. Proclamations of amnesty were being issued 'wherever circumstances admit'.[132] In January 1899 Cardew confidently despatched:

> . . . I have the honour to report that the disturbances have been most completely suppressed throughout the Protectorate, that with a few exceptions all the rebel chiefs have either surrendered themselves or been apprehended, that a general amnesty for all offenders has just been proclaimed, that the natives are returning to their towns and villages and cultivating their lands, and they have accepted the house tax as an accomplished fact, and that I am informed from every direction they are paying readily wherever it has been imposed.[133]

The last remnant of resistance was in the extreme east of the Protectorate, where Nyagua's son, Mogbi, was in alliance with the Kissi. He eventually submitted in August.[134]

The suspected ring-leaders were detained as political prisoners—three in number, namely, the *Beh Sherbro* (Gbanna

[129] CO 267/441/229, 240, Cardew to SS (18 October 1898).

[130] CO 267/441/229, 238, 257, Cardew to SS (20 October 1898).

[131] CO 267/441/Tel., 29 Nov. 1898, Cardew to SS.

[132] CO 267/441/Conf. 89, Cardew to SS. In spite of this the actual number hanged is difficult to determine, and may probably never be known.

[133] CO 267/445/15, Cardew to SS, 1899.

[134] CO 267/445/Conf. 19; CO 207/447/Conf. 60, Cardew to SS, 1899.

Lewis), Nyagua, and Bimba Kelli of Mokelle in Imperreh. Nyagua's release and return was mooted, there being insufficient evidence against him and the *Beh Sherbro*. Nathan, the acting Governor, was in favour of Nyagua's return:

Nyagua is probably the most powerful chief in the Protectorate, his administrative influence extending over the larger part of Panguma district. He has undoubtedly done good service to the Government of this Colony in the past, and in the case of the late disturbances was clearly under arrest at the time the disturbances broke out in his country. He was arrested on suspicion of disloyalty and of making preparations for attacking the Frontier Police in his town of Panguma. *I am by no means convinced that these suspicions were justified*, and I would call . . . attention to former instances . . . in which similar suspicions entertained of this chief were afterwards found to have rested on but slight foundations . . . Captain Blakeney . . . arrested Nyagua . . . his views from reports he made at the time show a want of confidence between the chief and the District Commissioner. I have reason to believe that *the Panguma District is considerably disorganised by reason of Nyagwa's absence* from it. I have asked [the DC] . . . whether he considers it desirable that Nyagwa should return. If he replies in the affirmative, I propose to reinstate Nyagwa as Paramount chief.[135]

Unfortunately, the District Commissioner, C. E. Birch, who a year earlier had not been unfavourable to Nyagua, was now opposed to his release because it would be considered an act of weakness which 'would increase Nyagua's power and influence', and as the chief was already so powerful, his return, quite contrary to the views of Nathan, would 'unsettle the district'.[136]

As for Gbanna Lewis, the only reason which seems to have been behind official hostility towards him, was his use of the Poro to prevent trade. Even Nathan, so sympathetic to Nyagua, was not prepared to release him, for while all believed that there was sufficient 'evidence that the "one word poro", which started the Mende rising' was the work of the *Beh Sherbro*, the allegation was not substantiated at all. Thus the real reason seems to have been that 'the trade importance is too great to risk any further trouble on the mainland',[137] because the *Beh Sherbro* had previously used the Poro to stop trade.

135 CO 267/446/Conf. 8, Nathan to SS, 1899 (emphasis added).
136 CO 267/446/Conf. 41, enc., Birch to Col. Sec., 1899.
137 CO 267/446/Conf. 8, Nathan to SS, 1899.

In March, Ordinance No. 3 of 1899 was passed, legalizing the detention and banishment of Gbana Lewis, Nyagua, and Bimba Kelli as political prisoners. Bai Bureh was also to be exiled. While awaiting their banishment to the Gold Coast, Bimba Kelli died of dysentery, but the rest were exiled on 30 July.[138]

Failure of the resistance

The character of the Mende war goes a long way to explain the reasons for its defeat. The target of their onslaught seems to have been anyone who appeared to propagate the cause of the administration. Cardew characterized them as being 'among the lower type of savages [and] they are cannibalistic in their tendencies'.[139] Yet he omitted the ruthlessness of the conquest and the use of methods that would not have been tolerated in Europe. The Mende 'fought as a disorganised rapacious rabble, incapable of sustained opposition, but formidable in a sudden offensive against unsuspecting opponents'.[140]

The Mende underestimated the resources of the administration. They thought that a short vicious engagement would win permanent victory. The 'remarkable feature' of the rising, as Cardew wrote, was 'the simultaneousness and secrecy with which it was effected. It was most unexpected and entirely unsuspected.'[141] After the first onslaught the movement degenerated into a series of uncoordinated attacks on British traders, agents, or posts. There was no overt leadership like that of Bai Bureh. But even if they had, 'guerrilla warfare would only have staved off the inevitable', because West African society, being agrarian in nature, could not finance a long-term war against the industrialized society of Europe with infinitely more resources.[142] The nature of the Mende war was consistent with traditional methods, but completely unsuited to the novel European situation—and therein lay the fatal miscalculation.

On the other hand, Cardew had 'every confidence in the resources of the Government and in the ability of the Officer

---

[138] CO 267/445/67; CO 267/447/230; CO 267/447/Conf. 54, Nathan to SS, 1899.
[139] CO 267/438/Conf., 28 May 1898, Cardew to SS.
[140] Fyfe, *A History*, p. 572.
[141] CO 267/438/Conf. 34, Cardew to SS, 1898.
[142] M. Crowder (ed.), *West African Resistance* (London 1971), p. 15.

Commanding the Troops' to win the war.[143] The Mende were vastly inferior in weapons. Their swords, cutlasses, sticks, and a few trade guns were no match for British fire-power. It was not expected that the resistance would be long drawn out and consequently, no gunpowder was stored in anticipation.[144]

Lastly, there was the role of the 'collaborators'. Only three chiefs willingly co-operated with the administration. Not surprisingly, they all owed their positions to the administration. Nancy Tucker of Bagru was the mistress of Sgt. Edward Coker, who installed her as 'provisional chief' of Bagru in 1897. It paid her well to collaborate, for she got confirmed as Paramount Chief after the war of 1898. Madam Yoko was recognized by the British administration in Freetown, and her people never failed to remind her that she was a sell-out and a colonial product. Only the police saved these quislings from massacre. Thomas Neale Caulker, however, was not lucky enough to escape. A 'usurper', he was disliked by the people. Moreover, his mother was said to have been a 'slave', but the administration installed him. So when the war broke out 'the rightful chief went down to Shengay with his warboys and killed Neal Caulker'.[145]

Momoh Kaikai only collaborated under duress. Had not the police been quartered in his town, he would in all likelihood have resisted.[146] The Temne chief, Fula Mansa of Yoni, was conspicuous for his part in collaborating with the administration. Having been arrested for his part in the 1887 Yoni disturbances and exiled to the Gold Coast (present day Ghana) for seven years, it was he who informed Captain Sharpe of Karene that the chiefs had decided not to pay the tax. When the flying columns were formed, he contributed over 1000 warriors and was himself killed fighting for the British.[147]

The Europeans proved very skilful in forging alliances among African states and in exploiting local conflict situations to weaken the resistance movement. As has been rightly pointed out, 'if one determinant of the outcome of the scramble for

[143] CO 267/438/Conf. 34, Cardew to SS, 1898.

[144] CO 267/438/Conf. 32, Cardew to SS, 1898.

[145] CO 267/439/Conf. 45, enc. 4, memo by J. A. Cole; Governor's confidential despatches, 94/1911, enc. Fairtlough.

[146] Wallis, *West African Empire*, p. 153.

[147] Fyfe, *A History*, p. 582.

Africa was the vastly superior technological strength of the European powers, the other was Africa's political disunity . . . .'.[148]

Interpretations of the war

(a) The house tax

In June 1898, when there was fair hope of overcoming the resistance movement, Sir David Chalmers was appointed as Royal Commissioner to enquire into the disturbances with the following terms of reference: whether the hut tax together with all its implications caused the war; whether 'the scheme of administration' adopted was best 'to promote the development of the country while preserving the rights of the natives'.[149] This was in accordance with precedent—to hold an imperial inquiry into the causes of the outbreak. Moreover, representations had been sent to Chamberlain 'while the affairs of the Protectorate were in a critical state'.[150]

Before Chalmers came out in July, he wrote in a private letter: 'I know I am well enough known not to be the sort of man who would make a trimmed report.'[151] His view was that indigenous rulers were independent contracting powers whose rights were to be preserved. Official circles in Freetown thought him partial. An antipathy therefore developed between him and Cardew—the Governor feeling that the Commissioner was interfering in his administration, while the latter felt that the former was inhibiting him in his duty. Chalmers, for instance, suggested a variation in the terms of Bai Bureh's surrender, but Cardew 'respectfully deprecated' the interference.[152] While the inquiry was on, the Colonial Office allowed Fairtlough's account of the war to be published in *The Times*, thus prejudicing the 'impartial commission' and making it a 'superfluity and an embarrassment'.[153] By the same time,

---

[148] E. Stokes and R. Brown (eds.), *The Zambezian Past* (Manchester 1966), p. xx.

[149] Chalmers Report, I, pp. 4–5.

[150] CO 267/438/Conf., 28 May 1898, Chamberlain to Cardew.

[151] Quoted in J. A. Chalmers, 'In Defence of Sir David Chalmers', *The Nineteenth Century*, March 1900, p. 488.

[152] CO 267/440/Conf. 81, Cardew to Chalmers, 1898.

[153] Chalmers, 'Defence', pp. 488–9.

Cardew had won the Colonial Office over to his view that the tax must be retained, and that it was not the cause of the war.[154]

However, the Royal Commissioner concluded that the tax being 'obnoxious to the customs and feelings of the people' and collected in a 'sudden, uncompromising and harsh manner' was the 'moving' cause of the 'insurrection'.[155] Frontier Police activities had vexed and irritated the chiefs for a long time. Indeed the tax can be seen more correctly as the precipitant which exploded a powder-keg of accumulated grievances. Cardew was probably right in seeing the tax mainly as the 'exciting cause' or the 'pretext'. The tax was not burdensome, and the chiefs admitted this before officials and even Chalmers. Nor can it be said that the people were opposed to taxation *per se*. All through their historic experience, the people had been used to paying taxes to their rulers to uphold the political institution economically. It was an accepted institution to pay tax willingly, as Nyagua testified before Chalmers.[156] It is thus inadmissible that 'taxation for administrative purposes was quite unknown' as well as the obligations economically to uphold the political institutions.[157]

The real objection was that the Freetown administration had no right to tax houses. Taxation on houses implied a rent, and therefore no right of ownership. In one of the petitions to Cardew, the chiefs stated that 'the Government will take the country from them . . . our own true fear is that paying for our huts naturally means no right to our country'.[158]

(b) The role of the Poro

How the resistance was plotted is an enigmatic problem and there are conflicting opinions even among contemporaries. No evidence was found against Nyagua and Gbanna Lewis who were said to have started the ball rolling. Fairtlough's account is not consistent. He says that the resistance started in Panguma, and later that the Bumpeh people rose first.[159] More

---

[154] CO 267/438/Conf., 28 May 1898, Cardew to Chamberlain.
[155] Chalmers Report, I, p. 73.
[156] Ibid., II, p. 334.
[157] Little, *The Mende*, p. 57; CO 267/438/Conf., 28 May 1898, Cardew to Chamberlain.
[158] Chalmers Report, I, p. 22, also pp. 48–9, 66–7.
[159] CO 267/440/Conf. 68, enc., Fairtlough to Colonial Secretary, 1898.

people believed that a few chiefs started the resistance, and 'the masses were compelled to follow'.[160] Cardew believed that it was started purely by 'one of the chiefs'.[161] Chalmers, the Royal Commissioner, concluded that the 'rising was brought about by the common action of a very large number of chiefs and others'.[162]

However, the alarming and incredible rapidity of the Mende war indicates that it was centrally planned, and in all probability through the instrumentality of the Poro. All the officials were sure of this.[163] Major Stuart reported that Gbanna Lewis arranged the meeting and sent out messengers carrying a half-burnt leaf. Those who accepted it were given a number of pebbles and directed to throw one away every day, and rise when the last was thrown. This account is fully corroborated by Revd. J. Abayomi Cole.[164] The chiefs planned the resistance and all Poro members were bound to take part, although many chiefs did not physically participate. Many others were attracted by the mere prospect of loot.[165] Thus, although some people collaborated with the administration, the mass of the people took part, and therefore the resistance can be seen as a mass movement, at least in operation, even if not in origin.

The importance of the Poro on this occasion has been challenged. It is argued that separate lodges were independent, and that the proclamation of the Protectorate altered the influence of the Poro. 'The frequent wars and raids between towns, the dispersed pattern of settlement, and the absence of any corresponding centralised political structure', reduce the instrumentality of the Poro to nought.[166] Cardew too believed that the chiefs 'lack cohesion and powers of organization, and there are too many jealousies between them for concerted action'.[167]

[160] CO 267/439/Conf. 54, and enc. 2, Revd. D. F. Wilberforce to Alldridge, 1898; Wallis, *West African Empire*, pp. 116–17.

[161] CO 267/438/Conf., 28 May 1898, Cardew to SS.

[162] Chalmers Report, I, p. 57.

[163] CO 267/436/Conf. 35, Cardew to SS, 1898; CO 267/440/Conf. 68, Fairtlough to Colonial Secretary, 1898.

[164] CO 267/448/War Office, 28 March 1899, enc. notes by Major Stuart; CO 267/439/Conf. 45, enc. 4, memo by J. A. Cole.

[165] Mannah-Kpaka, 'Memoirs', p. 32.

[166] G. C. Bond, 'The Contemporary Position of Chiefs in Sierra Leone' (London MA thesis, 1962), p. 20.

[167] CO 879/55/570/2, Cardew to Chamberlain, 24 December 1897.

The misguided nature of these assessments is apparent enough. It was Mendegla's 'peace poro' that brought an end to the wars in the Gallinas and its hinterland. That no centralized structure existed is a gross travesty. The Poro, more than any other institution gives continuity to Mende culture and a sense of unity to the Mende people. Without exaggeration, it facilitated the accomplishment of the concerted intention to resist.

(c) The Freetown Press

At the end of May 1898 Cardew explained bitterly that the Creole traders and press in Freetown incited the people to resist payment of the tax, fearing a possible imposition of such a tax on themselves. The month before Fairtlough made a search at Forodugu and found thirty copies of the *Sierra Leone Weekly News* in a chief's house, but they were three years old! Cardew caused the matter to be taken up by the Attorney-General who reported that there was not sufficient evidence 'to justify a prosecution for incitement to rebellion'. It was 'difficult to obtain exact legal proofs for these conspiracies', as Cardew admitted, but the officials believed them.[168] Dr. Berkeley, the District Surgeon of Bandajuma, reported in November that the chiefs admitted that the Creole traders had advised them not to pay the tax. One trader, he noted, was in the habit of reading the Freetown papers aloud and spreading the news of Bai Bureh's success.[169]

This factor cannot be ignored, but it has perhaps been quite exaggerated. The circulation of the papers was too small to have incited such a widespread movement as the Mende resistance. Chalmers dismissed the point altogether.

(d) Mori-men

Some observers attributed part of the blame for the resistance to mori-men. Every chief had his permanent mori-man, who was usually quite influential, 'and nothing of any consequence is entered upon without a reference being made to' him. Alldridge hoped that the administration would use the Frontier

---

[168] CO 267/437/Conf. 4, CO 267/438/Conf. 43, Cardew to SS, 1898; CO 267/438/Conf., 28 May 1898, enc. 1, Attorney-General to Governor; CO 267/440/Conf. 68, enc., Fairtlough to Colonial Secretary, 1898; Chalmers Report, I, p. 64.
[169] CO 267/441/275, enc., Berkeley to Colonial Secretary, 1898.

Police to destroy their 'mystic cults'.[170] Captain Wallis claimed that the 'mischief making of the Mori-men throughout the Hinterland' was one of the direct causes of the resistance. The chiefs, he explained, spent large sums of money in payment for their services and in making sacrifices for the success of the resistance.[171] The Royal Commissioner did not consider this factor. But the role of mori-men is a traditional one. It is not unlikely that they were consulted by individual chiefs, but to attribute a major cause of the resistance to the universality of their influence is suspicious.

(e) Creole dishonesty and oppression

'One of the causes which brought about the massacre', wrote Cardew, was the dishonest and oppressive treatment of the people by the Creoles.[172] Fairtlough argued that Creole activity deliberately aimed at retarding 'the progress of civilization' by preventing the circulation of coin and knowledge of its value. The official rate for carrying a load from Freetown to Panguma was twenty-one shillings, but Creole traders paid in kind—two pieces of cloth worth only about two shillings and sixpence.[173] Alldridge further adds that the cloth was so folded as to represent a larger quantity than was actually contained in the roll. The Creole traders extended the measures for a bushel and a gallon when buying from the people.[174] This factor did not feature in the Chalmers inquiry, and it is probable that the people did not take this cheating seriously, otherwise they would have responded unfavourably.

(f) The abolition of the slave-trade

Although Cardew had years before stated that slave-trading had ceased, he advanced that 'the chief cause is the abolition of slavery'.[175] Most officials agreed with this. There were complaints that the economic basis of chiefly authority was directly

[170] CO 267/401/113, enc. 2, Alldridge to Governor, 1898; Alldridge, *The Sherbro*, pp. 304–5 and *passim*. Mori-men are Islamic scholars who prophesy and prepare charms and amulets supposed to possess efficacious supernatural powers.

[171] Wallis, *West African Empire*, pp. 115 and 237.

[172] CO 267/441/Conf. 93, Cardew to SS, 1898.

[173] CO 267/440/Conf. 68, enc., Fairtlough to Colonial Secretary, 1898.

[174] CO 267/441/Conf. 93, enc., Alldridge to Cardew, 1898.

[175] CO 267/438/Conf. 28 May 1898, Cardew to Chamberlain.

undermined by the abolition of slave-trading.[176] This made the rising inevitable. Wallis continued emphatically that the war was 'not a "tax war" at all; it was a "slave war" '.[177] There is a serious contradiction here. Slave-trading, proclaimed ended long before the Protectorate, could not suddenly be the cause of the resistance years later. No doubt there were complaints about losing dependants under the new arrangements, but the reasonable inference is, as Chalmers wrote, that there was a 'general feeling of reconcilement with the change. That interference with slavery formed a material factor in the rising rests on no sound foundation.'[178]

(g) The missionary impact

Fairtlough charged that there was a bitter feeling against the missionaries because they opposed 'native customs of sacrifice and fetish, and because of their educating the children'.[179] Hudson, one of the first District Commissioners but later Attorney-General, saw the events of 1898 as a direct reaction to missionary activity. The leaders, 'former pupils', meant to 'wipe out the missionary entirely', because the missionary approach was wrong. It attempted to make a spiritual *tabula rasa* of the African before christianizing him. He questioned the possibility of pushing a people forward from 'utter darkness' and a 'crude form of devil worship to a belief in and comprehension of the highest and purest philosophy that the world has yet known'.[180]

The Revd. William Vivian made a rejoinder correctly drawing attention to the fact that the war was more complex, and that Hudson ignored that 'inflammable factor', the house tax. The treatment of missionaries was not peculiar to them. Christianizing influence was not negligible. Two of the four chiefs arrested by Carr at Mofwe were Christians. If the people had objected to the education of their children, they would simply have withdrawn them. Long before the Protectorate, the missionaries would have been easily evicted if they

---

[176] CO 267/440/Conf. 68, enc. Fairtlough to Colonial Secretary, 1898.
[177] Wallis, *West African Empire*, p. 207.
[178] Chalmers Report, I, pp. 53–4.
[179] CO 267/440/Conf. 68, enc., Fairtlough to Colonial Secretary, 1898.
[180] A. Hudson, 'The Missionary in West Africa', *Journal of the African Society*, July 1903, pp. 454–5.

had been disliked. Revd. J. B. W. Johnson destroyed 'devil houses' in the Bumpeh river area unmolested, without the people seeming to mind him.[181] But by preaching sermons exhorting the people to pay the tax, they became identified with the officials of the administration enforcing the tax. They thus appeared to be an arm of the administration. In the Maji Maji resistance to German rule in Tanganyika, missionaries were attacked 'because they were Europeans and all Europeans are the same'.[182] Vivian, however, ignored the deaths of the U.B.C. missionaries, because by the time he wrote, he was appealing for a resumption of missionary activity in the Protectorate. However, within six months of the cessation of the hostilities, the very people who destroyed the churches in a fury were working to rebuild the selfsame churches.

(h) Return to savagery

According to nearly all the contemporary assessments, the resistance aimed at destroying British rule and all other 'civilizing' influences and returning to savagery. It was interpreted, in fact, as 'the resentment of the savage to the encroachments of civilization'.[183] The position is maintained by modern writers that the resistance was 'to the whole impact of western cultural influences'.[184] But in fact, the people had been adjusting to the British presence peacefully, if somewhat uneasily, until the Protectorate Ordinance and its operation rudely entered the scene.

(i) Frontier Police brutalizations

The Frontier Police were a source of constant vexation to the chiefs owing to their indiscipline, extortion, oppression, violence, and 'objectionable tendencies', abusing their position and powers, being in fact 'little judges and governors'.[185] Dr. Edward Blyden attributed the rising to the oppression of the

---

[181] Fyfe, *A History*, p. 555.

[182] Quoted in J. Iliffe, 'The Organization of the Maji Maji Rebellion', *The Journal of African History*, viii, 3, 1967, p. 499.

[183] CO 267/438/Conf., 28 May 1898, minute by Mercer; Alldridge, *The Sherbro*, p. 153; CO 267/440/Conf. 68, enc. Fairtlough to Colonial Secretary, 1898; W. Vivian, 'The Missionary in West Africa', *Journal of the African Society*, 9, 1903, pp. 100–3; CO 267/437/Tel., 9 May 1898, minute by Selborne.

[184] Hargreaves, *Samuel Lewis*, pp. 91–2; idem, 'Sierra Leone Protectorate', p. 57; Corby, 'Mende Rising', pp. 19–20; Harrison, 'Twenty-seventh of April', p. 105; Davidson, 'Mende Chiefdoms'.

[185] Chalmers Report, I, p. 12.

Frontier Police and the arbitrary tyranny of the District Commissioners, but Cardew dismissed it as a 'very extravagant assertion'. Quite contrary to the truth, Cardew claimed that their rulers were more oppressive in pre-colonial times, the proportion between the two being 'the thickness of the little finger to that of the loins'.[186] Dr. Berkeley believed that nothing done by the Frontier Police 'gave the slightest encouragement to the insurrection'.[187] This is of course contrary to the truth.

The police caused much mischief with regard to the authority of the chiefs, and flagrantly misused their powers. Even before the Protectorate was declared, Cardew was forced to take action to discipline them. Apart from the ill-treatment they meted out to the chiefs and people, the class of persons who now came as police were mostly 'freed men who were slaves of the chiefs'. In 1898 Parkes admitted 'with regret' the conduct of the Frontier Police.[188]

Most vexing, and prominently brought before Chalmers, was police interference with women. It was reported that women were not safe unless accompanied by men. 'The police raped the women and deflowered the young girls.' The writer, Momolu Massaquoi from the Gallinas, was reporting to the Very Revd. the Dean of Chester. When reports were made to the officials, they replied that 'these men have not their wives here, hence they cannot help the wrong'. Cardew in fact used this explanation. However, in the opinion of the writer, 'this is the real cause of the rebellion'.[189] Police activities formed a veritable core of resentment.

(j) Cardew's character

Cardew's approach was that of a 'Victorian missionary rather than a modern administrator' who thought it his urgent humanitarian duty to civilize the savage, whose institutions had nothing 'sacrosanct' about them. Led by this sense of mission, he moved at a speed hardly justified by the available material resources.[190] Cardew knew that severe changes

---

[186] CO 267/440/Conf. 75, Cardew to SS, 1898.

[187] CO 267/441/275, enc., Berkeley to Colonial Secretary, 1898.

[188] Chalmers Report, I, p. 14; Mannah-Kpaka, 'Memoirs', pp. 37–8; CO 267/438/Conf. 43, enc. 4, Parkes to Governor, 1898.

[189] CO 267/451/Revd. Darby, 20 April 1899.

[190] Hargreaves, 'Sierra Leone Protectorate', pp. 60–2.

accompanying the British impact were vitally affecting society, and there were 'accumulated grievances'. But he lacked tact and patience. His approach was in fact that of a paternal military dictator, rather than that of an enlightened civil administrator. He knew the forces at work, but was uncompromising in his haste to get things done. The Protectorate Ordinance introduced more sudden and far-reaching changes and without allowing time for the people to adjust to them, Cardew insisted on immediate payment of house tax. Alternatively, he would have imposed a direct tax on something other than houses. Above all, Cardew did not do much to woo the rulers to the cause of the administration, although the Colonial Office advised it. Instead of passing a Poro Ordinance, he would have got the chiefs to use the Poro to collect tax.

As late as 1905, when the tax was accepted and paid as a *fait accompli*, the people could still not understand a tax on houses. 'The natives consider the assessment of a country as a tax on that country and not as a tax on each house. . . . The money is generally collected by levying a tax . . . on each farm and so the amount is made up, but inhabitants of houses do not pay it all.'[191] In the manner in which it was comprehended by the people, it was not much unlike the traditional taxes they paid. But sociological niceties found no place in Cardew's militaristic thinking. There was thus no serious effort to understand local customs. It has been advanced that this ignorance led to the fatal disaster.

. . . The mind of the negro is not a *tabula rasa* on which the white man may write what he pleases; white law is not to the negro so superior that he is at once pleased with it; on the contrary, the law which seems to us so just is often to him the grossest injustice. Every native tribe is bound together by a system of laws and customs, resting eventually on a religious basis; i.e. resting on certain ideas as to man's nature, his relations to his fellows and to the other world. On the basis of these ideas, different tribes have built up very complex systems of laws and observances, resting on and bearing witness to, certain habits of the mind. . . . The Hut Tax rising in Sierra Leone . . . was not due to any double dose of original sin in the native . . .[192]

[191] CO 267/475/48, Report on Panguma district.
[192] W. L. Grant, 'The Administration of Africa', *United Empire*, 1, 4, 1910, p. 284.

Thus the legal assumptions behind the Protectorate Ordinance were quite contrary to the existing indigenous legal system. Cardew dismissed local institutions and expected the people to see the rationale of European institutions. His lack of compromise was bound to generate conflict.

(k) The 'local crisis' and social revolution

On first contact, co-operation between Europeans and Africans is a more usual response than hostility. But as the contact increases and change intensifies, there appears to be what has been called the 'local crisis'—the pressure from above and beneath which sandwiches the local rulers. This 'local crisis' is both internal and external, 'and reflects the straining dislocation and displacement'. As the 'local crisis' deepens, co-operation becomes sour and when the position becomes finally intolerable, the rulers succumb to one pressure 'in order to resist the other reckoned more formidable'. Collaboration thus gave way to resistance.[193]

Reviewing the disturbances in a typically able dispatch, Cardew explained the 'local crisis':

The true causes, in my opinion . . . lie far deeper down, and they are a desire for independence and for the reversion to the old order of things such as fetish customs and slave-dealing and raiding. It is practically a revolt of the Chiefs, whose authority has been lessened and whose property has suffered through the abolition of slavery. They are sick of the supremacy of the white man . . . they see the old order of things passing away, the fear and reverence paid to their fetish customs diminishing, their authority going from them, their slaves asserting their independence, their children being taught by the missionaries a purer religion and methods of civilization, and on top of it all, comes the house-tax, which is the last straw that breaks the camel's back . . .[194]

The British impact was causing serious strains and stresses, and everything was moving in the direction of disruption of local society. When the Protectorate Ordinance was promulgated, it was tantamount to a social revolution, in the context of

---

[193] E. Stokes, 'Traditional Resistance Movements and Afro-Asian Natioanlism: the context of the 1857 Mutiny Rebellion in India', *Past and Present*, 48, August, pp. 103–4.

[194] CO 267/438/Conf., 28 May 1898, Cardew to SS.

a much undermined African society. The implications of the tax on dwellings symbolized the totality of this revolution. The most onerous part of this revolution, however, was the radical interference in the relations between rulers and ruled which also deprived the rulers of a vast part of their incomes. Their old world, so to speak, was vanishing. When this was symbolized in the house tax, they determined to resist. But it may not be far from the truth to say that it was more their internal sovereignty that the chiefs wanted to regain.

(l) Conclusion: the 'colonial situation'

All the factors enumerated above contributed to the war of 1898. Many had been in operation long before the Protectorate was proclaimed. Had the war been principally against any particular one, it is reasonable to suppose that it would have come earlier than it did.

It is likely that the movement began with limited objectives. But once it got started, it had the snowball effect which developed a xenophobic character. The movement went out of hand, because the leaders were anonymous and the arrangements secret. There were many mixed motives in the resistance movement. The rulers had been subject to much British influence—even control—before 1896, which they did not resent. But the Protectorate shattered this equilibrium, effected a virtual revolution by abrogating the internal sovereignty of the rulers, and symbolized this in the hut tax. Cardew's tactless methods, however well-intentioned, precipitated the war, which brought together for the first time in one determined effort that transcended the limits of their states, people who previously were thought to lack powers of organization and to be too divided to unite. The policy, however, was that of the British Government, as even Lord Selborne admitted.

The effect of the war was felt on both sides. The British feared a recurrence of the disturbances—hence the refusal to release Nyagua and Gbanna Lewis. The people too were made more fully aware of the power of the British Government. Collaborators and Resistors is an irrelevant dichotomy, for while collaborators gained short-term successes, all eventually lost. Structural and territorial fragmentation became a policy dictated by the 'colonial situation'.

The victory of the administration vindicated the new order, and the Colonial Office preferred Cardew's scheme to Chalmers's recommendations. Indeed even before the Chalmers Report was out, the Colonial Office had made up its mind.[195] Chalmers's criticism of Cardew's system was valid, but it is doubtful if his own proposal was any more realistic, particularly as the resistance movement failed, since it amounted in some respects to putting the hands of the clock back. The people accepted the tax as a *fait accompli*, and this was the buttress of the Protectorate administration. To abolish it would have been foolhardy, because any subsequent attempt to impose it would not have been without difficulty. In this respect, it was unrealistic of Chalmers to suggest the abolition of the tax. Cardew regretted the occurrences, but was convinced that he was acting in the interest of the people. In December 1898, he wrote in a confidential dispatch:

In the sense of the responsibility under which I rest for the initiation of the house-tax, no-one can more deeply deplore and regret the sad occurrences which have taken place, but I venture to hope that great good will result from the evil of the past . . .[196]

The rulers could never regain their pre-colonial position. With the British *pax*, they were set on the path of a different historical development.

The new order set the scene for that 'conflictive complex' that has been identified as the 'colonial situation'. Apart from emphasizing the exclusive position of a culturally and racially alien minority that dominated the African majority by its monopoly of physical force, this situation added more complexity to the pre-colonial 'plurality'. It is further characterized by the 'antagonistic . . . relationships between the two societies which [are] explainable by the instrumental role to which the dominated society is condemned'. No doubt the superior technology of the dominating society was bound to accelerate the process of change. The universalization of capitalism by the dominating power through colonialization geared the economy of the dominated society to the structure of the international capitalist system. Throughout the colonial period, these

[195] CO 267/441/Conf. 95, minutes at CO, 1898.
[196] Ibid., Cardew to Chamberlain, 1898.

various new phenomena added to the bewildering complexity of society.[197] The next two chapters will examine some of the aspects of the dynamics of the political process and the resultant cultural synthesis.

[197] George Balandier, *Sociologie actuelle de l'Afrique Noire* (Paris 1963); Pierre L. van den Berghe (ed.), *Africa: Social Problems of Change and Conflict* (San Francisco 1965); I. Wallerstein (ed.), *Social Change: The Colonial Situation* (New York 1966); Karl Marx and F. Engels, *On Colonialism* (Moscow 1968); Bernard Magubane, 'A Critical look at Indices Used in the Study of Social Change in Colonial Africa', *Current Anthropology*, vol. 12, No. 4–5, October–December 1971.

IV

POLITICAL FRAGMENTATION AND ADMINISTRATIVE OSSIFICATION

The 'colonial thesis' and the colonializing ethos

LITERATURE during the colonial period concerning colonial activities has tended to obscure the true picture of African society and the dynamics of the process of change. It usually tended to justify the existing situation. Thus we are made to accept as inherited from the remote past, traditions that only took shape as a response to, or as a direct result of, the 'colonial situation'. That colonialism was established by the method of 'divide and rule' has been rejected by colonialists and scholars alike, and the opposite proposition has been advanced. This colonial thesis, in short, states that the British did not dismantle large polities in Sierra Leone, which did not exist. Rather, there was a 'high degree of fragmentation'—the country being divided up into the numerous chiefdoms we know today, independent and having no common allegiance. It was the British who tried to carve larger units out of this political babel. This chapter will test this thesis.

The colonial interpretation may be excusable on the part of the officials, perhaps, on grounds that they could not have a better perspective since they were prime participants in the very process of colonialization, and being naturally eurocentric in outlook, they utterly believed in the rightness of their actions. Perhaps unwittingly, while professing to preserve the pre-colonial institutions, they radically altered their *raison d'être*, because in the new scheme of things such institutions had to conform to the ethos of the colonial situation. New norms were therefore introduced and the pre-colonial institutions could no longer remain 'pure' but had to respond to the wind of new challenges and novel situations in which they found themselves. Whilst the officials thought they were

preserving what they found in existence, they were totally misguided in their conception. This is not, however, to state that

MAP 7. ADMINISTRATIVE DIVISIONS, 1900

the officials were completely oblivious of the sort of changes
they were introducing, but they believed that they were not
radical to the extent of fundamentally altering the pre-existing
system. To them the changes were subtle and could not (as
was believed) effect radical changes. Yet paradoxically, radical

changes resulted, for the rationale of any changes had to fit into the new context of the colonial situation. This situation which in simplistic terms was the domination of society by a technologically superior minority, meant that the values of the colonizing society were used to judge institutions and actions of the colonized society. In most cases they were opposed and conflicting, but in the colonial situation, the metropolitan ethics prevailed. Thus traditional practices were condoned only if they were not 'repugnant to humanity and civilisation', which was the yardstick of the colonizing power.

Before the Protectorate was declared, it was in the interest of the Freetown administration with its colonial ambitions to prevent large territorial aggregates either from asserting and exerting themselves or, in the case of a declining polity, from seeking to recuperate. When formal rule was proclaimed, the handful of colonial officials, in order to carry out their functions which were grotesquely disproportionate to their numerical strength, had to depend largely on their ability to secure local allies. As Hatch has said, 'Thus conflicts between rival African societies [or any factions for that matter] . . . were exacerbated. . . . The general effect of this imperial impact, therefore, was to aggravate fragmentation within African society and to exacerbate hostility between communities'.[1]

Within this framework of the colonial situation, Balandier has explained:

The colonised society is *ethnically divided* [and even within an ethnic group there are divisions]. These divisions have their root in indigenous history, but are utilised by the colonial power, and complicated by the arbitrary character of the colonial boundaries and administrative subdivisions.[2]

Arbitrary chiefdoms and the policy of 'divide and rule'

Indeed the colonial boundaries and administrative subdivisions were arbitrary. In 1925 the Colonial Secretary T. N. Goddard admitted that, 'the division of the Protectorate into provinces, and of the provinces into districts, *is arbitrary*, and has been dictated by considerations of administrative

[1] John Hatch, *Britain in Africa*, p. 197.
[2] Georges Balandier, 'The Colonial Situation', in van den Berghe, *Africa*, p. 42.

efficiency, due regard being paid to the necessity for including in one district, *where possible*, chiefdoms comprising one tribe or section of a tribe'.[3] Unfortunately, it was not possible to group chiefdoms of 'one tribe or section of a tribe' into the Ronietta district, which comprised Mende and Temne chiefdoms. But the district boundaries could have been redrawn to avoid this. As a colonial official, Goddard may have been honest in his belief that the 'boundaries of the chiefdoms, however, are fixed by prehistoric tradition and native custom, and although disputes constantly arise as to sections of inter-chiefdom boundaries . . . the government does not interfere with chiefdom boundaries unless invited to do so . . .'. The only exception, he added, was the break-up of the Kpaa–Mende state.[4] The position was reiterated by Fenton, a former Chief Commissioner of the Protectorate, that the chiefdoms had been treated as independent of each other, and that although Government in a few cases divided them up or carved new ones, the general pattern of the administration was to preserve the chiefdoms as they were in 1896.[5] Nothing could be a more absurd travesty of historical facts than this, as the evidence points to the exact contrary. However, the effectiveness of this colonial interpretation of African history can be judged by the way it has succeeded in misleading modern scholars. Professor Hargreaves has noted that the 'establishment of the Protectorate implied an arbitrary work of political unification'.[6]

In his recent study of colonial rule in West Africa, Professor Crowder asserts that, 'the British being anti-assimilationist and empirical in spirit, did not, like the French, wish to restructure the countries they administered, only to reform them gradually. Thus chiefdoms were not broken up, except in the obvious case of Ashanti . . .'. He continues that, 'there had never been any traditionally larger unit of centralization' in Sierra Leone other than the 'chiefdom', of which states there were some 200.[7] Professor Little makes the same point.

There was an absence of central authority on any large scale,

[3] Goddard, *Handbook*, p. 103 (emphasis supplied).
[4] Ibid., p. 104.
[5] Fenton, *Outline of Sierra Leone Native Law*, pp. 2–3. See also J. R. Cartwright, *Politics in Sierra Leone, 1947–1967* (Toronto 1970), p. 29.
[6] 'Sierra Leone Protectorate', p. 59.
[7] M. Crowder, *West Africa Under Colonial Rule*, pp. 212 and 225.

although a few fairly important 'hegemonies', like that of Nyagua, were conspicuous and might have expanded still further had not the British 'solidified' existing chiefdoms boundaries. In some cases chiefdoms were connected with each other by family ties which can still be traced in the ruling houses concerned . . .

It is possible that the British found this rather high degree of fragmentation convenient, and even encouraged it, if only for military reasons, in the early days.[8]

Professor Crowder did no primary research on Sierra Leone, but Professor Little's shortcomings may be explained, *inter alia*, in terms of his anthropological methodology, which is inadequate for arriving at historical conclusions. He regards the 'chiefdoms' as autonomous units within a 'hegemony' rather than as sections within a state structure. Although the coastal states were in decline when the British moved in, the 'high degree of fragmentation' is to be explained meaningfully within the context of the colonial situation, not in terms of a purely pre-colonial phenomenon. So also is the 'ruling house' system, and Little's admission that connections between chiefdoms can be traced through family ties of the 'ruling houses' may prove that the families belonged to one territorial unit before they were fragmented into separate chiefdoms, this fragmentation being a colonial phenomenon. According to one Chiefdom Speaker, who is an accredited local historian,

there were then no chiefdoms [before 1896] as they are now termed. Great warriors had ownership over extensive areas. But after the 1898 rebellion the British Government thought it best to split up these areas into chiefdoms, thus ultimately creating a lot of chiefs. This plan they thought would finally weaken the powers of any individual chief, as they indirectly planted disunity in the country.[9]

Although admittedly during the latter half of the nineteenth century the coastal states were in a period of political decline, they nevertheless maintained clear state structures; the *Beh Sherbro* for instance, was not a smashed romantic image as is likely to be supposed, for as late as 1896 the coronation of the *So Kong* of Imperreh, 'was presided over by the Bai Sherbro, the paramount chief, the Suzerain of the whole Sherbro country'.

[8] K. Little, 'Mende Political Institutions in Transition', *Africa*, XVII, i, Jan. 1947, pp. 16–17.

[9] Sahr Matturi, MS. on 'History of Jaiama Chiefdom' (n.d.), p. 11.

At the same time he exacted tribute from the various Sherbro divisions, and in 1897 a dispute between Jong and Imperreh had to be referred to him for settlement.[10]

In 1938, Neil Weir, a District Commissioner, while admitting that 'the chiefdom is the unit in the Sierra Leone Protectorate', frankly gave his opinion that 'it is probable that it is largely an artificial unit and is not part of any indigenous system'.[11]

Within the tentative reconstruction of Mende states described in Chapter I, there were nine states by 1880. In 1899, just after the 1898 war, the 'Records of Paramount Chiefs' listed twenty-seven Paramount Chiefs for the area under review.[12] In 1912 they had multiplied to eighty-two,[13] and the high-water mark was reached by 1924 when there were 115, although this included a few Kono chiefdoms with headquarters at Panguma.[14] Thus it was within the context of an already well-established colonial society that Goddard defined the political position of the chiefdoms:

Each chiefdom is entirely separate and independent, and although there is natural cohesion between chiefdoms composed of peoples of the same tribe and situated in the same locality, no paramount chief can claim pre-eminence over other paramount chiefs . . . either by reason of the area of his chiefdom, the wealth of his people, or the antiquity of his house.[15]

By this time the position had become ossified, and there was no more of the pre-colonial fluidity. There is thus no doubt that it was part of the colonial strategy to fragment in order to establish firmly the colonial hegemony. Once it was established, a reverse process began—that of amalgamation. In 1946 the chiefdoms in the same area under review had diminished to about 106,[16] and in the following year to about ninety-nine.[17]

[10] T. J. Alldridge, *Transformed Colony*, p. 270; Bonthe District, Confidential Minute Papers, 157, 1910; Sherbro District Commissioner's Letterbooks, Alldridge to Colonial Secretary 1896, SLGA.

[11] N. A. C. Weir, 'Native Administration Notes, Sierra Leone, 1938', para. 6, MSS. Afr. S. 1151, in Rhodes House Library, Oxford (hereafter referred to as RHO).

[12] Records of Paramount Chiefs, 1899, SLGA.

[13] Information Regarding Protectorate Chiefs, 1912, SLGA.

[14] Goddard, *Handbook*, p. 104.   [15] Ibid., p. 105.

[16] *Sierra Leone Protectorate: Chiefdoms, Capital Towns, Chiefs' Names, Tribes* (Freetown 1946).   [17] *Sierra Leone Protectorate Handbook* (Bo 1947).

Thus a clearly discernible picture emerges of a systematic policy of 'divide and rule'. Within two decades of the colonial occupation, the entire country had been fragmented into the minute 'independent' chiefdoms that have survived and are so familiar a feature of today's local administration. When this historical fact was openly denied by Sir Andrew Cohen in 1959, he was merely trying to give a colonial administrator's rationale in an age of decolonization. Having earlier correctly stated that British policy stressed 'localism and not central institutions' in the early phase,[18] he later shows the contradiction in colonial policy when he comes out with the colonial apologia: 'It is sometimes assumed that British policy in Africa is based on the principle of divide and rule. This is not correct. The policy is, rather unite, and let them rule.'[19]

At the time, Sir Allan Burns, in a partisan and aptly titled book was defending British policy in similar terms: 'So far from following the policy of *divide et impera*, we have encouraged the inhabitants of the colonies to look beyond the boundaries of tribalism to a larger nationalism.'[20] This interpretation ignores the historical antecedents and only refers to the post World War II period. As the statistics above show, amalgamation became an important policy by World War II. Before that it was one of de-amalgamation. The changing circumstances during and after the war necessitated emphasis on 'central institutions', denied hitherto.

Early fragmentation

It has been argued[21] that, following the completion of the annexation of the coastline, the two interesting points that emerge are the striking imperviousness of the officials to the pre-colonial territorial aggregates and their attempts to create sovereign entities of the sub-units of the states. The officials preferred to deal directly with the sub-rulers who were then made to sign treaties on behalf of specific territorial units. These were then virtually recognized as independent, and the

---

[18] Sir Andrew Cohen, *British Policy in Changing Africa* (London 1959), p. 27.
[19] Ibid., p. 55.
[20] A. Burns, *In Defence of Colonies* (London 1957), p. 72, also pp. 73, 75.
[21] Chapter II above.

signatories as independent rulers. The effect of this colonial action, whether it arose out of a genuine misconception of the situation or from conscious design, was to increase the desire and determination of the chiefs to be independent of the total state structure. With the kings effectively limited to the sections they directly administered, the chiefs came to assume a position of equality with their kings. But the situation could sometimes be more complex than this. The Gallinas example is a case in point where the chiefs were struggling to acquire the *Massaquoi*—in other words, sovereignty. The resultant turmoil was conducive to colonial expansion.

Even before the Protectorate was formally declared, the administration in Freetown was arrogating to itself the supreme political position, which in effect meant that within the colonial structure, the pre-colonial polities which hitherto had been central governments in their own right were converted into units of local administration. The administration would readily spot and immediately frustrate any attempts at political integration or territorial aggrandisement. For instance after the Sofa expedition, the land from Tungea to the Bafi river in Kono was granted to Vonjo, a Chief in the Kpaa–Mende state, by Col. Ellis. Cardew was completely opposed to giving effect to the arrangement. While reminding the chief that the administration had not ratified the grant, Cardew continued:

. . . I was not prepared to recommend that he (Vonjo) should be supported in any attempt to coerce the people in the ceded country, and I directed him not to do so. . . . I do not think it would be politic to make *chief Vonjo, who is of the warrior caste, too powerful.*[22]

Fragmentation was a necessary pre-requisite for the successful implantation of *Pax Britannica*.

In the upper Mende country, in addition to Kai Londo, the 'most powerful chiefs' who were in fact kings, were Makavoray, Nyagua, and Mendegla. Entering into treaty relations with these kings in 1890 would not only secure their alliance but 'have a beneficial effect on trade and the peace of the country will be assured beyond the limits defined by the Frontier Road'.[23] Yet three years later, realizing that Nyagua was

[22] CO 267/408/117, Cardew to SS, 1894 (emphasis added).
[23] Dispatches, 137, Hay to Kurtsford, 31 March 1890, SLGA.

probably the most powerful ruler of the Sierra Leone hinterland,[24] the administration determined to fragment his authority
and territory. In March 1893 three and a half years before the
formal declaration of the Protectorate, Governor Fleming
publicly humiliated Nyagua, an act calculated to break his
power and to fragment his territory. Addressing an assembly of
chiefs at Bandasuma at which there were about 3,000 people,
Fleming thought that there was some 'uncertainty' existing

regarding the position of the chief Nyagwah and as to his powers
with which he is invested as regards other chiefs. [Therefore] I
desire to state that he like the others, who are present today, is a
Treaty Chief for his own country only having entered into a Treaty
similar to those entered into by other chiefs. That as such Treaty
chief he possesses no great[er] powers in so far as the Queen's
Government is concerned, than the others do, that he is only
recognised as the chief of the district to which he belongs, and that
in matters relating to treaties the other chiefs should not receive
instructions or orders from him.[25]

This was certainly an incitement to the sub-chiefs to revolt and
assert their autonomy. Within the new scheme of things, there
was no place for African sovereignty. The administration was
assuming sovereign powers, and kingly titles were clearly obnoxious to the general ethos. All traditional rulers were now
becoming chiefs, even if they had been kings. The assault on
Nyagua, however, proved ineffective until after the 1898 war.

With the formal declaration of the Protectorate in 1896,
African sovereignty, which had been gradually undermined
during the past decade, was finally lost. Kings were henceforth
no more to be heard of, and all treaty chiefs were recognized
as equals and designated 'Paramount Chiefs'. The Ordinance
defined a Paramount Chief as 'a chief who is not subordinate
in his ordinary jurisdiction to any other chief'.[26] Sovereignty
'of the most exalted rank' was now vested in the colonial administration. Although previous kings could still maintain their
traditional relations with their subordinate chiefs, it was those
in whose territories treaties had been signed with many sub-
chiefs who suffered the first blow of fragmentation, for their

[24] Cf. Records of Paramount Chiefs, 1899, p. 213, SLGA.
[25] CO 267/401/113, enc. 1, Fleming's address to chiefs at Bandasuma.
[26] The Protectorate Ordinance, 1896, Cap. II.

sub-chiefs were elevated, and their kings relegated, to the equal rank of Paramount Chief. Thus the delicate federal structure of most states was shattered.

This process was perhaps most clearly seen within the Sherbro state, in which his sub-chiefs had emerged as fairly strong in relation to the *Beh*, during the period of political decline in the nineteenth century. The Records of Paramount Chiefs 1899, listed the following chiefdoms and their chiefs who all formerly belonged to the Sherbro state.

Ronietta District

Chiefdom	Paramount Chief
Shenge and Cockboro	Madam Sophia Neale Caulker
Bagru and Mokassi	Madam Nancy Tucker
Mano Bagru	Sey Lolo
Bompeh	Canray Bah [Caulker]
Ribbi	Pa Kaini
Imperi	Mr. Wilberforce
Mabanta	Bannafema
Timdale	. . . No Paramount Chief at present . . .

Bandajuma District

Krim Country	Momo Ja of Pujehun
Jong	Queen [?] Betsy Gay

It is striking that no mention was made of the *Beh Sherbro* or his successor or his office. In 1910 the son of the exiled *Beh Sherbro*, Kong Cuba, petitioned for the return of his father. Apparently, a paramount chief had been appointed on Sherbro island where the *Beh Sherbro* resided, in the person of Fama Yani, a rival of the ex-*Beh Sherbro*. But his authority seems to have been limited to the island. Yani was arrested for obstructing trade in 1897, but it was later alleged that 'he was made a cat's paw by Gbanna Lewis', the *Beh Sherbro*.[27] The petition was rejected as 'it is absolutely essential that the Government should prevent Gbanna Lewis or his successor or his representative to laying claim to any of the territory in the Protectorate'. Governor Probyn was afraid that

. . . if Gbanna Lewis returns, the people will regard him as the head

[27] CO 267/526/Conf. (A), 20.11.1910, enc. Fairtlough to Col. Sec.

of a pagan tribal authority, and not as a Christian and the importance of the fact that the people will thus regard Gbanna Lewis is due to the peculiarity of the tribal laws respecting succession and the choice of chiefs . . . the return of Gbanna Lewis will enable his son Kong Cuba, alias Herbert Lewis . . . to commence scheming for the overthrow of Fama Yani, the present paramount chief.[28]

In the Gallinas where colonial intervention had prevented the solution to succession struggles, the contestants were each now recognized in their own sections as Paramount Chiefs. Momo Kai Kai became Paramount Chief of Malene Chiefdom, Francis Fawundu of Gallinas and Tunke, 'Queen Nyarroh' of Barri, Momo Fofi of Lower Gallinas, Boakei Mina of Boma as paramount chief of Western Gallinas. Momo Fofi, elected headman of Gendema, the capital of the *Massaquoi*, in 1885, was reported to have 'succeeded chief Jaia Siacca'.[29]

Nominal successor to King Jaya Siaka, Momo Fofi inherited nothing more than a bare fraction of the Gallinas territory. This arrangement perhaps suited all the parties concerned. For the British, it prevented the re-emergence of any strong power. As for the contestants for the imperial title, none lost face, as there was no real successor. Each was firmly entrenched in the territorial unit he had ruled before, and it is possible to believe that, considering the mutual jealousy that existed at the time of the struggles, a contestant would have preferred no victor at all than to see himself lose. Thus rivals would have preferred a situation in which all of them actually lost the struggle. This was bound to introduce an element of parochialism.

Mendegla's state was also easily fragmented. Although he was succeeded by Gbatekaka in 1890, many of his sub-chiefs had signed treaties with Alldridge, and were now recognized as Paramount Chiefs. Gbatekaka himself was limited in his jurisdiction to Gaura proper, which was his nuclear political unit. Those who signed treaties in the other component units of his predecessor's state were each confirmed as Paramount Chief: Amara Samawa of Tunkia, Joseh of Koya, Suway Gayeh, brother of the late Hakawa who signed the treaty, of Dama.

The same process was discernible in the other polities. Only

[28] CO 267/526/Conf. (A), 20.11.1910, Probyn to SS.
[29] Records of Paramount Chiefs, 1899, SLGA.

two of Makavoray's sub-chiefs signed treaties. He himself died in 1897, and was succeeded by Sandi, who was recognized as Paramount Chief of Tikonko. But it was not the same Tikonko over which Makavoray exercised jurisdiction. The two sub-chiefs, Hotagua of Bo and Fakondoh of Baoma, who had signed treaties as well, had their territories separated from Tikonko. By 1899, however, both had died, but Hotagua was succeeded by Bongay, and Fakondoh by Gbolie. A considerable territorial unit, however, remained for the time being under Sandi of Tikonko. Nyagua, being more remote from British influence since his territory stretched much further inland to the north-east, alone signed a treaty on behalf of his own country. No sub-chief of his had signed one. Thus, until he was exiled, he was still the sole Paramount Chief of 'Bambara West'. The fragmentation process in his empire came a little later.

Madam Yoko the most loyal and unflinching collaborator of all the Protectorate rulers, was recognized as Paramount Chief of 'Mendi', or more correctly, of Kpaa-Mende. For the next two decades a semblance of unity was maintained over this state, but it did not escape eventual fragmentation in 1919, probably as part of the general administrative reorganization of the Protectorate in 1920. Administratively this process came in a sudden rush. By contrast, Kai Londo's state was fragmented by a gradual process of erosion that spread over two decades, but by the time of World War I, the process had been completed. Thus within two decades of colonial rule, the hinterland had been fragmented into the minute chiefdoms that are so familiar a feature of today.

Vendetta against the 1898 war

This fragmentation process has been partly explained as a deliberate colonial strategy to destroy strong states and exploit local conflicts so as to maintain the colonial dominance. To some extent also, it can be partly explained as a brutal vendetta after the 1898 war. Cardew minuted that 'chiefs who had either levied war against Government, or instigated others to do so, cannot be condoned'.[30] So that those who collaborated with the

[30] Minute Papers, Confidential, 52/1898, SLGA.

administration were installed as chiefs, and in many instances, this implied a degree of territorial fragmentation. Sophia Neale Caulker, Nancy Tucker, D. F. Wilberforce, Boakei Mina and many other chiefs owed their position to the administration, which had become the source of the legitimacy of traditional authority.[31]

Cardew was adamant in his determination to blot out towns which had taken a conspicuous part in the war. Addressing the Colonial Secretary in a letter on 28 July 1898, Cardew wrote:

Please inform the DC Kwalu that owing to the atrocious murder of the two Missionaries... at Taiama, I consider that place ought never to be allowed to be reinhabited, that the buildings should be razed to the ground and the site of the town blotted out. The DC will be so good as to take the necessary action when opportunity offers to effect this. Rotifunk which was the scene of so many murders of Missionaries ought to be treated in the same way, but for the fact that the Missionary Society of which the victims were members possesses considerable property in lands there and wishes to resume work amongst the natives as soon as the disturbances are quelled, but I think a zone round the Mission Station should be cleared of all native buildings and shall be glad if the DC will carry this out when practicable.[32]

Cardew would have liked to do the same at Shenge, where Thomas Neale Caulker who was 'loyal' was murdered, but the Missionary Society was as anxious to resume work there as at Rotifunk.[33]

In point of fact, Taiama had been destroyed by Col. Woodgate in May 1898 with great loss of life.[34] The site remained deserted for a year. This revenge policy was hardly one to gain the confidence of the people, but rather led to a deterioration of the situation. The people 'seemed cowed but sullen', and the situation was more unsatisfactory in that 'in the Taiama–Mende country . . . the people are still mostly hiding in the bush'. Acting Governor Nathan was of the opinion 'that a revengeful attitude on the part of the Government should now cease',[35] after it had been carried out for a year. It is significant

---

[31] Records of Paramount Chiefs, 1899, SLGA; see also next Chapter.
[32] CO 267/447/Conf. 46, enc., Cardew to Col. Sec., 1898.
[33] Ibid.
[34] CO 267/447/Conf. 49, enc., Ag. DC Hood to Secretary Native Affairs, 1899.
[35] CO 267/447/Conf. 45, Nathan to SS, 1899.

that when Cardew went on leave, no one of his subordinates acted as governor, but Chamberlain sent Nathan out directly from England, a sensible man with a mind of his own very different from Cardew's.

Referring to a plea from Madam Yoko herself, Nathan informed the Colonial Office:

. . . I was petitioned by Madam Yoko, Paramount Chief of the Taiama–Mendi country, to allow the rebuilding of the Taiama towns . . . [which] had been forbidden by Sir Frederic Cardew . . .
The Ag. DC is of opinion that the petition should be granted as the Taiama country is, at present, in a most unsatisfactory and unsettled state, the natives hiding in the bush, and what was formerly an important trade centre remaining a desolate waste. . . . Fori Vong who was chief of Taiama at the time . . . was . . . hanged . . . the order against the rebuilding of Taiama should be rescinded.

The Colonial Office agreed with Nathan.[36]

In July 1899, five important leaders of Taiama, 'Makiah, Kokoyah Karbengwi, Kongo Momoh, Beriwah Pessima, Boku Kundeto', approached Dr. Hood, the acting District Commissioner, with regard to the rebuilding of Taiama. They drew attention to the following points for a reconsideration:

1. Taiama was destroyed with great loss of life by Col. Woodgate . . .
2. Foravong The Chief . . . suffered death . . .
3. Taiama was the largest collection of towns in the Protectorate and the centre of trade and Mohammedanism consequently there is considerable loss of revenue both directly and indirectly.
4. The Amnesty apparently should cover the Taiama people.
5. The fact of the forefathers of the natives being buried on the site of Taiama fills them with the greatest desire to rebuild there and nowhere else.[37]

As a medical officer Dr. Hood welcomed the opportunity to rebuild as 'it would afford . . . an excellent opportunity of instructing the natives how to lay out a town . . .', the sanitation aspect doubtless being uppermost in his mind.[38]

Nathan agreed with Hood, and suggested that the Taiama

---

[36] CO 267/447/Conf. 46, Nathan to SS, 1899.
[37] CO 267/447/Conf. 49, enc., Ag. DC Hood to Secretary Native Affairs, 1899.
[38] Ibid.

towns be rebuilt on the old site. This inflamed the wrath of Cardew who fulminated:

I cannot concur in this recommendation and suggest that the matter should be left in abeyance till my return to the colony . . .

The Secretary for Native Affairs seems to have been unaware of the fact that I also gave orders against rebuilding two other towns, viz: Bumpe, where some native missionaries were killed and the plot of the Mendi rising hatched; and Bambaiya, where Mr. Hughes, Asst. D.C. was murdered. My decision with respect to Bumpe, which was a town of equal, if not greater, importance to Taiama was received without question and I was informed that it was being rebuilt on another site at the time I visited Bandajuma District last February. I have no information with respect to Bambaiya.

. . . I think from a political point of view there should be some such memorial as the obliteration of their sites to mark the sense of the Government at the horrors of which they have been the scenes.[39]

Chamberlain, however, partly motivated by economic considerations, would not wholly agree with Cardew. He saw the urgency of the sanction being given if trade was not to suffer. Cardew capitulated:

. . . I concur in the necessary sanction being given to Madam Yoko to rebuild that town, as I should be very averse to any decision of mine having the effect of delaying or postponing either the return of the natives to their ordinary avocations or the complete restoration of their confidence in the Government.[40]

It is to be inferred that it was in similar bitterness, related to the nature of the Mende war, that Nyagua's territory was fragmented. While he was sent into exile in 1899, he recommended that a trusted servant of his, Farma, be put in his place, thinking that his banishment was temporary and that he would soon return.[41] Farma was appointed by Cardew in September 1900 and he received a commission and a staff.[42] However, a report of 1908 makes it abundantly clear that the process was completed by that time. There were rumours that certain inhabitants were plotting to loot and raid trading

[39] CO 267/451/Cardew, 24 July 1899.
[40] CO 267/451/Cardew, 15 August 1899.
[41] Revd. Dr. Max Gorvie, personal interview, March 1973; Record of Commissioner, Chief and Distribution of Sticks of Office, 1894–1901, SLGA.
[42] Record of Commissioner, SLGA.

stores at Blama and Hangha, both on the railway, and which were formerly within Nyagua's state. Governor Probyn, reporting, explained:

The chiefdoms affected are situated in the area formerly governed by Chief Nyagua. The latter took a prominent part in the Rebellion of 1898, and was deported by the Government; *the area under his dominion was divided by the Government into chiefdoms*, and the people were called upon to elect paramount chiefs in *the new chiefdoms thus created*. The paramount chiefs thus appointed after the rebellion have always been disliked by the Nyagua family, and the plot may be regarded as an attempt by some members of the Nyagua family to bring discredit upon the chiefs.[43]

Demilitarization of the administration and the introduction of the Court Messenger Force

Certainly order was most important to the administration. An important priority of the colonial state was the maintenance of law and order. While the fragmentation process may be said to have become institutionalized, it was necessary to obtain the absolute confidence of the people. Thus when King-Harman took over as Governor from Cardew in 1900, his first concern was to restore confidence in the people by demilitarizing the administration.

At the end of that year, information reached the Governor from the Protectorate that far from the universal peace portrayed by Cardew, there was 'in two districts at least, profound discontent . . .', and threats were being openly expressed of resistance to the collection of the house tax. King-Harman was well aware that the tax was being collected under 'arbitrary and . . . irritating conditions . . . which undoubtedly tend to keep alive a resentful spirit among the people'.[44] The Frontier Police were mainly responsible for this, and the Acting Inspector-General, H. G. Warren, reported on their indiscipline as late as 1901:

They sit down with their detachments in a town and in a week or so have so made friends with the inhabitants and in a short time 'Women palavers' arise not only between the Frontiers and the

[43] CO 267/502/Conf. 29, March 1908, Probyn to SS.
[44] CO 267/457/33, Probyn to SS, 1901.

people, but in many cases with the big men of the town and even the paramount chiefs.

There the Frontier uses his position as a Government Official for the purposes of terrorising those with whom he has disputes. Bribes are freely given and it is very difficult, in fact impossible to stop it.[45]

Warren concluded by suggesting the abolition of out-stations and the concentration of the Frontiers at headquarters.

King-Harman took pains to remedy the situation. Certain places along the frontier, customs stations, centres of trade, and areas of disaffection were to retain detachments of police for the time being. But he gave strict orders to have the posts relieved every month. The rest of the Frontier Police were concentrated at headquarters where the District Commissioner was, and the frequent patrols undertaken were always under European officers.[46]

To pursue the administrative demilitarization to its logical end, King-Harman introduced Court Messengers to take over the civil duties of the Frontiers, whose connection with the civil administration was now only in the provision of escorts in connection with collection of house tax. The District Commissioners agreed that the Court Messengers were sufficient to meet civil requirements.[47]

The Court Messengers evolved as a 'Force' into which they were formally constituted by ordinance in 1907, having constabulary powers, and under the direct orders of the District Commissioner. This was a curious and extraordinary body; in addition to police duties its members performed a multitude of other tasks. Their administrative duties were more important, for with major crimes being infrequent and minor ones effectively handled by the chiefs, no 'District could have been run without the Force'.

They suppressed minor disorders, assessed house tax, kept order during boundary disputes and were the connecting link between the District Commissioners and Paramount Chiefs. . . . They interpreted for Government Officials, escorted them on tour, organised carriers, guarded buildings, specie and stores, carried public mails

[45] CO 267/457/33, Probyn to SS, 1901, enc., Warren to Colonial Secretary, 1901.
[46] CO 267/458/195, Probyn to SS, 1901.
[47] CO 267/459/304, Probyn to SS, 1901.

and supervised numberless constructional works which ranged from small shacks to motor roads—and even during the Second World War to air fields.[48]

At first nominated by Paramount Chiefs, the members of the Force increasingly came to be drawn from ex-servicemen after World War I, since they were 'ready-made' and required little training. With changing conditions especially after World War II, it was expected gradually to phase out the Force in the 1950s. Until it disappeared, it was a 'unique force—probably the cheapest peace force in the Empire'.[49]

The bisection of Bompeh and Banta

However, once confidence had been restored, the fragmentation policy could be continued without fear of resistance. In this regard there are a number of instances, albeit isolated, but which nevertheless may help to reveal a more or less general pattern, of the deliberate bisection of territorial units of appreciable size during the early phase of colonialism. According to the Caulker Manuscript,

. . . Richard Canary Bah Caulker of Bompeh [Sherbro] . . . was one of the ring leaders [of the war of 1898]. . . . Perhaps his hostility to the Government at this point was partially due to the fact that Ribbi, which had from time immemorial formed part of the Bompeh territory, was torn from his control and made into a separate chiefdom in 1897 . . .[50]

Similarly, in 1905, the Banta Chiefdom was bisected. After the death of Bimba Kelli in prison while awaiting banishment in 1899, Bangali Margai was installed as Paramount Chief by the colonial administration over the Banta Chiefdom. His brother Stribey, a wealthy man, lent money to the sub-chiefs and demanded free labour in default of repayment. It was alleged that he had given £42 in loan, but had extorted forced labour from the people far in excess of the amount lent, which the chiefs could not prevent. On investigation the District Commissioner recommended that it was impossible for Margai

[48] 'The Court Messenger Force', article in proposed 'Sierra Leone Encyclopedia' (1949), RHO.
[49] Ibid.; also N. C. Hollins, 'A Note on the History of the Court Messenger Force', *Sierra Leone Studies*, 18 (1932), pp. 78–80.
[50] The Caulker Manuscript, I, *Sierra Leone Studies*, IV, Oct. 1920, p. 24.

to continue to be Paramount Chief of the Mokele section; Governor Probyn

. . . discovered . . . that Stribey . . . had been, for a considerable period, in the habit of forcing the inhabitants of the towns of the sub-chiefs, to do work for his own personal benefit without payment. The evidence on this point was so conclusive that paramount chief Bangali Margai realised the impossibility of his remaining paramount chief over the Mokelli District.[51]

On the recommendation of the District Commissioner, Governor Probyn authorized the people of Mokele to select a Paramount Chief over their own section, and he deposed Margai from that section. The Paramount Chief there took the title of Bimba Kelli, having been 'confirmed . . . as paramount chief of the residue of the Banta Chiefdom'. There were thus two Paramount Chiefs, and each was supplied with a complete list of his respective towns and villages. This was not a boundary dispute.[52] Evidently this action suited two parties—the Mokele people and the colonial administration. For the latter it was indeed a crucial opportunity not to be missed, to bisect a territory, so as to generate or exploit local conflict and maintain dominance. As such the two sections would now become rivals, and the administration was assured of an ally any time it wanted. For the Mokele people, it is reasonable to infer that having been deprived of their lawful traditional ruler, they would have welcomed the opportunity to revive the dignity. In this situation it was theoretically possible for Mokele to lay claims over the whole of Banta Chiefdom, appealing to historical precedent which would only serve to exacerbate more conflict. Margai certainly lost, but it was not a total loss. He owed his position to the colonial administration, and in view of this, it was perhaps best in order to uphold him in his authority, to remove from his control that portion of his territory which was disaffected and likely to flare into open rebellion.

The District Commissioner in making his recommendation, obviously seems to have realized that the Mokele people were apparently antagonized beyond a *rapprochement*. To uphold their product and to institutionalize latent conflict in the colonial interest, the Banta Chiefdom was bisected.

[51] CO 267/473/305, Probyn to SS, 1905.
[52] Ibid.; Decree Book, Ronietta Dist., 1905, SLGA.

Irredentism and colonial abortion

It seems reasonable to argue that fragmentation or dismantlement, having become an institutionalized policy of the colonial power, was vastly contradictory to any attempts to amalgamate fragmented units. The administration readily intervened and suppressed any irredentist movements.

(*a*) The case of Mandu and Dia

For instance, Dia had originally been part of Mandu, but was separated from it in 1902, confining the chief Kabba Sei to the Mandu section only. Bobo Tamba was made Paramount Chief of Dia. This is strikingly similar to the bisection of Banta. However, when Comber became Paramount Chief of Mandu, he intrigued in 1916 to get the two chiefdoms reunited. This happened just after the death of the Chief of Dia, Manyeh.

The District Commissioner quickly intervened and effectively frustrated the plan.[53]

However, to claim a one-sidedness in this process is to distort the true picture. The internal dynamics of the society adapted in an advantageous manner in the new situation. It was thus possible once there arose opportunity for gain, for anyone to take the chance to exploit the new situation. The perpetuation of internally localized conflicts was paradoxically at the same time a vital strategy for the consolidation of colonialism, and for the maintenance of *Pax Britannica*. 'Paramount Chiefs' lost status and power in the traditional context by becoming agents of the British Government. Thus internal dissensions which they had previously been able to control became uncontrollable by them, the dissidents appealing to British authority over the heads of the Paramount, and sometimes securing from the British paramount status for themselves.[54]

(*b*) Momolu Massaquoi and the bid for a greater Gallinas

An illustrative case happened in the Gallinas in 1906.[55] Ostensibly a boundary dispute between the Gallinas Chiefdom as it had become under the colonial contraction, and the Chiefdoms

---

[53] Decree Book, Railway Sub-District, p. 298, SLGA.
[54] See G. Balandier, *Political Anthropology* (Penguin, 1972), p. 161.
[55] The following account is taken from Decree Book, Bandajuma District, SLGA, pp. 22–7, 31.

of Soro and Gbema, the whole matter was in fact due to the irredentist claims of Momolu Massaquoi, Paramount Chief of the Gallinas Chiefdom.

Gbesay Kai Luseni and Murana, Paramount Chiefs of Soro and Gbema respectively, advanced their claim to all towns on the left bank of the Moa River as being part of their territories. They admitted that in some former period, Manna the Gallinas king, had settled some of his people and built towns for them there. But the point of contention was that Manna had not acquired ownership over the land, but had received it as a favour. The Soro and Gbema people on account of their marriage ties with Manna, did not interfere with the ownership of the land, but their rights had been recognized on repeated occasions by the customary small presents given by the Gallinas people in the disputed towns to the Chiefs of Soro and Gbema.

On the other hand Momolu Massaquoi claimed that he had a right to the land as chief and 'successor of Prince Manna of Gendima'. He then entered on a historical account in respect of his claim. He narrated that the claim could be dated to the Lugbu war, when Lalu or Dabemeh country was entirely separate from Soro and Gbema. After a dispute between Soro and Lalu, the latter became a refuge for runaway slaves from Soro, Gallinas, and the neighbouring territories. This war spread and involved Gallinas, Krim, Makpele and other countries. At its conclusion, the Lalu people were either killed or dispersed and, as the Soro people could not pay the indemnity claimed, the Gallinas under King Manna took possession of Lalu, and kept it thereafter. The Chief asserted emphatically that the land was part and parcel of Gallinas, and consequently descended from one chief to another. The war in question probably took place around the mid-nineteenth century, when Manna was building and organizing the Gallinas state.

The chiefs to the dispute admitted that they were 'all closely related and all members of the Massaquoi house, the ruling house in Gallinas or Jaiahun chiefdom'. Momolu Massaquoi was the grandson of King Jaya, who was the brother and successor to Manna; Gbesay Kai Luseni, son of Manna, while Murana's father was a brother of Manna's father Siaka, and Murana married Manna's daughter. Besides, there were other relationships. Manna's wives, the mother of Luseni among them, were daughters of chiefs and headmen of Soro. In the traditional context, they were all of the same family. The relationships between the contenders can be illustrated as follows:

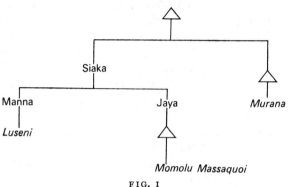

FIG. I

Dr. Maxwell, the District Commissioner who investigated the case, favoured the side of Luseni whose claim, 'whether true or not, is self-consistent', while that of Massaquoi was 'self-contradictory'. Luseni admitted the ownership of certain towns in Soro by Manna and his family, and he brought forward the names of several towns which were still the property of Manna's descendants, but which nevertheless recognized the Soro Chief, and these towns were not far away from those which refused to recognize his authority. Maxwell thought that Massaquoi was contradicting himself when he put forward different claims: first by right of conquest, secondly by the failure of the Soro to pay indemnity for the Lalu war, and thirdly as being the property of Manna and not Luseni. In actual fact these claims reinforce each other as well as Massaquoi's claim, but Maxwell was interested more in the 'logic' of the arguments than in the cultural setting. He was therefore at a loss to understand why Soro should pay an indemnity for the Lalu war if Lalu were outside Soro, and if other people, such as the Krim, also suffered by their slaves running away to Lalu. To him the war appeared to have been waged 'for the suppression of a common nuisance, a revolt of slaves against their masters, and it is difficult to understand why one party and one party only should benefit in this war, for it is claimed that Manna was the only person who gained land . . .'.

From the kinship and territorial relationships already explained, it is reasonable to suppose that Manna's state comprised all the territories whose rulers were now parties to the dispute. Moreover, it is implicit from the account that apart from the slave trade from which Manna apparently derived most of his revenue, he made efforts to expand his territory by conquest. All the territory in question should therefore more properly belong to the direct successor of Manna. The very mixed-up nature of the situation lends support to the hypothesis that if Manna *was* the first *Massaquoi*, all the territories in dispute belonged to him: '. . . there is no natural boundary whatsoever between Soro and Gbema; that Gbema itself has towns on the left bank of the Moa, and that Gpaka and Gallinas are mixed up and alternate with no other'.

Maxwell's bias is apparent when he contradicts himself by quoting the admission of Luseni that Lalu was part of Soro. He was certainly in difficulty deciding this matter:

Between these two conflicting traditions it is difficult to decide, but the one advanced by Bese Kai Luseni has the merit of self-consistency—that advanced by Momo Massaquoi is self-contradictory. We are thus drawn to the third view that the towns owned on the left bank of the Moa are possessions of a family and not part of a chiefdom.[56]

If the towns were possessions of a family then it is Maxwell who would not admit that the towns belonged to the territory of the family that owned them, in spite of the fact that he was well aware that 'the possession of certain lands in his [Manna's] family would not abrogate chiefship rights though of course, these rights would not be pushed to an extreme considering the relationships existing. I hold it established that *chiefship rights have been formerly maintained by their assertion* . . .'.[57]

It would thus appear that Maxwell himself was biased when he ruled against Massaquoi for attempting to maintain his chiefship rights by asserting them. He held it as a point against the chief that he had administered oaths to his witnesses, and frankly opined before summarizing his finding:

It has been previously decided that the position claimed by Momo

---

[56] The following account is taken from Decree Book, Bandajuma District, SLGA, pp. 25-6.   [57] Ibid. (emphasis supplied).

Massaquoi as Paramount Chief of all Gallinas peoples in succession to Manna and Jiah is untenable. . . . *It is also unnecessary to settle the exact position Manna and Jiah occupied. Whatever it was, the chief at Gendema is merely now chief of Gallinas and has no position of authority over other Vai chiefdoms.*[58]

Thus an abundant display of *Realpolitik* is implicit in the commissioner's finding, as he ignored the cultural background and history. The colonial administration had accelerated the disintegration of the Gallinas state in order to facilitate the colonial occupation. The parochialism exercised in this process generated potential sources of internal conflict, as is demonstrated by the dispute just investigated. No ruler recently elevated to the position of Paramount Chief would, in the nature of traditional politics, without the intervention of the colonial administration, readily agree to abdicate his authority and territory to another who laid irredentist historical claims. When Maxwell entered his finding, it was clear that he was reaffirming the colonial situation, and was interested in maintaining the divisions to allow the colonial administration ample elbow-room for political manœuvre and intrigue in order to maintain the colonial dominance.

There is no evidence that the land in question on the left bank of the Moa forms part of Gallinas chiefdom. The land and towns in question must be considered part of the Soro and Gbema chiefdoms and must show respect to these chiefs as paramount chiefs. The Gallinas people occupying these towns shall not be disturbed in their ownership and shall be treated in all respects like Soro and Gbema peoples so long as they show allegiance to the properly constituted chiefs. Any failure on their part to do so and any attempt to transfer this land to another chiefdom shall be regarded as a defiance of the settlement and shall be dealt with accordingly.[59]

The following month, April 1906, Momolu Massaquoi was deposed in 'view of the gross misgovernment that has undoubtedly been going on in the Gallinas chiefdom for a number of years'.[60] On 24 April, he was given only eight days to go into exile. The chiefs were asked to elect a Regent. It turned out that it was none other than Kai Luseni of Soro, who according to Maxwell's previous ruling should not have had any hand

[58] Ibid., pp. 24–5. [59] Ibid., p. 27.
[60] CO 267/484/79, enc., Maxwell to Col. Sec.

in the government of the Gallinas Chiefdom, who 'presented Momo Gotto in the name of the people as Regent'.[61]

It is thus possible to assume that the colonial administration considered Momolu Massaquoi a dangerous chief. He persistently tried to reclaim the other dismembered sections of the Gallinas, but was always ruled against. In 1903 Dr. Hood had ruled against him; in 1906 Dr. Maxwell ruled against him. Apparently it was thought better to remove the chief, who in view of his previous stubborn activities, would be likely to disturb the colonial peace. Whether or not the charges against him were proved beyond all reasonable doubt, it is obvious that the colonial administration mistrusted this chief. As an educated African—particularly an African educated in the United States—Massaquoi was inevitably suspect to the colonial authorities, who feared such people, once they had ceased to be useful to them. D. F. Wilberforce of Imperreh, installed after the 1898 war, suffered a similar fate once he had completed the work of 'pacifying' the country. At all events the colonial administration would not permit Massaquoi to reclaim so large a territory, and it exploited the feeling of resentment by the Paramount Chiefs of Soro and Gbema against Massaquoi. It is even quite likely that the administration itself incited the chiefs and people to prefer charges against this chief in order to have a semblance of legal basis for removing him. As long as there appeared prospects for gain, anyone who felt he had the opportunity took the chance to exploit the new situation. Thus the continuation of internal local disputes was at the same time functional in the consolidation of colonialism.

Integrity and disintegration: the paradox of Kpaa–Mende

In spite of the bitter memories of the activities of the Mende in the 1898 war, the administration was reluctant to apply its fragmentation policy to the territory claimed for its appointee, Madam Yoko. For despite the fact that technically subchiefs of hers, such as Quee of Jama, Kargobai of Damballa, and the Taiama chiefs had signed treaties, the colonial administration tried to uphold her in authority more than she could actually exercise. This was to make inevitable the break-up

[61] Decree Book, Bandajuma District, p. 31, SLGA.

of the Kpaa–Mende state after her death. But for the present, the Records of Paramount Chiefs merely named Yoko as Paramount Chief of 'Mendi', implying thereby Kpaa–Mende. There was no mention of Quee, or Kargobai, or their successors.

But it can be said that once the balkanization of the traditional states had begun, it tended to have a snowball effect in terms of the internal dynamics of the society. Ambitious headmen put forward claims as Paramount Chiefs, knowing well that if they argued their case logically and claimed the 'hereditary right', which the administration set as a yardstick for measuring the legitimacy of any claims, there existed possibilities of their success. It is not being claimed that this was exactly what happened in the Kpaa–Mende state. But ever since the recognition of Yoko as chief, depending on the support of the colonial administration rather than on the Mende political system, factors were generated which began to work gradually in favour of the disintegration of the state. The administration's effort to uphold her could not arrest the process of internal decay which the very fact of Madam Yoko's ascendancy had set in motion. While the colonial administration favoured her, her sub-chiefs, in the technical sense that they were rulers of territorial units within the state of which she was ostensibly the head, virtually ignored her and conducted their affairs in due obedience to the indigenous pattern. To them the position she held in the eyes of the administration was an innocuous one, a kind of ambassadorial status to negotiate their external affairs, with which the real chiefs had practically nothing to do. Quite apart from the fact that most of her sub-chiefs had demonstrated their independence during the 1898 war, by the early phase of the colonial administration they had become virtually autonomous, and were only kept within the state structure in an uneasy alliance due to the support Yoko received from the Freetown administration.[62]

This tendency was clearly discernible even before Yoko died, and it can be concluded that the colonial administration was merely delaying the inevitable. In 1905 there is reference

---

[62] Abraham, 'Traditional Leadership', Chaps. I and VI; Darrell Reeck, 'Innovators in Religion and Politics in Sierra Leone', *International Journal of African Historical Studies*, V, 4, 1972, pp. 606–8.

to Lunia, Vanjelu, and Bagbeh as chiefdoms.[63] These three were in fact sections of the Kpaa–Mende state furthest east, and therefore the remotest from central pressure, let alone control. Thus even during the reign of Madam Yoko, they had asserted their autonomy. While the colonial administration wanted to uphold Madam Yoko, it nevertheless had to be realistic. But where circumstances permitted, it did much to delay the collapse of a decadent edifice. It was realized that Vanjelu 'properly belongs to Gba Mendi, and will probably be merged in that chiefdom shortly'.[64] With this attitude prevailing, the Paramount Chief 'Momoh Gittai [was] deposed and deported for oppression'. The chiefdom was then merged with Kpaa–Mende 'and Mika Goro put in charge under Madam Yoko'. This event occurred in February 1906, six months before Madam Yoko died.[65] Vanjelu thus lost its paramountcy, albeit temporarily.

On the death of Madam Yoko, her brother Lamboi 'was unanimously selected as successor . . .' on 21 August 1906.[66] Ten days later, His Excellency 'approved of chief Lamboi's appointment on six months' probation'. Ninety-five chiefs and sub-chiefs signed their acceptance.[67]

The advent of Lamboi was not conducive to the continued policy of the administration to uphold the chiefdom in gratitude for the support and alliance of the late Madam Yoko. Meanwhile the sub-chief of Moyamba Section, Momoh Gulama had died and in July 1907 'Chief Lamboi and all men of note' elected Mboyawa in 'place of his late brother'.[68] This was perhaps one of the few memorable events that Lamboi participated in with regard to the exercise of his authority, for, a year or two later, he was struck down with paralysis that lasted nearly a decade before he died. In the dry season following the election of Mboyawa, Lamboi made a tour of his chiefdom. According to Ranson,

The story is told that at Senehun in Kamajei chiefdom [apparently

[63] Intelligence Diary, Moyamba District, 1906, p. 15, SLGA.
[64] Ronietta District, Decree Book, 1908, pp. 20, 27, 70, SLGA.
[65] Moyamba District Intelligence Book, p. 34, SLGA.
[66] Intelligence Diary, Moyamba District, 1906, pp. 10, 14, SLGA; Moyamba District Intelligence Book, p. 34, SLGA.
[67] Ronietta District Decree Book, 1905, SLGA.
[68] Intelligence Diary, Ronietta District, 30. 7. 1907, SLGA.

not a chiefdom then], he discovered a witchcraft gown hanging on a tree and attempted to grip it. As he did so, Lamboi became paralysed and the infirmity stayed with him all his life . . . he was unable to rule any longer by himself, so Kpungbu Kangaju chief of Bauya, came from Kongbora [section] to Moyamba to act as Regent.[69]

By 1910 it had become apparent that it would no longer be possible to save Kpaa–Mende from disintegrating. While Lamboi was still alive, the administration would show him gratitude on account of his late sister, but there were clear indications that the inevitable would be conceded as conditions worsened. Thus the Ronietta District Report of 1910 stated:

Proposals were set on foot to break-up the Gbah–Mendi chiefdom. The chiefdom as it at present exists, is not an historic unit, but is the product of a fusion of a number of formerly independent chiefdoms under one administration. Even before Madam Yoko's death it was felt that the cohesion of the chiefdom would suffer on her demise. Her brother the present chief Lamboi however, has succeeded in retaining the country intact, but with weakening power, chief Lamboi is now paralysed, and as there is no fitting successor to take his place, it has been felt desirable to meet the inevitable reorganization of the chiefdom. Chief Lamboi was himself one of the first to suggest this step and is using his influence to bring it to a successful issue. Beyond a single meeting held at Taiama in October at which all the sub-chiefs were present, no further steps have as yet been taken.[70]

Primarily internal factors were gradually making for the erosion of the political structure and its disintegration into its component parts. But the officials were blind to the fact that the situation as it existed by 1910 was the result of a slow process of disintegration, necessitated in the first instance by the ascendancy of Madam Yoko, and secondly by the colonial impact. To say that the various sections were formerly independent chiefdoms fused together for administrative purposes under Madam Yoko, is to show a complete misunderstanding of the pre-colonial state system. It is possible to conjecture that had a strong king succeeded Movee instead of Madam Yoko,

[69] B. H. A. Ranson, *A Sociological Study of Moyamba Town, Sierra Leone* (Zaria 1968), pp. 21–2.
[70] CO 267/531/238, 5 May 1911, Report of Ronietta District for 1910.

the colonial administration would have had to contend with a strong power, and could have precipitated the disintegration of the state only by consciously dismantling the federal structure. The 1910 Ronietta Report considers the sections to have been previously independent because of the very nature of their existence at the time and the manner in which they operated.

However, once the process of internal decay had begun, owing partly to the external colonial impact and partly also to the internal dynamics, it is difficult to believe that it could have been arrested. While it may be true that Lamboi 'did not possess the capacity for ruling that his sister had', the process of internal dissensions cannot be attributed to him. It was a legacy bequeathed to him. Thus while 'the union of the chiefdoms [sections] has rather slackened, at the same time more settled conditions have tended in the same direction, namely to the restoration of the several chiefs as themselves paramount rather than subject'.[71]

Although the Regent Kangaju who followed Lamboi tried as hard as he could, it was impossible for him to control the affairs of the state and to halt the process already well advanced.

The Regent Kangaju is a very willing man and is readily accepted by the people and sub-chiefs. The task is however, rather too large for him. It has been thrust upon him rather than sought, and he loyally tries to do the work, though not equipped for the same by nature.[72]

Once Kangaju had moved from Bauya to Moyamba, the people regarded his jurisdiction as extending effectively over the Moyamba section alone, while retaining only 'residuary powers' with regard to the other sections of the state. Since he was clearly a senior chief, because he was Regent Chief of all Kpaa–Mende, the people tended to ignore Mboyawa, the chief of Moyamba. It was thought that Kangaju was exercising Mboyawa's authority. This was bound to generate conflict. In pre-colonial politics, the king was also the chief of his own section of the state. This obviated any duplication in the exercise of administrative authority. Thus, since Kangaju was

[71] Information Regarding Protectorate Chiefs, 1912, SLGA.
[72] Ibid.

senior, the people looked up to him rather than Mboyawa. The administration, impervious to the nature of the indigenous constitutional practice, was at a loss to understand this development. To them, Mboyawa and Kangaju represented different levels of authority that were quite clear. To the people, it was a conflicting situation, and they therefore chose to resolve it by accepting the authority of Kangaju, the senior. The two levels of administrative jurisdiction were meaningless to them. The administration was forced to intervene and positively clarify the position. Therefore,

A meeting was held at Moyamba on the 5th July [1915] to explain to the people the exact position of sub-chief Buyawa. It was pointed out that sub-chief Buyawa although he had been selected as successor to the late Momo Grama [Gulama] as sub-chief of the Moyamba section had not, especially in recent years, been upheld in his position by the Paramount Chief or the Regent Chief, and that the people instead of looking up to him as their immediate head to a great extent ignored him. It was pointed out that this state of things was harmful to the country. The Regent Chief acting for the Paramount Chief, who was incapacitated, was unable to obtain the assistance from the sub-chief he was entitled to. . . . It was pointed out to the people that sub-chief Buyawa was in future to be looked up to as sub-chief of the Moyamba section.

It was further plainly explained to them that Chief Lamboi had for many years been unable to perform the duties of Paramount Chief owing to the state of his health and that Kangaju had during these years been in the position of Regent Chief, having been recognised by the Government, and they were given to understand clearly that they were to look to him as the virtual head of the whole Gpa–Mendi chiefdom, he acting as the Regent Chief for the Paramount Chief Lamboi.[73]

Nevertheless, it is doubtful whether the administration succeeded in this until Kangaju returned to Kongbora as Paramount with the break-up of the state in 1919.

By this time, the situation had deteriorated seriously, and the administration was forced to take notice of it. The Report on Ronietta District for 1914 clearly states that

. . . the Gpa–Mende chiefdom nominally under chief Lamboi who is paralysed, is extremely loosely held together. It is quite anticipated that on the demise of this chief, *many of the sub-divisions will*

[73] Ronietta District Decree Book, 1915, SLGA.

clamour for separation which, without doubt, will have to be conceded. This great chiefdom (probably the greatest in the whole of the Protectorate) comprises twelve sub-chieftaincies . . .[74]

The process of disintegration long begun was now reaching its logical conclusion. The District Commissioner tended to lay some blame on Kangaju for being 'rather weak and disinclined to exert his authority', and therefore 'would recommend the Gpa-Mendi being split up on the death of Lamboi'.[75] This was a rather unfair assessment of Kangaju, for the District Commissioner ignored the actual forces at work, which made Kangaju perhaps nothing more than a victim of the circumstances set in motion from two directions: from the colonial administration, and from the internal politics of the society. The state had in all manifestations disintegrated into its component units.

The death of Lamboi was probably long awaited. On 26 December 1917 the last king of Kpaa-Mende died, and the Regent Kangaju continued in office.[76] But there is evidence of intrigue against him. In April 1919 a certain F. B. Combo drew the attention of the administration to the state of affairs in which

. . . those who are set up to administer the Government are not going according to the rules of our country and customs. Those who have the right to rule are always shut out, through by bad advices [*sic*] given to the District Commissioners. I believe that when a King dies, his son is to succeed him.

Now in the case of Madam Yoko . . . [she] left her brother to succeed her. For sometime this brother fell sick; so he got one of his men Kangaju . . . to assist him in managing the affairs of the country tending that after his death his sons will succeed him.

Now Kangaju seeing that . . . [Lamboi] is dead, wants to take the right of the crown from the boys. *Now this Kangaju was the one who 'oined in the raid of 1898 together with Boyawah. . .*[77]

The writer was certainly misguided in his opinion that in customary law succession is from father to son. On the contrary, it is collateral, from brother to brother, more or less.

[74] CO 267/564/89, enc. (emphasis supplied).
[75] Moyamba District Intelligence Book, pp. 14–15, SLGA.
[76] Report on Ronietta District, 1917, CO 267/577/76, enc.
[77] CO 267/548/F. B. Combo, 7.4.1919 (emphasis added).

Moreover, he was trying to discredit the Regent by alleging that he was active in the 1898 war. All this is evidence of intrigue. Governor Wilkinson caused an investigation to be made. The District Commissioner, Ronietta District, reported that the sons of Lamboi, in whose interest Combo was ostensibly writing, had disclaimed any knowledge of him. Lagao Lamboi, the eldest surviving son of the late chief Lamboi, was staking a claim for the chiefship, but dissociated himself 'entirely from the petition and states that "Combo" is evidently an assumed name'.[78]

There seem to be grounds for believing that a proper successor was sought to Lamboi, and in the election, probably in October 1919, Kangaju and Lagao Lamboi were contestants. Kangaju is reported to have been elected as Paramount Chief, while Lagao lost. The latter 'states now that as the people did not want him, he is content to "sit down" under paramount chief Kangaju . . . who is a relation of his'. There is also reason to believe that Lagao petitioned earlier stating his claims but that Wilkinson replied that 'Paramount Chief Kangaju had been elected by the people and that I was not prepared to interfere with the people's wishes'.[79]

There is perhaps more ill-feeling in the post-Lamboi period of politics than is hinted at in the above paragraph. A more detailed study will highlight this. Later in the year 1919, 'the Gpa Mendi country was divided into thirteen chiefdoms . . .'.[80] It is, however, possible to surmise that the division of the state into thirteen chiefdoms already existed in reality, and in the light of the proposed administrative reorganization of 1920 it was only logical to go ahead and, in the interests of administrative efficiency, make the *de facto* division *de jure* as well. As Goddard explained in 1925, 'the division was made at the instance of the Government, as it was found that the area was too large to allow of efficient administration by one Tribal Authority'.[81]

But this seems an oversimplified explanation. The area had been administered by one 'tribal authority' since pre-colonial times. The installation of Yoko, with no traditional authority,

[78] CO 267/583/455, Wilkinson to SS, 1919.   [79] Ibid.
[80] Report on Ronietta District, 1919, CO 267/586/173.
[81] Goddard, *Handbook*, p. 104.

as Paramount by the British, caused the kingdom to break up. Even after the break-up of the state, dissatisfied groups in the potential conflict situation would stake claims to territory, chiefship, or autonomy. After all, in all other parts except Kpaa-Mende, before 1920, the people had seen the administration recognizing minority claims and splitting up territories.

Availing themselves of the opportunity of perhaps getting a chiefdom of their own, the people of the Mokori section of Fakoi Chiefdom, formerly a section of Kpaa–Mende, made claims to independence in 1921. It seems that only the previous year they had made similar claims which were not admitted by the District Commissioner Hollins. Thereafter they adopted 'a policy of passive resistance'. These people claimed that seventy-five years earlier they were under the Taiama chief, and that he had given them the bush they were currently occupying. But in Madam Yoko's time, they came under Kwellu (now Fakoi). Paramount Chiefs Kangaju of Kongbora, Mboyawa of Kaiyamba, Nuyaba of Gbo, Yoki of Nyawa–Lenga, Lappia of Seilenga, Molu Briwa of Kori, and Yavana of Kowa were present at a meeting at Moyamba in April 1921 at which the Mokori people 'were given clearly to understand that they had no right to independence and must remain under Farkoeh chiefdom'.[82]

The balkanization was already sufficient for the purposes of the colonial administration, but even after the precedent was set, internal conflicts were still latent. The exploitation of such situations for personal self-aggrandisement was becoming burdensome to the administration once colonial dominance was firmly established.

From greater to smaller Luawa

There is a more complete set of evidence regarding the dismantlement of Kai Londo's state. On the polity itself, there is no lack of written material,[83] but it is necessary to give a brief

[82] Moyamba District Decree Book, SLGA.

[83] N. C. Hollins, 'A Short History of Luawa Chiefdom', *Sierra Leone Studies*, 14, June 1929; W. R. E. Clarke, 'The Foundation of Luawa Chiefdom', *Sierra Leone Studies*, n.s. 8, June 1957; Protectorate Literature Bureau, *Kailondo Kɛɛ Ndawa* (Bo: Bunumbu Press, 1953); Max Gorvie, *Our Peoples of the Sierra Leone Protectorate* (Lutterworth Press, 1944); A. Abraham and B. Isaac, 'A Further Note on the

resumé of how Kai Londo extended and consolidated his empire by conquest, before examining the dismemberment of the state, for the colonial administration undid just what Kai Londo had done.

N. C. Hollins, the District Commissioner, who examined the history of Luawa and wrote on several indigenous customs, gave in the Pendembu District Intelligence Book perhaps the best brief account of the formation of Kai Londo's state. The account is of further interest in illuminating the pattern or nature of the political system before the period of state expansion through conquest or the demonstration of power that began about the mid-nineteenth century. The people were already organized into states, but the states were numerous and had no large political framework of the kind known by the 1880s. In all probability state formation in this region was a historically recent phenomenon,[84] and the organization into larger polities was a movement of the nineteenth century. It is also highly likely that the way in which the states expanded reflected their hierarchical and bureaucratic character. The minor states which were conquered or brought into the larger polities of the latter nineteenth century retained their basic organization. Sometimes the king appointed one of his own warriors to be the chief of a subjugated state, but once he had done this, the king left the administration entirely in his hands. Thus the state took on a kind of federal character composed of the various sections or units that had been brought into a new political machine. The section was divided into subsections, each under its own chief, and so logically down the ladder to the village level. Even the village, if large enough, was divided into compounds, and each compound head was a chief in his own right. The process of creating larger polities out of the smaller states created a situation of flux and fluidity. As Hollins recorded,

Previous to the time when Ndawa of Bandajuma (old W.A.F.F.H.Q.

History of Luawa Chiefdom', *Sierra Leone Studies*, N.S. 24, Jan. 1969; K. Wylie, 'Innovation and Change in Mende Chieftaincy, 1880–1896', *Journal of African History*, 2, 1969; A. Abraham, 'Traditional Leadership'; Alldridge, *The Sherbro*; M. McCall, 'Kailondo's Luawa and British Rule' (York University D.Phil. thesis, 1975); K. Wylie, 'The Politics of Transformation: Indirect Rule in Mendeland and Abuja' (Michigan State University Ph.D., 1967).

[84] Abraham, 'Traditional Leadership', Chap. II.

Railway District) raided this part of the country, and Kailundu became famous as a warrior, and drove him out, the country was divided into a great many chiefdoms owing allegiance, in varying degrees, to any chief who for the moment had sufficient power to enforce it . . .

Kailundu's . . . father Dori, originally lived in the Wunde country near Koendu (close to Dukono) but came over and settled south of the Moa river at the town of Komadu, near Mano. He was taught war by Pauwo Bundu of Giema. . . . Kailundu . . . united and made [the country] strong, and all the chiefs in it owed their power and wealth to him . . .

When Ndawa of Bandajuma raided and ravaged the country, burning Giehun, Nyandahun etc. chiefs Masa, Pauwe, Bundu, Bona, Jimmi, Segba and Bundeh met with Kailundu to discuss what should be done. Kailundu asked the others what they would give him if he defeated Ndawa and they all swore to make him chief of the whole country should he defeat him. Kailundu agreed and defeated Ndawa at Ngiehun. . . . After this Kailundu was accepted as Paramount chief . . . later he built Kanre Lahun [Kailahun]. . . . [He] raided Vahun, in the Guma country. . . . Kai Kai chief of Tungi, came to Kanre Lahun and agreed to sit down under him. He made war on Towe (Shaffa) of Tengea, and compelled Tengea to recognise him as paramount chief. . . . He carried the war further east into the Gbah country (Bandi's), took the chief Fobawuru prisoner to Kanre Lahun and killed him there, because he would not agree to sit down under him. He joined Kafina . . . crossed the Mafessa with him, after a battle at Wulade, and helped Kafina to make the tribe east of the Mafessa sit down to him. Later he carried war into the Bande country, and defeated them at Popalahun, and made them submit to his rule . . . in 1895 Kailundu died.[85]

This account sketches the creation of a greater Luawa state under Kai Londo. The new polity was not, however, to survive its architect.

Kai Londo was a firm ally of the colonial administration, and Alldridge personally admired the king, apparently because he was amenable to his colonial designs.[86] But it was in the interest of the colonial administration, in order to establish the colonial peace, to dismantle the state structure of their ally's empire, particularly as it comprised various ethnic units. In 1896 a few months after the death of the king, a successor was still not found. Cardew who was on a tour of the interior in March seized upon this as

a convenient opportunity *for rearranging the tribal limits* of the Luawa and Bombali [Kpombai] peoples, who were under Kai Lundu and of *excluding therefrom certain* Kissi towns which also paid him allegiance. I decided before approving of any appointment to ascertain for myself the exact limits of the Luawa and Bombali tribes, and with this object I left here on the 6th instant . . . I have thus been able to determine the precise limits of these districts on the Kissi side, which is of most importance . . .

The policy of excluding from these districts any Kissi towns is desirable for two reasons:

1. Because it is very doubtful whether the chiefs will transfer their allegiance to any successor of Kai Lundu, and a tribal fight might ensue in an effort to compel them, and

2. Because two at least of these towns be within the Liberian sphere of influence. This is even the case with the eastern portion of Luawa and Bombali, and it is doubtful, Major Grant informs me, whether the true position of Kare Lahun itself may not be found east of the 13° West of Paris . . .[87]

By the time Cardew had determined the extent of Kai Londo's state, the 'principal persons' had agreed on a successor, Fa Bundeh, 'who was Kai Lundu's Prime Minister and General, and is certainly the strongest man in the country'. Cardew had an interview with Fa Bundeh and informed him that he would only recognize him and 'approve of his appointment' if he gave up his claims to the more distant parts of the state, and confined his jurisdiction to Luawa proper and Kpombai. Fa Bundeh agreed to the 'limitations imposed' and consented not to exact allegiance from Kundo, Kangawa, Foya, and others.[88] Thus the state of Kai Londo was by 1896 contracted virtually to the core from which the king had expanded his authority.

Apart from this, a very ugly anomaly arose on the delimitation of the international frontier. In this situation, the principal actors were more concerned with matters of European diplomacy than with African politics. Before the boundary was agreed upon, Cardew, not wanting to cheat an ally of the

[87] Dispatches, Cardew to Chamberlain, Conf. 19, 10 March 1896, SLGA (emphasis added).
[88] Ibid.

administration who had proved so loyal, warned the Colonial Office:

I venture to suggest that in the demarcation of our territory between the source of the Niger and the Liberian frontier, tribal limits should be followed as far as possible, and I would specially recommend that the territory of Kai Lundu should be kept intact [after judiciously pruning it of undesirable territories] . . .[89]

In spite of this warning and recommendation, the result of the negotiations between Britain and France in 1894 fixed the boundary along a straight line 13° west of Paris. No African interests were here considered, for the division cut Kai Londo's territory into two.

After ascertaining the true position, Cardew addressed the Colonial Office on the subject, drawing attention to the ugliness of the situation.

. . . it will be seen that a large section of the district, comprising perhaps the most important parts, falls within Liberian territory.
    Such a partition is most unfortunate, for the part cut off comprises of the theatre of the warfare that has for 4 or more years been going on between Kai Lundu and the Kissi, Bandemeh and Bandeh chiefs. The Liberian Government has no power to quell these disturbances, and moreover, the combatants do not acknowledge its authority, and this Government is precluded from interfering by the fact that the disturbed area lies to the East of 13° west of Paris. Thus we are unable . . . to assist a loyal chief who is pressed by numerous foes, and have to tolerate warfare on our confines which ruins the trade of the country, and moreover the incongruity exists that this chief is called upon to give a divided allegiance on the one hand to Great Britain and on the other to Liberia. It is obvious such a state of affairs must be fraught with great inconvenience to the proper administration of affairs in this quarter of the Protectorate and the partition of his country by an arbitrary line entails a peculiar hardship on chief Kai Lundu. I venture to suggest if practicable, a readjustment . . . of the frontier . . .[90]

In the following year Cardew, with grave apprehension, ventured to suggest a way of solving the problem—'a give-and-take principle for the rectification of that frontier'. The partition of Luawa and Kpombai, he further warned the

[89] CO 267/408/131, Cardew to SS, 1894.
[90] CO 267/417/Conf. 40, Cardew to SS, 1895.

Colonial Office in apprehension of the imminent division, 'is most unworkable and unsatisfactory'.[91]

Cardew was not only motivated by humane consideration for the suffering that was brought on Kai Londo by the arbitrary division of his territory, but he was also concerned to maintain the colonial peace. This meant, *inter alia*, that those areas from which war was fermented, must be effectively controlled, so as not to prejudice trade. The Liberian Government was effete, and could not control its own hinterland. Therefore, Cardew feared, if the theatre of war were allowed to go to Liberia, it would continue to afford 'a case of operations for warfare in our protectorate'.[92] This was no groundless anxiety. In February 1896, Momoh Bahoni, a Gbandi chief from the Liberian side, attacked and burnt two towns in Kpombai, part of which was in Liberian territory, but the greater part in the British sphere.[93]

Alldridge greeted the situation with misgivings, but he accepted it as a *fait accompli*:

This is one of these curious divisions that sometimes arise in boundary delimitations, as it had so divided the Luawa country that one half, from the town of Gehun, is British, while the other half is Liberian. In consequence of this division, the chief of Luawa is just now, so to speak, divided; his residential town being Kanre-Lahun in Liberia, while Gehun in the British Protectorate is also part of his territory.[94]

In this dilemma a genuine concern was manifested by Hemming at the Colonial Office. With a diagrammatic representation to illustrate his point, he minuted:

It is the people from [the eastern half] that Col. Cardew wants to deal with. They don't cross the boundary to the British side, but they attack Kai Lundu on the Liberian side, and he being very naturally utterly unable to comprehend how his territory can be divided between Great Britain and Liberia, looks to us as the strongest power to protect him, and when he is told this cannot be done, he threatens to throw off all allegiance or connection with us. This it is very desirable to prevent.[95]

[91] Dispatches, Conf. 19, 10 March 1896, SLGA.
[92] CO 267/412/Conf. 84, Cardew to SS, 1894.
[93] Dispatches, Conf. 19, 10 March 1896, SLGA.
[94] Alldridge, *Transformed Colony*, p. 130.
[95] CO 267/421/Foreign Office, 5 September 1895, minute by Hemming.

In trying to solve this problem, the Colonial Office was hamstrung by the Foreign Office's concern about relations with France rather than by the practicality of the situation. For the man on the spot, the problem was urgent and desperate, and consequently it needed a desperate remedy. Cardew's reactions can be better imagined than described, when after being invited to attend a conference at the Foreign Office to suggest a solution to the boundary problem, he reported to the Colonial Office:

> . . . it was found at the conference that a solution of the question was attended with considerable difficulty owing to the fact that a cession of Liberian territory for the purpose could not, under the Franco-Liberian agreement of 8th December 1892, be made without the concurrence of France, and that Great Britain was precluded . . . from acquiring territory to the east of the 13th degree of longitude west of Paris. It was felt by those present at the conference that any adjustment of the frontier in the direction suggested by me must be obtained from the French Government as a favour . . .[96]

Thus, for all that he could do to rectify the irrationality of the partition, even with regard to the colonial interest, Cardew lost the game. No face-saving device could be accepted. In view of the recent history of the territory in question, the British were guilty of a breach of faith. The British Government had done just what it restrained Kai Londo from doing in the Treaty of 1890. Neither Kai Londo nor his successor was rewarded for his loyalty to the British Government. Instead, the British association had brought political disaster to the state, which now became no more than a pawn on the chessboard of the European diplomatic game. The King's position was conflicting, contradictory, and downright intolerable. This state of affairs was highly conducive to the disintegration of the state. While Fa Bundeh found himself in a position from which it was difficult to take any effective action against the enemies who constantly attacked him, the colonial administration only intervened if there was actual violation of what had been appropriated as British territory. Being so divided the chief was hampered on every side, and his lack of power to enforce his authority meant that ambitious sub-chiefs would take advantage of the situation to assert their independence.

[96] CO 879/43/497/38, Cardew to CO.

The approach of the colonial administration in these circumstances had a very weak character, for it could not itself rectify the situation.

In spite of his recognition by Cardew and his consistent loyalty to the British, it is very depressing to find Fa Bundeh petitioning in 1906 to be brought under British protection, because Liberian officials were beginning to invade his capital. The position he required needed no petition in the light of the 1890 treaty and the way in which the Protectorate was proclaimed. What Fa Bundeh sought in 1906 ought in fact to have been his by right. But the Colonial Office refused to accept the chief's petition.[97] This is one of the most disgraceful and depressing episodes in the colonial history of Sierra Leone.

The situation became especially difficult for Fa Bundeh when, early in 1907, Lieutenant Lomax arrived in Kailahun to set himself up as Liberian District Commissioner, although there were British Frontier Police in the town. The recurrent maladministration of Liberian officials led the British officers forcibly to eject Lomax at the end of 1907. The British were left in *de facto* occupation of Luawa. A temporary boundary between the areas administered by Freetown and Monrovia was agreed in 1908, which gave the whole of Luawa to Britain. In 1911 this was officially recognized, and on 26 March the Union Jack was officially hoisted in Kailahun, but Kissi Tengea remained under Liberia. In compensation the 'Morro-Mano triangle' in the south-east was added to Liberia. A joint commission demarcated the present boundary of the 'Kailahun salient' in 1913 and 1914, and this was confirmed by Anglo-Liberian treaty in 1917.[98]

By 1914 the last straw was being supplied to break the camel's back, i.e. the final dismantling of the remnants of Kai Londo's state into the 'independent' chiefdoms that we know today. Serious dissatisfaction arose in the remnant of the mutilated Luawa Chiefdom among the Kissi sub-chiefs of the Paramount Chief Boakei Bundeh. After a not admirable record as trouble-maker between 1906 and 1912, during which time he was twice banished, his election was nevertheless

[97] CO 267/486/Conf., 21 July 1906, Probyn to SS.
[98] CO 267/530/Conf., Haddon-Smith, 9 April 1911; Hollins, 'Short History of Luawa Chiefdom', p. 24.

secured in January 1912, and 'at first he gave promise of being a satisfactory ruler'. However, within a short time, his condescending attitude towards the Kissi sub-chiefs gave rise to a veritable storm of protest. While it cannot be denied that the movement for separation might have been welcomed by the Kissi sub-chiefs, it is difficult to swallow the pseudo-rationalization of both the District Commissioner and the Governor that 'whatever they may have said when Kanre Lahun territory was ceded to Great Britain, the Kissi chiefs were never really subject to either Kai Lundu or Fa Bundeh. The bond between them was a kind of offensive and defensive alliance . . . and Kai Lundu was the acknowledged head of the alliance but was only "primus inter pares".' In further support of this justification, the Governor added:

It is quite possible that when Kanre Lahun territory was ceded, the Kissi chiefs, in their anxiety to come under British rule may have stated or allowed it to be believed that they owed allegiance to Fa Bundeh, or their real position of an offensive and defensive alliance and nothing further may have been misunderstood.[99]

The District Commissioner who inquired into the matter, W. D. Bowden, confessed that it was necessary in order to understand the existing political situation to take into account the 'various historic facts'. But, he continued,

I have not seen them set out in any paper as yet, but will give a very short sketch of what I gathered has been the history of the Kanre Lahun chiefs. My source of information is Gobe, the speaker of late chiefs Kai Lundu and Fa Bundeh and also now of Bockari Bundeh.[100]

The information and conclusions arrived at were plainly misguided. The picture which was given of Kai Londo's state seems to be the only one which runs contrary to all the documentary and oral evidence available.[101] He claims that Kai Londo and his sub-chiefs were all 'of equal rank'. Besides this, there is reason to doubt the credibility of this account in the light of subsequent events. Gobeh was elected as Paramount Chief after Boakei Bundeh was deposed. It is highly likely that

[99] CO 267/557/Conf., 14 April 1914, Lord Harcourt to Gov. Merewether.
[100] Ibid., enc., D.C. Railway District to Col. Sec., 27 March 1914.
[101] Cf. the detailed entry of D.C. N. C. Hollins in the Pendembu District Intelligence book cited above, which was quite impartial.

at the time Gobeh was intriguing to gain the position, and perhaps saw his chance by falsifying the 'historic facts' so as to accelerate, to his own advantage, the break-up of the territory. It is even more unfortunate that Bowden should have relied *solely* on his testimony. The only rational argument advanced by the District Commissioner was that the area was too large 'to be effectively administered by one chief', but in comparing it to the Kpaa-Mende chiefdom 'which it equals almost exactly in size', Bowden was guilty of a gross exaggeration.[102] By 1914 Luawa was perhaps just about a quarter of the size of Kpaa-Mende. It was already by this time decided to break up Kpaa-Mende on the death of Lamboi, and drawing upon this, Bowden 'strongly' advised 'that the Kissi chiefdoms be separated from the Luawa chiefdom'.

The arguments presented did not succeed in blinding the Secretary of State for the Colonies to the inconsistency between the previous reports and the pseudo-rationalization contained in the current proposals, although he was not averse to the policy of breaking up the territory. Lord Harcourt told Governor Merewether:

I note from Mr. Bowden's memorandum that it is now considered that the Kissi chiefs were never subjects of the paramount chief of Luawa but that their predecessors entered into a defensive–offensive alliance. . . . It is clear however, that *when the Kanre Lahun district was ceded by Liberia, a very different view was taken of the relationship between these chiefs.* Sir Leslie Probyn in his confidential despatch of 23rd September 1907 indicated that *the lower Kissi chiefs were under the jurisdiction of the Paramount Chief of Luawa* and Lord Crewe in his confidential despatches of 18 January and 11 March 1909 emphasised that chiefs were not to be allowed to acknowledge paramountcy of the Luawa chief merely in order to come under British protection.

I concur however, in your view that apart from other reasons the Luawa chiefdom is too large. . . . In view however of the circumstances attending the cession of the chiefdom by Liberia, I consider that it would be desirable to retain some semblance of the authority of the chief of Luawa as suggested in paragraph 20 of Mr. Bowden's report.

Otherwise I approve of the proposals in your despatch.[103]

[102] CO 267/557/Conf., 14 April 1914, enc., D.C. Railway District to Col. Sec., 27 March 1914.
[103] CO 267/557/Conf., 14 April 1914, Harcourt to Merewether (emphasis supplied).

However, in spite of the rationalization, it is reasonable to accept the view of Governor Merewether that 'the fact remains that the present position of affairs is very unsatisfactory, and the Kissi chiefs are in no mood to submit to Bokari Bundeh's arrogant pretensions'.[104] This situation was exacerbated by the fact that contrary to constitutional practice, Boakei Bundeh was a 'young boy whom [the Kissi chiefs] helped to make chief', but he was 'now fining [them] in a way his father never attempted to do'.[105] This distortion of pre-colonial constitutional practice was a direct attribute of the colonial situation.

The partition of Luawa was not immediately effected in 1914, although it was agreed upon in principle. Boakei Bundeh was warned to behave himself properly and that 'further maladministration on his part would lead to his deposition and banishment'.[106] The *coup de grâce* came in 1916. There were further accusations of maladministration against Bundeh, and both Bowden and the Governor thought it best to depose the chief, and to effect the final and definitive partition of Luawa. The chief himself petitioned the Secretary of State for the Colonies that the 'country be allowed to remain in the same state that it was under his late father ... before he died, and not be divided'. But looking at it from the point of view of internal politics, the decision to partition the territory but to make the Luawa chief a kind of senior chief who could hear appeals, had been made publicly at a gathering in Kailahun in June 1914. If anything, this hardened the determination of the Kissi sub-chiefs to break away totally and assert their autonomy. When matters came to a head in 1916, there was only one course of action open—to depose Boakei Bundeh and to separate the Kissi chiefdoms finally from Luawa.[107] Perhaps if Boakei Bundeh had been deposed earlier and a more mature and elderly chief had been found to succeed him, there would not have been that inside drive to effect the final separation. But the quasi-independence of the Kissi chiefs in 1914, coupled with the further maladministration of Boakei Bundeh, created a very strong internal drive for partition. This was quite in accord with the policy of the colonial administration.

[104] CO 267/557/Conf., 14 April 1914, Harcourt to Merewether (emphasis supplied).
[105] Ibid., enc., Bowden to Col. Sec.
[106] CO 267/571/Conf., 17 May 1916, Wilkinson to SS.   [107] Ibid.

The 'counter-colonial thesis'

Thus by 1920 the whole country had been fragmented into over 200 chiefdoms, yet all previous interpretations of this phenomenon have simply restated the colonial thesis that the multitude of tiny chiefdoms that we know today are pre-colonial—even 'prehistoric'—units. By claiming to have been upholding pre-existing institutions through that very elusive and fleeting—if not meaningless—phenomenon popularly known as *Indirect Rule*, British policy has succeeded, through its mouthpieces, in misleading scholar after scholar into simply reaffirming the colonial interpretation. Walter Barrows is only the most recent in a chain of scholars to support this proposition. He makes the very suspicious statement that 'rapid and automatic disintegration . . . did not ensue in the aftermath of colonial interference with Mende political institutions', and then goes on to assert categorically that 'the contrary is more accurate'.[108] Barrows may be partly correct in that theoretically he takes an antithetical position to most 'displacement models', which view the colonial period as a conflict situation in which the traditional society collapses and the colonial power carefully guides and directs the society along a pattern of change, the end result of which has been carefully worked out and determined by the colonial power. Indeed no part of Africa has been totally free from the effect of Western contact, but it would be a wild and unfounded assumption to believe that any society had completely succumbed to it. But he nevertheless goes wrong, for there was rapid territorial disintegration, which can be seen in the light of Mende political institutions, and which cannot be ignored. To assert that 'Mende chiefdoms emerged *from the early colonial period* as more stable and durable entities than their pre-colonial forebears'[109] is not only a false claim, but takes no notice of the instability of the 'chiefdoms' under early colonial rule. The fluidity of the pre-colonial system, to which Barrows rightly draws attention, did not automatically give way to the ossified system that characterized the high tide of colonial rule. The pattern was more complex than this. Pre-colonial fluidity was first replaced by 'colonial fluidity' before the period of

[108] W. Barrows, 'Contemporary Mende Chief', p. 7.   [109] Ibid., p. 6.

ossification set in that was to characterize the remainder of the colonial period. This was most apparent in the sphere of the functional role of the paramount chief.[110]

The existing fragmentation attracted Raymond Buell in 1928 when he was examining the 'native problem' in Africa. In his view, 'certainly the object of gradually building up a Mende or a Temne nation out of the various tribes [chiefdoms] into which these people are now divided is desirable'.[111] At the high tide of colonial rule, this was rather in tune with the ethos of *Indirect Rule* but it passed virtually unnoticed.

In the light of the foregoing exposition in this chapter, the only conclusion to be drawn is the counter-colonial thesis— that large polities existed in the pre-colonial period, but dismemberment was a systematic policy practised by the colonial power to weaken states and kings, so as to facilitate the implantation of colonialism. Rivalries were generated or exacerbated between and within societies and exploited in the interest of colonialization. The present chiefdoms are not traditional entities, but a result of the fragmentation process. Basil Davidson's verdict is invariably right—that the 'central effect' of colonialism 'was one of dismantlement. Within its new frontiers, it took apart; it did not put together again.'[112] The fall of the African political humpty-dumpty was an act of colonialism.

Administrative reorganization, 1906–8

Meanwhile, as the process of territorial fragmentation was going on, the colonial administration was restructuring the dismembered parts into administrative units, the boundaries of which have changed as circumstances have dictated. In 1896 the whole of the Protectorate was divided into five districts, and the first major reorganization of administrative boundaries came in 1906. The first administrative division was effected by an Order in Council on 20 October 1896, which delimited the boundaries of the following five districts that then constituted the Protectorate: Karene, Koindagu, Panguma, Ronietta, and Bandajuma.[113] Each district was placed

[110] See section below and next chapter.
[111] R. L. Buell, *The Native Problem in Africa*, vol. i, 1928 (London, 1965), p. 866.
[112] B. Davidson, *Which Way Africa?* (Penguin, 1967), p. 35,
[113] See map 8.

in the charge of a District Commissioner, who communicated with the Governor through the Secretary for Native Affairs. This latter post was held by an African, J. C. E. Parkes, and in many instances the District Commissioners ignored him and communicated directly with the Governor through the Colonial Secretary.[114] When Parkes died in 1899, it was only too natural that the Colonial Secretariat should absorb his department. The District Commissioner's staff was small, consisting generally of a clerk, an interpreter, a gaoler, and from four to ten Court Messengers, and as circumstances permitted, a District Surgeon.

(a) Boundary disputes

This rudimentary administration proved ineffective before long. There was a proliferation of boundary disputes, which assumed a degree of prominence following the effective intervention of the colonial power. As the process of fragmentation progressed, boundary disputes were bound to escalate. When Governor King-Harman made a tour of the Protectorate early in 1901, he was quick to notice the ferocity of such disputes. When he visited Bo and Tikongoh, 'the chiefs . . . expressed themselves to me as being satisfied with the administration of the country and only desired to have *definite boundaries* fixed between their respective spheres of influence'. At Moyamba the only complaints preferred related to the absence of boundaries and to encroachment on each other's territories.[115]

These complaints were the inevitable result of the break-up of the pre-colonial states, which itself generated forces of change and fluidity. Indeed the Decree Books in which the officials entered their findings, reveal the almost incessant boredom of settling these boundary disputes that formed a crucial feature of the duties of the District Commissioners. When a people belonged to one state, there was no need to define their parochial units definitively, for as they were all subjects of one king or state, very few problems arose for instance as to farming land. But with the break-up of the pre-colonial states, freedom of movement with regard to farming

[114] Fyfe, *A History*, p. 544.
[115] CO 267/457/60, King-Harman to SS, 1901.

land was particularly affected. Boundary delimitations separated the people, but as they crossed these artificial administrative divisions to farm as before, the movement was regarded as 'encroachment'. The same 'bush' which hitherto had been cultivated without qualms became a 'bush' in dispute, once

MAP 8. ADMINISTRATIVE BOUNDARIES, 1907–19

the people who farmed it came to be regarded as subjects of separate and independent territorial entities. Thus the territorial disintegration generated forces of conflict and dispute which made it necessary to demarcate boundaries clearly. The people never failed to avail themselves of the opportunity of the presence of the Governor to revive irredentist claims to territory, or make appeals against previous decisions of District Commissioners.

On another tour in 1903, King-Harman held a meeting at

Bandajuma with Paramount Chiefs 'who had come in to meet me, and whose business with me was principally confined to laying claims on each other's territory . . .'. At Moseylolo in Bagru, the old chief Sey Lolo

. . . has a grievous and long-standing complaint as to the boundary of his territory, which was fixed some few years ago by the District Commissioner and against which he has always protested. I have had more than one petition from him on the subject . . . and have not been able to give him any satisfaction in the matter. I have, however, never been convinced that full justice has been accorded to him . . . and I intend to make another effort to arrive at the correct state of affairs. These boundary questions are exceedingly difficult to unravel, the rival claimants for territory being always ready to produce any amount of evidence to support their respective contentions; and although in very many cases the District Commissioners have succeeded in arriving at satisfactory agreements among the parties concerned, there have been and are still some disputes in which it has not yet been possible to obtain mutual accord. I recognise that these questions are of vital importance to the natives, and that it is of the utmost consequence that, in our dealings with them, their proprietory rights should be rigidly and strictly preserved; . . . I propose to reopen and to re-examine judgements which appear to me to have been arbitrary and hasty.[116]

Moving on from Bagru to Gbamgbatoke in Banta, the Governor was reminded of the 'inevitable question of boundaries' by Chief Margai, who urged a restitution of the old boundary with Imperreh, and 'complained that English law was being intruded on their native land customs'.[117]

The colonial peace did not immediately guarantee territorial stability, for with the territorial dismemberment going on, boundary disputes proliferated. The population was certainly increasing but given even the present population of Sierra Leone (about 3 million) compared with its land area (28,000 sq. miles) it is improbable that population pressure early in the century was a major cause of land disputes. In pre-colonial times, particularly in the nineteenth century, boundary disputes never featured prominently. If they did arise, they were settled by war, and ownership was acquired by right of conquest. This method of settling the matter was now rendered anachronistic with the imposition of colonial hegemony. It thus became

[116] CO 267/467/36, King-Harman to SS, 1903.   [117] Ibid.

the responsibility of the colonial power to settle these disputes, which may perhaps be seen as a direct function of the colonial *pax*. Until this problem was solved, well into the colonial period, and the situation thereby concretized, the early phase of colonial rule was as much a period of fluidity as the era just preceding it, the difference being in dimension.

(b) Problems of tax collection

This being one of the manifestations of the new process of social change that was generated by the colonial administration, Governor King-Harman was much concerned for 'the proper and effective administration of the Protectorate'. A contrastingly pacific man who detested the military methods of his predecessor, King-Harman, was enraged at the violence and corruption of the Frontier Police and Court Messengers who continued to register huts and assist chiefs to collect tax. He drew attention to the 'arbitrary' and 'irritating' conditions under which the Frontier Police and Court Messengers collected tax, 'a class of persons arbitrary in their procedure and irritating in their treatment of the people'. The chiefs, too, in some cases exacted more than the tax demands. The Governor therefore discontinued the employment of these personnel in collecting tax in 1901.[118]

(c) The 'development of the Protectorate' and the need for more efficient administration

Moreover, the administration was no more than a rudimentary structure. For the five districts covering an area of about 28,000 sq. miles and an estimated population of about $1\frac{1}{2}$ millions, there were in 1901 only four District Commissioners, one Assistant District Commissioner, four District Surgeons, and fourteen police officers. The progress of the railway construction, too, was causing quite noticeable social problems. King-Harman therefore gave his opinion that

. . . it is quite impossible to keep pace with the development of the Protectorate or to cope with the increasing requirements of the people. . . . Expenditure is necessary not only to develop the country,

[118] CO 267/457/Conf. 9, King-Harman to SS, 1901.

but to satisfy the people that the Government is not established to plunder them but to benefit them . . .[119]

The Governor 'urgently required' a man of some administrative experience, but 'not necessarily a military man', to serve as District Commissioner, and also four Assistant District Commissioners and two District Surgeons.[120]

The completion of the rail line to Baiima in 1905 and the changing pattern and volume of trade were further main reasons behind the administrative reorganization of the districts in 1906. The line passed through the Ronietta district from the colony, and after passing Mano, traversed part of the Bandajuma district and entered the Panguma district where its terminus was. It was obvious to the Governor that the area traversed by the railway after Mano should be in the jurisdiction of one District Commissioner. The problems of the 'railway chiefdoms' were quite different from other areas, and to ease the administrative burden and make the administration more efficient, it was necessary to have all the railway chiefdoms beyond Mano in one district.[121]

Governor Probyn further suggested in the same year the creation of a Sherbro district to include the 'Timdale [Temide] and Imperri Chiefdoms in the Ronietta District and all the chiefdoms adjacent to and on the north of the Kittam river'. The Sherbro district that existed at the time with its capital at Bonthe was part of the colony along with that strip of coastline ceded for fiscal purposes in the 1880s. Trade from the proposed Sherbro district naturally flowed into Bonthe, and the anomalous situation existed whereby inhabitants of Turner's Peninsula (technically in the Sherbro district of the colony) regarded as their Paramount Chiefs people who were part of the Bandajuma district of the Protectorate.[122] This shows that in the administrative proposals the colonial administration placed its own convenience first. However, the effect of this proposal would have been to alter the Sherbro and Bandajuma districts, which, in the opinion of the Governor, would be very 'important districts within the Government', since the bulk of trade would come from them. The Governor was hopeful that 'the pressure of trade will force ever increasing numbers of Sierra

[119] CO 267/457/61, King-Harman to SS, 1901.   [120] Ibid.
[121] CO 267/478/262, Probyn to SS, 1906.   [122] Ibid.

Leone [Creole] traders to settle in the Mendi and Sherbro towns in the two districts'. The District Commissioners of the two districts would each require additional assistance.

The Governor further proposed a sub-district in the Bandajuma district, to consist of the railway chiefdoms, i.e. 'the chiefdoms adjacent to and situated to the north and south of the Railway' which should be under a 'European Political Officer'. Effect was given to the adjustment of these boundaries as proposed, in April 1906.[123]

Although this change was found to work satisfactorily, it was discovered later in the year that 'the change did not go far enough'. Considering ethnic divisions this time, it was discovered that a small portion of the Sherbro people were left in the Bandajuma district, which it was now decided should be transferred to the Northern Sherbro district.[124]

The development of feeder roads for the railway was having similar effects on the chiefdoms they traversed. Therefore it was necessary to add these chiefdoms to the railway chiefdoms then placed in the Bandajuma district. This enlarged Bandajuma district would then comprise 'the whole of the Mendi east of Bo', and it was proposed to name it in the future 'Railway district'. The Kono chiefdoms of the existing Panguma district should be lumped into the Koinadugu district, and as little of the existing Panguma district would then be left, a new district should be formed to be called 'Central district' which would ultimately include:

(a) that part of the southern portion of the Karene district which includes the Bombali–Temne and the Mapaki–Temne–Limba country,

(b) the lower portion of the Limba country which is now included in Koinadugu . . .

(c) Temne chiefdoms forming part of the North-east portion of Ronietta . . .[125]

Thus this new Central district would comprise those portions of the existing Panguma, Koinadugu, Karene, and Ronietta districts that were furthest from their respective district headquarters.

The following month November 1906, all the Mende

[123] CO 267/484/99, Probyn to SS, 1906.
[124] CO 267/488/394, Probyn to SS, 1906.   [125] Ibid.

chiefdoms in the Panguma district except Bambara (west) chiefdom, were transferred to the new Railway district. The proposed inclusion of Kono into the Koinadugu district was shelved, and Kono became part of the Central district.[126] The Bandajuma and Panguma districts disappeared from the administrative map. The new Railway district comprised forty-six chiefdoms, of which twenty-two belonged to the former Bandajuma district, and twenty-four to the former Panguma district. The railway had increased the importance of chiefdoms adjacent to it. Bandajuma consequently became unsatisfactory as the capital as it was thirty-three miles away from it. Therefore the capital was shifted to Kenema which had several advantages; in addition to being the best site, it had the best water-supply and was 'practically speaking the geographical centre of the district'.[127] The rearrangements reflect a policy backed by economic considerations. 'Railway district was seen as one economic unit comprised of chiefdoms north and south of the main line. Central location was one reason for Kenema being chosen as administrative base.'[128]

The Central district itself was never constituted as originally proposed. It was intended to incorporate five chiefdoms from the Karene district, and four from Koinadugu. In 1908 these proposals were cancelled, and the Central district then consisted of six chiefdoms taken over from the Ronietta district, and three formerly in the Panguma district. The Central district thus had only nine chiefdoms, although at the beginning of the year it still had jurisdiction over Bambara (west) chiefdom. But in March, Bambara and the Kono chiefdoms were taken over by the Railway district.[129]

Behind this administrative reorganization was the implicit assumption that the pace of change would be far greater in the chiefdoms affected by both the railway and its feeder roads, thus causing more problems. The best way to handle this situation was to incorporate into one district all the chiefdoms likely to be so affected or already so affected, so that the situation could be better controlled from one headquarters. Every

[126] CO 267/489/444, Probyn to SS, 1906.
[127] Bandajuma-Railway District, Report for 1906.
[128] A. M. Howard, 'Administrative Boundary Changes', p. 30.
[129] Report on Central District, 1908; and Report on Railway District, 1908.

effort was made to keep the situation under control, and the sanguine nature of the Railway District Report of 1910 shows how far the problem was being controlled. New phenomena associated with the market-oriented economy introduced by the Western impact, and the consequent rise of new economic and social relations, required a kind of co-operation between the traditional authorities and the administration:

While trade has increased, there has been no increase in serious crime . . .

In native administration the attitude of chiefs and people and their relations to the Government are full of encouragement for the future. Chiefdoms are being organised and the abuses are fewer and less gross than in the past. Chiefs are as a rule managing their own affairs better and at the same time are co-operating with the Government on the more important matters. There is much to be done yet, but it has to be remembered that before the Railway, the greater part of the District was the darkest and most backward part of the whole Protectorate.[130]

This indeed reflects the prevalent attitude of the belief in the civilizing influence of European trade and commerce. Socioeconomic change was speeded by the colonial state.

Administrative reorganization, 1919–20

After World War I, the administrative reorganization of 1906 proved inadequate. Goddard maintains that the existing system was 'defective in practice, as it led to much duplication of work, and to a lack of both uniformity and continuity of policy'.[131] Governor Wilkinson suggested the division of the Protectorate into three provinces under Provincial Commissioners. After consulting with the leading District Commissioners, the Governor was guided in his decision by 'considerations of language, race, and communications'.[132] As such the Northern Province would contain no Mende chiefdoms, nor would there be any Temne chiefdoms in the Southern and Central provinces.

The Sherbro, Gallinas and Krim chiefdoms are confined to the Southern Province; the Kissi and Kono chiefdoms to the Central;

---

[130] Report on Railway District, 1910.
[131] Goddard, *Handbook*, p. 103.
[132] CO 267/583/432, Wilkinson to SS, 1919; Goddard, *Handbook*, p. 103.

the Yalunka, Koranko, Limba, Lokkoh and Bullom chiefdoms to the Northern. All this will make for efficiency and good feeling.

It is the same with transport. Communications in the Central Province turn on the main railway line and its feeder roads; those in the Southern, on the Sherbro waterways. Ultimately it should be possible to bring every sub-district within a few hours journey of the Provincial headquarters. . . . It is desirable that district centres should be readily accessible . . . and I may have to recommend that all headquarters townships should be either on a railway, motor road, or navigable river . . .[133]

Each Province should be divided into four or five districts, each with a resident District Commissioner. Only the Provincial Commissioners, however, were permitted to communicate directly with the Secretariat. The proposals were approved by the Colonial Office and effected in May 1920. The Southern Province comprised four districts: Bonthe, Gbangbama, Puje-hun, and Sumbuya. The Central Province also comprised four districts with a total of sixty-nine chiefdoms: Kenema, Pendembu, Moyamba (created out of the recently fragmented Kpaa-Mende state), and Kono, the headquarters of which remained at Panguma.[134] Although Panguma was in a Mende chiefdom, it nevertheless remained the headquarters of Kono, presumably on historical grounds, for in pre-colonial times Nyagua had conquered and subjugated the entire southern half of Kono, which became incorporated into his polity.[135] The Southern Province comprised forty-six chiefdoms, but in 1922, Pujehun district was divided and a Mano river district separated from it, thus giving the Southern Province five districts.[136] In 1928 the Kono district was divided into two, and a Panguma district created. This of course was barely a tiny fraction of the territorial area of the first Panguma district.

This administrative reorganization is ample demonstration of the administration's responses to the pace of change taking place at the time. Socio-economic developments rendered necessary the agglomeration of chiefdoms sharing common features and problems to be administered from one centre.

[133] CO 267/538/432, Wilkinson to SS, 1919.
[134] Annual Report on Southern Province, 1920; Annual Report on Central Province, 1921.
[135] Records of Paramount Chiefs, 1899, SLGA.
[136] Goddard, Handbook, pp. 104–5.

Certainly this would avoid duplication, as Goddard suggested. Moreover, as the transport infrastructure developed, it became imperative to relocate the various administrative centres so as to make the best use of such development. The remoteness of any administrative headquarters would hinder efficiency, and the mind of the Governor was still influenced by a rather unfortunate incident when a District Commissioner, Colonel Warren, died because of the difficulty of getting medical aid to him in time. All administrative headquarters therefore had to be readily accessible.[137]

Administrative reorganization, 1931

Within a decade of this arrangement, a new proposal was set on foot. It was a response to the increasing pace of socio-economic change. This new adjustment was primarily concerned with the Southern and Central Provinces. It was decided to amalgamate these, and there was 'a general consensus of opinion in favour of this course'. The plan was hatched by the Senior Provincial Commissioner, W. D. Bowden, 'who has an unrivalled knowledge of the administrative problems of the Protectorate, and the suggestion has now been endorsed by a joint report made by the three Provincial Commissioners . . .'. The development of motor roads in the Southern and Central Provinces rendered the presence of two Provincial Commissioners unnecessary since it would now be possible for one Provincial Commissioner to perform the duties of two.

Therefore the acting Governor, M. A. Young, recommended that as from 1 January 1931, the Protectorate be divided into two provinces, Northern and Southern. The former would remain as previously constituted, while the latter would in effect be constituted of an amalgamation of the existing Southern and Central Provinces.

. . . the new Southern Province will be divided for administrative purposes into eight districts, the reduction from the present total of ten being effected by the absorption of three of the existing districts which adjoin them, and the creation of one new district. The new district will consist of parts of the present Kenema, Panguma and Moyamba districts and will have its headquarters at Bo. . . . It is

[137] CO 267/583/432, Wilkinson to SS, 1919.

indeed the natural headquarters town of the new Southern Province . . . the Provincial headquarters . . . will be moved to Bo.

The three districts which will be absorbed are the Sembehun district, which will become part of Moyamba district, the Panguma

MAP 9. ADMINISTRATIVE BOUNDARIES 1920–30

district, which will be divided between Bo, Pendembu, and Kenema districts, and the Mano river district, which will be administered as part of the Pujehun district.[138]

The Sembehun district, however, was not wholly absorbed into the Moyamba district. The Bonthe district (originally proposed as Shebar district) was to absorb the southern portions of Sembehun while the northern portions were to be absorbed by the Bo district since they would be easier to administer from Bo in view of the improving communications.

[138] CO 267/631/File No. 9462, Young to SS, 1930.

This obliterated the Sembehun district altogether and the southern province now consisted of seven districts. With regard to the obliteration of the Sembehun district, C. E. Cookson, the acting Governor, explained:

The general effect will be to dispense with one district, without making Bo District (in which Bo itself will be more centrally placed) any more difficult to administer and without putting too great a burden on the District Commissioners of the other districts affected.

This scheme will tend not only to simplify administration of the new Southern Province, but also to economy in the matter of administrative officers . . .[139]

The new Southern Province now consisted of the following districts: Kono, Kenema, Bo, Moyamba, Bonthe, Pujehun and Kailahun. The Pendembu district headquarters had been moved to Kailahun in 1928 and so it took the name of the district in the reorganization. There was therefore a direct relationship between the socio-economic changes and their concomitant problems and the pattern of administrative reorganizations.

Administrative reorganization, 1939

Further changing circumstances convinced Governor Jardine in 1938 that another reorganization of the Protectorate administration was necessary. He suggested abolishing the two posts of Provincial Commissioner, to be replaced by a post of Secretary for Protectorate Affairs. The functions of this officer, who should be in the Secretariat, would be similar to those of a Secretary for Native Affairs as understood in Tanganyika and Nigeria. His duties would be to advise the Governor on 'native affairs' in the Protectorate and on the organization and dispositions of the Administrative service. Thus in this 'capacity, he would be the eyes and ears of the Governor in the realm of native affairs'. This suggestion was prompted by previous experience, which since 1932 had shown the importance of the presence of a Provincial Commissioner in Freetown 'for discussion, consultation and attendance at Executive Council meetings . . .'. By this arrangement the Governor would be

[139] CO 267/632/File No. 9549, Cookson to SS, 1931.

brought into closer touch with 'native affairs', while at the same time the Colonial Secretary would be relieved of some of the burden of work which he had.[140]

Apart from efficiency there were socio-economic motives at work:

> . . . with the still greater development of motor roads and for a variety of other reasons, it is both unnecessary and extravagant to divide so small a Protectorate into two Provinces . . . both under a Provincial Commissioner drawing £1,400 a year. . . . I would prefer to revert to the pre-war system of administration by districts with the inclusion in the Secretariat of an officer to be styled Secretary for Protectorate Affairs.[141]

Administration by districts rather than by Provinces seemed to the Governor to be an ideal arrangement considering the conditions existing in the Protectorate. There was a diversity of peoples and a multiplicity of tiny independent chiefdoms, and there were the 'varying agricultural and mining interests' which were becoming prominent by the late 1930s. It was hoped that the imminent introduction of the 'Native Administrations' would ease the further problem of the administrative officer personally collecting house tax in cash and 'make the comparatively small administrative units in direct touch with the headquarters of Government of more practical value than provincial units'. The development of mining interests during the 1930s created further social problems, to solve which it was necessary to have colonial officials in closer liaison with the local units. Administrative officers with pre-1920 experience agreed that Protectorate administration on a district basis 'allowed more time for supervision of native affairs', quite apart from the fact that it was just as efficient as the Provincial system and allowed more opportunity for training junior officers.[142] It is probable that had not the mining sector come into prominence in the 1930s, there might not have been this need to alter the Provincial system.

The Colonial Office approved of these proposals in principle The following year, 1939, Jardine submitted detailed proposals. The Protectorate was to be divided into four large districts

---

[140] CO 267/665/File No. 32212, Jardine to SS, 1938.
[141] Ibid.   [142] Ibid.

which would in turn be divided into sub-districts, corresponding closely to the existing administrative units. Kenema district
would include Kenema, Kono, and Kailahun districts, with
headquarters at Kenema; Bo to include Bo, Pujehun, Bonthe
and Moyamba districts, with headquarters at Bo; Makeni to
include Bombali, Koinadugu and Tonkolili districts, with
headquarters at Makeni; and finally Port Loko to include
Port Loko and Karene districts with headquarters at Port
Loko.

Each district was to be under a Senior District Commissioner
to be styled 'Commissioner' and the sub-districts would be
under District Commissioners. The Colonial Office approved
of the scheme which took effect from January 1940.[143] This
administrative reorganization did not alter the existing boundaries between administrative divisions. Except for the abolition of Provincial Commissioners and provinces, the new
districts and their Commissioners were to all intents and purposes provinces and Provincial Commissioners, while the
sub-districts were the same pre-existing districts under District
Commissioners. The only innovation of any practical administrative utility was the inclusion of the Secretary for Protectorate
Affairs in the Colonial Secretariat. This ensured greater liaison
between the central administration as the Secretary for Protectorate Affairs could easily get relevant information from
the Protectorate and supply such information at Secretariat
meetings. This arrangement, with reference to the southern
half of the country, has practically remained till today. The
only subsequent alteration was in the northern area, where
Karene was altered and absorbed into the new Kambia
district.

*Conclusion: from asset to liability—fragmentation in retrospect and
'Native Administrations'*

By the period of World War II, the world was at the threshold
of what has been called 'decolonization'. This in effect amounted to practically nothing more than the politico-legalistic
disentanglement of the colonial powers leaving intact all the
colonial institutions which had been unsuited even to colonial

[143] CO 267/665/File No. 32212, Jardine to SS, 1938.

circumstances, and were even more unsuited to post-colonial circumstances. At first best suited to exacerbating socio-structural divisions, to breaking up polities and creating rivalry between families, all most conducive to the establishment of the colonial hegemony, the fragmentation process began to

MAP 10. ADMINISTRATIVE BOUNDARIES, 1931–9

become a liability once it had served its intended purpose—the full establishment of all the institutions of colonial domination. Once the colonial power had been firmly entrenched in a position of unchallengeable superordination and maintained law and order by its monopoly of force, it was necessary to utilize the institutions of colonialism in other spheres than main-tenance of law and order. Thus by the 1930s, with the colonial power fully established, the emphasis shifted from the main-tenance of law and order to various forms of 'development'.

But development to any appreciable degree at the local level presumed the existence of viable local political units. But the fragmentation process of the first two decades of colonial rule had obliterated any viable units. By the time of the 1931 reorganization, there were 116 chiefdoms in the Southern Province.[144]

Some of the chiefdoms were ridiculously small, averaging only a few square miles. Concern began to grow in official circles about this state of affairs which made it extremely difficult, if not downright impossible, to initiate any development projects at the chiefdom level. The first indicators in this direction were on the socio-political plane. In a memorandum on agricultural policy by Mr. A. H. Kirby, the Director of Agriculture, in 1931, official attention was drawn to the subject of political or administrative amalgamation in the interest of socio-economic development.

In connection with the work thus indicated, for the native to progress in agriculture, sanitation, education, and all the matters with which we so nearly desire him to help to endow himself, it is necessary for him to add to his powers and resources by amalgamation of chiefdoms into strong native authorities doing the work for themselves under guidance.[145]

The Governor, A. Hodson, was aware that the agriculturalist was not the first to moot this proposal. He admitted the desirability from points of view other than that of the agricultural officer, but from the information he had, he was convinced that 'the time is not yet ripe to move in this matter. It is one which will require much study and consideration, and any undue haste is to be deprecated.'[146]

The move in this direction would have received more urgent consideration if political problems had also been involved. However, the first experiment, which proved abortive, was made two years later. In Kailahun there were three minute chiefdoms which it was decided to amalgamate. The Paramount Chief of Kunjo Chiefdom died in 1928, and of Horahun in 1931. These Chiefdoms were purposely left in the charge of Regents, so that on the death of the chief of Tongboma 'the

---

[144] Annual Report, Southern Province, 1931.
[145] CO 267/635/File No. 9654, memo by Kirby on agricultural policy, 1931.
[146] CO 267/635/File No. 9654. Hodson to SS, 1931.

tribal authorities of the three chiefdoms would consider the question of amalgamation dispassionately, and without the fear of any one chiefdom being absorbed by the others and losing its identity'. The chief died in May 1932, and the three chiefdoms 'flatly refused to consider amalgamation and each elected a chief'.[147] Having once encouraged the people into secession from their greater political units, it was indeed to be expected that after a few decades of autonomy, a chiefdom would be loath voluntarily to surrender its identity. It was, as it were, a position that was already legitimized, and to reverse the legitimate position by destroying a chiefdom already existing in its own right, needed more than persuasion. Pressure was necessary. But that did not come until the advent of the Native Administrations in 1937.

Native Administrations were an attempt to introduce Lugardian style *Indirect Rule* directly from Nigeria. The main features included salaries to Paramount Chiefs, a chiefdom treasury, and a more defined local court system. The officials called this 'organised local government'.[148] The Native Administrations, if anything, were intended to serve the purposes of 'development', firstly in the political sphere, and then in other spheres. Thus it was in the best interests of the Native Administrations to create greater, and therefore more viable, political units from the bewildering number of existing chiefdoms.

Their success was limited. There were 146 chiefdoms in 1962 compared with 217 in 1925. In the context of this chapter, this limited success is to be partly explained as the by-product of the fragmentation process. This process diverted ethnic energies away from conceiving of larger political units other than the tiny chiefdoms which came to be traditionally accepted now. The people themselves seized advantage of this situation for reasons of personal self-aggrandisement. After three or four decades, this state of affairs came to be generally accepted and legitimized. The colonial administration had encouraged 'inward looking at the local level'.[149] Parochialism became a crucial factor in the lives of the people, and this led the people

[147] Annual Report on Southern Province, 1933.

[148] L. W. Wilson, 'Native Administrations', in 'Material for a projected Encyclopaedia of Sierra Leone and notes for a diary of important events in the territory from 1900', MSS. Afr. S. 383–90, Box 2, RHO.

[149] Kabwegyere, 'Politics of State Formation', p. 66.

themselves to resist amalgamation, although it would have been in their own interest. But who, formerly a Paramount Chief with a staff of office symbolizing the dignity, would readily and voluntarily capitulate his office and staff to another Paramount Chief and then become subject to him? Power-consciousness became an integral part of colonial parochialism, itself the result of the breaking up of the pre-existing polities. This cancer has still not found a cure even in the post-colonial era, and is partly responsible for retarding post-colonial development.

In its attempt to create viable units from the bewildering number of chiefdoms that it had created, the colonial administration did not resort to force or administrative directives to effect its object. It gave the people an option. It is no surprise that this course of action failed because of the prevalent parochialism. How this parochialism came to be engendered in the institutions of the political structure will be considered further in the next chapter.

V

THE POLITICS OF
COLONIAL CHIEFTAINCY

Kilson's theory of political change

A SOCIETY is said to be in a process of political change when, as Easton says, 'support has shifted from one set of authorities to a different set, in which . . . the central character-istics with regard to the way in which power is used have all undergone change'.[1] The process begins as soon as the support begins to shift. However, Martin Kilson argues that political change cannot be limited to authority or power alone. There-fore, to find a concept more diffuse in its meaning, he has come out with the use of *modernization* as an analytical tool. He defines the term as 'those social relationships and economic and tech-nological activities that move a social system away from a traditional state of affairs in which there is little or no "social mobilisation" among its members'.[2] Of particular importance in this social system is the establishment of a cash nexus 'in the place of a feudal or socially obligatory system, as the primary link relating people to each other, and to the social system, in the production of goods and services in their exchange'.[3]

Martin Kilson is inconsistent and jejune in his 'analytical concept' of modernization when he equates it with political change. 'The establishment of a colonial state', he stresses, 'is the beginning of both modernization and political change . . .'[4] This is very reminiscent of Karl Marx, who saw all non-Western societies as static. Writing about India in 1853, he

[1] David Easton, 'The Perception of Authority and Political Change', in Carl Friedrich (ed.), *Authority—Nomos I* (Cambridge, Mass., 1957), p. 171.

[2] M. Kilson, 'African Political Change and the Modernization Process', *The Journal of Modern African Studies*, I, 4, 1963, p. 426.

[3] Ibid., p. 427.

[4] Ibid., pp. 427–8. See also Szymon Chodak, 'Some Aspects of the Theory of Modernization as applied to sub-Saharan Africa—A Case Study', *Africana Bulletin* (Warsaw), 7, 1967, for a perpetuation of the fallacious myth.

saw Indian history as 'the history of successive intruders who founded their empires on the passive basis of that *unresisting and unchanging* society'.[5] Since these societies lacked inner dynamism that made for change and therefore history, Marx concluded that the universalization of capitalism through imperialism was a necessary evil working in the interest of ultimate socialist revolution. In this context, he justifies British rule in India since 'whatever may have been the crimes of England, she was the unconscious tool of history in bringing about that revolution'.[6]

To Karl Marx, new forms of social organization only come into existence because of the dynamic nature of the process of production, which is always changing and subverting its own existence. Marx's arguments may be equally applicable to Africa, for in his social analysis he makes undifferentiated references to all non-Western societies. These non-Western societies seemed to Marx to lack any internal mechanisms for change. This particular interpretation of history when applied to Africa is now generally accepted to be quite simplistic, and is very unfortunately one of the inconsistencies or paradoxes in Marx's philosophy of history.[7] This does not, however, fundamentally undermine Marx's more important theses or formulations which have general validity.

That political change cannot be limited to power or authority alone is questionable, for politics is the art of government, and government is the exercise of authority and power. Moreover, political change can be the reverse of modernizing. The disintegration of a state is certainly political change, but not, one would have thought, 'modernization'. It is rather myopic to agree with Kilson that the proper analysis of African political change must begin with the imposition of colonial rule. African societies had been undergoing political change as defined by Easton for centuries before the imposition of colonial rule. This was the result of their own inner dynamics. This, moreover, may be equated with 'modernization' especially in its economic emphasis, since cash nexuses were gaining ground

[5] Karl Marx and Friedrich Engels, *On Colonialism* (Moscow 1968), p. 81 (emphasis supplied).

[6] Ibid., p. 41.

[7] Shlomo Avineri, (ed.), *Karl Marx on Colonialism and Modernization* (New York 1969), pp. 1-31.

in West Africa from at least the tenth century onwards. That 'fundamental political innovations occur in response to' the imposition of colonial rule[8] is admissible enough, but that this was synonymous with modernization is hardly acceptable except in a very negative sense. Although a study of the economic aspects of modernization is outside the scope of this work, it is worthwhile to note that, until the 1930s when the mining boom began, no major colonial economic investment project was undertaken in Sierra Leone except perhaps for the construction of the railway. It may not be far from the truth to state that the major economic effect of the railway was nothing more than the stepping up of an existing and modernizing economic system. The socio-economic forces unleashed by major investment projects as an aspect of the modernization process more properly belong to the post-1930 period in the history of Sierra Leone. The 'endeavour of the colonial oligarchy of officials, technicians, and entrepreneurs, to create and maintain the framework of a market or money economy as a basic means for introducing the natural and human resources of an African territory into the world market system'[9] is not appreciably noticeable in Sierra Leone before the 1930s. The major interest of the Sierra Leone administration after the abortive resistance of 1898 was to maintain peace and stability, and it was very wary of introducing measures, particularly in terms of entrepreneurship, that might lead to unsettling the social conditions and therefore disturbing the serenity of the British *pax*. Until the 1930s the modernization process in its economic dimension was perhaps only an extension of the pattern of the old coast trade and equally of the pre-European internal trade. This admittedly meant an increase in the volume of exported produce as well as imported manufactured goods.

With regard to the political aspect of modernization, it is difficult to accept the view that 'the particular features of colonial political change that render it "modern" in the context of indigenous African societies are (1) the process of rationalization and (2) the increase in access to political authority and power on the part of the average person'.[10]

---

[8] M. Kilson, *Political Change in a West African State: A Study of the Modernization Process in Sierra Leone* (Cambridge, Mass., 1966), p. 281.

[9] Ibid.   [10] Kilson, *Political Change*, p. 8.

While it is accepted that a key feature of African political change in the colonial period is the method by which the indigenous rulers adjusted to the colonial state, and that this cannot be equated with modernization, Kilson goes completely wrong in attributing the 'spread or dispersal of power' to the colonial administration, as far as indigenous political authority is concerned. In fact, as will be shown later in this chapter, the colonial administration fossilized the method of acquiring political power in the traditional context by the creation of socially regimented 'Ruling Houses' which excluded the 'average person' from the vistas of power and authority even if he had the ability and was qualified for leadership.[11] In this sense, the traditional society was 'modern' and the colonial state was 'antiquated' in circumscribing traditional avenues of power to limited groups of persons.

This is not, however, to deny the modernizing role of the colonial state, but merely to draw attention to the fact that such a concept can be simplistic if not properly seen in historical perspective.[12] Therefore it is proposed to examine the pre-1930 period in the context of political change as distinct from political modernization. Until 1937 the Sierra Leone administration was not committed to any policy of political development, which makes it conceptually plausible to examine the period in the context of political change only.

Colonial interference and the abrogation of pre-colonial sovereignty

For several years before the declaration of the Protectorate, the intervention of colonial officials in the political affairs of the interior brought added impetus to political change. The kings held both power and authority, but the gradual interference in their affairs and the acceptance of the superior power of the officials was having imperceptible corrosive effects on the power of the rulers. Although actuated by self-interest, the officials posed as altruistic neighbours genuinely interested in the welfare of the indigenous people who took them in good

---

[11] See generally Abraham, 'Traditional Leadership', *passim*.

[12] Kilson, *Political Change*, admits this and attempts to examine political change in a historical dimension, but the result has not been quite successful because his historical method is shallow.

faith. It is not surprising then that the rulers readily took the arbitration of the officials for granted, and this perhaps marks the beginning of the shift of power from the African rulers to the colonial state.

Through all the devious methods used to lure the rulers into the colonial net, the officials had succeeded by 1890 in creating a state of affairs whereby the power of the administration based in Freetown was accepted far inland. One of the most subtle yet dangerous mechanisms used was stipends. The stipendiary rulers were the 'Good Friends' of the administration. But acceptance of the stipends had unfortunate consequences. Acceptance limited the power of the rulers, since as a condition of acceptance, they began to submit their disputes to the administration for arbitration. Moreover, the rulers felt obliged to accept the authority of the administration, which had the same effect of limiting their powers. Acceptance of stipends was in fact a symbol of change. But apart from these things, the mechanism made the administration interested in any succession to a stipendiary rulership to the extent that, in the final analysis, the officials were determined to influence its outcome.

In 1884 for instance, when William Tucker signed a declaration reaffirming British jurisdiction over his territory, the stipend was to be paid to the person who held the office 'during Her Majesty's pleasure'.[13] All these trends can be illustrated.

About 1890 Vonjo, technically a sub-chief of Madam Yoko, had a dispute with Nyagua. Warriors belonging to Vonjo plundered towns and killed people belonging to Nyagua. Nyagua sent to Vonjo to 'make good of his people whom he had killed', and to restitute the property looted, otherwise he would retort in like manner. Vonjo sent to Nyagua to apologize, but the King would not accept any apologies. War seemed imminent, and then Frontier Sub-Inspector Johnson intervened. His arbitration was readily accepted by both parties.[14]

The settlement of this dispute by a Frontier Police Sub-Inspector without any difficulty shows that the power of the administration was being gradually accepted, and that even if they had wished to, indigenous rulers would not readily resort

---

[13] Hertslet, *Map of Africa*, pp. 52–3.
[14] Diary of Events, Native Affairs Department, 7, 1892, SLGA.

to traditional methods of redress in the face of colonial intervention. Perhaps the rulers found it easier to accept the new role the administration was assuming because, though it limited their powers, it did not yet appear to threaten the exercise of their authority over their people.

Again, there were reported threats of disturbances after the death of King Mendegla in 1890. Dama was not disturbed by this occurrence, but Jawe and Gaura quarrelled over the property of the deceased king, and determined to fight. Moreover, the rival factions disputed the place of burial. War fences were therefore being built. Private Garber, the policeman stationed at Gorahun, visited the places and ordered that the fences be destroyed. The order was immediately complied with. Sub-Inspector Betts was later sent there to settle any further disputes, and he was there when the question of succession was settled.[15]

The question of the succession was not settled without colonial interference. Alldridge, who was signing treaties further up country, reported the death to the Governor, who replied that on his homeward journey, the Travelling Commissioner should take part in the 'coronation ceremony'. The various chiefs assembled at Joru and elected a successor, in which Alldridge participated. Gbatekaka of Kpuwabu was elected.

The succession had been established by a general consensus of opinion. . . . The late chief had a grown-up son, who was not even named; this will show that primogeniture is not a sine qua non to a succession in Mende Law, and that chiefship is not hereditary. . . . There was no relationship between the late chief and the chief who was proposed as his successor.[16]

Alldridge accepted the succession, notified the Governor, and advised that it be approved. From his report the Governor was pleased to 'learn that this choice was a judicious one, the chief in question being a man of both determination and influence in the country', and accordingly submitted to the Secretary of State for the Colonies on the advice of Alldridge, that 'it would be politic to *recognise him formally* as successor of Mendingrah and a stipendiary chief of this Government'.[17]

---

[15] Dispatches, 478 and 518, 1890, SLGA.
[16] Alldridge, *The Sherbro*, pp. 244–5.
[17] Dispatches, 518, 1890, SLGA (emphasis added).

Although the choice was not Alldridge's personal one, the indications are that by gracing a traditional succession with colonial recognition, the ultimate source of legitimacy was shifting to the colonial state. This shift becomes more discernible in the case of Kai Londo's successor, five years later. As noted in the last chapter, Governor Cardew visited Kailahun in 1896. The successor, Fa Bundeh, accepted Cardew's terms, and the Governor publicly announced his approval of Fa Bundeh's succession, 'subject to the limitations of his authority . . .'.[18] Concluding his dispatch on this subject, the Governor made very instructive comments. 'As it may be remarked that no relative of Kai Lundu has been appointed to select him [*sic*] I may mention that he is not an hereditary chief. . . . Kai Lundu . . . acquired power and influence by his sword and subsequently became chief. He has one son . . . a youth . . . quite unfitted to succeed; besides *a chieftainship is not usually given to a son.* . . .'[19]

In Kono too there was a similar intervention on the part of the colonial authorities. Kono itself was roughly divided into two spheres of influence—the northern under Suluku of Kayima, and the southern under Nyagua of Panguma. When Cardew first toured the country in 1894, he requested the rulers to meet him. Two in particular, the rulers of Kainkordu and Koranko respectively, had never effectively recognized the suzerainty of either Nyagua or Suluku. Being on the eastern periphery of Kono, these rulers were quite remote from the political centres of gravity controlled by either Nyagua or Suluku. Many rulers refused to come to see Cardew. Therefore he unilaterally recognized the ruler of Kainkordu, Gbenda, who came to see him, 'as chieftain of this portion of the Konoh country'. Thus in the new colonial scheme of things, Cardew had *created* a Paramount Chief who was recognized as superior to the other rulers who failed to see His Excellency.[20]

For the people nearer the coast and therefore under much greater influence from the colonial administration in Freetown, pressure was exerted much earlier. As noted in Chapter II, the terms of Rowe's treaty of 1876 after the Keningbo war

[18] Dispatches, Conf. 19, 10 March 1896; Conf. 21, 23 March 1896, SLGA.
[19] Dispatches, Conf. 19, 10 March 1896, SLGA (emphasis added).
[20] Records of Paramount Chiefs, 1899, p. 224, SLGA.

showed that the administration was determined to impose its own peace. After severely punishing the culprits, the treaty stipulated that anyone breaking the terms 'shall be deemed to have forfeited the right to the government of his country and that consequently, the administration could depose him and appoint another person to govern it'. Rowe wanted to threaten the rulers and his action shows exactly what the colonial administration could do.

These instances demonstrate that the administration was gradually abrogating pre-colonial sovereignty. Ultimate power lay with the administration, and the kings became chiefs, exercising only that authority which the colonial administration chose to allow them. This position was crystallized after the declaration of formal rule, when the position of chiefs came to be defined by Ordinance.

Certain aspects of the principles of the pre-colonial power system should now be stated.

. . . The political system was fluid to allow anyone the channel to achieve it by merit through the manifestation of the greatest skill in leadership. Where there appears to be hereditary succession, it was more a coincidence than a consciously accepted principle in Mende law of succession, because the late chief's son must have had better opportunities to train in leadership. But even at that, his succession was influenced by the outcome of a consensus. The question of 'royalty' was not a consciously primary consideration.[21]

Thus kinship might be a factor, but not necessarily the most important factor in succession to sovereign political office. It was not an all-pervasive basis for political leadership. The Mende authority system was a largely secular affair, and because of its flexibility, it has been described as a 'more practical and less defined institution: it meets a need and it is a child of events; it is less bound by ceremony, and less deeply rooted in the past', and does not rest upon 'quasi-religious bases'.[22] Nearly any influential person could make a bid for leadership, though at the level of ultimate political sovereignty, women were excluded.[23] This is not to deny, however, that women held minor political positions.

21 Abraham, 'Traditional Leadership', p. 178.
22 Hollins, 'Mende Law', p. 25.
23 Ibid., p. 28; Abraham, 'Traditional Leadership', Chaps. I and VI.

Period of colonial liquidity

This political picture quickly altered with the imposition of colonial rule, which accelerated the pace of political change. Right from the Protectorate Ordinances of 1896–7, a series of serious political changes were set in motion at high velocity, the effects of which may justify characterizing the period up to about 1910 as one of colonial liquidity. This colonial fluidity quickly froze into 'tradition' and the propagation of the new colonial traditions through colonial writings has not only blurred our understanding of the pre-colonial system, but has seriously distorted the true traditions of the people. It is thus not surprising that recent writers who have been unable to pierce through the gloom of colonial literature, have fallen victim to its propaganda, with the unenviable result that they have still come out with distorted historical interpretations. From about 1910 until the introduction of 'Native Administrations' (generally believed to be modern local government based on Lugardian style *Indirect Rule*), the policy of the administration in relation to the indigenous political system was an *ad hoc* one. In other words, there was no plan for political development.

The Protectorate Ordinance and the indigenous authority system

The 1896 Protectorate Ordinance was the most important single documentary precipitant which quickened the pace of political change. Unequivocally establishing the hegemony and suzerainty of the colonial state, the document in one single stroke destroyed the hierarchies of the pre-colonial state systems. Central governments in their own right, the pre-colonial states were converted into units of local administration, and the policy of fragmentation admirably fitted this pattern. The very existence of the colonial state implied the reduced status and prestige of the traditional rulers, and perhaps it is reasonable to agree that 'the index of the success of the Administration, is the index of the decreasing authority of the chief over his subjects', who could now report their chief to the colonial District Commissioner.[24]

[24] K. A. Busia, *The Position of the Chief in the Modern Political System of Ashanti* (London 1951), pp. 109–10, 117.

The Protectorate Ordinance defined a 'Paramount Chief' as 'a chief who is not subordinate in his ordinary jurisdiction to any other chief,' and a 'chief' was defined to include 'a paramount chief and such other chiefs and headmen as are by native customary law the councillors or assistants of any such paramount chiefs'.[25] With regard to the exercise of judicial authority the Ordinance limited the jurisdiction of the chiefs to

a. All civil cases arising exclusively between natives other than cases involving a question of title to land;

b. All criminal cases arising exclusively between natives other than cases of murder, culpable homicide, rape, pretended witchcraft or matters or offences relating to secret societies . . . or cases arising out of faction or tribal fights, and all matters made offences under the provisions of this ordinance . . .[26]

Thus excluded from the jurisdiction of the chiefs were all matters involving 'non-natives', and much of their criminal jurisdiction. It may be said that the jurisdiction of the chiefs was reduced by more than half. Besides, the ordinance sought to bring the chiefs within firm control as subordinate agents for realizing the aims of the colonial state. Thus, it was made an offence for any chief to 'defy or neglect to promptly obey' any orders issued by the Governor. Moreover, it was similarly made an offence for any chief to exceed the bounds or limits of the jurisdiction circumscribed by the Ordinance. Above all the Governor was empowered to depose chiefs at will and to appoint replacements, subject to the approval of the Secretary of State.[27]

All jurisdiction covering areas in which rapid socio-economic change was expected was removed from the chiefs. Kilson states this point confusingly:

. . . the legal system . . . was related to the colonial authorities' conception of the colonial situation. The changes expected of this situation, especially the rise of the market economy and related

[25] Protectorate Ordinance, 1897, Part I, Clause II.

[26] Ibid., Part II, Clause V.

[27] Ibid., Clauses LXXIII, LXVII, LXXVI. Cf. the Gold Coast Native Authority Ordinance of 1935 which defined a 'chief' as 'a person whose election and installation as such in accordance with Native Law and Custom is recognised and confirmed by the Governor by notification in the Gazette . . .'.

institutions, could hardly be obtained with relative efficiency without the type of judicial arrangements established.[28]

The colonial authority directly took charge of matters affecting the economic activity of foreigners such as those involving a title to land, commercial contracts and debts, agricultural and mineral concessions, etc. This was because the African, as Lord Hailey explained, was thought to be inexperienced in 'all contractual relations involved in commercial transactions based on a money economy', which consequently made him a stranger to the legal methods of the 'modern individualistic and industrialised society'.[29] But this was a misconception. The coastal people in particular had been trading with Europeans for a long time, and therefore had been in contact with a cash economy and its contractual obligations for centuries. Lord Hailey, however, like Lugard and others before him, did not realize this, because they saw the establishment of colonial rule in apocalyptic terms, as the sudden introduction of civilization into barbarism.

The new arrangement sought to integrate two different social systems with different, if not conflicting, systems of law into one system. This piece of social engineering presumed constant adjustment by the indigenous institutions as the pace of political change quickened. The ultimate source of traditional authority was shifted to British law. In the final analysis, it was the Governor who decided who was a chief. The use of this external non-traditional means to uphold traditional legitimacy 'was dysfunctional to the maintenance of traditional authority'.[30] An unstable political situation resulted from this superimposition of British over African authority, and according to Apter, 'the most disruptive element . . . was introduced by transmuting traditional legitimacy into legitimacy derived from Great Britain'.[31] Thus the attempt to uphold the organizational structure of indigenous social life without impairing its efficiency did not work, and the institution of chieftaincy without being destroyed nevertheless declined. The chiefs had none of their traditional sovereign powers—indeed, power now

[28] Kilson, *Political Change*, p. 17.
[29] Lord Hailey, *An African Survey* (London, 1938), p. 295.
[30] Apter, *Gold Coast in Transition*, p. 151.
[31] Ibid., p. 123.

belonged to the colonial state. They exercised only the authority which the colonial state allowed them to exercise, and the residual authority of the British Crown decided the question of chieftaincy. Yet the institution was meant to retain its 'traditional' character. Herein lies one of the most enigmatic problems of colonial history. Thus in the colonial chief, 'the frailty of conflicting authority is strong . . .'.[32] When Alldridge visited Upper Bambara Chiefdom about a decade after the declaration of the Protectorate, he was quick to notice that 'Chief Kutubu . . . a highly progressive and intelligent personage . . . evidently feels the importance of his position as a native ruler, while realising the necessity of implicit obedience to all Governmental instructions'.[33]

From African to colonial chieftaincy

The implications of the suzerainty of the colonial state over traditional authority did not take long to unfold. The policy of the colonial administration was laid bare with devastating brutality after the abortive resistance struggle of 1898. The chiefs who were recognized and listed in 1899 as Paramount Chiefs nearly all owed their position to the administration. Service to the community, which in pre-colonial times was the basis for acquiring political power and authority, was now transmuted to service to the colonial state in order to acquire colonial traditional authority.

The victory of the administration in the 1898 war confirmed the primacy of the colonial state. With the ringleaders exiled or hanged, 'chiefs Government could rely on were confirmed or installed in the centres of the Mende rising . . .'. Since the house tax precipitated the war, official policy favoured those who were likely to be good tax collectors. Therefore, 'when District Commissioners, anxious to instal loyal chiefs, put in their own nominees, they seemed to their subjects, not lawful rulers, but tax gatherers masquerading as chiefs'.[34]

The 'Records of Paramount Chiefs' put out immediately after the 1898 war, listed twenty-seven Paramount Chiefs for

---

[32] Max Gluckman, *Custom and Conflict in Africa*, p. 53.
[33] *A Transformed Colony*, p. 176.
[34] Fyfe, *A History*, pp. 604 and 606.

the area under review, nearly all of whom owed their position to the support they had given to the administration during the war. So that even if a chief was a chief by pre-colonial standards, his chiefship was now thrown into a different context. Pre-colonial chiefship belonged to the past; a new kind of chiefship was now the order of the day. Pre-colonial chiefs who retained their positions after 1898 either must have supported the administration, or at least must not have done anything appreciably to discredit or undermine the new suzerainty. This was exactly the pattern that operated in Ashanti in the then Gold Coast. 'After the rising of [1900] the candidates who were known to have been loyal to the Government were elected as chiefs even though they had no title in native law and custom to the offices.'[35]

Of the twenty-seven new (colonial) chiefs listed in 1899, five were women—i.e. roughly one-fifth. Arranged by districts, there are annotations relating to each new Paramount Chief. In Imperreh, Revd. D. F. Wilberforce was made acting Paramount Chief by the District Commissioner, and this was approved by the Governor in September 1899. In approving the 'election' of Mr. Wilberforce, the Governor explained:

Mr. Wilberforce who was a member of the American Mission, and is a man of education, did good service at the end of last year in bringing to justice the murderers of the late Mr. Hughes [Creole assistant District Commissioner] and also in arranging for the meeting of the Imperri Chiefs at which the amnesty was proclaimed. This year Mr. Wilberforce has already collected about £720 out of the £750 due as house tax from the Imperri.
In these circumstances, I have approved of the election.[36]

Wilberforce was clearly a product of the situation. A collaborator in the 1898 war, he was also vigorous in collecting house tax. These circumstances justified his being made Paramount Chief. Service to the colonial administration, not African society, was now the ultimate criterion for acquiring authority.

Although Cardew wrote of his 'election' there is evidence of duress. Governor King-Harman reported in 1903 that his election was 'due . . . to the fear of the people of reprisals on the part of the Government, and to the hope that his civilization

---

[35] Busia, *Position of Chief*, p. 105.
[36] CO 267/447/257, Cardew to SS, 1899 (emphasis added).

and knowledge of the English language would enable him to plead more effectually in their behalf'. To the people the most rational course was to 'elect' Wilberforce in 1899, even though in more normal circumstances they might not have had him as Paramount Chief. Therefore, as King-Harman continued, 'after . . . the dread of punishment was removed, a strong party was formed in the country against Wilberforce . . .'. His popularity was gone and the people were clearly out to get him removed. But he was a colonial product and the colonial administration was pledged to uphold it's creation. It was King-Harman himself who 'took occasion to strengthen his position . . .'. Once the colonial administration supported a chief, it was difficult for the wishes of the people alone to alter his position easily. Yet even though Wilberforce enjoyed the confidence of the administration, Governor King-Harman could not help confessing that the chief 'will need constant support in order to enable him to maintain himself in his position . . .'.[37]

In the Bandajuma district the most important of the new chiefs seems to have been Momoh Kaikai of Bandajuma. Major A. R. Stuart noted shortly after the 1898 war that Kaikai became the most prominent figure in the Bandajuma district 'owing to his steadfast loyalty to the British Government in 1898'.[38] In the Records of Paramount Chiefs, Kaikai is returned as the 'chief of Kittam and Malene District, and is the leading and most influential chief therein'. In November 1898 he received a silver medal and chain 'for his loyal services during the 1898 disturbances. . . . He was very useful to the District Commissioners of Sherbro and Bandajuma in 1898 in bringing over many of his people to quell and quieten the peninsula at the end of the disturbances.'[39]

The Gallinas and Tunke countries were ruled by Francis Fawundu, who succeeded his father in 1894 and was recognized by the Governor. Fawundu was suspected of subverting the colonial state and, as noted in Chapter III, was wilfully deposed by Cardew, without actually having committed an offence, early in 1898. The Records, however, show that he

[37] CO 267/467/36, King-Harman to SS, 1903.
[38] CO 267/448/W.O., 28 March 1898, Notes by Stuart.
[39] Records of Paramount Chiefs, 1899, p. 157, SLGA.

was arrested 'as it appeared that Francis Fawundu was using his influence . . . to induce the Mendies to rebel against the Government'.[40] The true facts as noted in Chapter III were that the King refused to accept the colonial suzerainty. However, there was not sufficient evidence to substantiate the charge brought against him. In January 1899 he was reinstated by Cardew when he at last agreed to accept the colonial supremacy.[41] Despite Fawundu's earlier claims to rule by traditional right and legitimacy, he was now clearly a product of the new situation. Whatever his previous claims, his authority now stemmed from the colonial administration which had deposed and later reinstalled him. After his reinstatement the chief could do no more than play the role of a colonial product. Therefore he seemed 'from this date to have once again become loyal and of good behaviour'.[42]

In Koya, the signatory of the 1890 treaty, Joseh, was arrested in 1898 because he 'was very active as a disturbing element which in due course broke out in open rebellion'. He was sentenced to be deposed and imprisoned as a ringleader. When a general amnesty was proclaimed, he was released and allowed to return to his country and resume the Paramount Chieftainship.[43] The Chief of Koya now owed his position to the administration, which ultimately decided its legitimacy.

In the chiefdom created as western Gallinas the chief was Boakei Mina, who 'has always remained a loyal chief'. His position was clearly stated to have been given him by the administration, and for remaining loyal during the 1898 war he was chosen to take charge of Fawundu's country when the latter was arrested. After the amnesty and return of Fawundu, Mina was 'presented with £10 by the Government in recognition for services rendered'.[44]

Momoh Jah of Pujehun, lower Krim country, was arrested and sentenced to three months imprisonment with hard labour before the 1898 war broke out. When he paid the house tax the sentence was rescinded, and 'from this date, that Chief . . . rendered valuable services to the Government in leading the friendlies and securing the pacification of the country'. He was

[40] Ibid., p. 162. [41] CO 267/445/Conf. 1, Cardew to SS, 1899.
[42] Records of Paramount Chiefs, 1899, p. 162, SLGA.
[43] Ibid., pp. 173-4. [44] Ibid., pp. 186-7.

highly spoken of and conjectured to be the successor to his brother, Momoh Kaikai, who was about eighty-seven years old at the time.[45]

Sandi succeeded at Tikongoh to Makavoray's truncated state in 1897 and is stated to have been loyal during the 1898 war.[46] But the Chief of Koranko (Baoma) 'is very little known, [and] seems to have been loyal during the 1898 disturbances'.[47] He succeeded Fakondoh, the signatory chief. But more specifically, Chief Gbolie of Baoma 'is Paramount Chief having been recognised as such after the Mendi rebellion in 1898'.[48]

In Panguma district Nyagua was still recognized as ruler of his vast state, although he was shortly to be exiled. In Bambara (east), the Chief Momoh Babawo was supposed to have had a hand in the war of 1898, but 'is now loyal and a good friend in the interests of the Government'. Fa Bundeh still remained ruler over the remnants of Kai Londo's state and the switch in the source of his authority to the colonial state was apparent in his recognition by Cardew even before the Protectorate was proclaimed. Jawe and Mandu countries were grouped together under Kabba Sei. This chief, actually of Mandu, had suffered at the hands of the administration even before the 1898 war, although he claimed innocence. He was reinstated as Chief of Mandu only a few weeks before the outbreak, in which he took no part.[49] 'He seems to have profited by his past experience, as during the Mendi rising of 1898, he remained loyal to the Government and was of great service . . .'.[50] Vandi Saawai, who signed the treaty on behalf of Jawe, died about 1897 and Kabba Sei claimed chieftainship over the area, which was disputed by Vandi Von of Nyeama. Momoh Babawo was also claiming the chieftaincy. In the meantime, however, Kabba Sei was recognized as Paramount Chief of both Mandu and Jawe, apparently in view of his support of the administration.

Apart from chiefs who gave or were made to give active support to the administration, there was another category of Paramount Chiefs who were recognized as such because they

[45] Records of Paramount Chiefs, 1899, pp. 191–2, SLGA.
[46] Ibid., p. 197.   [47] Ibid., p. 199.
[48] Intelligence Book, Panguma District, 1905–8, p. 51, SLGA.
[49] Abraham, 'Traditional Leadership', pp. 48–53.
[50] Records of Paramount Chiefs, p. 217, SLGA.

were believed to be harmless. This opinion stemmed from the fact of their old age, and consequently they were not thought to have played any active part in the 1898 war. Chief Bongay of Bo is reported to have been a very old man and seemed to have been 'neutral' in the war. The lower Gallinas was under Momoh Fofi, who was elected to the headship of Gendema, the *Massaquoi* capital, during the struggles for the *Massaquoi* crown. He is thus said to have succeeded King Jaya. He was also the brother of King Manna, and because of his longevity, 'did not have sufficient control to stop the rising of his people'. The successor was already being considered in the person of his grandson, Massaquoi.[51]

In Gaura the role of the colonial administration in Gbate-kaka's succession has already been noted. 'He is not supposed to have joined in person in the rebellion of 1898 owing, it is said, to his having been very sick for some years past.'[52] In Dama the signatory chief was dead by the time of the 1898 war, and his successor Soway Gayeh 'is supposed to have been neutral . . . although several of his smaller sub-chiefs with their following joined the rising . . .'.[53] In Mano Bagru, Seh Lolo was 'a very old man, [and] nothing seems to be on record about him'.[54]

Two of the twenty-seven Paramount Chieftaincies listed in 1899 were vacant, because the chiefs had fallen victims of the 1898 war. These chiefdoms were Mabanta and Temide. A third may be added, although the ruler (Nyagua) is listed. Although recorded as the Chief of Bambara (west), Nyagua was soon exiled to the Gold Coast where he died in 1906.

'Colonial products'—women Paramount Chiefs

One striking phenomenon which stands out clearly in this new scheme of things is the high incidence of women hold-ing political authority of the highest order within the tradi-tional context. From this time onwards, women have held the office of Paramount Chief till today,[55] but it has resulted in a

[51] Ibid., pp. 195, 185–6.   [52] Ibid., p. 165.
[53] Ibid., p. 169.   [54] Ibid., p. 8.
[55] Women Paramount Chiefs are only found in the Mende-dominated southern half and not in the northern part of the country. A hypothetical explanation is to be found firstly in the character of the 1898 war, and secondly in the nature of the

misinterpretation of the pre-colonial system of the Mende. The colonial authorities themselves gave popularity to this new phenomenon, which soon fossilized into a tradition that has ever since been accepted without question.

Perhaps Sir Harry Luke was the first colonial authority who began the publicity. When he compiled his *A Bibliography of Sierra Leone* in 1910, he obviously was influenced by events of the previous decade to conclude that among the Mende and the Sherbro, women could become Paramount Chiefs, although he added: 'in the absence of a suitable male'. Because of this he characterized the Mende as 'rough and ready', and 'more practical' than the 'conservative Temnes'.[56] Five years later K. J. Beatty, who sat on the commission of 1912 to try so-called cannibals, took up the publicity and stated more categorically that 'as there is no salic law to prevent such a course' among the Mende, 'women are *frequently* elected to the chieftainship'.[57] Indeed the emphasis on frequency represents an increase in the incidence of the elevation of women to Paramount Chieftaincies, which may be contrasted with the care Sir Harry Luke took to qualify such acquisition of authority by women. Indeed having become so familiar a feature of the early phase

political systems. The Temne war was a highly organized guerrilla war which, with perhaps one exception, did not claim any innocent victims. Indeed, Bai Bureh was highly respected, and he found sympathy in Britain for the way he conducted his campaign. (See Abraham, 'Bai Bureh'.) There was thus no threat of a vendetta and a wholesale replacement of chiefs in the north. On the contrary, the Mende war was a brutal and ill-organized onslaught against 'westerners', and it claimed many innocent victims. The administration determined to punish them severely. Many chiefs were exiled or hanged. Those who escaped could not come forward to claim their chiefships. The people thus put forward women as chiefs to the administration in order to escape further punishment. The administration accepted and upheld them. Apart from this, Mende chiefship is largely a secular affair, whereas Temne chiefship is heavily ritual. Generally a Temne chief is made a chief for life, and cannot be legally deposed in customary law. The coronation of a successor cannot be performed without the head of the deceased chief, on which much ritual ceremony has to be performed, to ensure the continuity of the office and legitimize the successor. Very rigid rules are observed which preclude women. The absence of this strict ritual made it possible to legitimize the authority of women in the Mende areas. Although Sherbro chiefship is very similar to Temne chiefship, it was possible to have women chiefs there because of the decline and consequent weakening of the institution throughout the nineteenth century, and also because of the dominating Mende influence with its secular chiefship character.

[56] H. C. Lukach, *A Bibliography of Sierra Leone* (Oxford 1910), pp. 25–6.
[57] K. J. Beatty, *Human Leopards* (London 1915), p. 110 (emphasis supplied).

of colonialism, the claim was categorically made that women could achieve the highest political office in pre-colonial times.

By the 1930s, women Paramount Chiefs were already an accepted tradition. Thus Dr. Easmon reiterated the same colonial thesis that there were pre-colonial women Paramount Chiefs, when he wrote about the *Massaquoi* crown, the existing incumbent being a woman then.[58] Modern writers have been heavily influenced by this colonial tradition which they have accepted without question. Weight was further lent to it when the Chief Commissioner of the Protectorate put out an official document reaffirming the position. First published in 1939, the *Outline of Native Law in Sierra Leone* in its second impression in 1951, stated under 'Constitutional Law' that it appears

(a) that the custom of the northern tribes has been against the idea of a woman becoming a Paramount Chief;

(b) that Mendies were formerly not unwilling to accept women as Paramount Chiefs; but there is now a considerable body of opinion that they are not suitable, though so far as is known, custom would not bar them;

(c) that Gallinas, Krim and South Sherbro custom has not been repugnant to the idea of women becoming Paramount Chiefs.[59]

In the same year, the anthropologist Kenneth Little in his study of the Mende, was more categorical when he asserted that women occupied the dignity in pre-colonial times on 'exactly the same basis of power and authority as men'.[60] At the same time McCulloch, another anthropologist who was influenced by Little, stated the position with a little more caution. 'Occasionally today, as in the past, a woman may succeed to the chieftainship among the Mende.'[61]

Until 1971 this thesis was not seriously challenged. Christopher Fyfe only mentioned *en passant* that women chiefs owed their positions to the colonial state and proceeded to give a catalogue of them.

Yoko was only one of several women rulers who owed security or crown to the government. Rowe gave Nyarro of Bandasuma special protection [Bandasuma was declared 'neutral' in 1885].

[58] M. C. F. Easmon, 'The Massaquoi Crown', *Sierra Leone Studies*, o.s. xxii, (1939), 86.

[59] J. S. Fenton, *Native Law*, p. 4.

[60] Little, *The Mende*, p. 195.

[61] M. McCulloch, *Peoples of Sierra Leone* (London 1950), p. 16.

Betsy Gay of Bogo owed her crown to official connections. Commandant Laborde installed a woman, Kona Kambe, as chief in the Bagru, but after his death, her right was contested, and she was deposed. Madam Yata, sister of Prince Mana and Jaia, was officially recognised by 1890 as having charge of the Massaquoi territory.[62]

Nancy Tucker of Bagru was forcibly installed by the Frontier Police in 1897 over territory to which she had no claim whatsoever, except that she had been domiciled there for some time while trading; essentially she was installed because she promised to bring in house tax for the territory in question.[63]

The first categorical challenge to the thesis that women had a historical right to claim a Paramount Chieftaincy came in 1971.[64] It was shown that women chiefs among the Mende 'are products of colonialism'.

Despite the fact that some writers have overstated the political role of women as occupying the post of chief on 'exactly the same basis of power and authority as men' both in traditional and modern times, it must be remembered that in the political organization of Africa as a whole, the role of women is in general, a limited one—their primary concerns being, productive activities. Women do not dominate politics even in matrilineal systems.[65]

Quite recently a belated attempt has been made to salvage the crumbling thesis. Citing only three examples, Carol Hoffer makes the pretentious claim that 'For the Mende and Sherbro . . . there is a long tradition of political activity on the part of women'. Evidently she was referring to 'Paramount Chieftaincy' which in the pre-colonial context, may be said to have been kingship, implying sovereignty of the most exalted rank. With the example of three women signing treaties, the writer precipitously jumps to the premature conclusion that she has succeeded in refuting 'the hypothesis that women chiefs in Sierra Leone are the creation of British colonialism put forth by Arthur Abraham . . .'.[66]

So much of the current misinterpretation stems from a

---

[62] Fyfe, *A History*, p. 484.
[63] Ibid., pp. 553, 558; Minute Papers, Native Affairs, 13/1898, SLGA.
[64] Abraham, 'Traditional Leadership'.   [65] Ibid., pp. 11–12.
[66] Carol P. Hoffer, 'Mende and Sherbro Women in High Office', *Canadian Journal of African Studies*, VI, ii (1972), p. 151 n.

misunderstanding of the pre-colonial state systems. Within the reconstruction made in Chapter I, only Madam Yoko can be said to have achieved, albeit only theoretically, the position of authority equivalent to kingship before the proclamation of the Protectorate. All the other women referred to in the documents as 'Queens' more correctly held subordinate offices within the state structure, rather than offices of suzerainty in their own right. With the greater pressure of the colonial officials in Freetown, greater cognizance was taken of these women political rulers who were made to appear suzerain and were almost all referred to as 'Queens'. Taking into consideration the gradual tilt in the focus of legitimacy to traditional authority by the 1890s, it is plausible to argue that the elevation of women in the eyes of the colonial officials tended to endow them with the attributes of suzerainty. The process of political fragmentation to consolidate British colonialism aided this tendency. Moreover,

It may be plausible to argue that if women chiefs were 'colonial products', then part of the explanation may be sought in the formidable influence and prestige of Queen Victoria. Many traditions recall that the white men . . . confessed that they were servants of the 'Great White Queen' who had the greatest empire in the world. Perhaps in imitation, women candidates were put up. Perhaps too, colonial agents wanted pliable instruments to deal with.[67]

(a) Madam Yoko

Before dealing with other women chiefs, it is necessary to examine Madam Yoko's political position as the only woman supposed to have had control over one of the pre-colonial states (not a division of it). For her Hoffer makes the very ahistorical claim that 'Madam Yoko used both diplomacy and warfare to bring 14 separate chiefdoms under her personal hegemony'.[68] No evidence whatever is adduced to substantiate this spurious claim. Before the advent of Madam Yoko, the Kpaa-Mende state existed as a 'territorial' state based on the Wunde society—a society more powerful than the Poro, which cannot admit a woman. It was war and warriors that accounted

[67] Abraham, 'Traditional Leadership,' p. 13.
[68] 'Mende and Sherbro Women,' p. 153.

for the importance of a state in the later nineteenth century, and the Wunde in particular was a society organized for war.

That Madam Yoko was the creation of the colonial administration is no subject for dispute, as has been clearly proved.[69] Perhaps what must be highlighted, is the very dramatic way she rose to becoming a 'Queen' in the colonial conception. In 1879 when William Budge made his visit into Mende country, he discovered that Yoko was one of the widows of the late King Gbanya and was head woman of Mowoto, 'a small town about two hours journey from Senehun on the way to Tyama'.[70] When Laborde undertook his trip into Mende country from 11 December 1880 to 21 January 1881, he made no mention of Yoko. Although head woman of Mowoto, she was apparently insignificant. Her name only appeared on Laborde's map as head woman of Mowoto.[71] The successor to Gbanya of Kpaa–Mende was Movee of Senehun, although we are told that Yoko was recognized by Rowe as successor to Gbanya.[72] This drastically simplifies the story.

In 1895 a petition was sent by the people of Bompeh town in Sherbro protesting against Madam Yoko's suzerainty. What at this time was the Kpaa-Mende capital, Senehun was technically Sherbro country, although incorporated into Kongbora section which was added to Kpaa-Mende in return for a wife given to Chief R. C. B. Caulker of Shenge.[73] The people unhesitatingly stated that

It was . . . to our entire surprise when report reached us in the year 1887 . . . that *Madam Yoko was appointed by Sir Samuel Rowe* to take charge of the Senehoo district. This woman came thirteen years ago [i.e. 1882] as a fugitive from the Mendi country to the Bompeh to seek safety and protection to [*sic*] him [R. C. B. Caulker], from her pursuers; during this time, there was a headman over Senehoo, appointed by his late father Mr. Canray Bah Caulker, named Bhangya [Gbanya]. She was given him as his wife; and after the death of this [Gbanya] she returned to [Caulker] as her adopted

[69] Abraham, 'Traditional Leadership', Chapter VI; also Reeck, 'Innovators', pp. 606–8.

[70] CO 879/17/214/18, enc. 5.

[71] CO 267/344/60, enc., map by Laborde.

[72] Fyfe, *A Short History*, p. 123; Fyfe, *A History*, p. 484; M. C. F. Easmon, 'Madam Yoko; Ruler of the Mendi Confederacy', *Sierra Leone Studies*, n.s. 11, December 1958, p. 167.

[73] Abraham, 'Traditional Leadership', pp. 127–8.

father, and was under his parental care for sometime; there we knew her. But how came this woman to the notice of the Government as to be promoted, to the entire government of Senehoo . . . is a mystery to us.[74]

The mystery lies in the fact that while the Bompeh people looked to tradition, Madam Yoko looked to the administration, which at this time was more powerful. The petition was to no avail.

Since the time of Gbanya, Yoko had some influence in official circles in Freetown. After Gbanya's death she fully exploited the situation, so much so that although Movee was successor to Gbanya and based at Senehun, Yoko was placed in charge of Senehun in 1882 under a special arrangement with Governor Havelock. Thereafter Yoko was described as the 'sub-chief of Senehun'.[75] A clever schemer, Yoko thereafter began to undermine the authority of Movee by attempting to settle disputes on her own account and quickly appealing to the administration to solicit their assistance.[76] Support was whipped up in favour of Madam Yoko in official circles when Movee died in 1884.

Yoko quickly reported disturbances to the Governor early in 1884 and was given special credit for protecting British traders. Havelock sent her two constables 'for your own benefit as well as for the traders and other British residents in your town'. By May 1884 she was officially described as the 'Principal Lady of Senehun', and a little later as 'Queen of Senehun'.[77] For all practical purposes, Madam Yoko as the ruler of Kpaa-Mende was the creation of the British administration and the basis of her power lay in protecting British interests and in being doggedly loyal to the administration. When Cardew made his first tour of the hinterland in 1894, he did not fail to observe that 'Queen Yoko . . . bears the character of being *very loyal*'.[78]

This unprecedented situation had important consequences. In all probability, Yoko's power was limited and she could not control all the sections of a state created by war and held

[74] CO 267/510/A. Walker, enc. 2, 1908 (emphasis added).
[75] GALB, 53/95, 29/84, SLGA.
[76] Ibid., 19/83.
[77] Ibid., 39/84, 85/84.
[78] CO 267/408/117, Cardew to SS, 1894 (emphasis added).

together by the Wunde. Her power must have been conceptual
—existing in the minds of the officials—rather than practical.
True when a sub-chief died, the administration commissioned
her to take part in the election of a successor.[79] But for all
other purposes, those who were technically her sub-chiefs just
ignored her and carried on their own affairs. In fact one of her
sub-chiefs, Kamanda of Bauya, openly defied and challenged
her. In the confrontation, the British administration came to
the rescue of Madam Yoko, for after the Yoni expedition of
1886, Kamanda was arrested and imprisoned. This act on the
part of the administration did not scare other chiefs into submission to Yoko and trouble still persisted. An important case
in point is the continuing conflict between Moigula and Vonjo,
both technically sub-chiefs of Yoko, which was only resolved
with the intervention of Makavoray of Tikongoh, outside
Kpaa-Mende.[80]

Madam Yoko's power was upheld by the colonial administration, which elevated her to the position and did not rest in
customary constitutional law. Yoko knew where the source of
her authority lay and was therefore unflinching in her loyalty
to the administration. Yoko herself admitted in a letter to the
Superintendent of the Native Affairs Department that 'it was
through the Government that I am looked upon as their leader'.[81] When it was decided to go to war in 1898, Yoko was not
informed or consulted and she was one of the first targets of
the warriors. That she escaped with her life was due to the
advice of a relative who had taken part in the war delibera-
tions; she took cover in the Frontier Police barracks. Dr. Hood
the district surgeon of Ronietta, who was acting District
Commissioner during the collection of the house tax reported
that 'the majority of her sub-chiefs are not loyal to her, and
pay little attention to her orders until my assistance has been
rendered'.[82]

Again . . . during the disturbances, although forsaken by most of her
people, she stuck to the government and did great work in bringing
about peace and quietness in the District as also in aiding in the

[79] See for instance, Records of Paramount Chiefs, 1899, p. 50; GALB, 623/95,
749/96, SLGA.
[80] Abraham, 'Traditional Leadership', pp. 143–50.
[81] Minute Papers, Native Affairs, 366/93, SLGA.
[82] Minute Papers, Confidential, 1/98, SLGA.

arrests of several important chiefs who were responsible for the rising. For these loyal services, she was decorated by H.E. the Governor 15.9.98 with a silver medal and chain.[83]

Apart from the support she received in return, Cardew personally thanked her for her help in the 1898 war. As he minuted, '... Yoko to be informed that I much appreciate the loyal manner in which she has acted throughout the present crisis'.[84]

It is thus difficult to see how Madam Yoko could have brought '14 separate chiefdoms under her personal hegemony', and to assert that she was 'the greatest of the Mende chiefs' is not only historically wrong but also a gross and an unpardonable travesty.[85] As a counter-hypothesis, it can be stated that Madam Yoko's elevation to the headship of Kpaa-Mende was dysfunctional to the maintenance of the integrity of the state. Lacking traditional legitimacy to buttress her position, the various sections of the state rather tended to go each their separate way, since there was no legitimate traditional leader to look up to. To the chiefs, themselves products of a war-tradition, Yoko was a puppet who mattered little. Yoko could not control Kpaa–Mende, and this process of separation due to the policies of independence which tended to be followed by Yoko's sub-chiefs marks the beginning of the disintegration of the Kpaa–Mende state.

As noted in Chapter IV, this process was almost becoming a tradition, for in the early 1900s the administration itself did not know that Vanjelu, for instance, was Kpaa-Mende and hitherto an integral part of the state!

To say that Yoko integrated the Kpaa-Mende state reveals the limited and myopic anthropological methodology of Hoffer, who has failed to pierce through the gloom of colonial literature and propaganda into the true traditions of the people. It also shows an imperfect reading of the documents, a misinterpretation or else a misrepresentation of the historical facts. Far from integrating the state, Yoko's advent as 'Queen' of Kpaa–Mende began a period of disintegration of the state as each chief came to depend less on the centre. Yoko was a

---

[83] Records of Paramount Chiefs, 1899, pp. 50–1.
[84] Minute Papers, Native Affairs, 135/98, SLGA.
[85] B. H. A. Ranson, *A Sociological Study of Moyamba Town, Sierra Leone* (Zaria 1968), p. 19.

creation of the British, and was maintained in her position by the British administration.

(b) Other 'Queens'

Apart from Madam Yoko, no other ruler who wielded authority over any of the pre-colonial states was a woman. Certainly there were women political figures, but they held subordinate political ranks in the state structure. All oral traditions collected by the present writer emphatically make the point that women in pre-colonial times could never be suzerain. In this context, Hollins rightly discovered that

. . . strictly speaking, a woman cannot be elected as chief [implying the suzerainty inherent in kingship] in Mende; that a few women have been put up to Government and accepted as such proves nothing. In the Mende country of old, the chief had to take his oaths and hold his more important councils in the Poro bush: this excluded a woman from holding the post. The so-called women chiefs were to some extent dummies. Again, a chief was primarily a leader in war, and there were no amazons among the Mende.[86]

Oral traditions emphasize war as a most important aspect of politics, and this was not the concern or domain of women.

However, officials made references to 'Queen Nyarroh of Bandasuma' in Barri country, with whom a peace treaty was signed in 1885, and not in 1889 as Hoffer says. In 1889 Alldridge, while travelling through upper Mende country, passed through Mendekelema, the headwoman of which was Mammy Lehbu, the sister of King Mendegla. Alldridge referred to her as 'Queen'. Mammy Lehbu had influence and prestige due to her age and also to her being the sister of the King. But this in no way made her a 'Queen', nor did she sign any treaty. In the case of Ɖalɔ (Nyarroh) of Bandasuma, she also never signed a treaty in 1889. At the meeting convened in her town, it was Mendegla who was invited to sign a treaty.[87] Thus Carol Hoffer deliberately twists the evidence in a vain attempt to uphold her thesis by stating that Alldridge 'specifically reported making treaties of peace and amity with two women chiefs in 1889',[88] which he did not.

[86] N. C. Hollins, 'Mende Law', p. 28.
[87] Alldridge, The Sherbro, pp. 166 ff. and 181.
[88] 'Mende and Sherbro Women', p. 151.

Before 1896 it seems to have been a common practice by the colonial officials to refer to all women with any degree of political authority as 'Queen'. Women as heads of towns are not uncommon, and there is no gainsaying that they held such minor posts of political authority among the Mende. But to refer to them as 'Queens' is not only a misnomer, but a falsification of their true political positions and roles. Dalɔ certainly had influence over a few towns that could be marked out distinctly as a country within Mendegla's state. It seems as if her husband was the town Chief of Bandasuma, and when he died, she took the position.[89] Thereafter, she fell in love with Boakei Gahiŋ of Tunkia country (under Mendegla) who gave her Teweyoma, Samatia, and Gawulema which became the Barri country.[90]

Dalɔ remained on very good and friendly terms with the colonial administration. 'Owing to her loyalty during the rising of 1898, her town Bandasuma was attacked and even besieged by an armed force . . .'[91] The administration supported her and confirmed her position as Paramount Chief in her own right after the war of 1898.

The Records of Paramount Chiefs say very little about 'Queen Betsy Gaye' of Jong beyond her being a 'great trader' and 'loyal during the 1898 disturbances'.[92] However, after the Jong disturbances of 1882,

Betsy Gay and other chiefs then apologised, blaming the Fula and Susu. Within four years she was crowned Queen of the Jong herself, less from hereditary right than from her known influence with the colony government.[93]

The other women chiefs, Sophia Neale Caulker of Shenge and Nancy Tucker of Bagru, were more emphatically colonial products, the result of collaboration with the administration in the 1898 war. Mrs. Caulker was made chief after her husband, who insisted that his subjects pay the tax, fell the first victim at the hands of his own family. Thomas Neale Caulker was not particularly liked in the Caulker family circle of Shenge

[89] Records of Paramount Chiefs, 1899, p. 177.
[90] Oral interviews at Joru, Gorahun, and Bandasuma, May 1973.
[91] Records of Paramount Chiefs, 1899, p. 177.
[92] Ibid., p. 193.
[93] Fyfe, A History, p. 440; also CO 267/349/207, Havelock to SS, 1882.

because his mother was a 'slave', and the administration virtually installed him. It is understandable why Mrs. Caulker was made to succeed her husband.[94]

Before the 1898 war, Nancy Tucker was installed in 1897 as acting Paramount Chief of Bagru. A trader-settler in Sembehun,

. . . she began by entertaining all Court Messengers and other Native Officials, and later extended her hospitality to European officials. In 1898 war came, and when it was over, all the chiefs were deposed and substitutes had to be selected by the Government, which was done very hastily. Nancy was by now well known, so she was made chief . . .[95]

Later in 1898 Nancy had to escape for her life to Kwellu 'owing to her loyalty to the Government'. She remained there until the end of the war. Subsequently, she 'proved most useful in bringing many offenders to justice'.[96]

Thus the assertion is made again that all women Paramount Chiefs were colonial products. In pre-colonial times, no woman could acquire political power of the highest order, although women held subordinate political offices. It was after the Protectorate and the 1898 war that the supporters of the administration were elevated to the position of Paramount Chiefs—the highest traditional political office that could be achieved under the colonial umbrella. In this sense, women Paramount Chiefs were like men Paramount Chiefs after 1898, because all owed their positions to the colonial state in the final analysis. But unlike men, women holding supreme political office were a colonial creation. The men were generally aware of the fact that the administration had a weakness for readily accepting women as chiefs. So, after the 1898 war, it has been plausibly argued that

often the male powers behind the scenes put forth a woman under the theory that the British—whose monarch was a member of the fair sex—would deal more tolerantly with her than with a man.[97]

The position is well supported by oral information and

[94] CO 267/446/184, Nathan to SS, 1899; Records of Paramount Chiefs, 1899, p. 1.

[95] F. W. H. Migeod, *A View of Sierra Leone* (London 1916), p. 189.

[96] Records of Paramount Chiefs, 1899, p. 5.

[97] W. L. Barrows, 'Local-Level Politics in Sierra Leone: Alliances in Kenema District' (Yale University PhD thesis, 1971), p. 60.

there is much documentary support too. In what became Wandoh Chiefdom, Madam Fangawa became chief after the 1898 war. Her husband had murdered some Frontier Police and, to escape punishment, surrendered the country to his wife, described as 'a wise and able chief, very staunch to the Government'.[98] She gave provisions to the administration during the war.

Similarly, it is related that in Bagbeh Chiefdom, Madam Marbajah, 'a crafty woman but seemingly a fair chief with her people, . . . was put forward as big chief after the rising when the real men chiefs wished to hide . . .'.[99]

In Lekpeyama Chiefdom too Chief Bundu of Tene was deposed by the administration and Madam Baiya Gelu was selected as chief. She was not related to him, but once she had been made chief, the dignity continued in her family in the female line and up to the time Migeod was travelling in the 1920s.[100] The administration deliberately encouraged women Paramount Chiefs. At the end of May 1908 Paramount Chief Makavoray of Bumpeh was made to resign because he was an 'unsatisfactory ruler'. In his place, the Section Chief of Yengema, Madam Boi Nessy, was installed.[101] In Nongowa Chiefdom, which was broken out of Nyagua's state, Madam Humonya was treated as 'a sort of Paramount chief of the other Paramount chiefs of the district'.

This Nongowa case is most illustrative. In 1918 there was a revolt against Humonya and, in one of her petitions written by lawyer H. Graham on 26 January 1920, there is a very graphic description of the position. Faba, the father of Nyagua, appointed Gbow, his brother-in-law, to 'administer the Nongowa section'. Gbow died in 1897 and, after the 1898 war, the people were afraid to elect a chief. 'Subsequently, the British authorities sent to ask that a chief be appointed but no man would come forward—they were all afraid.' In this extremity, the people requested Madam Matolo, one of Faba's wives, to take the position. She was readily accepted. She was succeeded by her daughter Humonya when, owing to senility, she abdicated in

[98] Intelligence Diary, Railway District, vol. III, SLGA.
[99] Ibid., Railway Sub-District, vol. III, p. 102.
[100] Migeod, *View of Sierra Leone*, pp. 93-4.
[101] Intelligence Book, Panguma District, 1905-8, p. 61, SLGA.

favour of her. The letter categorically states that 'the foregoing explains how women came to be Tribal Rulers in the Mendi country'. As a general phenomenon, the advent of women chiefs as heads of chiefdoms may be said to have begun after the Protectorate was proclaimed, and particularly after the 1898 war.[102]

(c) Impostors

Knowing full well the readiness of the colonial administration to have women as Paramount Chiefs, some women took advantage of the situation and made out claims to territory for themselves. A woman called Kona Kambeh intrigued successfully to get Commandant Laborde to secure official recognition for her as 'chief woman' of East Bagru. A letter was written to Laborde on 24 May 1884 purporting to come from the other chiefs, in which they acknowledged Konah Kambeh as 'Chief Woman'. In 1886, after the death of Laborde, Kona Kambeh caused trouble, and the chiefs petitioned for her removal and 'emphatically denied' ever having written the letter of 24 May 1884. The letter was fictitious and the signatures were forgeries. Kona Kambeh had told the writer to sign the names of the chiefs, thus deceiving Laborde into recognizing her and her jurisdiction. She was tolerated in her short reign mainly because the people thought she had the support of the Commandant. The chiefs unanimously asked for her deposition from 'the position of Chief woman of Bargroo to which she was never elected and which she gained by fraudulent representations'.[103] She was accordingly deposed. But this incident also shows that it was possible to intrigue for traditional leadership through the colonial administration even before the latter later became the ultimate source of that authority. Kambeh readily seized upon the obsessive weakness of the administration for women chiefs for purposes of personal aggrandisement. It is possible that had she not caused trouble to whip up opposition against her, she might well have succeeded, like many others, in carving out a Paramount Chiefdom in which her descendants might be reigning even today.

[102] Nongowa Chiefdom, Paramount Chief Elections, 1898–1926, SLGA (hereafter Nongowa Chiefs); Intelligence Diary, Railway District, vol. III, p. 1, SLGA.
[103] CO 267/364/312, Rowe to SS, 1886.

Another impostor nearly succeeded in carving out a chiefdom for herself, but for the fact that it clashed with a stronger interest. Madam Nyebo claimed the Kagboro country, and started posing as acting Paramount Chief. When three chiefs, all women, came to meet Nathan in June 1899 at Moyamba after the war, the acting Governor was not sure whether Nyebo had been recognized by the administration as Paramount Chief or whether she had been duly elected by the people. The country she claimed was part of the country over which Sophia Neale Caulker had been recently recognized as Paramount Chief. She therefore disputed Nyebo's claim, and Nathan decided that an investigation must be made.[104]

J. C. E. Parkes threw doubts on Nyebo's claims and, after the investigations, her right was refuted and Kagboro was regarded as part of Shenge.[105] Fairtlough passed the decision of the administration to Sophia: '. . . the Government cannot recognise Madame Neghbo as Paramount Chief of the Cockboro which position has always been held by the Caulker family. Madame Neghbo will therefore consider herself as subchief to you in every way.'[106] It is possible that had Nyebo's claims not been contested by one who had far stronger support from the administration, she might well have succeeded then in carving out a country for herself.

(*d*) Disregard for the authority of women

Nevertheless, despite the support received from the administration, the authority of women chiefs was generally precarious. Less then a decade after the 1898 war, this had become quite manifest. As early as 1903 Governor King-Harman on a visit in the Panguma district realized the precarious position of Madam Matolo. In order to prop her up, he sent her a small brass staff 'with an expression of my hope that, with such a token of the support of the Government, she will find no further difficulty in enforcing her authority over her sub-chiefs and other subjects'.[107] In 1907 the Paramount Chief of Lugbu complained that her authority was being disregarded.[108]

[104] CO 267/447/Conf. 45, Nathan to SS, 1899.
[105] Records of Paramount Chiefs, 1899, p. 1.
[106] CO 267/511/Conf., 5 Jan. 1909, Fairtlough to Caulker, enc.
[107] Nongowa Chiefs, SLGA.
[108] Decree Book, Bandajuma District, p. 107, SLGA.

Madam Fangawa, to whom her husband had abdicated the rulership of Wandoh, was 'at constant variance with her people'.[109] In 1903 Governor King-Harman reported sadly about 'Queen' Dalɔ of Bandasuma:

. . . the Paramount chief is a poor weak creature, quite unequal to the task of governing her country, and the District Commissioner has been obliged to appoint a deputy to assist her. . . . She resents this interference with her authority; but as she herself informed me that her people would not obey her, I did not see my way to interfere in the matter.[110]

Madam Humonya was no exception. Her sub-chiefs were not loyal to her and 'they took undue authority upon themselves'.[111] Thus, it is not unreasonable to conclude that the administration had to support constantly the institution of their own creation—women chiefs—until it became generally acceptable. As such, there was a general instability in the early days of the colonial period when, after the threat of punishment for the 1898 war had gone, the men tried to oust the women chiefs. This situation was inevitable, and it only ceased when the practice became precedent and was subsequently legitimized by the people voluntarily accepting the institution, well into the colonial period. Until this point was reached, women chiefs as colonial products needed constant bolstering from the colonial authorities.

As to Madam Sophia Neale Caulker, who gained victory over Nyebo in 1899, the administration failed ten years later to keep her going in the face of a revolt. Being too old and ill, the chief was unable to perform her functions, which she delegated to her speaker, George Domingo. The people of Kagboro revolted because they were not given the opportunity to elect a regent, contrary to customary law. George Domingo too had succeeded in personally antagonizing a lot of people. Rather than get a regent appointed, Governor Probyn thought it politic to get Sophia deposed and an opportunity given to the people to elect a new chief. Sophia was of the opinion that the District Commissioner, Fairtlough, was instigating the revolt against her. Nevertheless, on 8 February 1909, the representa-

[109] Intelligence Diary, Railway District, vol. III, SLGA.
[110] CO 267/467/36, King-Harman to SS, 1903.
[111] Intelligence Diary, Railway District, vol. III, SLGA.

tives of Kagboro and Shenge elected Seh Lebbi from Kagboro to be the Paramount Chief of the two districts.[112]

New Traditions

Women Paramount Chiefs were such a familiar sight in the early days of colonial rule that within two decades the institution had gained legitimacy, and therefore hardened into tradition, which colonial officials justified. Earlier than Sir Harry Luke, Dr. J. C. Maxwell in 1906 attempted to give administrative legitimacy to the new institution, thus making it appear an old tradition.

In a memorandum, Maxwell set out the reasons why 'women have been selected as chiefs':

(1) because the woman has either been the only child of the chief or the oldest person fit to succeed

(2) because she was the wife of a chief and acted as regent for him during illness and was then chosen to succeed him

(3) because there were rival male claimants of equal strength, and to avoid internal disturbances both have waived their claims in favour of a woman

(4) because the influential men of the chiefdom were afraid of their own powers being restricted if they selected a man.[113]

These reasons are based on observations of local politics in the colonial period and can lay no claim to pre-colonial validity. However, although women Paramount Chiefs were colonial products, they had been accepted into the traditions of chieftaincy perhaps by 1910 and after, beyond which period it is fruitless to continue the debate. It became accepted without misgiving that men and women could become Paramount Chiefs among the Mende and Mende-dominated peoples.

In the matter of handling chiefs, the two years between the proclamation of the Protectorate and the defeat of the Mende in the war of 1898 were a time of immense fluidity. At that time, the only source of legitimacy for political authority was service to the colonial state. From this time also, it was possible

[112] CO 267/508/594, Probyn to SS, 1908; CO 267/511/Conf., 5 Jan. 1909, Probyn to SS; CO 267/512/Conf., 17 Feb. 1909, Probyn to SS.

[113] CO 267/503/209, enc., memo by Maxwell, 1906.

to get women chiefs integrated into the traditions of the people. After peace and quiet were restored, the liquidity of the situation was similarly bound to freeze. While it was known and accepted that the colonial state was the ultimate source of traditional authority, the administration wanted this ultimate source to become only a matter of remote control, a residual authority, since it was not only undesirable but also impossible to rule 'directly'. A new set of traditions emphasizing the ultimate suzerainty of the colonial state had to be integrated with the old customs in so far as they were compatible with the maintenance of colonial hegemony. Until this integration was well under way, 'the general position with regard to the status of Paramount chiefs, [was] for many years . . . indefinite'. This was because with many chiefs hanged, exiled, or imprisoned after the 1898 war, the administration had to find successors. 'Subsequent experience has shown that many "successors" had no real claim to their positions and were accepted by Government for no other reason than that they should be vigorous in the collection of the House Tax', as a Chief Commissioner explained in 1949.[114]

The British had the further task of clearly delineating succession to this new type of traditional authority having its *raison d'être* in the colonial state. By 1937 one of the greatest British paternalists, Margery Perham, realized that African methods of succession were more complex than the British had previously imagined. There was no simple, neat, clearcut manner. 'The occasions when the Government has tried discreetly to tip the scale in favour of what seemed by our standards the most likely ruler have not always been so successful as to encourage the practice.' Therefore strict primogeniture was not a hard and fast rule and the administrations resorted to 'appointing [rulers] freely in the traditional way'.[115] This seems somewhat paradoxical, but it gives the clue to the colonial pattern. Whatever the method used to obtain a chief, he must not be unsuitable to the colonial administration for any reason whatever. This reaffirms the primacy of the

[114] L. W. Wilson, 'Memorandum—Election, Appointment, Recognition, and Deposition of Paramount Chiefs', in 'Material for a projected Encyclopaedia for Sierra Leone', Box 3, MSS. Afr. s. 390, Rhodes House Library, Oxford, paras. 17 and 18 (hereafter Wilson, PC memo).

[115] M. Perham, *Native Administration in Nigeria* (London 1937), p. 46.

colonial state whose interests must be served by all institutions under its aegis.

Indeed in Africa as a whole, rules are rarely found which indicate clearly a single definite successor. Even if the rules were clear, they operated uncertainly in practice.[116] Until the British learned this lesson by trial and error, they tried to find a neat system, somewhat similar to their own succession system. The policy of upholding the institution of chieftaincy through which alone the British could rule peaceably was never questioned. No colonial official ever suggested abolishing the institution. That a definite set of customary laws and government existed was accepted and recognized. 'For the just and peaceful administration of this country', wrote Wallis, 'we have had to take into consideration the influence of the chiefs over their people, and the power they are able to wield through the agency of their own courts . . .' He hoped that, strengthened by 'the best laws and the highest principles which modern science and modern thought have to give', it would be possible to achieve a gradual development 'strictly on African lines'.[117]

Throughout, however, there was no consistent policy—only that all activities of the officials were to be in the interest of the colonial state and not necessarily of the subjects. Whatever the confusions, contradictions, puzzles, and inconsistencies of the period, colonial interest stands out as the overriding constant. After the imbroglio of 1898, there was a genuine need to have certain principles followed in respect of the most important 'traditional' institution in the scheme of local administration. But the language of the officials themselves was sufficiently confusing as to convey a picture of a confused situation. Wallis stated that the Paramount Chief was 'appointed to this position either by the right of succession, by election, or, in exceptional cases, by the nomination of the British Government'.[118] It is difficult to reconcile appointment with election and right of succession. This, however, shows the complexity of the situation, which suited the administration since it could apply the rule that best served its interests at any particular time. But

[116] Gluckman, *Custom and Conflict*, p. 46.

[117] C. B. Wallis, 'In the Court of the Native Chiefs in Mendiland', *Journal of the African Society*, XVI, 1905, pp. 399, 405, 409.

[118] C. B. Wallis, 'Tribal Laws of the Mendi', *Journal of Comparative Legislation and International Law*, III, 4, 1921, p. 228.

throughout the colonial period there is to be found either emphasis on, or lip-service to, hereditary succession and ruling houses.

Governor Probyn's principles of local administration

In this complex situation, Sierra Leone, however, found a spokesman in Governor Probyn. Without putting them into legislation or legal document, he spoke and wrote freely about the principles of administering the Protectorate. He, perhaps, gave shape to the policy that obtained in Sierra Leone as far as was practicable. In a lecture given before the African Society, Probyn reiterated that the chiefs, being the 'natural leaders of their people', were the best qualified agents through whom to achieve the aims of the colonial state. Although he stated earlier that there were no kings but only chiefs—this being true only after the Protectorate was proclaimed—Probyn drew attention to the democratic basis of the chieftaincy institution. Chiefs were chosen from a 'ruling family' by a consensus of the elders. It was the man they thought would best direct the affairs of the chiefdom who was chosen. The chief could not take any important decisions without 'the consent and advice of his principal men'.[119]

Probyn was not very sympathetic with the Christian missions because of their approach. 'There is no more religious man than the pagan of the West Coast', yet the missionary had to smash his 'traditional belief' and 'elaborate religion' before making the slightest effect. The Africans, as a matter of fact, were not perfectly aware of the mission of *pax Britannica*. This ignorance, coupled with their religion, made it difficult to achieve rapid progress. 'The great secret . . . in dealing with the West Coast is enormous patience and determination to go very slowly.' To achieve further improvement, it was necessary to have freedom of conscience and lack of 'tyranny', not tyranny of the individual, but 'of a class of special interests, of preconceived opinion'—which must be a reference to the missions.[120]

The Governor envisaged the existing situation as one in

[119] Leslie Probyn, 'Sierra Leone and the Natives of West Africa', *Journal of the African Society*, VI, 23, 1907, p. 251.
[120] Ibid., pp. 252–8.

which the King of Great Britain and his authorities represented a great Paramount Chief of all the Paramount Chiefs, and therefore 'we should act towards the chiefs not as a European power, but rather as a wise and experienced native Paramount Chief'.[121] In 1904 the report on the Blue Book stated the position:

The Government of the country is carried out through the chiefs. The authority of the chiefs is upheld and every encouragement is given to them to adhere to their native customs and laws, provided these are not repugnant to civilised ideas of justice.[122]

Following this up, Probyn sent a dispatch in 1906 explaining that the administration 'only claim at excercising a controlling influence' over the chiefs who in point of fact governed the Protectorate.[123] The Governor was well aware of the rapid change that the society was undergoing as a result of erecting the alien cultural superstructure of the colonial state. Perhaps from altruistic motives he attempted a codification of the law to regularize the position of the chiefs *vis-à-vis* their people.

The effect of the rebellion and the abolition of slavery [internal slave trade] has been that a doubt has been created as to the relative position of the chiefs and their people: the influx of Freetown traders, acquainted solely with colonial law, necessarily tends to produce friction.[124]

The Protectorate Native Law Ordinance, 1905

In 1905 an 'Ordinance to simplify, modify, and give effect to Native Law in the Protectorate of Sierra Leone in certain cases' was passed, referred to in short as The Protectorate Native Law Ordinance, 1905. The Ordinance was divided into eight parts. The first part constituted three-tier assemblies of chiefs: Local, District, and General Assemblies. The General Assembly would give advice on legislative proposals affecting the Protectorate. The District Assemblies would form 'a body from which the District Commissioner will be able to select chiefs to assist in settling boundary disputes'. The Local

---

[121] Ibid., p. 255.
[122] CO 267/479/347, enc., Report on Blue Book, 1904.
[123] CO 267/484/Conf., 30 May 1906, Probyn to SS.
[124] CO 267/477/202, Probyn to SS, 1905.

Assemblies, functionally more important, would 'serve as a means whereby the actual working of a law can be foretold and, indirectly, they will serve as a medium through which the publication of a law can be effected', since the real difficulty in Protectorate administration is to get the inhabitants to understand what is intended in all legislation.

Part II was more controversial in that it sought to regulate the rights of Paramount Chiefs and other chiefs with regard to labour and thus 'prevent [them] from attempting to reintroduce a system indistinguishable from slavery'. The Governor was empowered to make regulations for this purpose. The people were not to be made to work for the chiefs to the extent of preventing them from cultivating their own farms. Clause 18 gave rise to controversy:

It shall be lawful for a Paramount Chief in his capacity as chief and for the other chiefs in a Paramount Chiefdom, with the consent and approval of the District Commissioner, to commute the labour which they are entitled to have supplied for the purpose of working their farms or buildings or repairing their compounds, to a fixed tithe or share of the crops harvested by the people or of the produce collected by the latter . . .

This commutation was a change in customary law but was intended to introduce a 'more business-like system'.

The Colonial Office accepted the bringing of the Ordinance into operation, but with the advice that Section 18 should not be enforced until it had been further considered.[125] Probyn asked, however, to be allowed to experiment in one or two chiefdoms only 'as the wisdom or unwisdom of the change could be ascertained to a large extent by experience'.[126] This was approved.

Parts III to IV inclusive were intended to deal with problems and matters arising from the presence of 'non-natives' within the jurisdiction of the chiefs. For the first time, the Ordinance used the term 'Tribal Authority' to mean 'Paramount Chiefs and their Councillors and men of note or Sub-Chiefs and their Councillors and men of note'.[127]

[125] CO 267/477/202, Probyn to SS, 1905; CO 267/482/Tel., 3 Jan. 1906, SS to Probyn.
[126] CO 267/482/42, Probyn to SS, 1906.
[127] Protectorate Native Law Ordinance, 1905, Sec. 58.

In December 1907 Probyn sent a report on the experiment in two chiefdoms—Wunde and Yoni. He claimed that the experiments were successful and, although commutation was optional, the people were much in favour of it preferring it to the time lost in making 'manja' farms. The Colonial Office, however, felt that there was not sufficient evidence to decide in favour of making Section 18 universally operational. More information was requested.[128]

The general opinion of the District Commissioners was against introducing the measure; the only exception was G. W. Page, District Commissioner of Sherbro and Northern Sherbro district. But Probyn seemed to have a special interest in the matter. Major Fairtlough drew attention to the success of the experiments, but cautioned that this was not sufficient index for universal or compulsory application. Although Probyn agreed with him, he still favoured commutation.

It would be most impolitic to make the adoption of the tithe system compulsory, but as pointed out by Dr. Maxwell . . . tithe system is already recognised and worked by the natives as an alternative to the system by which labour is given upon the chief's farm [in contra–distinction to labour on public works].[129]

The Colonial Office was very cautious in its reply.

If . . . the principle of commutation has been recognised to some extent by the natives themselves it may perhaps be better for the colonial Government itself not to interfere at this stage, but to leave matters to develop naturally, until the time arrives when Govern-ment is called upon to give legal recognition and enforcement to an established custom.[130]

Thus by 1909 the commutation debate was over. Probyn's enthusiasm to push the reform was neutralized by general official opinion that it was best to leave things alone while they were in a process of change without precipitating that change. The colonial state itself, consciously or unconsciously, was an agent of change, and it was undesirable to escalate changes to the detriment of the colonial state which was feared in this case.

[128] CO 267/498/567, Probyn to SS, 1907, and enc., memo by Maxwell.
[129] CO 267/512/107, Probyn to SS, 1909; also CO 267/517/524, Probyn to SS, 1909, and encs., D.Cs to Governor.
[130] CO 267/512/107, SS to Probyn 1909.

K

Erosion of chiefly authority

However, despite the passionate efforts to uphold the institution of chieftaincy, the activities of the administration and the inevitable progress of social change were steadily undermining the institution. The chiefs although generally supported by the administration were in a position of little authority as the colonial administration had usurped most of it, and were unable to enforce their authority over their subjects in the traditional fashion. This came to official notice as early as 1904. When C. B. Wallis took over the Sherbro district, he reported to Governor King-Harman, on the strength of reliable information, that there was grave dissatisfaction in the district. Briefly enumerated, this situation arose out of the loss of control of the chiefs over their people; interference by the police; 'no recognition by the Government of the ancient laws and customs of the chiefs and people . . .'; the large exodus of people into Liberia which the chiefs could not arrest because of lack of sufficient authority and the interference of the police. The Governor blamed Alldridge, Wallis's predecessor in office, for causing this state of affairs. Spending most of his time at Bonthe, he hardly visited his district. 'Mr. Alldridge has pursued', the Governor opined, '. . . an absolutely wrong policy in not supporting and encouraging the chiefs and in ignoring the fact that although the Sherbro, for political reasons, forms part of the Colony, the people . . . are identical with their close neighbours in the Protectorate.'[131]

Perhaps Alldridge is altogether not to blame for this crisis. He was acting within the law. If Sherbro ought to be administered as the Protectorate, then there seemed to be no reason to keep it technically as part of the colony, when in fact, in every characteristic, it was like the Protectorate. This is just an example of one of these irrational decisions made and kept to for no reason but colonial convenience during the establishment of the colonial regime and which then survived as onerous relics.

Wallis, like a true soldier, had in 1904 recommended the following:

Support of the Chiefs. The laws of the district as regards their

[131] CO 267/472/Conf., 8 Apr. 1904, King-Harman to SS.

relations with their people to be . . . like those in the Protectorate. Chiefs to act as Police and Detective Officers of Customs at the small stations and to receive a percentage upon all smuggled goods captured by them. . . . An arrangement with the Government of Liberia to give us their assistance in preventing British subjects from being shipped from Liberian ports.[132]

The following year it was decided to place the whole of the Sherbro district outside Bonthe, Bendu, and York Island 'under the tribal system'. Governor King-Harman gave priority to this reform.[133] Alldridge, back from leave, was instructed to proceed with the re-creation of the Paramount Chiefs. The Commissioner was optimistic that when it was completed, 'I do not doubt that it will be an excellent institution, of considerable utility to the Government, as well as to the people, if properly supervised.' The people received the matter extremely well.[134]

Alldridge held large meetings at the headquarters of each of the 'chiefdoms' and announced the decision. The people were then asked to consult together to choose their Paramount Chief at a subsequent meeting. Alldridge showed much energy in this task and got the people to elect their chiefs in all areas except Krim country.[135] The administration recognized these chiefs for a probationary period. Later on, the people of Krim chose Charles W. Tucker as chief over one portion, while Governor Probyn, on a visit to the Sherbro, appointed Francis Fawundu as Paramount Chief over the remaining portion. 'In both cases,' wrote the Governor, 'the tribal rule has now passed back to the families which in olden days ruled the two portions of the country in question.'[136] Evidently, the Governor was assuming that pre-colonial government of the indigenous people was through institutionalized 'Ruling Houses' consisting of certain circumscribed families. This further implies some kind of hereditary succession.

[132] Ibid., enc., Wallis to Col. Sec.
[133] CO 267/486/263, Probyn to SS, 1906.
[134] CO 267/475/43, enc., Report on Sherbro District.
[135] CO 267/477/Conf., 17 Apr. 1905, Probyn to SS; CO 267/486/263, Probyn to SS, 1906.
[136] CO 267/486/263, Probyn to Sp, 1906.

'Ruling Houses', the 'hereditary' right, and new methods of succession

However, the situation was fluid and it was difficult to find clear-cut rules of succession. The most important factor in making a ruler was the unanimous choice of the elders of the potential subjects. The elders could be induced in their choice by several motivating factors, but service to the community was at the root of everything. Anyone, therefore, had an opportunity to be a leader and a ruler. This was quite distinct from ownership of land which was vested in families. Acquisition of political authority at a level higher than the village and the acquisition of land and property through inheritance were mutually exclusive phenomena.[137] Perhaps a confusion of these two, together with a sprinkling of one or two instances of son succeeding father in political office, crystallized the image of 'Ruling Houses' to the colonial officials.

In his report on the Bandajuma-Railway district for 1906, Dr. Maxwell pointed out the uncertainty in the matter of elections. He had left the people themselves to elect their own chiefs and, if they so wished, with the aid of outside chiefs. Observing these successions, Maxwell reported that '. . . in some cases there is a well-established hereditary succession, in others the chief must belong to one of two tribes or clans, while in others, no rule as to succession seems to have been established'.[138] Unfortunately, Governor Probyn was, about the same time, generalizing that chiefs were chosen from 'Ruling Families'.

The idea of Ruling Houses has tended to be perpetuated as a genuine traditional system. As early as 1890 Alldridge noted that neither hereditary succession nor primogeniture was a law in Mende succession. In 1896 Cardew also emphasized that a *chiefship* is not usually given to a son and that Kai Londo was not a hereditary chief. Yet the colonial officials, eager to create a neat system out of the pre-colonial dynamics, insisted on or invented principles that were not altogether indigenous to the Mende system. While Cardew was refuting any claims to hereditary succession by Kai Londo, N. C. Hollins maintained that in virtue of his preserving and maintaining

---

[137] Interviews at Gaura and Jaiama-Bongor, May 1973.
[138] CO 267/493/144, Report on Bandajuma-Railway District, 1906.

Luawa, Kai Londo 'and his family should be looked upon as the Ruling House of Luawa'.[139] During a disputed succession in Lugbu in 1907, the 'tribal authority' held that the chiefship 'could not be claimed as a right by the eldest son', a decision with which the assessor chiefs, who usually assisted the District Commissioner at elections, perfectly agreed.[140] In 1909 Probyn, who had earlier stated that chiefs came from ruling families, reminded the Secretary of State for the Colonies that 'the family of a Paramount Chief had no vested right to inherit the chiefdom'.[141] Kenneth Little is thus wrong when he asserts that the post of chief or ruler of the chiefdom is according to tradition 'to be regarded strictly as the possession, in the male line, of the descendants of the original founder . . . usually the first born'.[142] What is being stated here is clearly recognizable as a colonial development.

It does appear that while the officials tried as much as possible and practicable to create a neat pattern in the matter of successions, their adherence to hereditary succession and ruling families was circumvented when it was in the interest of the colonial state. A system does seem, however, to have developed under the colonial regime; a system, however flexible, the rules of which came to be more or less these: firstly, a Paramount Chief had to be approved by the colonial administration. Secondly, if the elders chose a man who was acceptable to the administration then no problem arose. But, thirdly, if the elders chose a man unacceptable to the administration, then the latter tended to take the initiative, and would very often choose the descendant of a previous chief and impose him on the elders.

In the Sherbro, far from upholding the institution of the *Beh Sherbro* and allowing his descendants the opportunity of holding the dignity, the administration deliberately demolished the institution. Although the policy of fragmentation militated against reviving the power of the *Beh Sherbro*, the institution might nevertheless have been upheld with limited reference to Sherbro island only. As events proved, however, it was in the

---

[139] D.C. N. C. Hollins of Pendembu District to Commissioner of the Southern Province, 24 May 1924, Kailahun District Records.
[140] Decree Book, Bandajuma District, p. 107, SLGA.
[141] CO 267/511/Conf., 5 Jan. 1909, Probyn to SS.
[142] Little, *The Mende*, p. 181.

colonial interest to destroy the institution. Gbanna Lewis, the *Beh Sherbro*, was exiled by administrative order as the chief architect of the 1898 war although no legal evidence could be procured against him.

In 1905 his son petitioned to have Gbanna Lewis back, but this was firmly rejected, as noted in Chapter IV above. It was feared that the return of the King would afford his son an opportunity to whip up support against the colonial incumbent, Fama Yani. The former rival of Gbanna Lewis, Fama Yani, was content to have his authority limited to Sherbro Island only, whereas there was the possibility that Lewis would lay irredentist claims to the whole of Sherbro territory. This would have unsettling effects on the Protectorate administration. Therefore it was better to have Fama Yani than to follow any rigid principles with regard to having Gbanna Lewis back. In 1914, however, Yani was convicted and sentenced to two years imprisonment for possession of 'Borfima', the medicine of the 'Human Leopard Society', and was therefore deposed.[143]

Besides, there were also other local political interests militating against Gbanna Lewis's return in which Fairtlough and Page were personally involved. The part Gbanna Lewis was supposed to have played in the 1898 war was still fresh in the minds of these officials, and it was still believed that 'his offer to assist the D[istrict] C[ommissioner] was a treacherous one and was part of the conspiracy' to enable him to get arms and furnish the 'rebels' with them. Page maintained that the agitation to get Lewis back was started by a Mr. Williams of Mokolo who wanted to get rid of Fama Yani.[144]

Where convenient, the administration adhered to hereditary succession in so far as this can be taken to mean claim based on descent from a former ruler. In Luawa, the pattern of succession reveals the flexibility of the colonial principles. When Fa Bundeh died in 1912, his son Boakei Bundeh contested with Momoh Banya, the son of Kai Londo. With the help of Chief Kutubu of Pendembu, Boakei Bundeh was made chief. Four

---

[143] CO 267/526/Conf. (A), 20 Nov. 1910, Probyn to SS, and enc., Fairtlough to Colonial Secretary.

[144] Sherbro District Records, Confidential File, 1/1899, 'Deposition of Gbana Lewis'. I am grateful to Mr. Christopher Fyfe for supplying this information.

years later, he was deposed for misrule. Then Momoh Banya offered himself again, this time against Gobeh who was a 'trusted messenger' Kai of Londo. 'Momo Banya received the most votes, but in view of his comparative youth, was induced to stand aside for the venerable Gobe.'[145] It is doubtful whether Momoh Banya was any younger than Boakei Bundeh, but Gobeh played his cards well and claimed to be the 'first cousin' of Kai Londo.[146] It must be noted that there is no indigenous term for 'cousin'. Cousins are all referred to as brothers. But by claiming a tenuous relationship with Kai Londo, Gobeh succeeded in getting his right recognized by the administration. He thus created another 'ruling house' in addition to the Kai Londo-Banya and Fa Bundeh houses.

In Baoma Chiefdom too the administration created a new ruling house in 1915. The three ruling families reached a deadlock in the matter of finding a successor. Dembi, not a member of any of the existing ruling houses, was, however, chosen as a convenient way out of the impasse. Thereafter, it was settled by the elders that in the future the Paramount Chief should be from the original three ruling houses. But,

should . . . some member of another well-known Baoma-Falle family have rendered such service to the country as to merit the reward of a chiefship, he could not be disbarred from election.
. . . It was recognised that Dembi had no claim to the chiefship by Falle birth, but he formed a convenient way out of the impass [*sic*] the three families had got into and so accepted by the Government . . .[147]

It was implicit in this that in the colonial period, birth was certainly a criterion for accession to a Paramount Chieftaincy. But as it suited their convenience, the administration could circumvent this 'principle' and appeal directly to the precolonial principle of service to the community. This circumstance assumes all being well with no colonial interests at stake. However, Dembi succeeded in founding another ruling house in Baoma that still holds the chiefship today.

There is an even more illuminating example from Jawe. When Vandi Von of Nyeama died, Kponie of Folu was chosen

[145] Hollins, 'Short History of Luawa', p. 25.
[146] Decree Book, Railway Sub-District, p. 303, SLGA.
[147] Ibid., p. 291.

as his successor in 1906. Jaya, the son of Vandi Von, contested the validity of the election and claimed the chiefship in succession to his father. In the inquiry that was held, it was shown that there had been no regular succession in any one family and that Jaya's claims were inadmissible, while Kponie was found to have been 'appointed' by the people 'in the usual manner'. The following year Kponie died and was succeeded by his brother Gombukla. Another dispute arose and the settlement was entered in the decree book:

(1) That the chief be chosen as formerly from the Bobor house.
(2) That Gombukra of Foru—brother of the late chief Gbonnie be elected as chief of Jawi.
(3) That as the chiefship has sometimes been in the Nyeama family to avoid further disputes, it is agreed that the chief shall be chosen alternately from the Foru and Nyeama families, the next chief to be chosen from the Nyeama family.[148]

Clearly, this arrangement was influenced by the officials. Only one chief had come from Nyeama, but the arrangement recognized a ruling house from there. This position was clearly demonstrated in a petition by Lahai Conteh, Gombukla's successor, against his deposition in 1913. Lahai Conteh explained that Vandi Von was the son of a Muslim stranger, Vandi Gbey, who used to make charms for the Chief of Jawe, an ancestor of Lahai Conteh. After the 1898 war the country was unsettled and in consequence Kponie, 'the rightful successor', waived his right in favour of Vandi Von, 'a much older man, who had grown up as a foster brother of Kponie's [and] was the person deputed to treat with the District Commissioner at Bandajuma for the settlement of the country and the regular payment of the hut-tax'. In two subsequent elections after the death of Vandi Von, the claim of Jaya, his son, was turned down 'partly on the ground that his father Vandi Von was not regarded as the founder of a separate royal house', but if anything, a member of the Folu family by adoption.[149] Moreover, the idea of having a neat alternate succession is a colonial one. But as often happened the fate of these arrangements, even when entered in the degree book, lay

[148] Pendembu District Decree Book, pp. 4–6, 10, SLGA.
[149] CO 267/556/112, enc., petition of Lahai Conteh by Sam Barlatt to SS, 1914.

in the hands of the District Commissioner. A successor might not even know of the entry in the decree book, or if he did he could ignore it for various reasons.

When Gombukla died, he was succeeded by his nephew Lahai Conteh, who was deposed after a petition that the election was irregular. There seem to have been some fishy circumstances surrounding Lahai Conteh's case. Evidently the 1907 arrangement was not invoked at the election, but after the petition it was discovered and invoked against him. It was then agreed that the alternating principle should operate which automatically disqualified Lahai Conteh from offering his candidature.[150] Foray from Nyeama was then elected and since then no one has invoked the 1907 arrangement with the consequence that the chiefship has not alternated back to Folu up to the present time. Apparently, no official was thereafter ever aware of the arrangement at any subsequent election.

A similar situation obtained in Lekpeyama Chiefdom, where a tripartite agreement was made to rotate the chiefship among the ruling houses. But the administration did not allow this arrangement to govern subsequent elections. So much depended on the local District Commissioner. Thus in 1945 the District Commissioner turned down the claims of the two ruling houses in the Tunkia Chiefdom that they had agreed to alternate: 'I cannot imagine . . . a Temne custom to intrude into a Mende election.' Two years later, the decision was reversed by another District Commissioner. Five years after that, a new District Commissioner disallowed the agreement as a 'Temne custom' and allowed the Paramount Chief to be elected from the same house as his predecessor.[151]

The primacy of hereditary principles was a colonial innovation and does not feature prominently in pre-colonial political affairs, although it was a factor of minor importance. The British, however, in seizing upon descent as a criterion for political succession ossified the recruitment system to Mende political office and limited the choice of leadership to a circumscribed group which now comprised the 'ruling houses'. However, this innovation became rapidly integrated with the

[150] CO 267/557/183, enc., Bowden to Col. Sec., 1914.
[151] See Barrows, 'Local-Level Politics', pp. 69–70.

traditional political institutions which were not rejected. This invention has been described as 'the most important innovation of the early colonial administration', and judging from the point of view of most development theories, the foisting of ascriptive rulership in place of the achievement-orientated practice of the traditional system 'was a regressive step'.[152]

From an examination of the decree books, it is clear that the sub-chiefs and headmen were made to choose the Paramount Chief by a unanimous decision. All being well, where no colonial interests or prejudices were at stake, the administration then graced the choice with its formal recognition by 'appointment'. In short, the people elect, the administration appoints! The residual authority of the administration was exercised in the matter of withholding recognition or deposing a chief.

The pattern and effect of depositions

In general there were two types of depositions: those in which proceedings against the Paramount Chief were initiated at the grassroots in the form of a petition or revolt; and those initiated by the administration outside the chiefdom structure. This latter method of deposition was vested by law in the Governor under the Protectorate Ordinance of 1896 and subsequent amendments. Depositions of Paramount Chiefs seem to be another colonial innovation, and one is extremely reluctant to agree that the Mende 'had often ousted' their rulers.[153] The former type of deposition seems to have been of more common occurrence than the latter, at least after 1914.

During the first fifteen years or so of colonial rule, depositions were a common theme in the Governor's dispatches to the Secretary of State for the Colonies. It is entirely untrue that the process of deposition was 'extremely complicated and rarely resorted to'.[154] Indeed one is impressed by the alacrity of the administration in deposing chiefs for the slightest offences during the early phase of colonial consolidation. In 1906 Dr. Maxwell warned against 'hasty depositions of chiefs, who with

[152] See Barrows, 'Local-Level Politics', pp. 62–79.

[153] Ibid., p. 93. Chiefs might have been deposed, but this writer certainly has no evidence for deposition of kings in the pre-colonial period.

[154] Crowder, *West Africa Under Colonial Rule*, p. 225; also Buell, *Native Problem*, p. 864.

all their faults are very frequently popular in their chiefdoms and always command a considerable following'. He advocated a humanistic approach based on the development of a sense of respect for law and order as the cure to maladministration of the chiefdoms rather than frequent depositions.[155]

The advice was favourably received by Probyn, who authorized the District Commissioners to impose a fine on chiefs in cases in which 'a chief commits a fault of omission or commission which cannot be overlooked but which does not merit the full penalty of deposition'. The fines were not to exceed £10 and were to be subject to the Governor's approval. In this arrangement, the District Commissioners were to intimate to the chiefs in default that they were being fined in lieu of deposition. When this was acted upon in 'one or two cases with good results', the Governor formally asked the Colonial Office to recognize the 'system'. The Colonial Office readily approved.[156] In Standing Instruction No. 10 of 1910 concerning the deposition of chiefs, it was not intended to prescribe the procedure by law in connection with the deposition of a chief. But in the majority of cases requiring deposition, 'the necessary preliminaries will be an enquiry held by the District Commissioner into the conduct of the chief and a report to the Governor . . .'. The two circumstances under which an inquiry should be held with a view to deposition were

(a) Deliberate disobedience of important instructions given by the Government to the chief, or acts of other defiance indicating actual or intended rebellion.

(b) Persistent and flagrant misgovernment of his chiefdom and oppression of his subjects.

Apparently, the frequent incidence of depositions tended to create a power vacuum as the new incumbents could not readily command the respect of, and effectively exercise authority over, their subjects.

Yet even these measures did not blind the officials to the steady deterioration in the position of chiefs whose institution the administration was pledged to uphold. It seems to have

---

[155] CO 267/493/144, Bandajuma-Railway District Report, 1906.
[156] CO 267/497/Conf., 5 Nov. 1907, Probyn to SS.

been one of the ironies of Probyn's Governorship that while he championed the cause of upholding the institution of chief-taincy, the effect of their diminishing position gradually became apparent. In 1910 Dr. Maxwell sent the following to the Colonial Secretary:

It must be admitted that the ordinances affecting the Protectorate, while necessary from the point of view of civilisation, and while recognising the continuance of chiefs' rule, have (with the exception of the Protectorate Native Law Ordinance 1905) in many directions tended to have a detrimental effect on the position of chiefs. The chiefs have certainly been given security from attack, but their powers over natives have been diminished, their former power over non-native residents in the chiefdoms taken away and the sources of wealth of many destroyed by the clauses dealing with slave dealing. Unless some provision is made, these factors will operate to a greater extent in the future.[157]

Dr. Maxwell further cautioned that if the chiefs were allowed to be reduced to poverty, then it would be difficult to preserve 'tribal rule', which was one of the objects of the Protectorate Ordinances. He suggested two ways of 'providing against the deterioration of the chief's position'; first, the chiefs should receive sufficient stipend from the administration and so render themselves less dependent on traditional sources of income; second, the principle of direct contributions by their subjects to the chiefs should be more effectively recognized.[158] As late as 1915 Captain W. B. Stanley, following the conviction of eleven people for defying the authority of the Paramount Chief of Banta Chiefdom, entered in the decree book:

At the present time it appears to me that cases of this nature are unfortunately far too frequent in this [Ronietta] District, and that it is of the utmost importance that the Paramount Chiefs should receive the support of the Government and if possible be brought to assert their own authority.[159]

The administration did not take these suggestions lightly. It was the policy to rule through the chiefs, and if these chiefs as adjuncts of the new colonial administration were weak to the point of not being able to assert their authority they would be undermining the very existence of the colonial state. The

[157] CO 267/524/436, enc. 1, Maxwell to Col. Sec. 1910.   [158] Ibid.
[159] Ronietta District Decree Book, 22 Nov. 1915, SLGA.

Blue Book Report for 1911 outlined the new principles of Protectorate administration:

The principles underlying the administration of the Protectorate have been to recognise, as between natives, the use of native customary law; to preserve the authority of the native rulers; to strengthen the just and lawful exercise of that authority, while preventing all acts of aggression; and to grant to all non-natives in the Protectorate the protection of the English law . . .[160]

In the same year, the Annual Report on Railway District noted with apparent pleasure that no deposition took place in the district. It was usual to depose nearly every year.

The politics of administration—chief relations

From this time onwards the general policy was to uphold the chiefs in their positions and to protect them if need be. Until World War II, there were a few glaring depositions, but they represent extreme cases in which the people had become so dissatisfied that there was no other way out. The administration itself was now in a rather ambivalent position—pledged to uphold the chiefs and posing at the same time as the protector of the people against 'oppression'. On the whole, perhaps, it is fair to say that the administration only stepped in during the most revolting 'oppression' of his subjects by a chief. Otherwise, it was more or less a policy of *quieta non movere*.

But the administration was still the final arbiter in the matter of Paramount Chief elections. Where all was well, the District Commissioners forwarded the report of the election of a Paramount Chief by the elders to the Governor, but they frequently used the term 'appointment'. This was generally followed by a routine recommendation of 'confirmation on the usual six months probation'. In 1912, Dr. Maxwell minuted that while the Governor had power under the Protectorate Ordinance to depose a chief,

there is no provision in the Protectorate Ordinance requiring the Governor's confirmation as an essential to the election of a chief, and apparently, the intention is that the election should remain, as it had been in the past, entirely in the hands of the natives, while at

---

[160] CO 267/541/308, Bluebook Report, 1911.

the same time, the power of deposition possessed by the Governor enables any unsatisfactory person to be forthwith got rid of.[161]

Maxwell further stated that with regard to succession there was provision in customary law to allow a chief to be elected outside a ruling family, 'but it is understood that such appointment confers no subsequent rights on his family, and that on his death, the chiefdom reverts to the original family'. This was purely theoretical, for, as already seen, the chiefship remained in the Demby and Gobeh families as ruling houses instead of reverting to the original houses. Thus far from maintaining what was thought to be simply the pre-colonial system, such innovations as choosing a chief outside what had become a ruling house in colonial times gave opportunity to the incumbent during his period of office to 'create' a ruling house of his own family. Although the administration was justified by Maxwell in taking such a course of action provided the chiefship reverted, subsequent events have shown that it was easier to create a new ruling house than to obliterate the claims of the descendants of an 'outside chief' simply through the system of reversion. In most instances, the Commissioner presiding at the next election was not even aware of recorded precedents. Much therefore depended on local circumstances and individual administrators.

(a) The injustice to Lahai Conteh

In the case of Lahai Conteh, already cited, an election was conducted in 1913 in which he received 1,178 votes of households while Foray received 1,216. But it was discovered that some of Foray's supporters had secretly sworn 'to allow the real power to be exercised by another person who was objectionable to the Government'. Under the advice of the assessor chiefs who usually assisted at elections, the Acting District Commissioner declared Lahai Conteh elected. The action of the District Commissioner was certainly high-handed, but it was alleged that the assessor chiefs were bribed.

The Foray faction were disaffected and behaved in a manner not altogether conducive to the good order of the chiefdom. In fact Lahai Conteh complained of their 'insubordinate

[161] Quoted in Wilson, PC memo, para. 20.

intentions', but they made representations to the District Commissioner against Lahai Conteh. As discontent in the Foray camp continued, a letter was sent by the Acting District Commissioner to Lahai Conteh in November 1913, stating that he was coming to Daru with three assessor chiefs to discuss a certain matter. In his petition against his deposition, Lahai Conteh explained:

At that meeting the Acting District Commissioner announced that, although he was perfectly satisfied that your petitioner had not been guilty of bribery at his election and your petitioner had given the Government no cause for complaint since his election, yet he would declare your petitioner to be no longer chief, and he then proceeded to order a new election.

At the close of the election, at which a hitherto unknown feature was introduced—namely the taking of votes per capita rather than per headmen, your petitioner was declared to have lost the poll and was forthwith deposed.[162]

Lahai Conteh accused Foray of bribing the assessor chiefs and drew the attention of the Governor to the fact that he had been deposed in an illegal manner—no charges having been preferred against him for disobedience, misgovernment, oppression, 'or any other of those offences which might well entail the severe punishment of deposition'.

One crucial point in the petition was that once a chief had been declared elected he could not by law be disqualified from his office by regular proceedings for deposition. This was not followed in Conteh's case which afforded the major legal issue in support of him, although the Attorney-General advised that the first election was void and that there was therefore no need to depose the petitioner.

Even at the Colonial Office there were serious misgivings about this case, particularly concerning the suspicious nature of official involvement. Rather than allow a legal battle to go ahead which showed signs of favouring Lahai Conteh, the Colonial Office, anxious to avoid any forensic imbroglio, was content to 'leave the Executive to manage their matters, rather as questions of policy, than questions of law'. Further, 'if the claim [of Lahai Conteh] were to be looked at from a purely

[162] CO 267/556/112, enc., Barlatt for Conteh to SS, 1914.

legal standpoint, there is a good deal to be said for the [peti-
tioner]'. Faced with this impasse, Lord Harcourt was content
to take no action in the matter but to leave it to the Sierra
Leone administration.[163] As a matter of fact, a double injustice
had been done to Lahai Conteh: firstly, for having had him
elected; and, secondly, for deposing him. This episode shows
how much local circumstances and personalities determined
what actually happened at the grass roots level, the variables of
which complicate matters considerably.

(b) The problematic election of Joe Kwi

In 1936 an almost similar situation arose in Lower Bambara
Chiefdom over the election of Joe Kwi. In 1933 James Kwi,
son of Nyagua and father of Joe Kwi, had been elected Paramount Chief by the votes of thirty-three out of forty-six elders.
The other two contestants received four and nine votes respectively. In December 1934 the chief died. In the subsequent
election, there were four contestants including the brother
of the late chief. After the election had failed to arrive at a
decision, the Provincial Commissioner gave notice to the
Tribal Authority to get a chief within twelve months, under
the Protectorate (Amendment) Ordinance of 1934 which empowered the Governor to appoint a chief if the Tribal Authority
after due notice failed in that duty. Accordingly, in 1936, the
election centred round Kwi Gbole (brother of the late chief)
and Joe Kwi (son of the late chief). The former received the
votes of one section chief and forty-three Tribal Authorities,
while the latter received those of six section chiefs and forty-
eight Tribal Authorities. However, when a count was taken
on houses, 4,242 votes turned out to be in favour of the former,
while only 3,120 showed for the latter.

It was shown that Kwi Gbole had been previously convicted
of a criminal offence and sentenced to three years imprisonment, while Joe Kwi 'has a clear record'. It seems as if the
Acting Commissioner Southern Province, J. S. Fenton, was
more favourably disposed towards Joe Kwi. '. . . Literate, . . .
formerly employed by the Survey Department . . . I believe he
would make a satisfactory chief.' Fenton therefore recommended

---

[163] CO 267/556/112, enc., Barlatt for Conteh to SS, 1914.

him to be appointed by the Governor under Ordinance No. 10 of 1934, Section 7A (2).[164]

This gave rise to misgivings at the Colonial Office. The numerical majority was for the candidate 'the Governor does not nominate'. S. Robinson opined that the 'Governor can depose a chief for subversive conduct, but I do not find that he can debar a candidate for previous misconduct'. Another official expressed suspicion about a candidate who had the majority of the elders, and 'I should be apprehensive that the Elders were influenced in their choice by a desire to have the weaker man over them'. Whatever these qualms and the suspicious nature of the entire proceedings, the Colonial Office thought it best to leave it to the 'local authority'.[165]

(c) District Commissioner's choice or popular will?

In these cases, it was the local official who determined the outcome of the traditional power contest. It is reasonable to argue that much actually depended on the local District Commissioner and whether or not he acted contrary to policy, there would be no official consequences unless colonial interests were involved. The District Commissioners installed chiefs and it is reasonable to suppose that in an appreciable number of instances the Governor was not even informed. In 1914 when Fawundu was exiled from Northern Sherbro district, the chiefdom remained vacant for some time because the District Commissioner had 'not yet been able to find a suitable successor'.[166] It was his own personal choice rather than that of the people that was important here.

In 1916 after the deposition of Amadu Kaikai, Major Fairtlough appointed Lahai Swaray as Regent Chief of Pujehun without the consent of the Governor or that of the sub-chiefs and elders. Some of the latter protested and Swaray sentenced them each to six months imprisonment, which Fairtlough confirmed. As Swaray's oppression became unbearable, two deputations were sent to the Governor, who transferred Fairtlough, and the succeeding District Commissioner settled

---

[164] CO 267/655/512, File 32156, Fenton to Col. Sec., 1936.
[165] Ibid., minute by Locker at CO.
[166] CO 267/565/262, North Sherbro District Report, 1914.

the matter. But there was a lesson behind this. As the Governor explained:

The most unsatisfactory feature in this incident is its illustration of the dependence of political officers upon interpreters and court-messengers. I fear that this is inevitable, while the study of native languages is backward; but things are improving in this respect.[167]

Fairtlough's explanation that Swaray was the senior sub-chief and that no charges were pending against him is not totally convincing. After his dethronement, Swaray was described as 'an unimportant sub-chief who took charge of the Panga–Sowa chiefdom when charges were pending against the Kaikai faction'. Governor Wilkinson candidly stated that: 'I am afraid that this unimportant sub-chief was forced most irregularly upon the people, and that he attempted to secure his position by ways that were even more irregular . . .'[168] It is likely that a number of incidents like this occurred without the knowledge of the Governor, where the incumbent did not incur such displeasure in the people he had been appointed over that a revolt followed.

When Amadu Kaikai was allowed to return from banishment in 1925, he offered his candidature for the vacant chieftaincy and won the poll after a keen contest. It was thought politic and just to cancel the order for his deposition and have his re-election recognized. It was believed he was a victim of the circumstances which led to his banishment in 1916 and, now that he was back from exile, it would be unwise to act contrary to the popular will.[169]

From these accounts, it is clear that no consistent policy was followed, but this is not to suggest that there was no policy at all. The manner in which chiefs were chosen represented an enigma even to the people themselves since a number of alternatives existed which did not necessarily seem consistent to the people. In 1931 while on tour in the Protectorate, Governor Hodson received requests from gatherings of chiefs that 'the old system of election of chiefs by selection and not by vote might be re-introduced'.[170] Evidently the chiefs did not like the

---

[167] CO 267/572/Conf., 28 Oct. 1916, Wilkinson to SS.
[168] CO 267/574/Conf., 24 Jan. 1917, Wilkinson to SS.
[169] CO 267/607/Conf., 3 Mar. 1925, Slater to SS.
[170] CO 267/635/File 9694, Hodson to SS, 1931.

voting system, but preferred the old system by which the elders and men of note unanimously chose their leader. The frequent changes in the method of choosing chiefs were confusing to them.

(d) Colonial tenure of office: strengthening the chiefs

The chiefs, once given the support of the administration, were quite secure in their tenure of office. The determination to uphold the chiefs and the institution of chieftaincy was not a hollow policy. The administration made sure that more control or restraint was now being exercised over the chief at the same time as his tenure became more secure. True enough, most of the powers of the chiefs had been whittled down and the only way to ensure further control was to reduce their powers still further, although the support of the administration meant security of tenure and greater authority. As a result, the traditional sanctions and the checks and balances on chiefly powers were undermined, but the British supplied an administrative check. Captain Stanley, in his report on the Ronietta district, 1915, stated the position thus:

. . . it will be seen at the present day, many checks and restrictions on oppression exist which in former days were unheard of . . . whereas in former days it took a revolt or tribal war to remove a chief, at the present time oppression or misconduct results in his downfall; his actions are naturally to a large extent, regulated by this vital change in circumstances. At the present day moreover, and especially in this District, the chief is surrounded by a non-native population who watch his every action, and who are only too willing to advise his subjects to report him to the Government, or to report him themselves should his judgements, through greed or any other motive, become oppressive.[171]

The powers of the chiefs had been drastically reduced, and the greatest restraint in the exercise of their authority stemmed from the ultimate sanction of the colonial state which could depose them. All the same, the rather paradoxical situation arose that while a chief's powers were but a shadow of the pre-colonial ones, the chief who enjoyed the confidence of the administration, and therefore the security of his tenure in office, could oppress his people without the traditional sanctions

[171] CO 267/571/182, Ronietta District Report, 1915.

operating. The function of control was taken over by the colonial state and while it sought to preserve the chiefs, it found itself at the same time safeguarding the rights of the subjects who could no longer operate the traditional sanctions against their chiefs.

From 1916 to 1942 there were in all less than ten depositions. In general, the administration was not ready to depose a chief just for any offence, as in the early days of the Protectorate. However, it was discovered that there was a large discrepancy between the paltry fine of £10 introduced in 1909 as an alternative to deposition and the ultimate penalty of deposition. In 1927, therefore, the fine was raised to the maximum of £100, but it was now the Provincial Commissioner and not the District Commissioner who was entitled to inflict it, subject to the approval of the Governor. This policy was intended to give further support to the chieftaincy institution, since the increase in wealth over the previous decade or two and the fall in the value of money made £10 a ridiculous alternative to deposition. In his report on the bill, the Attorney-General stated in no uncertain terms that part of the motivation in passing it was the 'anxiety to save chiefs from the full penalty of deposition'.[172]

When Amadu Kaikai was deposed and banished in 1916 from Panga–Sowa Chiefdom, subsequent requests by the ex-chief to return to his home were refused by the Governor. The successor was an old man, Sam French, and in order to uphold him, Kaikai was refused permission to return to Panga–Sowa. He was, however, permitted to return in 1923 after the death of Sam French because 'the main reason for his exclusion—i.e. to prevent intrigues against Sam French—no longer existed'.[173]

Unless a chief lost the confidence of the administration or there was blatant and flagrant oppression on his part, he was upheld in his position. In 1915 there was a plot by the headmen against the Paramount Chief, Komai, of Koya Chiefdom. Charges of oppression and extortion brought against him proved unfounded on investigation by the District Commissioner. The headmen were then ordered to apologize, which they failed to do. They also refused to hand in their house-tax

[172] CO 267/618/File 4008, Attorney-General's report, 1927.
[173] CO 267/607/Conf., 3 March 1925, Slater to SS.

in person and assaulted a court messenger sent by the chief to summon them. The District Commissioner had to go to Koya himself with a small escort to arrest the headmen who had been flouting the authority of the chiefs.[174]

In Pujehun district in 1931 there were several internal disturbances. The District Commissioner proposed to banish three elders opposed to a Paramount Chief, but the Provincial Commissioner reversed the decision after an inquiry. This severely embarrassed the chief, as the opposition gained from the dispute. The District Commissioner felt bewildered since complications arose in relation to his administrative and political task. The neighbouring chiefdoms were affected and similar revolts arose as the minorities became very active. Appeals were made to the Governor to redress grievances or oppression mostly of an economic nature—to reduce levies and chiefs' demands for labour. When these were attended to, political demands followed. The Governor realized the difficulty faced by the District Commissioner in these circumstances—with only a rudimentary staff it was impossible for him to exercise sufficient administrative control over the politics of these chiefdoms. The officers, 'whose first business is to maintain order, and who have therefore to arbitrate and control', thus had a heavy work load. It was a difficult situation even for the Governor, but by the end of the year 'very great improvement has occurred in the internal politics of the chiefdoms of Pujehun District . . .'.[175]

In Dama Chiefdom, the administration actually banished the opposition to the Paramount Chief in 1934. The five ringleaders, Braima Nomo, Foday Kabineh, Momoh Kanneh, Braima Kraji, and Ibrahim Fogbawa were banished from the four districts of the Southern Province—Kenema, Kailahun, Bo, and Pujehun. These leaders migrated with their followers to Liberia, where a Liberian newspaper carried apparently exaggerated reports. The migrants related a story of oppression and extortion in which the Provincial Commissioner had treated them indifferently, upholding the authority of the chief.

The Foreign Office was jittery at the report of oppression in a British Protectorate, especially as investigations were being

---

[174] CO 267/565/Conf., 10 Ap. 1915, Intelligence Return for First Quarter.
[175] CO 267/637/File 9799, Annual Report on Southern Province, 1931.

conducted against the Liberian Government for cruelty at the same time. The Governor refuted the Liberian newspaper report as exaggerated and said that the article was 'dangerous and misleading'. In October the Acting Governor told the Colonial Office that the Provincial Commissioner had furnished him with information that 'all the five deportees and all the voluntary followers who went into Liberia crossed back without exception into Nomo chiefdom on October 5'. The five leaders subsequently returned to Liberia with their wives, but their followers stayed in Sierra Leone and there was reason to believe that they would return to Dama.[176] Whatever the variations in details, it is evident that a group opposed to the Paramount Chief enjoying the confidence of the administration was banished on grounds of disturbing the peace.

(e) Internal revolt: Achilles' heel of strengthening chiefs

These instances of upholding the authority of chiefs and the institution of chieftaincy need not lead to the conclusion that the administration carried out a blind policy of upholding chiefs irrespective of their actions or the circumstances. Indeed, there are instances in which chiefs who enjoyed the confidence of the administration but faced a dangerous revolt from within were deposed. In upholding the authority of the chiefs, the administration was not totally blind to the interests of their subjects. In nearly all the depositions after 1914, the main reason was the 'oppression and extortion' of the subjects by the chiefs.

'Oppression and extortion', however, is a phenomenon that needs some amplification. With the superimposition of the colonial state, new vistas of socio-economic opportunity and vanity were open to the chiefs and the people. In particular, new items were made available for addition to the traditional status symbols. Imported gin or a motor car was an impressive addition to a bevy of wives or dependants. Consequently, the chiefs as the local rulers of their people were in an advantageous position and, to meet the challenges of this situation, increased the traditional demands they usually made on their people. In principle, there was nothing new or wrong in this. If the demands were now increased, it was not unlike a

[176] CO 267/646/File 22054; CO 267/648/File 22143, 1934.

pre-colonial situation of emergency which necessitated increased demands.

But with the new social-status consumption commodities came Western ideas of justice and 'good government', all represented by the colonial state. The rather ironical situation arose when by responding to the new circumstances through increasing the traditional demands on their people, the chiefs found themselves being judged by Western values and facing the possibility of being charged with 'oppression and extortion'. But they were merely taking the opportunity of advancing themselves in a sector that was called forth in the first instance by the very existence of the colonial state. Certainly as local leaders of their people, they wanted more labour and more taxes to get more money to purchase themselves the new Western commodities that would enhance their status. But the unlucky ones defeated their ends in this pursuit. Certainly there were new opportunities but new limitations too.

In October 1914 Governor Merewhether deposed Paramount Chief Bundu of Lekpeyama Chiefdom in consequence of a report on an inquiry held against him. District Commissioner Bowden found the complaints of the people 'well founded, and that the chief has been exceeding his rights for some years. . . . He is a man of greedy and selfish character, which finds expression in a positive lust for money and overindulgence in gin and women.' These failings made him an unsatisfactory chief who could not be maintained in the face of internal revolt. Certainly he had also lost the confidence of the administration.[177]

In Bongor Chiefdom, the Paramount Chief, Soko, was found guilty in an inquiry in 1915 of 'persistent and flagrant misgovernment'. Addicted to drink, he was said to have had a bad record in the past and nearly all the chiefdom was unanimous in their wish to have him deposed. Again, sandwiched between internal revolt and loss of confidence by the administration, the chief was deposed.[178]

In the case of Boakei Bundeh of Luawa, despite repeated warnings from the administration to reform his ways, his persistent failings made it impossible to keep him in office any

[177] CO 267/560/564 and enc., Merewhether to SS, 1914.
[178] CO 267/564/34, Merewhether to SS, 1915.

longer. Apart from seducing women and exacting extortionate fines, Boakei Bundeh succeeded in antagonizing virtually the whole chiefdom to the extent that 'hostility to him is so great as to create a risk of revolt or riot'. Among all the sub-chiefs only one supported him. The Governor was quite satisfied that Bundeh had 'governed very badly' and his fines were 'cruelly oppressive'. Considering his past record, which was bad, and his disregard of all warnings, the Governor deprived him of his authority as Paramount Chief in 1916 to avert a political catastrophe in the chiefdom.[179]

The people of Wunde Chiefdom brought thirty-seven charges against their Paramount Chief, Boima Dowi, in 1917. An inquiry was held into nine charges which proved the chief's guilt of 'oppression by excessive fines and levies of money'. He levied money for the war effort which he converted into his personal use; gave a man's wife to one of his followers and made the husband believe the woman was dead; fined a village because a girl had been killed by lightning; and a host of other offences. The Governor was convinced that he was unfit for the post of Paramount Chief and accordingly deposed him.[180]

Paramount Chief Boima of Bo was deposed in 1925, having been found guilty of eleven charges of oppression and misgovernment. He alienated the chiefdom to the extent that he was personally unable to carry on the administration, which was done by his speaker. His loss of support among his people impeded the work of the administration and although he was given ample opportunity to resign, he recalcitrantly refused and was quite unrepentant for his misdeed. He was deposed.[181]

Another deposition took place in Bongor Chiefdom in 1927. The Paramount Chief, Amara Kai, had had two previous inquiries made into his conduct, but having given assurances that he would rule in a 'constitutional' manner he was not deposed. Failing to honour his promises, a serious revolt threatened and 'the whole chiefdom was unanimous in its desire for Amara Kai's removal'.

The recent investigation . . . revealed, among the many abuses of

[179] CO 267/571/Conf., 17 May 1916, Wilkinson to SS.
[180] CO 267/574/Conf., 29 Jan. 1917, Wilkinson to SS.
[181] CO 267/608/Conf., 4 May 1925, Slater to SS.

his position that have characterised the chief's rule, such flagrant departures from native law and custom as the institution of Courts presided over by men of no responsible position in the country, the withholding from his Tribal Authority of their legitimate share of public funds, and disregard of the advice of the Elders and Advicers of the chiefdom, the attempted pledging of the chiefdom regalia, and other discreditable efforts to obtain money to feed the chief's avarice, and lastly a wanton breach of the laws of hospitality in connection with the wives of litigants and others.[182]

On the two previous occasions in 1916 and 1919 when inquiries had been held, Amara Kai's rule had been found anything but satisfactory. In fact on the second occasion Hollins recommended his deposition, but this was not carried out. In 1924 a 'settlement' was made 'for the better government of the country'. But not long afterwards, complaints began about the chief's misrule and extortion. On this last occasion the Provincial Commissioner reported that 'the Tribal Authority, representing the whole of the people, are united in their determination to get rid of him. It is not a question of faction, or even of a preponderating section.' Thus it was useless to attempt any reconciliation between the chief and his people; there was no choice but to depose him.[183]

Nine charges were preferred against Momoh Rogers of Kpaka Chiefdom in 1932, the resultant inquiry being the seventh into his conduct since he was made chief in 1916. On the previous six occasions he had not been deposed because the administration intervened to reconcile his people. But in 1932 'the present enquiry . . . has disclosed a state of affairs that the Government cannot tolerate. He has systematically plundered his people, defied native institutions, and flouted Government decrees.' Governor Hodson deposed him.[184]

In 1924 the chiefs of Nongowa and Lunia respectively were deposed after being found guilty of similar serious offences.[185] Then in 1942 the Paramount Chief of Fakunya, Yamba Kunyafoi, after ten years in office was deposed 'for persistent drunkenness and incapacity, together with interference with other

[182] CO 267/622/File 4671, Byrne to SS, 1927.
[183] Ibid.
[184] CO 267/636/File 9760, Hodson to SS, 1932.
[185] CO 267/603/106 and encs., Slater to SS, 1924; CO 267/603/Conf., 15 Jan. 1924, and encs., Slater to SS, 1924.

members of the Tribal Authority . . .'. His conduct in the inquiry was proved to be 'subversive of good government'. He had evidently lost support of the Tribal Authority.[186]

In all these incidents the Paramount Chiefs had to be removed because they had lost the localized base of their support and no amount of administrative support would have kept them without the risk of disorder. Thus from about 1914 all the depositions follow the second category enumerated above—that initiated at the local level within the chiefdom structure. Before 1914 all the depositions came straight from above as an administrative act. It is evident that the policy of upholding the chiefs, while generally practised after 1914, was not, however, a guarantee against deposition if a chief obviously overreached himself in his vain excesses. In such circumstances even the administration was bound to lose its confidence in the chief if he was guilty of maladministration and oppression, since the administration took over the championship of the rights of the subjects who could no longer exercise traditional sanctions within the structure of the colonial state. It is the administration that appears rather to have been in the ambiguous position of having at the same time to uphold the authority of the chiefs against their subjects and yet champion the rights of the subjects against the oppression of their chiefs. But since the chiefs had become employees of the administration, the latter had the right to dismiss them if they so misgoverned as to cause serious trouble among the subjects.

(f) Favouritism and partiality towards Madam Humonya

The deposition of Madam Humonya in 1918 is an illustration of the apparently ambiguous position of the administration. Madam Humonya was 'appointed' Paramount Chief of Nongowa in 1908, in succession to her mother. She received special support from the administration and, using this to her personal advantage, before long won a reputation for petty tyranny. However, discontent remained bottled up for fear of the consequences to whoever dared bring a complaint against the chief. In fact, as has already been noted, she was treated as 'a sort of Paramount Chief over the other Paramount Chief of the District'. She cleverly managed to keep good and strong relations

[186] CO 267/680/File 32123/2, Conf., Stevenson to SS, 8 July 1942.

with the Governor in Freetown and this made her position virtually impregnable. In spite of the despotic manner in which she treated her subjects and the extortionate demands made on them, which the older people still remember vividly, no one would dare make a report against her.

But her impregnability became fragile and vulnerable when W. D. Bowden took charge of the district as District Commissioner and was not well disposed to condone the maladministration of Madam Hunonya. As Bowden himself wrote in the Railway District Report for 1917, 'discontent which had been growing for a number of years in the Nongowa chiefdom . . . found a voice' in this year. But marshalling the support of the Governor behind her, Humonya was to get Governor and District Commissioner in a confrontation over her deposition. As the discontent in Nongowa neared a showdown in 1917, the presence of Bowden, who had an intimate knowledge of the chiefdom, was increasingly felt to be dangerous to the continuance of Humonya's regime. The chief knew that Bowden was bringing serious charges against her administration, and she too complained that the Commissioner was hostile to her and was encouraging intrigues against her which made it difficult for her to enforce her authority over her people. After an audience with the Governor, Humonya's attitude to Bowden became 'defiant and openly rude', the Commissioner complained. Two complaints against the Commissioner were forwarded to the Governor, and, in November 1917, the latter visited Kenema and held a public meeting. The Governor intimated to Bowden that he wished the latter to inquire into charges levied by the chief against six principal men of the chiefdom.

The result of the inquiry was not favourable to Humonya as it recommended banishment for two men, one of whom was her 'paramour'. Bowden believed that it was under the chief's influence that the Governor rejected the findings and decided to hold another inquiry himself. The results were the same. Rather than deal with Humonya, the Governor, R. Wilkinson, summarily transferred Bowden to the Ronietta district on the ground that the Commissioner had denied responsibility for the peace of the chiefdom since the two men were not exiled as he had recommended.

However, even the Governor's inquiry revealed widespread

dissatisfaction and that 'for years past very serious abuses had been going on'. Madam Humonya was found guilty of (1) failing to appoint a speaker and arbitrarily choosing two men as her principal councillors; (2) appointing sub-chiefs for the five sections of the chiefdom without consulting the wishes of her people, contrary to customary law; (3) oppression arising from excessive demands for labour, heavy death-duties, extortionate fines, and severe 'stocking', a kind of imprisonment in which the feet were pilloried. On all three counts, it was decided respectively that the chiefdom should choose a speaker, and Amara Jumu of Hangha was chosen, while the two unofficial councillors were banished according to the wishes of the people; the people should choose their own sub-chiefs; no more state farms were to be made, each section giving in lieu fifty bushels of rice; death-duties were to be abolished; fines and fees were to be entered in a book and receipts issued; no person should be 'stocked' for more than seven days.

After the departure of the Governor, a fresh complaint was lodged before the new District Commissioner, Lt.-Col. H. G. Warren, that the people did not approve of Madam Humonya's twenty-five messengers and a clerk and wanted them dismissed. Warren considered this a matter that rested entirely with the wishes of the people and the messengers were dismissed. Humonya was told that she could retain the clerk, but only in a private capacity and his emoluments should not be paid from public revenue.

Despite these severe disclosures of maladministration, it seems as if, once the administration was fully in support of her, Humonya could maintain her throne. In other cases where a chief in such circumstances had lost the confidence of the administration, deposition was only too swift in coming. Evidently, Humonya had lost the confidence of her people but not yet that of the administration. She could therefore maintain her throne, albeit perilously.

In December 1918 the new speaker, Amara Jumu, had a violent quarrel with the chief and, in consequence of a charge of assault brought against him, was banished. Actually, Amara was suspected of spearheading the opposition to Humonya and his banishment was a temporary victory for the chief. However, it was believed in local circles that Amara

was most popular and would be elected chief if allowed to
contest for the office, but the Governor was averse to allowing
his candidature. At any rate, a meeting of the Tribal Authority
voted to have Humonya resign the chiefship. Her lawyer,
Sam Barlatt, later described the incident as one in which the
chief was 'coerced into resigning her chiefdom against her
will' and he believed that 'she had not lost her ancient popularity amongst her people'. This extravagant view is a piece of
propaganda without foundation as subsequent events proved,
but that was precisely the lawyer's function for which he was
paid. The lawyer, however, succeeded in getting Humonya
eligible for re-election.

In August 1919 the election was held at Kenema, 'at which
Boakei Kekura of Kenema was elected chief, the whole of the
headmen voting for him with the exception of twelve headmen
who voted for Madam Humonya'. The chiefdom comprised
over 170 towns and villages and of the twelve headmen who
supported Humonya ten were her dependants or had close
connections with her. Amara Jumu was not allowed to contest,
but local opinion was vindicated when he secured election five
years later on the deposition of Boakei Kekura. Apparently,
the Governor did not want to allow a formidable rival to
Humonya, whom he supported and to whom he had granted
more than ordinary concessions. The Governor gave her ample
opportunity to whip up her last resources to secure re-election,
but in the face of popular dislike and hatred, the administration
could not foist Humonya on the people. The lady, however,
was rather too ambitious, and J. Craven, the District Commissioner who conducted the election, opined that 'judging from
Madam Humonya's attitude, I think it likely that she will
endeavour still to assert her claim to the chieftaincy in spite of
the fact that the whole chiefdom is against her'.[187]

This saga reveals the difficulty that the administration with
its residual authority would face if it supported a chief who had
lost the total confidence of his people. In fact it has been said
of Humonya that 'because of her despotism and cruelty, [she]
is still considered to be the worst chief in chiefdom history and
many people vow that they will never support another woman

[187] The entire Humonya episode is to be found in 'Nongowa Chiefs'; CO
267/577/Conf., 17 Mar. 1918, Wilkinson to SS, and encs.

for chief'.[188] Humonya's case shows that it could be extremely arduous to depose a chief who had lost the support of her people, but it also shows that the residual authority of the administration could only delay the inevitable. In the face of a severely violent opposition, the administration had to give way although it retained the ultimate source of legitimacy to chiefship.

The residual authority of the colonial administration

The matter of the residual authority of the administration was quite vague and various amendments were made to the Protectorate Ordinance to 'tidy up' the ambiguities. In 1912 Dr. Maxwell had drawn attention to the fact that the Protectorate Ordinance did not require the Governor to confirm an election which was intended to be conducted in the traditional manner. But the Governor's power of deposition enabled him to dispose of an unsatisfactory chief.[189] Governor Merewhether subsequently issued an order that there was objection to reports of elections being submitted to the Governor for *information*, but not for approval. But the previous practice of gazetting the 'approval' or 'confirmation' continued until 1924, when Governor Slater pointed out that there was no legal authority for the Governor to 'confirm' a Paramount Chief when the latter was succeeding a deceased predecessor. The Gazette notice was therefore changed only to notify the election, not confirm or approve.

When the amendment to the Protectorate Ordinance was being carried out in 1918, a subsection was added stating in addition to deposition by the Governor of a chief 'who in his opinion is unfit for the position and to appoint a person to be chief in his place', that the alternative of a fine instead of deposition could be imposed on a chief whose conduct is 'subversive to the interests of good government'.[190] The power of 'appointing' a chief by the Governor was only exercised once in 1914, when Merewhether appointed Abraham Tucker as Paramount Chief of Jong. The previous incumbent, Bunting

---

[188] D. Simpson, 'A Preliminary Political History of the Kenema Area', *Sierra Leone Studies*, N.S. 21, July 1967, p. 59.

[189] Wilson, PC memo, para 20.

[190] Protectorate Ordinance (Amendment) No. 12 of 1918, 80(2).

Williams, had been tried for several charges but was acquitted for insufficiency of evidence. But the court recommended his expulsion. The chiefdom was then temporarily placed in the charge of Abraham Tucker, whom the District Commissioner recommended to be permanently appointed. Therefore the Governor formally deposed Bunting Williams and, 'as Abraham Tucker is not a native of Jong Chiefdom and would probably not be elected if an election was held in the ordinary way', the Governor appointed him Paramount Chief under Section 80(1) of the Protectorate Ordinance 1901.[191] Obviously the Governor acted in the interest of the colonial state and the situation was not incompatible with its assumption of sovereignty after the Protectorate was proclaimed. Similar to the circumstances in the 'appointments' of chiefs after the 1898 war, the wishes of the people were of minor, if any, consideration.

No difficulties in the legal position seem to have arisen until late 1933 when, for over two years, a Tribal Authority was unable to reach agreement in finding a successor to a deceased chief. It then became necessary to introduce legislation to cover this contingency. Although the administration was pledged to upholding the chiefs, legislation concerning them was still excessively vague.

Clause 3 of the Protectorate (Amendment) Ordinance of 1934 for the first time made legislative provision for the election of chiefs and empowered the Governor to appoint a chief in the event of an abortive election. The Ordinance further added that no person elected to the position should perform the duties of chief unless he was first approved by the Governor and a notification was published in the Gazette.[192] This amendment implied that the Governor could therefore disapprove a duly elected chief and that, if the Tribal Authority failed to elect another chief twelve months after being asked to do so, the Governor could summarily appoint a chief. It seems as if this amendment aimed at meeting contingencies that now became apparent owing to the general progress of socio-economic change, but which had not been foreseen earlier, and also at tightening administrative control over the chiefs. In

[191] CO 267/561/617, Merewhether to SS, 1914.
[192] CO 267/641/File 22054, Attorney-General's Report.

1936 this section was invoked for the first time when, after Tankoro Chiefdom had failed for fifteen months to get a chief, the Governor appointed Sahr Gando as Paramount Chief. This was the second time the Governor directly appointed a Paramount Chief.[193]

Also for the first time since the Protectorate was proclaimed, the amendment made the first reference in legislation to the ordinary duties of a Paramount Chief: '. . . such chief shall generally maintain order and good government among the natives residing, or being in the area over which the Tribal Authority exercises jurisdiction.' This amendment is in contradistinction to others relating to elections or appointments of chiefs following misbehaviour, etc. The Chief Commissioner for the Protectorate, L. W. Wilson, was at a loss to understand why this omission was suddenly given legislative rectification, but guessed that the Attorney-General realized that it was necessary to provide some legal machinery for the election of chiefs before making provision for failure or neglect to bring about such election.[194] The truth, however, is that the Colonial Office drew the attention of the Governor to the loop-hole, which the latter admitted was an oversight and which was therefore rectified.[195]

But the position was still that the Governor could not withhold recognition of a chief duly elected by the elders of the chiefdom. No difficulties arose, however, but the Tribal Authorities Ordinance No. 8 of 1937 was passed to cover any eventuality. This Ordinance marks a turning-point in Protectorate administration, for it was the first attempt to apply to Sierra Leone the principles of 'Native Administration' on Nigerian lines. Apart from the general shift towards the so-called Lugardian system by this time, this step was further necessitated by the general socio-economic change over the previous four decades and its related problems which made the existing policy inadequate. In particular, since about World War I, the policy of the administration towards the chiefs and their duties had been one of *laissez-faire*, a kind of *quieta non movere*. It

[193] CO 267/655/File 32148, Moore to SS, 1936.
[194] Wilson, PC memo, para 24.
[195] CO 267/646/File 22054, Correspondence relating to the Protectorate (Amendment) Ordinance, 1934.

was realized by the 1930s that the previous policy was totally inadequate, especially as the general policy to uphold chiefs had bred such abuses in chiefdom administration that a drastic overhaul was necessary. The new measure gave the Governor power 'to control the whole machinery of tribal administration', and the Ordinance 'was clearly intended to effect a radical change in native Administration in the Protectorate', as L. W. Wilson put it.[196]

The time had thus come when, as in 1898, expediency suggested a radical change. In a very real sense none of the chiefs under colonial rule was legitimate since the source of their authority had now been converted from indigenous African institutions to British law. Even if the chief satisfied all the pre-colonial pre-requisites, his right to rule now depended on the colonial authorities. But the British did try at least to give a semblance of traditional legitimacy to colonial chiefship by first giving the people the right to choose their chief before he was recognized. Although this was not followed in all cases, it emerges as a general pattern.[197]

Conclusion: Dilemmas of the chief and the administration

The imposition of colonial rule abrogated the sovereignty of pre-colonial rulers; the kings were relegated to the position of chiefs. This implied also that their powers were taken over by the colonial state and they were only allowed the exercise of such authority as the colonial state allowed to be devolved on them. This automatically meant that the chiefs had become agents of the administration. Thus the ultimate source of their authority rested not so much on popularity or on the rendering of services to the community but on the power of the British Government. This put chieftaincy out of the reach of traditional sanctions that should be exercised by the governed.[198] Moreover, the institutionalization of ruling houses limited the

---

[196] Wilson, PC memo, para 28(4).

[197] Cf. M. Crowder and O. Ikime (eds.), *West African Chiefs* (University of Ife Press, 1970), pp. xi-xiii.

[198] Cf. L. Mair, 'Chieftainship in Modern Africa', *Africa*, ix, 3, 1936, p. 311; St. Clair Drake, 'Traditional Authority and Social Action in Former British West Africa', in Van den Berghe (ed.), *Africa: Social Problems*, p. 519.

opportunities for acquiring chiefship to purely ascriptive criteria in contrast to the traditional achievement-oriented system.

In the first phase of colonial consolidation, the administration used its power to depose chiefs until the institution was weakened. This was undesirable because the administration was creating difficulties for itself by weakening its agents. Therefore the policy of upholding the chiefs became a major object of colonial policy right through the 1930s. The depositions that occurred during this period were in effect the result of internal revolt by the subjects of a chief coupled with a loss of confidence by the administration.

In this *laissez-faire* period in which the chiefs were upheld, their privileges were enhanced although their powers were curtailed. Considerable economic advantages accrued to the chiefs from their position as tax-collectors and the payment of traditional tribute in cash or in produce that could be exchanged for cash.[199] Embezzlement of house tax and extortion of money in the name of the administration were common complaints and, in all cases of deposition of chiefs throughout the colonial period, oppression had been connected with excessive economic demands by the chiefs from their people. In this process the chiefs were acting not only as agents of change but as active participants in the process of 'modernization'. As in Western Nigeria, the chiefs were thus an important group in the process of 'modernization' in so far as their wealth tied them to the cash nexus of a market-oriented economy.[200] The position of the chiefs as the traditional élite 'enables them to retain traditional authority while simultaneously pursuing wealth and power in the modern sector of colonial society'. They thus had a much greater share than the ordinary man in the process of modern social change.[201] The new functions which the colonial state imposed on the chiefs in this wise further enhanced their privileges as direct agents of the administration.

'Because they have dissociated these privileges from the

[199] Cf. J. Cartwright, *Politics in Sierra Leone*, p. 30; V. Dorjahn, 'The Changing Political System of the Temne', in Wallerstein (ed.), *Social Change*, p. 197.

[200] M. Kaniki, 'Traditional Authority and Early Colonial Policies in Sierra Leone' (Birmingham MA, 1967), pp. 52–3; Kilson, *Political Change*, pp. 59–60; P. C. Lloyd, 'Traditional Rulers', in J. Coleman and C. Rosberg, *Political Parties and National Integration in Tropical Africa* (University of California Press, 1964).

[201] Kilson, *Political Change*, p. 53.

corresponding responsibilities, those in authority have sometimes failed to see that under modern conditions tribute paid
to the chiefs is coming to be just that one-sided burden that it
was sometimes thought to have been before.' But to add with
Lucy Mair that 'these same conditions make any effective
protest out of the question'[202] is an untrue and unfair assessment
of the whole situation. Even during the apogee of chiefly
authority, depositions took place as a result of oppression of the
people mainly through excessive economic demands. At the
zenith of chiefly power too there was no lack of restraint, as is
sometimes imagined,[203] despite the support of the administration. But certainly the traditional democratic basis of Mende
chiefship was radically undermined.[204] The traditional Mende
ruler was a 'constitutional monarch' and not 'an absolute ruler
of autocratic power' as Alldridge imagined.[205] In the colonial
context, however, the chief became the pivot of a number of
contradictions. He found himself in the contradictory position
of having to play two rather irreconcilable roles at the same
time, as agent of the administration to his people and as leader
of his people in their aspirations *vis-à-vis* the administration.[206]
The chief now 'becomes the pivot on which the new system
swings precariously'.[207] The remarkable fact is that the chiefs
succeeded so well in these incompatible roles.

But what is perhaps more remarkable is that the colonial administration was in a similar, if not worse, position of having to
play contradictory roles as well—not just the chiefs. Having taken
over the sovereignty of the chiefs, the colonial administration

[202] Mair, 'Chieftainship', p. 311; also Lewis, *Sierra Leone*, p. 68; L. Mair,
'African Chiefs Today', *Africa*, xxviii, 3, 1958, p. 198.

[203] Barrows, 'Local-Level Politics', p. 89.

[204] See Little, *The Mende*, pp. 183–5; Hollins, 'Mende Law', p. 26; Migeod,
View of Sierra Leone, p. 234; G. Padmore, *Africa: Britain's Third Empire*, pp. 112–13;
Apter, *Gold Coast in Transition*, p. 127.

[205] Alldridge, *Transformed Colony*, p. 193.

[206] See D. Middleton, *The Effects of Economic Development on Traditional Political
Systems in Africa South of the Sahara* (The Hague and Paris 1966), p. 16; Gluckman,
Custom and Conflict, p. 52; J. Beattie, *Bunyoro: An African Kingdom* (New York 1960),
p. 47; M. Fortes and E. E. Evans-Pritchard (eds.), *African Political Systems* (London
1940), p. 15; L. Fallers, 'The Predicament of the Modern African Chief', in S. and
P. Ottenberg (eds.), *Cultures and Societies of Africa* (New York 1960); G. Kingsley
Garbett, 'The Rhodesian Chief's Dilemma: Government Officer or Tribal
Leader?', *Race*, viii, 2, 1966.

[207] Fortes and Evans-Pritchard, *African Political Systems*, p. 15.

was nevertheless pledged to uphold them as instruments of colonial rule. By taking over sovereignty and the ultimate sanction to traditional authority, the colonial state undermined the existing traditional democracy and found itself in the curious position of having to protect the rights of the people who could no longer exercise traditional sanctions over their chiefs. The colonial state took over everything—the power of the chiefs as well as the sanctions of the people. Inevitably, it had to play the dual role of supporting the chief and at the same time defending his subjects. This latter contradiction stands out more remarkably in the Mende experience than even the dual roles of the chief.

In the absence of any plan of political development, it may be surmised that the inconspicuousness of the chiefly contradiction stems from their easy adaptation to the new situation, while the colonial administration was perpetually at pains to create a *via media*. Without putting forward a positive policy of political development until 1937, the administration of the Protectorate proceeded rather on an *ad hoc* basis. But the very superstructure of the colonial state implied political change and the Africans proved more adept at adapting to the new innovations than the administration at reconciling its contradictory roles. Especially with the belated introduction of Lugardian-style Indirect Rule the colonial administration was behaving more and more like a traditional paramount writ large, but in circumstances that were ever less relevant to such behaviour.

CONCLUSION

UNTIL fairly recently most studies of colonial Africa tended to treat the African past as ahistorical, static, and homogenous. Contact with the West was generally said to have started that complex of change bewilderingly known as 'modernization'.[1] Many studies until the 1960s centred on the activities of Europeans in Africa without seeking to bring out the African part in the processes of change. Africans, however, were not passive victims of the *pax Britannica*; they were indeed acted upon by the Europeans, but they also influenced the nature of the impact of colonial forces occasionally in directions not foreseen by the colonial authorities.

Among those writers who have considered the African role, there has been a tendency to discover a conflict or disharmony among the roles performed by Africans in the changing colonial situation. This study has shown that such tensions have been exaggerated. Apart from conflicts found in the exercise of political roles by African authorities, there were also conflicts in the colonial administration.

Like most African societies, that of the Mende, at the opening of the colonial period, was complex and fluid and it possessed well-grounded traditions. The last quarter of the nineteenth century had been a period of rapid social, economic, and political change which increased in pace with British intervention in 1896.

It was not a very difficult task for the British to establish domination over the hinterland. The basic British interest was in the continuing survival of the colony of Sierra Leone which had existed for over a century. Since by the latter part of the nineteenth century there was no imperial subsidy for the colony, the British relied heavily on customs revenue to finance the administration. But customs returns were dependent on the flow of trade from the interior and the wars in the interior were generally thought to be disruptive of trade and therefore to the accumulation of the revenue of the colony. The acute

[1] Kilson, 'African Political Change', pp. 247–8; Chodak, 'Theory of Modernization'; also Chapter V, above.

economic problems caused by the great depression of the 1870s were locally attributed to wars in the interior, and the administration, in a desperate bid to save the colony from financial strangulation, began a series of political manœuvres in the hinterland. These economically inspired political acts so entangled the administration that when the French threat appeared on the northern 'frontier' there was no alternative but to proclaim a Protectorate in the economic interest of the colony.

The proclamation of the Protectorate in 1896 shook the Africans by its provisions, which radically altered the traditional relations between themselves and the administration. The very fabric of their society was thought to be undermined. Cardew's concessions could not prevent the resistance of 1898 which sought to restore the traditional balance. British victory confirmed British hegemony. Thus the 'colonial situation' was ushered in.

Subsequent European domination, however, cannot be represented, as many writers have attempted, within a conflict or 'displacement/rejection' model in which the dominated society completely succumbs to the dominating society.[2] Instead of a confrontation of two hostile societies, dichotomous and conflicting in every respect, a striking level of coexistence and adaptation developed between them in several spheres. Thus the colonial period produced a new kind of system incorporating African and European elements. This renders inapplicable the dichotomous conceptualization of the change process as an innate conflict between 'modern' and 'traditional' institutions and values. Neither is the proposition of a universally 'eurhythmic' relation in the elements of change a kind of 'functional' approach in the process of socio-political change in contemporary developing societies very easy to sustain.[3]

British policy did not at the outset envisage or desire any major change. But the consequence was major social change. The British made use of existing institutions as the cheapest means of administering African peoples without causing any

[2] For a critique of such a model, see C. S. Whittaker, 'A Dysrythmic Process of Political Change', *World Politics*, xix, 2, January 1967, pp. 191–2.

[3] Ibid., p. 192. By implication Kilson (*Political Change*, p. 47) supports the 'harmonious' theory of change, when he states that with colonial rule, 'the political consequences of social change were rendered much more predictable'.

abrupt discontinuity with the African past. But the superordination of the colonial state meant the superordination of British law which was quite different from African systems of law. Therefore innovations were introduced that vitally affected traditional practice.

After the resistance of 1898 many loyalists were installed in chiefly positions most frequently contrary to Mende practice. Moreover, to establish further the colonial suzerainty large polities were fragmented. By thus breaking the power of real or potential opponents and at the same time making it possible to reward supporters with chiefships, the British altered the pre-colonial Mende political system.

The story is a complex one, fraught with intense intrigue in which Africans participated deriving advantages for themselves at the expense of rivals. The process of the establishment of European political control was not simply a British exercise, but one involving complicated interaction between Africans and the colonial authorities. These changes not only affected relationships among Africans but introduced new conceptions of traditional political roles. For instance, the position of the chief was altered and the notion of the 'colonial chief' was legitimized within two or three decades. But the main pre-occupation of the colonial administration in the early phase was to maintain law, order, and peace and to preserve the existing social fabric intact.

But the very establishment of colonial hegemony brought about changes not only in the relationships between Africans but in African political roles as well. However, the results of these changes on African societies were not always anticipated or even desired by the colonial rulers. Change was a complicated process of interaction between Africans and Europeans in which neither determined the resultant social order.

The attempts to remould indigenous political institutions without any sharp breaks with the past has led many writers[4] to discern a social system evolving which had major elements of disharmony and conflict among Africans. In many respects, it is argued, the colonial chief is the focus of this conflict,[5] being

[4] See Chapter V, above.

[5] Fallers, 'The Predicament of the Modern African Chief', p. 510; Fortes and Evans-Pritchard, *African Political Systems*, p. 15.

at one and the same time a representative of his people and an agent of the colonial administration. But it must be added also that, in the context of this study, the colonial administration was as well another focus of internal conflict, being simultaneously the protector of the people against their chiefs and the upholder of the traditional authorities.

The Mende chiefs did much to cushion the manifestations of the conflict and, perhaps, far from depicting them as playing contradictory roles they may be said to have developed a new kind of role, harmonizing, rather paradoxically, their role as traditional leaders of their people with that of agents of the administration. In this sense, they became a dual élite (traditional and modern), being in the forefront of local and national development.[6] But the colonial administration proved unable to resolve the conflict between its roles as protector of the subjects of the chiefs and as the ultimate sanction to chiefly authority. In other words, the contradiction here was in the attempts to 'modernize' on the basis of 'relatively unchanged sub-groups and on traditional attitudes and loyalties'.[7] This problem is as alive today as it was in colonial times.

Thus the colonial period represents a period of intense change and interaction between European and African institutions and values. The pattern of change, although in most instances dictated by the existence of the colonial state, took on a complex character that cannot be explained in terms of a *simple* change model. It cannot be said that the society as a whole followed a systematic pattern of change in the direction desired and directed by the colonial state. Neither can it be argued that Mende chiefs were unable to adjust to the conflicting situation and to create a new role for themselves. The chiefs have continued to be of vital importance in local and national life and, although overshadowed today at the national level, still remain important local indigenous political figures and will probably continue to do so for a considerable period to come. Every government in the post-colonial period has not only pledged itself to uphold the institution of chieftaincy, but has used it as

---

[6] Cf. P. C. Lloyd, 'Traditional Rulers', pp. 382–4. The Yoruba rulers succeeded in a strikingly similar degree.

[7] S. N. Eisenstadt, 'Political Development', in A. and E. Etzioni (eds.), *Social Change* (New York 1964), pp. 311–12.

the basis for local support. In striking contrast, however, has been the failure of the central administration to create a new role out of its conflicting situation and even today maintains *ad hoc* relations with the institution of chieftaincy. This may be well justified in the machiavellian game of politics, but for meaningful planning and development a systematic policy formulation on the issue, regulating and institutionalizing the relationships between the chiefs and the local political institutions, on the one hand, and the central political organs, on the other, is an urgent necessity.

SOURCES

Oral and documentary sources were used. Oral information is acknowledged in the footnotes.

I. OFFICIAL

A. UNPUBLISHED

1. Public Record Office, London.

   CO 267 Original correspondence. These are dispatches from the Governors of Sierra Leone to the Secretary of State for the Colonies and provide a most prolific source, especially in the enclosures. Three hundred and sixty-four volumes in all were examined from 1874 to 1945.

   CO 879 Confidential print. These documents were originally removed from the dispatches and printed for the Colonial Office and relate to important issues on which there was voluminous correspondence. The originals were then removed from the original correspondence, but some were simply cancelled.

2. Sierra Leone Government Archives, Freetown.

   a. Governor's Dispatches to the Secretary of State.
   b. Governor's Aborigines Letterbooks.
   c. Native Affairs Department Letterbooks.
   d. Decree Books.
   e. Intelligence Diaries.
   f. Records of Paramount Chiefs, 1899.
   g. Record of Commissioner, Chiefs and Distribution of Sticks of Office, 1894–1901.
   h. Information regarding Protectorate Chiefs, 1912.
   i. Nongowa Chiefdom: Paramount Chief Elections, 1898–1926.
   j. Minute Papers: Native Affairs Department Confidential.

B. PUBLISHED

1. Parliamentary Papers: vol. lii (1876).
   vol. lvii (1883).
   vol. lx (1899).
2. Bluebooks of Statistics, 1870–1900.
3. Royal Gazettes, 1880–1945.
4. Annual Administrative Reports of the Protectorate, 1900–45 (originally of individual districts, but later of the entire Protectorate, arranged by Provinces).

5. Books, pamphlets, etc.
Davis, R. P. M., *History of the Sierra Leone Battalion of the Royal West African Frontier Force* (Freetown: Government Printer, 1932).
Fenton, J. S., *An Outline of Sierra Leone Native Law* (Freetown: Government Printer, 1933).
List of Paramount Chiefs, 1914 (Freetown: The Secretariat, 1914).
Miscellaneous Information Concerning the Chiefdoms of the Sierra Leone Protectorate (Freetown: The Secretariat, 1943).
Sierra Leone Protectorate: Chiefdoms, Capital towns, Chiefs' names, Tribes (Freetown: The Secretariat, 1946).

II. UNOFFICIAL

A. UNPUBLISHED

1. Rhodes House Library, Oxford.

MSS. Afr. s. 388–90, L. W. Wilson, 'Material for a projected Encyclopaedia of Sierra Leone and notes for a diary of important events in the territory from 1900'.
MSS. Afr. s. 1151, N. A. C. Weir, 'Native Administration Notes, Sierra Leone'.

2. Theses and Typescripts.

Abraham, A., 'The Rise of Traditional Leadership among the Mende: A Study in the Acquisition of Political Power' (University of Sierra Leone MA, 1971).
Barrows, W. L., 'The Position of the Contemporary Mende Chief' (Paper presented to the University of Western Ontario Symposium on Sierra Leone, March 1971).
—— 'Local-Level Politics in Sierra Leone: Alliances in Kenema District' (Yale University PhD, 1971).
Bond, G. C., 'The Contemporary Position of Chiefs in Sierra Leone' (London MA, 1962).
Corby, R. A., 'The Mende Uprising of 1898 in Sierra Leone, as it related to the United Brethren in Christ Missions' (Western Illinois University MA, 1971).
Davidson, J., 'Trade and Politics in the Sherbro Hinterland, 1849–1890' (University of Wisconsin PhD, 1971).
—— 'The Southern Mende Chiefdoms and the Expansion of Sierra Leone, 1849–1898' (Birmingham University Centre of West African Studies seminar paper, 1972).
Davis, N. Darnell, *Chiefs and their Wars in West Africa* (n.p. 1876, printed for private circulation).
Harrison, J. S., 'The Twenty-Seventh of April: The Sierra Leone Wars of 1898' (City College of the City University of New York MA, 1972).
Kabwegyere, T. B., 'The Politics of State Formation: The Nature and Effects of Colonialism in Uganda' (Essex University PhD, 1972).
Kaniki, M. H. Y., 'Traditional Authority and Early Colonial Policies in Sierra Leone, 1896–1905' (Birmingham University MA, 1969).

Kaniki, M. H. Y., 'The Economic and Social History of Sierra Leone, 1929–1939' (Birmingham University PhD, 1972).

Lamboi, Ngolotamba, 'History of Madam Yoko: Kpa Mende Chiefdom' (1915, typescript in possession of its author).

McCall, M. J., 'Kailondo's Luawa and British Rule' (York University DPhil, 1975).

Matturi, Sahr [History of Jaiama Chiefdom, Kono] (n.d., typescript in possession of its author).

Newbury, C. W., 'Resistance and Adaptation to Colonial Rule in some Pacific Island Societies' (University of London Institute of Commonwealth Studies seminar paper, 1972).

Oroge, E. A., 'The Institution of Slavery in Yorubaland' (Birmingham University PhD, 1971).

Wylie, K. C., 'The Politics of Transformation: Indirect Rule in Mendeland and Abuja, 1890–1914' (Michigan State University PhD, 1967).

B. PUBLISHED

1. General.

Abraham, W. E., The Mind of Africa (University of Chicago Press, 1962).

Afigbo, A. E., 'A Reassessment of the Historiography of the [Colonial] Period', in Ajayi, J. F. A., and Espie, I. (eds.), A Thousand Years of West African History (Ibadan University Press and Nelson, 1965).

—— 'West African Chiefs During Colonial Rule and After', Odu, N.S., 5 April 1971.

Ajayi, J. F. A., 'The continuity of African Institutions under Colonialism', in Ranger, T. O. (ed.), Emerging Themes of African History (London: Heinemann, 1968).

—— and Austen, R. A., 'Hopkins on Economic Imperialism in West Africa', Economic History Review, xxv, 2, May 1972.

—— and Smith, R., Yoruba Warfare in the Nineteenth Century (London: OUP, 1963).

Akpan, N. U., Epitaph to Indirect Rule (London: Frank Cass, 1956).

Anderson, B., Narrative of a Journey to Musardu (New York: Green, 1870).

Anene, J. C., Southern Nigeria in Transition, 1885–1906 (OUP, 1966).

Apter, D. E., Ghana in Transition (New York: Atheneum, 1968).

Austen, R. A., 'The Abolition of the Overseas Slave Trade: A Distorted Theme in West African History', Journal of the Historical Society of Nigeria, v, 2, 1970.

Avineri, Shlomo (ed.), Karl Marx on Colonialism and Modernization (New York: Anchor Books, 1969).

Balandier, G., 'The Colonial Situation', in van den Berghe, P. L. (ed.), Africa: Social Problems of Change and Conflict (San Francisco: Chandler Publishing Co., 1965).

Bascom, W. R., and Herskovits, M. J. (eds.), Continuity and Change in African Cultures (University of Chicago Press, 1959).

Batten, T. R., Problems of African Development, Part II, Government and People (London: OUP, 1948).

Beattie, J., *Bunyoro: An African Kingdom* (New York: Holt, Reinart, and Winston, 1960).

van den Berghe, P. L. (ed.), *Africa: Social Problems of Change and Conflict* (San Francisco: Chandler, 1965).

Blackburn, R. (ed.), *Ideology in Social Science: Readings in Critical Social Theory* (London: Collins/Fontana, 1972).

Brown, Paula, 'Patterns of Authority in West Africa', *Africa*, xxi, 4, 1951.

Brunschwig, H., *French Colonialism, 1871–1914: Myths and Realities* (London: Pall Mall Press, 1966).

Buell, R. L., *The Native Problem in Africa*, i, 1928 (London: Frank Cass, 1965).

Burns, Sir Alan, *In Defence of Colonies* (London: Allen and Unwin, 1957).

Busia, K. A., *The Position of the Chief in the Modern Political System of Ashanti* (London: OUP, 1951).

Cary, J., *Britain and West Africa* (London: Longmans, 1946).

Chodak, S., 'Some Aspects of the Theory of Modernization as Applied to Sub-Saharan Africa—A Case Study', *Africana Bulletin*, 7, 1967.

Cohen, Sir Andrew, *British Policy in Changing Africa* (London: Routledge and Kegan Paul, 1959).

Collins, R. C. (ed.), *Problems in the History of Colonial Africa, 1860–1960* (New Jersey: Prentice Hall, 1970).

Coser, Lewis A., 'Social Conflict and the Theory of Social Change', *British Journal of Sociology*, iii, Sept. 1957.

Crocker, W. R., *A Critique of British Colonial Administration* (London: Allen and Unwin, 1936).

Crook, R., 'Colonial Rule and Political Culture in Modern Ashanti', *Journal of Commonwealth Political Studies*, xi, 1, 1973.

Crowder, M., 'Indirect Rule—British and French Style', *Africa*, xxxiv, 3, 1964.

—— *West Africa Under Colonial Rule* (London: Hutchinson, 1968).

—— (ed.), *West African Resistance* (London: Hutchinson, 1971).

—— and Ikime, O. (eds.), *West African Chiefs* (University of Ife Press, 1970).

Davidson, B., *Which Way Africa?* (London: Penguin, 1968).

Deschamps, Hubert, 'Et Maintenant, Lord Lugard?', *Africa*, xxxiii, 4, 1963.

Drake, St. Clair, 'Traditional Authority and Social Action in Former British West Africa', in van den Berghe, *Africa: Social Problems*.

Duignan, P., and Gann, L. H. (eds.), *Colonialism in Africa, 1870–1960*, 3 vols. (London: OUP, 1971).

Eisenstadt, S. N., 'Political Development', in Etzioni, A. and E. (eds.), *Social Change* (New York: Basic Books, 1964).

Fage, J. D. (ed.), *Africa Discovers Her Past* (London: OUP, 1971).

—— 'History', in Lystad, R. (ed.), *The African World: A Survey of Social Research* (London: African Studies Association, 1965).

—— 'Slavery and the Slave Trade in the Context of West African History', *The Journal of African History*, x, 3, 1969.

Fage, J. D., *States and Subjects in Sub-Saharan African History* (Johannesburg: University of Witwatersrand Press, 1974).

Fallers, Lloyd, 'The Predicament of the Modern African Chief', in Ottenberg, S. and P., *Cultures and Societies of Africa* (New York: Random House, 1960).

—— 'Political Sociology and the Anthropological Study of African Politics', *European Journal of Sociology*, iv, 1963.

Fisher, A. and H., *Slavery and Muslim Society in Africa* (London: Hurst and Co., 1970).

Fortes, M., and Evans-Pritchard, E. E. (eds.), *African Political Systems* (London: International African Institute, 1940).

Furnivall, J. S., *Colonial Policy and Practice* (London: OUP, 1948).

Gable, C., and Bennett, N. (eds.), *Reconstructing African Culture History* (Boston University Press, 1970).

Garbett, G. K., 'The Rhodesian Chiefs' Dilemma: Government Officer or Tribal Leader?', *Race*, viii, 2, 1966.

Gluckman, Max, *Custom and Conflict in Africa* (Oxford: Basil Blackwell, 1955).

—— 'Malinowski's "Functional" Analysis of Social Change', *Africa*, xvii, 2, 1947.

Grant, W. L., 'The Administration of Africa', *United Empire*, i, 4, 1910.

Hailey, Lord Malcolm, 'British Colonial Policy', in de Almada, Jose *et al.* (eds.), *Colonial Administration by European Powers* (London and New York: Royal Institute of International Affairs, 1947).

—— *Native Administration in the British African Territories, III and IV* (London: HMSO, 1951).

—— *An African Survey* (London: OUP, 1956).

Hatch, John, *The History of Britain in Africa* (London: André Deutsch, 1969).

Hertslet, Sir E., *The Map of Africa by Treaty, I & III, 1895* (London: Frank Cass, 1967).

Hopkins, A. G., 'The Lagos Strike of 1897: An Exploration in Nigerian Labour History', *Past and Present*, 35, Dec. 1966.

—— 'Economic Imperialism in West Africa: Lagos 1880–1892', *Economic History Review*, xxi, 1968.

—— 'Economic Imperialism in West Africa—A Rejoinder', *Economic History Review*, xxv, 2, 1972.

—— *An Economic History of West Africa* (London: Longmans, 1974).

Horton, R., 'Stateless Societies in the History of West Africa', in Ajayi, J. F. A., and Crowder, M. (eds.), *History of West Africa*, vol. i (New York: Columbia University Press, 1972).

Ikime, Obaro, 'Reconsidering Indirect Rule: The Nigerian Example', *Journal of the Historical Society of Nigeria*, iv, 3, Dec. 1968.

Iliffe, J., 'The Organization of the Maji Maji Rebellion', *Journal of African History*, viii, 3, 1967.

Kilson, M., 'African Political Change and the Modernization Process', *The Journal of Modern African Studies*, i, 4, Dec. 1963.

Kirk-Greene, A. H. M., *The Principles of Native Administration in Nigeria* (London: OUP, 1965).

Lloyd, P. C., 'The Political Structure of African Kingdoms', in Banton, M. (ed.), *Political Systems and the Distribution of Power* (London: Tavistock Publications, 1965).

—— 'Traditional Rulers', in Coleman, J., and Rosberg, C. (eds.), *Political Parties and National Integration in Tropical Africa* (Berkeley: University of California Press, 1964).

—— 'Kings, Chiefs, and Local Government', *West Africa*, 31 Jan. 1953.

Lugard, Lord, *Political Memoranda*, 3rd edn. (London: Frank Cass, 1970).

—— *The Dual Mandate in British Tropical Africa*, 5th edn. (London: Frank Cass, 1965).

Luke, Sir H., *Cities and Men*, vols. i and iii (London: G. Bles, 1953 and 1956).

—— *A Bibliography of Sierra Leone* (London: OUP, 1925).

McCall, D. F., *Africa in Time Perspective* (London: OUP, 1969).

Magubane, B., 'A Critical Look at Indices used in the study of Social Change in Colonial Africa', *Current Anthropology*, 12, 4–5, Oct.–Dec. 1971.

Mair, Lucy, 'African Chiefs Today', *Africa*, xxvii, 3, July, 1958.

—— 'Chieftainship in Modern Africa', *Africa*, ix, 3, 1936.

Marx, K., and Engels, F., *On Colonialism* (Moscow: Progress Publishers, 1968).

Meek, C. K., *et al.*, *Europe and West Africa: Some Problems and Adjustments* (London: OUP, 1940).

Middleton, J., *The Effects of Economic Development on Traditional Political Systems in Africa south of the Sahara* (The Hague and Paris: Mouton & Co., 1966).

Mockler-Ferryman, A. F., *British West Africa* (London: Swan Sonnenschein, 1900).

Nicolson, I. F., *The Administration of Nigeria, 1900–1960* (London: OUP, 1969).

Omer-Cooper, J. D., 'The Question of Unity in African History', *Journal of the Historical Society of Nigeria*, iii, 1, 1964.

Ottenberg, S. and P. (eds.), *Cultures and Societies of Africa* (New York: Random House, 1960).

Perham, M., *Native Administration in Nigeria* (London: OUP, 1937).

Perraton, D. H., 'The Man on the Spot: British Officials in Late Nineteenth Century Africa', in *Theory of Imperialism and European Partition of Africa* (Edinburgh University Centre of African Studies, Seminar Proceedings, 1967).

Rattray, R. S., *Ashanti Law and Constitution* (Oxford: Clarendon Press, 1929).

Roberts-Wray, Sir K., *Commonwealth and Colonial Law* (London: Stevens and Sons, 1966).

Robinson, K., and Madden, F. (eds.), *Essays in Imperial Government Presented to Margery Perham* (Oxford: Basil Blackwell, 1963).

Rodney, W., 'African Slavery and other forms of Social Oppression on the Upper Guinea Coast in the Context of the Atlantic Slave-Trade', *The Journal of African History*, vii, 3, 1966.

Special Correspondent, 'Native Administration: I, Foundations of Government', *West Africa*, 29 Sept. 1962.

—— 'Native Administration: 2. Northern Taxation and enterprise', *West Africa*, 6 Oct. 1962.

Stokes, E., 'Traditional Resistance Movements and Afro-Asian Nationalism: The Context of the 1857 Mutiny Rebellion in India', *Past and Present*, 48, 1970.

—— and Brown, R. (eds.), *The Zambesian Past* (Manchester University Press, 1966).

Tignor, R., 'Colonial Chiefs in Chiefless Societies', *The Journal of Modern African Studies*, 9, 3, 1971.

Tordoff, W., *Ashanti Under the Prempehs, 1888–1935* (London: OUP, 1965).

Touval, Saadia, 'Treaties, Borders, and the Partition of Africa', *Journal of African History*, vii, 2, 1966.

Twaddle, M., 'The Bakungu Chiefs of Buganda Under British Colonial Rule, 1900–1930', *Journal of African History*, x, 2, 1969.

Vansina, J., 'A Comparison of African Kingdoms', *Africa*, xxxii, 4, Oct. 1962.

—— *et al.* (eds.), *The Historian in Tropical Africa* (International African Institute, OUP, 1964).

Wallerstein, I. (ed.), *Social Change: The Colonial Situation* (New York: John Wiley, 1966).

Whitaker, C. S., 'A Dysrhythmic Process of Political Change', *World Politics*, xix, 2, Jan. 1967.

2. Sierra Leone.

Abraham, A., 'Some Suggestions on the Origins of Mende Chiefdoms', *Sierra Leone Studies*, N.S. 25, 1969.

—— 'Nyagua, the British, and the Hut Tax War', *International Journal of African Historical Studies*, v, 1, 1972.

—— 'Bai Bureh, the British and the Hut Tax War', *International Journal of African Historical Studies*, vii, 1, 1974.

—— 'The Pattern of Warfare and Settlement Among the Mende in the Second Half of the Nineteenth Century', *Kroniek van Africa*, 2, 1975.

—— and Isaac, B., 'A Further Note on the History of Luawa Chiefdom', *Sierra Leone Studies*, N.S. 24, 1969.

Alldridge, T. J., 'Wanderings in the Hinterland of Sierra Leone', *The Geographical Journal*, iv, 1894.

—— *The Sherbro and its Hinterland* (London: Macmillan, 1901).

—— 'Sierra Leone and its undeveloped Products', *Royal Colonial Institute, Proceedings*, xxxvii, 1905–6.

—— 'Sierra Leone up to date', *Royal Colonial Institute, Proceedings*, xl, 1908–9.

—— *A Transformed Colony* (London: Seeley and Co., 1910).

—— 'Sierra Leone and its Commercial Expansion', *United Empire*, ii, 5 and 6, 1911.

Banton, M. P., 'Economic Development and Social Change in Sierra Leone', *Economic Development and Cultural Change*, ii, 1953–4.

Beatty, K. J., *Human Leopards* (London: Hugh Rees, 1915).

Bokhari, Alimami, 'Notes on the Mende People', *Sierra Leone Studies*, June 1918 and Mar. 1919.

Butt-Thompson, F. W., *Sierra Leone in History and Tradition* (London: Witherby, 1926).

Cartwright, J. W., *Politics in Sierra Leone, 1947–1967* (University of Toronto Press, 1970).

'The Caulker Manuscript', I and II, *Sierra Leone Studies*, October 1920 and July 1925.

Chalmers, J. A., 'In Defence of Sir David Chalmers', *The Nineteenth Century*, Mar. 1900.

Clarke, R., *Sierra Leone* (London: James Ridgway, 1843).

Clarke, W. R. E., 'The Foundation of Luawa Chiefdom', *Sierra Leone Studies*, n.s. 8, June 1957.

Collier, Gershon, *Sierra Leone: Experiment in Democracy in an African Nation* (New York University Press and University of London Press, 1970).

Cox-George, N. A., *Finance and Development in West Africa: The Sierra Leone Experience* (London: Dennis Dobson, 1961).

Crosby, K. H., 'Polygamy in Mende Country', *Africa*, x, 3, July 1937.

Dalby, D. T. P., 'Language Distribution in Sierra Leone', *Sierra Leone Language Review*, 1, 1962.

Denzer, L., and Crowder, M., 'Bai Bureh and the Sierra Leone Hut Tax War of 1898', in Rotberg, R. I., and Mazrui, A. A. (eds.), *Protest and Power in Black Africa* (New York: OUP, 1970).

Despicht, S. M., 'A Short History of the Gallinas Chiefdoms', *Sierra Leone Studies*, Jan. 1939.

Dorjahn, V., 'The Changing Political System of the Temne', in Wallerstein, *Social Change*.

Easmon, M. C. F., 'The Massaquoi Crown', *Sierra Leone Studies*, 22, 1939.

—— 'Madam Yoko: Ruler of the Mendi Confederacy', *Sierra Leone Studies*, n.s. 11, 1958.

—— *Sierra Leone Country Cloths* (British Empire Exhibition Handbook, 1924).

Falconbridge, A. M., *Narrative of Two Voyages to the River Sierra Leone during the years 1791–1793* (London, 1802; Frank Cass, reprint, 1967).

Fyfe, C. H., 'European and Creole Influence in the Hinterland of Sierra Leone before 1896', *Sierra Leone Studies*, n.s. 6, 1956.

—— *A History of Sierra Leone* (London: OUP, 1962).

—— *A Short History of Sierra Leone* (London: Longmans, 1962).

—— (ed.), *Sierra Leone Inheritance* (London: OUP, 1964).

Gervis, Pearce, *Sierra Leone Story* (London: Cassell, 1952).

Goddard, T. N., *The Handbook of Sierra Leone* (London: Grant Richards, 1925).

Gorvie, Max, *Old and New in Sierra Leone* (London: United Society for Christian Literature, Lutherworth Press, 1945).

—— *Our Peoples of the Sierra Leone Protectorate* (London: United Society for Christian Literature, Lutherworth Press, 1944).

Greene, Graham, *Journey Without Maps* (Penguin, 1971).

'A Guide to Pujehun District', *Sierra Leone Studies*, Feb. 1932.

Hargreaves, J. D., 'The Evolution of the Native Affairs Department', *Sierra Leone Studies*, N.S. 3, 1954.
—— *A Life of Sir Samuel Lewis* (London: OUP, 1958).
—— 'The Establishment of the Sierra Leone Protectorate and the Insurrection of 1898', *Cambridge Historical Journal*, xii, 1, 1956.
Hoffer, Carol P., 'Mende and Sherbro Women in High Office', *Canadian Journal of African Studies*, vi, 2, 1972.
Hofstra, S., 'Personality and Differentiation in the Political Life of the Mende', *Africa*, x, 4, 1937.
Hollins, N. C., 'Mende Law', *Sierra Leone Studies*, June 1928.
—— 'A Short History of Luawa Chiefdom', *Sierra Leone Studies*, June 1929.
—— 'A Note on the History of the Court Messenger Force', *Sierra Leone Studies*, 18, 1932.
—— 'Notes on Mende Law', *Sierra Leone Studies*, 15, 1929.
Horton, J. A. B., *West African Countries and Peoples, 1868* (Edinburgh University Press, 1969).
Howard, A. M., 'Administrative Boundary Changes', in Clarke, J. I. (ed.), *Sierra Leone in Maps* (London University Press, 1966).
—— 'Economic History', in Clarke, *Sierra Leone in Maps*.
Hudson, A., 'The Missionary in West Africa', *Journal of the African Society*, July 1903.
Ijagbemi, E. A., 'The Freetown Colony and the Development of "Legitimate" Commerce in the Adjoining Territories', *Journal of the Historical Society of Nigeria*, v, 2, June 1970.
Johnson, L., *The Devil, The Gargoyle and the Buffoon* (New York, Kennikat, 1971).
Kilson, Martin, *Political Change in a West African State: A Study of the Modernization Process in Sierra Leone* (Cambridge, Mass.: Harvard University Press, 1966).
Lewis, Roy, *Sierra Leone* (London: HMSO, 1954).
Little, K., 'Mende Political Institutions in Transition', *Africa*, xvii, 1, 1947.
—— *The Mende of Sierra Leone* (London: Routledge and Kegan Paul, 1951).
—— 'The Political Function of the Poro', I and II, *Africa*, xxxv, 4, 1965, and xxxvi, 1, 1966.
—— 'The Mende Chiefdoms of Sierra Leone', in Forde, D., and Kaberry, P. M. (eds.), *West African Kingdoms in the Nineteenth Century* (London: OUP, 1967).
Loveridge, A. J., 'The Present Position of the Temne Chiefs of Sierra Leone', *Journal of African Administration*, ix, 3, July 1957.
Malcolm, M. J., 'Mende Warfare', *Sierra Leone Studies*, Jan. 1939.
Mannah-Kpaka, J. H., 'Memoirs of the 1898 Rising', *Sierra Leone Studies*, N.S. 1, Dec. 1953.
Migeod, F. W. H., *A View of Sierra Leone* (London: Kegan Paul, 1916).
Moore, Al. M., *Standing Orders and Regulations of the Sierra Leone Frontier Force* (London: Waterlow and Sons, 1890).
Newland, H. O., *Sierra Leone: Its People, Products and Secret Societies* (London: Bale and Danielsson, 1926).
Owen, N., *Journal of a Slave-dealer* (London: Routledge, 1930).

Probyn, L., 'Sierra Leone and the Natives of West Africa', *Journal of the African Society*, vi, 23, 1907.

Protectorate Literature Bureau, *Kai Londo Kɛɛ Ndawa* (Bo: Bunumbu Press, 1953).

Ranson, B. H. A., *A Sociological Study of Moyamba Town, Sierra Leone* (Zaria: Amadu Bello University, 1968).

Reeck, Darrell L., 'Innovators in Religion and Politics in Sierra Leone, 1875–1896', *International Journal of African Historical Studies*, v, 4, 1972.

Riddel, B. J., *The Spatial Dynamics of Modernization in Sierra Leone* (Evanston: Northwestern Press, 1970).

Siddle, D. J., 'War Towns in Sierra Leone: A Study in Social Change', *Africa*, xxxviii, 1968.

'The Sierra Leone Protectorate Expedition, 1898–1899', *Journal of the Royal United Service Institution*, xliii, 1, 1899.

Simpson, D., 'A Preliminary Political History of the Kenema Area', *Sierra Leone Studies*, n.s. 21, July, 1967.

Thomas, N. W., *Anthropological Report on Sierra Leone* (London: Harrison, 1916).

Thompson, D. C., *Sierra Leone* (British Empire Exhibition Handbook, 1924).

Vivian, W., 'The Mendi Country and some of the Customs and Characteristics of the People', *The Journal of the Manchester Geographical Society*, xii, 1896.

—— 'The Missionary in West Africa', *Journal of the African Society*, ix, 1903.

Wallis, C. B., *The Advance of Our West African Empire* (London: Fisher Unwin, 1903).

—— 'The Poro of the Mendi', *Journal of the African Society*, iv, 14, 1905.

—— 'In the Court of the Native Chiefs in Mendiland', *Journal of the African Society*, xvi, 1905.

—— 'Tribal Laws of the Mendi', *Journal of Comparative Legislation and International Law*, iii, 4, 1921.

Winterbottom, T., *Account of the Native Africans in the Neighbourhood of Sierra Leone*, vol. i (London, 1803).

Wylie, K., 'Innovation and Change in Mende Chieftaincy, 1880–1896', *Journal of African History*, 2, 1969.

3. Newspapers.

Sierra Leone Church Times
Sierra Leone Weekly News
Standard
The Times

INDEX